John Colet's Commentary on First Corinthians

A New Edition of the Latin Text, with Translation, Annotations, and Introduction

medieval & renaissance texts & studies

VOLUME 21

John Colet

John Colet's Commentary on First Corinthians

A New Edition of the Latin Text, with Translation, Annotations, and Introduction

Bernard O'Kelly

AND

Catherine A. L. Jarrott

medieval & Renaissance texts & studies
Binghamton, New York
1985

DISCARDED

Pegasus Limited for the Advancement of Neo-Latin Studies
has generously provided a grant to assist in the
publication costs of this volume.

Library of Congress Cataloging in Publication Data

Colet, John, 1467?–1519.
  John Colet's Commentary on First Corinthians.

  (Medieval & renaissance texts & studies ; v. 21)
  Translation of: Enarratio in Epistolam Primam S. Pauli ad
Corinthios; text in English and Latin.
  Bibliography: p.
  1. Bible.   N.T.   Corinthians, 1st—Commentaries.
I. O'Kelly, Bernard.   II. Jarrott, Catherine Anna Louise,
1925–   .   III. Title.   IV. Series.

BS2675.C5813   1985   227′.207   82–12403
ISBN 0–86698–056–3

This book is set in Bembo typeface,
smythe-sewn and printed on
acid-free paper to library specifications.
It will not fade, tear, or crumble.

Design and composition by
mRts

Printed in the United States of America

Contents

Preface

Professor Catherine A. L. Jarrott of Loyola University, Chicago, is responsible for most of the annotations in the present edition and for the index. Professor Jarrott also abridged the original text of my Introduction, reducing some of it to the notes on pp. 59–62, and she updated it in some respects. I am principally responsible for the Latin text and textual notes, the English translation, the Introduction, and those annotations in which my name appears in parentheses.

Professor Jarrott has made a welcome contribution to Colet studies. Many others helped in various ways and at various times in the preparation of this edition, but I can name only a few. I am especially indebted to Professor Herschel Baker of Harvard University, who first encouraged my interest in Colet, to the late Professors Douglas Bush and Hyder Rollins of Harvard, and to Professor Marcia Levin O'Kelly of the University of North Dakota Law School.

Professor Mario A. Di Cesare of the State University of New York at Binghamton and his colleagues at Medieval & Renaissance Texts & Studies have been most helpful and patient in bringing the book to completion. The staff of Cambridge University Library were kind in assisting me when I worked with Colet's manuscript, and Professor Jarrott and I extend to the Syndics of that library our thanks for their permission to reproduce here two folios photographically.

Bernard O'Kelly
University of North Dakota

hiiste se carere non intelligût/quoqz in ignorantia et infirmi =
tate. Se sapientes et potentes ee putant. Quorum sapientia
malicia [est] potentia impatientia. nobilitas et altitudo re =
uera ignobilitas et in Imum depressio est. atqz vt apud lucâ
inquit Saluator. ab ominatio apud deum quamobrem non abre
quidem videtur factum fuisse a deo: vt illo vulgo hominum
et quasi fece in fundo residentt longe a claritate/ postha =
bita: qui in tam altam obscuritatem non fuerint dêlapsi.
prius et facilius a diuino lumine attingerentur. qui fue =
runt qui minus in vallem mûdi miseriaqz descenderunt.q
altius multo extantes q̃ alij: merito priores exorto Justicie
sole illuminati fuerunt. qui supra multitudinem varietate et
pugnam huius humilis mundi: simplices sui similes, et quieti
extiterunt. tanto propiores deo quando remotus a mundo
distauerint. q̃d si deus ipse est ipsa nobilitas, sapientia, et po =
tentia. quis non videt petrum. Joannem. Jacobum et id genus
reliquos. etiam anteq̃ veritas dei illuxerat in terras. tâto
alijs sapientia et viribus prestitisse. q̃to [magis] abfuerint ab eorû illoqz
stulticia et impotentia. vt nihil sit mirum si deus cuius est
rbonis suis, meliores eligere, et accomodare. eos habitos stul =
tos et [impotentes] deligerit. quâdo quidem reuera vniuersi mundi no =
biliores fuerunt, a vilitateqz mundi magis seiucti, altiusqz ex =
tantes: vt quemadmodum id terre quod altius eminet ex
orto sole fatilius et citius radijs tangi tur. ita similiter sunt
necesse. prodeunte luce que illuminaret omnem hominem
venientem in hunc mundum: prius irradiaret eos qui magis
in hominibus eminuerint. et quasi montes ad hominû
valles extiterint. Ad alios autem qui sunt in imo. in regi

Introduction

I
Colet in History

When John Colet died in 1519, no work of his seems to have been so well known as was St. Paul's School. Well remembered also were his sermons, and in particular his firm and outspoken sermon to the Convocation of 1511 on "conforming and reforming," perhaps the finest statement of the century on the need for ecclesiastical reform and the manner in which it should proceed.[1] There is a foreshadowing in this: even today, except for those especially interested in the Tudor era, Colet's name seems ordinarily to be linked first with educational theories and practices in the sixteenth century, and then (perhaps more vaguely) with the ecclesiastical disputes and events that we call the English Reformation. Scholarly criticism has reflected the popular associations, often concerning itself almost exclusively with these two identifications of Colet as educator and reformer, instead of seeking a more integral understanding of Colet's mind or of the principles underlying his conclusions with regard to education and reform. He has long been known also as the intimate friend and adviser of men like Thomas More, Erasmus, John Fisher, Thomas Lupset, William Grocyn, Thomas Linacre, the chief scholars and Christian humanists of the realm. Immediately after his death, no one appears to have thought of him primarily as a writer.

A man as close in time and family friendship as George Lyly, William's son, could record with regret that his father's patron had left nothing extant in writing, and did not seem to have written very much.[2] Erasmus, to whom Colet had been very kind, and who thought he knew his English friend well enough to compose a short life of him, included in it the assertion that Colet had refrained from writing books.[3] Later, Thomas Harding, the Catholic controversialist, was to retort to his perennial adversary, Bishop Jewel: "As for John Colet, he hath never a word to shew, for he wrote no workes."[4]

Readers of Bishop John Bale's *Illustrium maioris Britanniæ scriptorum summarium* in the 1540's must have been surprised, then, to find listed under Colet's name no less than fifteen titles, and to see that one of these, the *Enarrationes in Paulum*,

covered fourteen "libros." Twenty-eight books are thus attributed to a man with never a word to show, a man who left nothing in writing. Bale cites Erasmus' testimony that Colet refrained from writing books, but adds (with a reticence of the sort that will always irk scholars) that "a certain friend" told him of the discovery, after Colet's death, of his unpublished writings in unbound pages hidden "in the most secret place of his library."[5]

Of the twenty-eight works Bale assigns to Colet, a few can be recognized as being books only in a very limited sense: one is really a letter from Colet to Lyly; a second is a letter to Erasmus; and a third designates the rules for admission to St. Paul's. Others in all likelihood never existed. Bale's national feelings made him sometimes overready to set down titles for the illustrious writers of Greater Britain. Several of the books did exist, however, and it is not at all unlikely that they were found after Colet's death concealed in his library; perhaps, too, the carelessness of schoolboys (or servants) accounts for the loss of others; moreover, Colet left written works that are not in Bale's list.

Had Colet allowed his writings to be published in his lifetime, he would have been recognized as an English philosophical and theological writer of the same general kind and of at least the same sort of relative significance as Pico della Mirandola and Marsilio Ficino in Italy. If his contemporaries had not read his major works, many of them had heard him speak, and had concluded with Thomas More that for generations there had not been in their midst "any one man more learned or holy." But his early death spared him the public involvement most of his learned friends and contemporaries, such as Fisher, Tyndale, and More, had to accept, and for the most part kept his thought from taking on the added interest that theirs acquired. From time to time in later years, of course, sectarian spirits sought to establish a retroactively combative affiliation for his memory, but no claimant to this day has found him on all points a comfortable comrade-in-arms.

For several reasons Colet's importance as a philosopher, a theologian, a moralist, and an exegete was for centuries obscured. Only in the latter half of the nineteenth century were his principal writings printed. The influence he had exerted in his lifetime by the spoken word soon became generalized and anonymous—as no doubt such influence must always become in an advanced culture—and then was overshadowed, and at last almost totally eclipsed, by tragic and momentous events that changed the course of history.

To a writer whose chief works are read neither by his contemporaries nor by the generations immediately following his own, perhaps there must always attach a certain remoteness, a distance, over and above that of time itself. Careful scholars must usually speak in conjectures, for one thing, when they discuss his influence on general currents of thought; they cannot with much assurance locate him neatly in a schematized system of dead schools, or relate his intellectual kin-

ships and allegiances; if they do not substitute personal enthusiasm for those more reliable guideposts, the reactions of the man's contemporary peers, they may be diffident about evaluating the intrinsic worth of his writings, wondering sometimes whether these were not much recognized at an earlier time simply because they were not, in point of fact, worth much recognition; and they cannot turn to the continuity of critical thought, the shifting emphases and viewpoints of thinkers in successive ages, in order to find some corrective for the intellectual biases, preoccupations, and natural bents of their own age, by which they must recognize themselves to be in some measure limited.

Between Erasmus' little biographical account (not in every respect a source to inspire confidence) and the work of Bishop Kennett and his literary heir, Samuel Knight, in the eighteenth century, not much reliable knowledge of Colet's life or thought was recorded in England or elsewhere. For the most part, the bibliographers and the writers of short lives offer as much legend and downright misinformation as fact. Bale's list of titles is followed by a dozen others, some longer than his and some shorter; some more scholarly, others considerably less so. Finally Kennett, and after him Knight, collected and sifted a great deal of information about Colet, and Knight's *Life* (1724) put readers in touch with some of the main lines of Colet's thought, if at second hand, and in a partisan, tendentious manner.

Knight's *Life* was reedited in 1823, with the "manifest errors" corrected and minor improvements made, but not until the latter half of the nineteenth century did Colet again become for scholars a subject of serious inquiry and research. Then the sympathetic work of Frederic Seebohm and of J. H. Lupton caused a more general interest in Colet's life and in his theology, at least; and his writings were at last published and translated, so that people could read them without having to journey to the manuscripts.

Lupton's admirable editions were small, however, and they have become in the natural course of events increasingly harder to find. In 1893, just twenty-six years after the first was published, Lupton noted that all were out of print. Reprints of Lupton's edition made by the Gregg Press in 1966 were unobtainable by 1974. Probably there are not many people who possess close or thorough knowledge of this writer who has so strong a claim to be considered the foremost thinker in England during the reigns of Henry VII and Henry VIII.

Yet one can read in almost any book that deals with the Renaissance in England encomia of Colet's mind and, frequently enough, courageous epitomes of his thought. Quite naturally, much more of Colet must remain outside these critiques than can fall within them. Notwithstanding the love Colet found for simplicity and for unity in his rich explorations of these concepts, he cannot be simplified without oversimplification, and his thought cannot be reduced to oneness without suffering also some degree of reduction to absurdity. The last

great exponent in Western Europe of a Christian world vision that was not in any significant way determined by the great controversies that left Western Christendom in fragments, he is best encountered with all his complexities of thought still upon him.

Apart from the thinning down and the occasional distortion that Colet has suffered at the hands of men writing about him in passing, as it were, the very few more particular commentaries that have followed the publication of his chief works have given varying importance to different aspects of his thought, sometimes rather arbitrarily. Even Lupton, with his deep insight into the works he loving-ly and carefully put within the reach of his contemporaries, found himself at times obliged to give a misleading emphasis to secondary issues in the treatises. His contemporaries he judged—and no doubt with justice—likely to be more intensely interested in whether or not Dean Colet was enlightened, forward-looking, and free from superstition than in whether or not he believed in the unity of the cosmos; they would be more concerned with any sixteenth-century English author's stand on purgatory than with his stand on the world of in-telligibles; they would be startled (as well they might) and perhaps upset, by Colet's assertions about marriage, and by his distinctly un-English views on the civil law and on lawsuits; their minds would be impatient to resolve the degree to which Colet had to be considered some sort of ultramontanist.

With tact as well as sincerity, then, and sometimes with a handsomely dispas-sionate wit, Lupton sought to remove or reduce any obstacles which might keep contemporary minds from knowing and contemporary hearts from loving his great and beloved Dean. "I have no desire," he writes, "to vindicate all that may seem visionary or over-strained in Colet's opinions . . . . My only wish is, that the reader may be placed at a right point of view, from which to estimate the opinions under consideration. This done, he alone will be responsible for the verdict given."[6] And when he has done all he can to place his readers at a right point of view in matters that might cause them uneasiness, Lupton adds:

> In conclusion, I would not have the reader suppose, from the above topics having been singled out for special notice, that they are what chiefly deserves his attention in these lectures. Most of them have been brought forward thus prominently, only as being likely to cause some stoppage to him in his progress. When once forewarned of them, let him rather dismiss them from his mind; and study, without interruption, the many admirable features of the work. Let him mark the ample and ever-ready command of Scrip-ture; the strong grasp, which will not be hampered by any bonds of tradi-tional interpretation; the bold denouncement of wrong-doing in the Church; the exaltation of Charity, as the only solvent of all difficulties; and, above all, that pure and lofty purpose, which would follow Paul, as he followed

Christ, through ways too arduous at times for the foot-step of ordinary
humanity.

(Pp. liv-lv)

The wording of this beautiful statement reveals that Lupton had met stop-
pages of his own in Colet's works; the passage indicates, too, how particular
were the main interests he found himself sharing with Colet. To these he naturally
gave most emphasis in his interpretations and comments; the perspectives they
helped him form can best be seen in the pages (and in the title) of the monograph
that is his last published work on Colet: *The Influence of Dean Colet upon the
Reformation of the English Church* (London and Cambridge, 1893).

Seebohm, with somewhat less detachment and candor, showed similar preoccupations.[7] What would help the readers of his day esteem Colet, the dedicated
"Oxford Reformer," he stressed and elaborated; what seemed in Colet's life or
writings to be at odds with the characterization, he explained or he dismissed.
This is not the only qualification one must (however gracelessly) put on Seebohm's
fine work. The dramatic and sometimes emotional quality of Seebohm's style
reflects an intention more frequently apostolic than academic. Seebohm observed
in his England of 1867 (and perhaps even more clearly in the England of 1887,
the date of the third edition) a crisis of faith and of religion in many ways parallel
to that which Colet, More, and Erasmus had attempted to meet. In the sixteenth century, those who could and should have listened carefully to the solu-
tions of the Christian Humanists, failing to do so, opened the way for what
Seebohm called "the tragedy of Luther" and "all the terrors of a religious con-
vulsion, which threatened to shake social and civil, as well as ecclesiastical, institutions to their foundations"; perhaps in the nineteenth century an earnest
restatement of the attitudes and ideals of the Oxford Reformers might serve a
troubled Christendom in ways not foreseen by those humanists themselves. A
"broad and distinctively *Christian* Reform"—this is what the Oxford Reformers
had wanted for their age, and this clearly is what Seebohm hoped to help bring
about in his own.

Seebohm, then, not only made Colet primarily a Reformer, and that in a
somewhat anachronistic sense; he also made his spiritual hero illustrate dichotomies
that can scarcely have entered his mind, and to bear arms in theological wars
he perhaps never dreamed of.

To this I must add that the close association of Colet's memory with those
of Erasmus and More, which Seebohm established rather too firmly, has been
an illumination of distinctly limited brightness. Emphasizing certain views and
ideals shared by Erasmus and Colet (and by himself), Seebohm in the main slighted
the radical and extremely important differences between their two minds. Theirs
was a splendid and a fruitful acquaintance, a warm and an affectionate friend-

ship; it was not, certainly, in every respect a harmony of singing birds. "It was probably at the instigation of Colet," writes Preserved Smith, "that Erasmus began an original Latin version of the New Testament."[8] Others have discussed the effects on Erasmus' thought of his association with Colet,[9] attributing to this association the genesis, at least, of much that is considered most important in the later works.

The love and esteem Colet felt for Erasmus, and his manner of directing and encouraging his friend in his endeavors, are all, I think, evident in the following passage from one of the letters. We do not have the letter Colet is answering, so we can only guess at the exact nature of the project to which Colet is referring in the first sentence:

> De philosophatione Christiana quod scribis verum est. Nemo est, credo, in orbe iam Christiano ad illam professionem et negocium te aptior ac magis idoneus, propter multiphariam tuam doctrinam; quod ipse non scribis, sed hoc dico quod sentio. . . . Non cessa, Erasme, sed quum dederis nobis Nouum Testamentum Latinius, illustra idem tuis expositionibus; et aede commentaria longissima in Euangelia. Tua longitudo est brevitas. Crescit appetitus, modo stomachus sit sanus, in lectione tuorum amantibus Scripturas. Si aperueris sensus, quod nemo te melius faciet, magnum beneficium conferes et nomen tuum immortalitati commendabis. Quid dico, immortalitati? Nomen Erasmi nunquam peribit, sed gloriae dabis nomen tuum sempiternae, et sudans in Iesu vitam tibi comparabis illam aeternam.

> (Your remarks about the pursuit of a Christian philosophy are perfectly just. There is no one, I think, in the Christian world of our own day better fitted for this business and profession than yourself, with the wide range of your learning; you do not say so yourself, I say it, because I really mean it. . . . Do not hesitate, my dear Erasmus, but when you have given us the New Testament in better Latin, go on to elucidate it with your explanations, and let us have a really long commentary on the Gospels. Length from you will seem short. In those who love Holy Scripture the appetite can only grow, provided their digestion is sound, as they read what you have written. If you make the meaning clear, which no one will do better than you, you will confer a great benefit on us all, and make your name immortal. Immortal, did I say? The name of Erasmus shall never perish, but you will win for your name eternal glory, and as you toil in Jesus, you will win for yourself eternal life.)[10]

Perhaps the most significant difference between the minds of Colet and Erasmus appears, however, in the last sentence. Colet was constantly preoccupied with

the *unum necessarium* — more, with sanctity — as Erasmus, he seems to have felt, was not. From the pleasing concept of an immortal name for Erasmus as a result of his scholarly labors, then, Colet passes gracefully to a reminder that eternal life for Erasmus is of considerably greater importance, and subtly urges him not to forget the real goal and purpose of his work.

Even greater directness in this matter appears in another letter, written a year later. Colet reproaches Erasmus for sending Reuchlin's *De arte cabalistica* to Fisher first, instead of to him, then adds drily that it came first to his hands anyway, and that he read it through before handing it on to the saintly Bishop. "I do not dare," he goes on, "to pass judgment on this book. I recognize my own lack of knowledge, and how blind I am in matters as abstruse as these, and when reading the works of so great a man. At the same time, it sometimes appeared to me as I read that here were greater miracles in words than in things. For (as the author instructs us)," Colet adds sardonically, "words in Hebrew have in their characters and combinations something transcending mere human knowledge." Then all lightness of tone is dropped, and Colet concludes his letter with these words: "Erasmus, there is no end to books or to knowledge. But our lives are brief, and there is nothing we can do with them better than to live them in innocence and holiness, and daily spend our efforts to the end that we may be purified, and enlightened, and made perfect. Now these Pythagorean and Cabbalistic matters of yours that Reuchlin writes about promise us such results as these; but in my judgment there is one way only by which we shall attain them: by an intense love for Jesus, and imitation of him. Leaving the roundabout and enigmatic ways, then, let us go the short way to the truth. Insofar as my own strength permits, that is what I wish to do. Farewell."[11] One senses sometimes in the correspondence that Colet feared at times that Erasmus' mind — or soul — might in some way mirror the rootless and homeless character of his physical life. With regard to Seebohm's "identification" of Colet with Erasmus, my only concern here is to warn the reader that if he approaches the works of Colet with the assurance that what he knows of Erasmus will help him directly in understanding Colet's mind, he may very easily be wrong. The same is true (although in different ways) of a prior knowledge of More, especially of More after the real beginning of the Protestant Revolt.

Since the deaths of Seebohm and Lupton, a number of writers have modified, added to, or gone counter to the lines of inquiry into Colet and interpretation of him that these authors established.[12] The history of the scholarly labelling of Colet is, of course, a long one, and sometimes a not very graceful one. Too many commentators have been much more concerned with whether they can marshall isolated texts to prove that Colet should be called a Protestant, or a Platonist, or whatever, than with the full and autonomous understanding of what he actually thought and wrote.

E. W. Hunt's *Dean Colet and His Theology* (London, 1956) is a balanced study which deserves mention both for the depth of its sympathetic insight into Colet and for the extent and scope of its understanding. It is a better general introduction to Colet than the biographies of Knight, Seebohm, or Lupton. Hunt clearly writes from an Anglican position, but he is at once more detached and less parochial in his reading of Colet than many others have been. No attempt is made to make Colet fit a historical Procrustean bed by lopping off those parts of his writings that will not be accommodated. Hunt has, to be sure, a name for Colet, the old one of "Christian Humanist," but he is more careful than most to have the term understood in its historical senses, rather than in any contemporary partisan sense (as though Christian Humanism were a quasi-political faction with a platform of minimum *credos* and policies). Although Hunt's emphasis in the definition is on Colet's Neo-Platonism, he does not make a label of the name and then reduce Colet to a size that the label will fit; nor does he pretend that one has communicated real knowledge simply by using it or establishing its aptness.

To avoid the oversimplifications and the distortions of emphasis that have arisen as side-effects of the attempts of many writers to identify Colet with this or that school or current in philosophy or theology, or to claim him for an intellectual tradition, or to assess his role as a seminal influence on his own or subsequent ages, I shall in the remainder of this introduction invite my readers to simply look at what Colet says, instead of speculating about what names best serve as complements of the verb *is* when Colet's name is used as subject. I shall confine myself, therefore, to a discussion of the principles and assumptions of Colet's thought, in their wholeness and coherence and, so to speak, in their intrinsic autonomy, as they are revealed in and relevant to the present work.

My concern, then, is not with what Colet means to us or to history. It is important, as Paul Oskar Kristeller has remarked, if we wish to understand the philosophy of the Renaissance, that we try "to separate the interpretation of the authentic thought of the period from evaluation and critique of its merits." The same scholar has warned us, too, of the "widespread tendency among historians to impose the labels of our modern time upon the thought of the past."

Similarly, I shall make no attempts to trace all the sources and analogues for every concept and proposition to be found in the work. Most of Colet's categories of thought and assumptions are to be traced ultimately, I think, to three main sources: the Bible, Plato, and Aristotle. Each of these sources, however, had had by Colet's time many centuries of tradition, accretion, and commentary of the most complex kinds; ideas and assumptions from them—and from sources independent of them and sometimes alien to them—had been blended and combined in the most intricate ways by thousands of fine minds and thousands of mediocre ones.

Colet's syncretizing mind, moreover, ordinarily transmuted and assimilated what he read, and only infrequently does one find direct or explicit borrowing from other writers, apart (of course) from the Bible. There is one rather long abstract from Ficino's *Platonic Theology* (Book XIV) on the love of God in the commentary on Romans, and in the present work there is a passage of direct paraphrase from Pico's *Heptaplus*. Lupton traces another passage in this work to the *Platonic Theology*.[13] In a less direct way, much of Colet's thought on the hierarchical nature of reality must be traced to the *Hierarchies* of the Pseudo-Dionysius.

In the introduction to his edition of the *Opuscula quaedam*, Lupton lists the authorities cited by Colet in his Pauline commentaries, with the number of times: Origen (7), Augustine (6), Jerome (5), Chrysostom (3), Ignatius (2), Ficino (2), Pico, Baptista Mantuanus, Cicero, Dionysius, Lactantius, Macrobius, Philo, Plato, Plotinus, Suetonius, Virgil.[14] To this one must add Aristotle, for the assigning to him (see below, p. 239) of the authority for the word ἐντελέχεια. The simple parading of names would, of course, be extremely misleading if from it the naive inference were drawn that Chrysostom, let us say, has somehow more to do with the nature of Colet's thought than Ficino or Pico, or that Virgil and the Pseudo-Dionysius have equal parts in it, or that because the name of Scotus is not there, he has no part at all.

One must, indeed, reject the validity of inferences based on the absence from Colet's writings of direct reference to Scholastic writers as authorities, and his expressed and reported impatience with these men, whenever these inferences are extended to the point of affirming or implying that Colet's own thinking is not influenced by (or as some would put it, free from) Abelard, or Peter Lombard, or Bonaventure, or Albert the Great, or Aquinas, or Ockham, or Roger Bacon, or Duns Scotus.[15] Colet had read these writers, or some of them, before he read others who were to seem to him more important. They formed his mind, and it would be outlandish to assert that some part of the structure of his thought does not come—proximately, at least—from them. Colet's hylomorphic preoccupations can be traced, for instance, to Aristotle, but they are colored by the discussions of the Schoolmen, and it is altogether probable that he first knew the concept from them. His acquaintance with the principle that "quidquid recipitur ad modum recipientis recipitur"—and perhaps his acceptance of it—may in all likelihood be traced to his reading of some Scholastic treatise, or of several of them, since the axiom is at the heart of Aquinas' psychological theories. It is, one might say further, a distinctly Aristotelian principle in its implications and intent, but one will not for this reason call Colet an Aristotelian; nor, on the other hand, will one draw inferences too swiftly from the circumstance that Colet would meet the axiom in Plotinus and Ficino also.[16] Similarly, Colet is in some measure indebted to Aristotle, and perhaps to his Scholastic followers, for his

views on causality (see below, pp. 44f) and on the hierarchy of the senses (pp. 55f).

In the matter of Colet's intellectual debt to the Pseudo-Dionysius — and this is surely one of the most pervasive, significant, and extensive that must be recognized in his writings — the impression has sometimes been given that between Erigena and the Florentine Academy the writings of the great Neoplatonizing Christian were ignored or lost sight of. The impression is, of course, a distinctly false one, as M. de Gandillac shows in the introduction to his edition of the complete works.[17] Discussions of Colet's thought that emphasize his debt to the Pseudo-Dionysius as though this were in itself a mark distinguishing him from thinkers of the centuries immediately preceding his own are bound to be to some extent misleading. Apart from the two commentaries on the *Hierarchies*, Colet's debt to the Pseudo-Dionysius appears most in *De Sacramentis*, where he is cited by name eight times. As Eugene Rice has pointed out,[18] Colet was acquainted with the view of Lefèvre d'Etaples that the Pseudo-Dionysius was not a Platonist, but an inspired Christian "uncontaminated by Gentile philosophy" whose Christian truths were pirated by Platonists without acknowledgement and falsely attributed to Plato.

Similarly, Colet's explicit references to and quotations from the Church Fathers and his silence about the Schoolmen have been presented as a further novelty of Colet's age, as though Schoolmen, when they were not quoting Aristotle, quoted only one another, passing over the patristic corpus in silence. One does not have to read very long in Scholastic works to see how distorted is such a view of their writings. Again, explicit allusions to Ficino and Pico, and a not infrequent community of interests with them, have been emphasized by one or two writers in such a way as to imply that they alone were Colet's principal sources. People who are alive at the same time often share common interests.

It is best, then, first to approach Colet's thought in its intrinsic coherence, relegating to a secondary place such considerations as his role in the development of intellectual history, content simply to recognize his indebtedness, direct and indirect, to almost every major thinker in the long tradition of European and Mediterranean speculation in matters philosophical and theological, while recognizing also that he is most particularly and overtly indebted to the Bible, to patristic writings, and to the Pseudo-Dionysius and his many commentators.

II

The Commentary on I Corinthians

This work is in most respects the best approach to Colet's thought. Paul's First Letter to the Corinthians lends itself admirably to an elaboration of the basic principles of Colet's philosophy and provides also many occasions for the applying of Colet's assumptions about history, theology, hermeneutics, and psychology. Although the nature of the work requires the reader to join, relate, subordinate, and in other ways systematize what is to be found here in discrete passages and fragments, it is the closest thing we have to a *systema* or a *summa* from Colet's pen. It is a much more nearly systematic work than the parallel commentary on Romans, while the commentaries on the Pseudo-Dionysius remain much closer to their author and the pattern of his thought.

I have found no sure way to assign a date to the composition of the work. Knight, Seebohm, Lupton, and many others followed the conjecture that this and its companion commentary on Romans are the only surviving texts of those used by Colet for the lectures at Oxford on Paul's Epistles mentioned by Erasmus. The conjecture was not unreasonable, but it had something of a fortuitous quality to it. Without Erasmus' account, that is to say, I think it unlikely that anyone would have thought either of the major commentaries intended as a lecture or a series of lectures. Jayne points to evidence in the All Souls manuscript of Ficino's *Epistolae* indicating that a commentary on I Corinthians was the seventh in a list of eight projects Colet planned to undertake between 1496 and 1505.[19] To this I can add from my study of the manuscript of this commentary that the work was not, apparently, composed all at one time. There is good evidence that Colet left it more than once for a length of time — perhaps a long time — and then took it up again.

A. The Text

MS Gg. iv. 26 in the Cambridge University Library is a large quarto volume bound in leather on board. It contains five works by Colet. The folios are numbered consecutively throughout, but 64, 65, 66, and 74 are missing from the foliation. Included in the volume are:

The Commentary on Romans (2r–61v)
A Letter to the Abbot of Winchcombe (62r–63v)

The Treatise on the Mystical Body (67r–73v)
The Commentary on I Corinthians (75r–153r)
The Commentary on the Celestial Hierarchy According to Dionysius
(157r–170v; 153v–156v, with additional notes 171r–172r)

A pencilled note by Henry Bradshaw, on fol. 172v, dated November 19, 1863, assigns the provenance of the volume to the Holdsworth Collection, "(1649) MS. 13.," while the bookplate on the inside cover reads: "University Library / Cambridge / From the library of Richard / Holdsworth, D.D., Master of / Emmanuel College. / 1664." Knight says—I do not know on what grounds— that the volume seems to have been the gift of Archbishop Parker, and was, with others of Colet's, "very probably bought by him of the Executors of Dean *Colet*, who were ordered to dispose of them by his *Will*."[20]

The text of the Commentary on I Corinthians is almost certainly Colet's holograph, although the handwriting varies greatly, showing at times much haste, at times much care. It is from significant variations in the hand in two or three places that I infer that Colet put the work aside perhaps for more than a few weeks at a time and then took it up again. The handwriting on fol. 150 differs sharply from that which precedes and follows; this text was almost certainly an earlier self-contained comment on particular points in Chapters XIV and XV of the Epistle, and no attempt was made to integrate its contents with what goes before (Colet's final comments on Chapter XIV) or with what follows (the regular beginning of Colet's comments on Chapter XV). In a few places throughout the work there may be evidence, I think, that Colet was suffering from fatigue or from ill health. The inexplicable omission of an obviously need- ed word here and there, together with the generally tidy composition of the folios, may indicate that in parts, at least, of the Commentary, Colet was writing from previous versions or drafts, but Chapter VII will be enough to indicate to the reader that the work was never entirely revised to the author's satisfaction.

In addition to a considerable number of emendations and insertions in Colet's own hand, there are a few by a later hand, one or two of them perversely wrongheaded, and all of them of purely grammatical import. These would ap- pear to have been added after Colet's regular scribe, Peter Meghen, used the manuscript for his transcription. On 97v, for example, Colet's "si magis bonum" has been correctly emended to "si maiori bono," but Meghen has copied the original and wrong case.

Meghen's handsome transcription of the text in Gg.iv.26 is to be found in the library of Emmanuel College, where it is numbered 3.3.12 (and not 3.3.16, as Lupton everywhere designates it). There is no difficulty in establishing the dependence of Emmanuel 3.3.12 on C.U.L. Gg.iv.26, nor is there any evidence, curiously enough, that Meghen had any other source to help him resolve what

difficulties and perplexities he found in reading Colet's hand. Colet cannot, then, have supervised the transcription, and he does not seem to have checked it after it was done.

The *monoculus Brabantinus* (as Meghen was called) was a very good scribe, but he left his copy in some respects unfinished. The initials are blank, and there are a good many empty spaces in the text, of which perhaps the majority seem to be for words Meghen either was unsure of or found some reason to query. There are some corrections, but these would seem to have been made on the spot, as it were; apparently he did not make any thorough revision of the whole.

Lupton, for his edition of 1874, made his own transcription of the text in C.U.L. Gg.iv.26, but had for consultation a copy of Em. 3.3.12 made by Seebohm.[21] It is hard to conjecture to what extent Seebohm's copy of Meghen's transcription may have influenced Lupton's reading of the original; certainly a few of his renditions seem to be drawn from the Seebohm copy. Thus where Colet has "habeare" (107v), Lupton reproduces instead "habearis," for no very cogent reason that I can see. On the whole, however, Lupton's dependence on Meghen is clearly negligible, even in those passages where Colet's hand is most difficult, and he does not repeat Meghen's mistakes and omissions, although he makes new ones of his own. Moreover, in a few instances where Meghen has read a difficult word or passage correctly, Lupton falls back on his own conjecture, with less satisfactory results.

The text presented here is that of C.U.L. Gg.iv.26 throughout, diligently compared, as editors could say in a more candid century, with that of Em. 3.3.12, and rather less diligently with Lupton's printed version. I have reproduced the text as exactly as possible within reason: I have not, that is to say, reproduced the contractions and abbreviations, and I have emended Colet's obvious slips, inserting between pointed brackets omitted letters, and recording in notes the original form where another sort of change has been necessary.

Latinists will be interested rather than disturbed by Colet's wealth of variant spellings, some of which were standard in his time, while others seem to be idiosyncratic. I have thought it worthwhile, therefore, to leave them unchanged, especially since Latin texts of the period that have not been normalized are not plentiful in print, and can be useful to scholars with an interest in these matters. When I have been in doubt as to whether a word is misspelt or simply given in a variant form, I have usually assumed that the second explanation is more likely, unless the word as it stands is not recognizable from the context.

What scriptural quotations Colet underlined I have italicized, but I have not exceeded my author, even for the sake of a well-established and generally useful tradition. He incorporates much more often than he cites; obviously not every scriptural word or paraphrase can be italicized. In my translation, I have tried to identify all of the principal biblical quotations and allusions.

Colet's marginal drawings I have reproduced, believing that they cannot fail to interest the reader and sometimes to illuminate the text, and that a reproduction, if generally accurate, is better than a verbal description. As much as possible, I have tried also to present the schemata in Chapters III and XII as Colet has them in his manuscript. I have not noted all Meghen's spelling variations,[22] nor his omissions and downright mistakes. Only when a variant reading is significant or suggestive have I made reference to it.

Both Meghen and Lupton omit Colet's marginalia, and these I have included. They are of two main kinds: the majority either summarize or serve as headings for the passages beside which they are written, in the traditional manner; a few are additions or insertions, and this is indicated in the manuscript by a line drawn roughly around them and pulling them to the text. These latter I have simply incorporated in their appropriate places, since clearly Colet meant them to be read thus. There is, of course, a slender possibility that he added them after Meghen had made his copy, but it is hard to imagine a reason for Lupton's failure to include them. Punctuation in Colet's manuscript is spare. I have therefore added paragraph divisions in many places, and such other marks of punctuation as might do no harm and might assist the reader's easier understanding. Chapter headings I have normalized (in the manuscript one finds "Caput II," "Capite 4," "Caput viii sequitur," all in a very offhand way) and I have supplied the titles for the first, sixth, and seventh chapters.

B. The Translation

Lupton's translation of this work possesses, as anyone who has read it will acknowledge, unusual felicity and poise of style. I was familiar with it long before I transcribed Colet's holograph myself, and in recording my indebtedness to it I can only pay a thankful tribute to a great scholar and an unusually gifted translator. In preparing my own translation, I have made no attempt to be significantly different from Lupton for the sake of establishing my autonomy as a translator. Where Lupton's English phrasing is exactly and felicitously adequate—as it sometimes is to a degree that will fill any translator with awe and respect—I saw no reason to torture synonyms or to juggle phrases.

Several considerations, however, inclined me to a largely independent translation rather than to a revision of Lupton's. For one thing, to revise a work with a style as graceful as Lupton's is a graceless undertaking, and one to make anyone reluctant. For another, one of the chief sources of beauty in Lupton's translation happens to constitute also a weakness in that translation. This is a pervasive anachronism of language which is often misleading, and generally unrepresen-

tative of the tone and character of Colet's original Latin. Lupton was at home and at ease with the beautiful rhythms and phrasings of the Authorized Version and the Prayer Book; he used them almost without trace of contrivance. They are not, however, the rhythms and phrasings of Colet's Latin, a clothing for thought tailored by other minds and hearts, and possessed of other — and not always parallel — strengths and weaknesses. I do not mean to say that Lupton in his translations consistently and in all respects biblicized Colet's style; so frequent and persistent, however, are the echoes from the two great mountains of religious and liturgical prose in English that the original sounds of Colet's thought are often counterpointed, at best, and perhaps more often lost altogether.

It was Lupton's practice also to use the Authorized Version almost invariably for the translation of Colet's biblical quotations, paraphrases, and allusions, even when these are a single word only. Now apart from the obvious weaknesses of this procedure in the matter of anachronistic flavors and tones, there are instances where the result is sheer absurdity. It is regrettable, let us admit, that the version of the Psalms in the Vulgate has the phrase "in cathedra pestilentiae"; but this is what Colet quotes, and there is little point in translating the phrase, as Lupton does, by "in the seat of the scornful." Again, to translate "omnis paternitas" (Eph. III:15) as "the whole family" is to mistranslate, and "Nemo Deum videt" is not adequately rendered by the words, "No man hath seen God at any time."

To avoid such difficulties as these, my own practice has been to try as well as I could to present literal translations for Colet's biblical Latin, whether quotation or paraphrase, and in so doing I have regularly consulted English translations of the Vulgate and commentaries on the Vulgate. In general, I have also in my translation borne in the forefront of my mind that the Latin of the Vulgate does blend with Colet's Latin as wine, in Lewis' phrase,[23] mixes with water; but where the Latin phrasing of the Vulgate would have had, in my opinion, a distinctly archaic or a dramatic or an otherwise special ring to it for speakers of Latin in the early sixteenth century, I have tried to transfer this quality to the English. My primary goal has been the accurate conveying of the sense as Colet is most likely to have understood it.

The reader should have at hand a copy of I Corinthians as he goes through the Commentary so that he can check on the degree of closeness with which, in any particular passage, Colet is following Paul. If an English translation is used for biblical references, a translation of the Vulgate is, of course, to be preferred.

Colet's Latin is not easy to translate. In the main, his syntax reflects what may be called (loosely, and with reservations) a Neoplatonist manner of thought, and his mind can find expression at once richer, more graceful, and more accurate in Latin than in English. This is principally because of the greater wealth of connectives and subordinating devices in Latin, and the far greater freedom

with which one can use them. At that, Colet's habit of sustaining continuities
of thought is unusual: the sentence, as such, is often of rather negligible importance in his writing. I do not think he tried especially to create the extraordinarily
long sentences that often occur in this treatise. The dialectic simply cannot let
a thought stand without a related thought, to which another again is too closely
linked to be divorced by a period, and so on and on, sometimes to the grave
dismay of the reader. More serious must be the dismay of the translator, because
he is bound by the primary conventions, at least, of another language; he must
seek to discern in the original language the relative degrees of emphasis given
to thoughts as well as their interrelations, and then try to transfer them as faithfully
as possible to his re-thinking of the thoughts in the second language. If the reader
will recognize this peculiar difficulty of the translator confronted by a style like
Colet's, he will be the more tolerant toward certain liberties I have had to take
in matters of punctuation (freer use of the colon, e.g., than contemporary purists
might approve), sentence structure, and diction. Faithfulness to Colet's precise
thought has been my first goal; my second has been to convey as much as possible not only what Colet says, but (with inevitable adjustments) the way he says
it. If there are any graces in my English translation, the reader will find they
were in Colet's Latin first, and I should like him to believe that at least half
the awkwardnesses in my translation can be traced to the same source.

C. Colet's Latin Style

George Lyly, after reporting that Colet left nothing in writing (see above,
p. 9 and n.), goes on to say, "sed purissimam *Latinæ* linguæ Elocutionem, eandemq;
Laconica Brevitate compositam ex . . . Epistolis colligere licet." Certainly Colet
thought it of the highest importance that men should write a pure Latin style,
rejecting "all barbary all corrupcion all laten adulterate which ignorant blynde
folis brought into this worlde and with the same hath distayned and poysenyd
the olde laten spech and the veray Romayne tong which in the tyme of Tully
and Salust and Virgil and Terence was usid."[24] "Blotterature," as Colet in the
next sentence describes the bad stuff written by the ignorant blind fools, "that
ffylthynesse," clearly stirs in him an ire that would do credit to the most ardent
of Renaissance Neo-Ciceronians.

Erasmus, however, with a tone of complaisant broadmindedness, implies that
Colet was almost equally impatient with the "trivial rules of grammarians," and
imputes to him the belief that "these were a hindrance to expressing oneself well,
and that that result was only obtained by the study of the best authors." With
gentle righteousness Erasmus adds: "But he paid the penalty for this notion himself.

For though eloquent both by nature and training, and though he had at his command a singularly copious flow of words while speaking, he would now and then trip in such points as critics are given to mark. And it was on this account, if I mistake not, that he refrained from writing books." He concludes: "I wish he had not so refrained; for I should have been glad of the thoughts of such a man, no matter in what language expressed."[25]

On the whole, George Lyly's inference from the letters was a sound one. Not only did Colet love the "purissimam *Latinæ* linguæ elocutionem"; he generally achieved it himself. There are indeed in his writings grammatical slips of the sort that "critics are given to mark," but the reader will see from the present work that these are very few, especially when he reflects that the Commentary was, as far as we can judge, never thoroughly revised or prepared for publication. On the other hand, that Colet should have been reluctant for stylistic reasons to publish this or any of the extant Latin manuscripts is also credible: in all things he was something of a perfectionist, and he had read a good deal of Latin by the best stylists. Ordinarily, Colet's Latin is inspired not so much by aesthetic considerations as by the principle of efficiency. What he has to say, he says almost always directly, adequately, clearly, and forcefully: "sufficienter et dilucide," as Pico says of Moses. Pico must have been the one among Colet's contemporaries to hold views on style most congenial to him and most like his own; the reader who comes to Colet from the *Heptaplus* or the *Oratio de hominis dignitate* will find himself more at home than one coming from the works of Erasmus.

By "laconic brevity" George Lyly probably meant nothing more than the freedom from polish and ornateness for their own sake which characterizes both Pico and Colet. Here is thought clothed to travel, not to impress or to delight. At the same time, the reader will observe that the qualities of eloquence (in the strict sense) adverted to by Erasmus are reflected in the present work. Often the style and manner are those of the spoken language rather than of the written. The tone is that of direct address, and the reader is made somehow to feel that he has a part in the words themselves comparable to the writer's, as though they were speaker and hearer, engaged in a dialogue of which only half is spoken aloud.

In addition, the manner is more often didactic than reflective, or persuasive, or simply conversational. Colet informs, explains, relates, comments, interprets, all as though directing his words to readers less well informed than himself and less well equipped for the purpose at hand. His didacticism is not, however, condescending; he is not here addressing himself to children or to the ignorant, and the work takes for granted both knowledge and intelligence.

If by laconic brevity Lyly intended also something approaching a Tacitean terseness discernible in more than one place in the letters to Erasmus, this, too, will be found not infrequently in the present work. There are also instances of

the traditionally English irony of understatement, and there is irony of other sorts, gentle as well as merciless, seemingly ingenuous as well as consciously urbane. The general tenor of the work is, however, no more Tacitean and no more ironic than it is florid. Directness, firmness, precision, and strength are the qualities the reader will find on every page, together with an extraordinarily adept manner of relating thought to thought and of sustaining the forward movement of an idea through hundreds of words, with consequent refinements of emphasis and always without artifice.

Occasionally, too, the style is lyrical and exalted; instead of moving onward, the sentences soar upward. Colet is capable of very considerable grace and rhetorical effectiveness, and sometimes his words do much more than communicate thought. I suspect, though, that against two or three passages in which Colet uses exclamation or apostrophe some readers may object that here is not only artifice but artificiality. I should defend such passages on the grounds that in them Colet is being simply literal, in a way; that here, too, is a very close correspondence between what his mind knows and what his pen writes. The passages to which I refer do not make their best impression when isolated, of course, and they have at times been excerpted to establish a point. The reader must also remember to make allowance for the potential intensity of convictions he does not share.

In one respect most balanced readers may well find themselves uneasy about Colet's Latin style. Like most of his contemporaries, he saw no reason to avoid the telling pun, even when it needed more than a little help from human ingenuity. In general, however, Colet's paranomasias are indeed telling, rather than merely or mainly pleasing: beneath them lie assumptions about correspondences between language and the reality it designates. Thus the extended play on *dominicus* and *demonicus* (pp. 216–18), is much more than a dubious *jeu d'esprit* or a rhetorical device for attaining a sharpened effect. In the words themselves, juxtaposed, Colet believes there is significant knowledge for the man who has eyes to see it—or, perhaps, ears to hear it. The consequences of such assumptions about language are to be observed also in the echoes, the chimings, which Colet's style prepares (sometimes elaborately) and fulfills in the reader's mind. I think they are not intended primarily as literary graces.

Yet for all its forthright efficiency, resourcefulness, and constant according of the primacy to statement rather than to ornament or wit, Colet's Latin style can scarcely claim an equal place with the styles of those writers of Latin whom Colet himself so earnestly wished to serve as models for the young. But it does deserve much more respect than has customarily been accorded it.

Mention may be made here of Colet's use of Greek in this treatise. To my knowledge, no one has yet found a way to establish definitively whether he ever achieved with the language a considerable ease, or a competence, or merely a gentleman's acquaintance. E. W. Hunt summarizes the direct evidence on the

matter from the correspondence of Erasmus:

> It would appear that what immediately stimulated him to set about learn-
> ing [Greek] was the publication of Erasmus' Greek New Testament in 1516.
> He wrote to Erasmus: "For my part I am so devoted to your studies and
> so charmed with your new edition, that it produces in me a variety of
> emotions. At one moment I am full of sorrow that I have not learned Greek,
> without which we are nothing; at another I rejoice in that light which
> is emitted by the rays of your genius." Later in that same letter he said
> that he was willing to learn it, "though I am almost an old man; remember-
> ing that Cato learned Greek when old, and observing that you, who match
> me in age, are now studying Hebrew." These words were written towards
> the end of June 1516. On 22 September of the same year Thomas More
> informed Erasmus: "Colet is already working hard at Greek with some
> help volunteered by my Clement"; and a week later Erasmus retailed the
> news to Reuchlin: "Colet is now, at his age, learning Greek."[26]

If we accept Jayne's inference that the present work was composed before 1505,
we may be surprised, noting the presence in it of Greek words in Colet's own
hand, to see that he was "learning Greek" more than ten years later, and that
his friends were speaking about him as though he had never before known any.
It is hard to say what part we must allow in these statements, and in Colet's
own, either for Colet's modesty — he thought his own Latin inadequate — or for
the standards of excellence he and his peers accepted in these matters.[27] In any
event, Colet uses Greek infrequently in the present work, but in a distinctly
illuminating way, and in a manner to indicate that there was more of it in his
head than a gentleman's interest or a dabbler's smattering of vocabulary.

D. Colet's Exegesis

Much that has been written on Colet's exegesis has been distinctly tendentious. In particular, Colet's commentaries on Paul have been compared in spirit,
procedure, and intent, not with medieval or other Renaissance works of exegesis
and exposition, but, unaccountably, with works of systematic theology like the
Sentences of Peter Lombard, the Summa Theologica of St. Thomas, or the Opus
Oxoniense (itself a commentary on the Sentences) of Duns Scotus. Obviously these
are not exegetical works, nor do they in any way represent medieval exegesis.
The Sententiarum libri quatuor, in Colet's time the most commonly used of the
compendia of systematic theology, is essentially a compilation (it has been said
that scarcely more than ten lines have been found to be original) of authorities —

scriptural, patristic, and some others—on the principal topics of Christian theology. The tone and intent of the work are clearly dialectical: Peter Lombard, inspired with the spirit of his master, Abelard, was a consummate dialectician, although he himself denounced what he called "the excesses of the dialecticians."[28]

During the four centuries following its composition (about 1150), this work had a very great influence, but it is a mistake to suppose that it supplanted the direct study of Scripture in the medieval universities. Nor must one suppose that the *catenae* (works in which patristic and other interpretations of each text were collated) were, for all their apparent popularity, the sole mainstay of scriptural study. There is no question, as I have said, that during the centuries immediately before Colet's time a dialectical approach to Scripture dominated formal study.

The spirit and methods of medieval exegesis can perhaps best be recognized in commentaries like those of Aquinas. A detailed comparison with Colet's work is not possible here, but it will be useful to draw some general lines between the present work and Thomas' commentary on the same epistle.[29]

It is to be noted first that Colet's commentary has much less of an academic ring to it than Thomas'. Thomas, like Colet, works his way through the Epistle chapter by chapter, but divides each of his own sixteen chapters into from two to eight *lectiones*. Each *lectio* analyses and discusses only a few verses. Thomas' methodological rigor does not, of course, permit him the digressions to be found in Colet, with the result that his commentary is easier to follow than Colet's, and in any given part more easily and more swiftly related to the text of Paul. Thomas has something to say about everything in the epistle, but Colet passes over some parts, and gives very scant attention to others.

While Colet readily abandons the exegetical discussion of Paul's meaning to pass to homiletic exhortation, using the words of the text as a starting point for the admonition or spiritual direction of his readers, Thomas confines himself to the meaning of the text, to allusions that will throw light upon the meaning, and to an impersonal exposition of theological and disciplinary applications that can be shown to be derived from or related to the words of Paul under discussion.

Thomas is much more within the tradition of interpretation than is Colet. That is to say, he quotes parallel and relevant texts from Scripture much more extensively than does Colet, and much more explicitly, giving the reference each time, and he cites patristic interpretations, when these are useful, much more often and much more rigorously. Again, Colet's language and categories of thought are often symbolic or mystical rather than scientific or even theological, in the customary senses of the word (see below, pp. 40f), while Thomas strives for conceptual clarity and precision, using the established terminology of tradition.

Colet was, of course, thoroughly familiar with the commonly accepted medieval doctrine of the four senses of Scripture. In fact, he discusses it at some length in Chapter V of the *Ecclesiastical Hierarchy*, grounding it in the ultimate reality

of God's universal order. The Christian hierarchy is a "bright image of the truth," and the Mosaic hierarchy is a "shadowing of the image"—in other words, a type of what is to come. The New Testament, on the other hand, is for Colet "wholly literal," with an important qualification: "inasmuch as the Church of God is figurative, conceive always an *anagoge* in what you hear in the doctrines of the Church; the meaning of which will not cease, till the figure has become the truth. From this moreover conclude that, where the literal sense is, there the allegorical is not always along with it; but, on the other hand, that where there is the allegorical sense, the literal sense is always underlying it."[30]

In the same way, one making a detailed comparison between the commentary of Colet and that of Aquinas would be hard put to it to say which uses the grammatical method more consistently and more thoroughly. They are about equally concerned (which is to say, not very much) with the ways in which versions other than the Vulgate, and in other languages, may add to or qualify understanding; interestingly enough, one finds (especially if the comparison is extended to include Thomas' commentaries on the other letters of Paul) that they take the Greek language into consideration to about the same extent and in roughly the same ways. On the whole, Thomas much more frequently concerns himself with the definition or explanation of Paul's terms than Colet does, and much more explicitly.

In view of these general points of comparison, I do not think it is particularly sound to seek to enhance Colet's historical importance by maintaining that his commentaries on Paul represent a notable break with the medieval tradition of exegesis because they are concerned with literal meaning, or because they occasionally mention Greek words, or refer to patristic authorities, or because they do not become involved in typological and metaphorical interpretations (in fact, they are almost always in some way involved with typology and metaphor). Even Colet's respect for the usefulness of grammar as distinguished from dialectic, a respect which makes itself evident not infrequently in the commentaries, is not, I think, a mark by which one may distinguish his exegetical methods from those of Thomas, whom one may safely take to be as characteristically medieval as anyone.

Colet's commentaries are, of course, much more than exegesis of specific books of the Bible: this one, in particular, is a discursive treatise on the most fundamental questions of metaphysics and soteriology, as well as an exposition of Paul. If we restrict our consideration of them for the moment to their exegetical scope and intention, I believe the most significant differences between them and the exegetical works of Thomas (taking these as representative of the Schools) are principally four.

First of all, and most obviously, Colet's commentaries are in a very real sense extra-scholastic. I have mentioned their discursiveness, their relative lack of

methodological rigor, and the impression they give the reader that they are written without much reference to the tradition of interpretation. Thomas addresses himself very clearly to academic, clerical readers, professional scholars with trained minds, or minds in the process of being trained. Colet, on the other hand, seems to have in mind readers who are approaching Paul as though for the first time, readers not particularly scholarly in any professional or traditional sense, and not by any means necessarily clerical, although in one or two places he speaks as though addressing priests alone. It would not be fanciful to say that Colet writes as though his words were to be read by all mankind, and not just by that relatively small number of people who, by reason of their native endowments, training, and interests, will be likely to spend their time reading commentaries on Paul's letters.

Secondly, Colet's exegesis is very different from that of Thomas because of its predominantly soteriological character. Thomas' theological assumptions are conceptual and metaphysical, while Colet's are largely symbolic (in a particular sense of the word) and soteriological. It is difficult to isolate and specify the ways in which this character makes Colet's exegesis different from Thomas'; to describe the one as Neoplatonist and the other as Aristotelian (or Thomistic) is to over-simplify matters. At this point, therefore, it is best simply to state the difference in general terms, and to postpone further inquiry to a discussion of Colet's soteriology in itself.

Thirdly, while to Aquinas Paul is simply "Apostolus," and highly impersonal, Colet makes his readers much more vividly aware of Paul as a real human being, judging, making decisions, and experiencing emotions.

Finally, Colet adverts much more frequently and much more consistently to the historical circumstances of Paul's letter than Thomas does. It is in this respect that one ought to recognize the nondialectical quality of Colet's commentaries.

The very general lines of comparison I have drawn here between the exegesis of Colet and that of Thomas are not intended to serve as bases for inferences about Colet's importance in the history of exegetical methodology, nor would I wish them to serve as confirmation for those studies that have treated Colet's approach to Scripture as something symptomatic of his age, and primarily significant for that reason. Perhaps it is best to leave to some professional historian of exegesis (there are not many of them) the task of locating Colet in the general pattern of pre-Reformation scriptural study and of assessing the extent of his contribution to subsequent developments. Only someone well versed in the very long and complex history of exegesis can successfully avoid the pitfalls of over-simplification and historical shortsightedness that are in the path.

Turning now from comparison to a direct discussion of Colet's exegesis, perhaps I should remark first that the reader should divest his mind of any connotations of a limiting sort that may attach to the words *explication* and *interpretation*. The

exegetical processes Colet displays in this work are operations of the mind no less creative, in the contemporary jargon, than most that culminate in writing. (Some people feel an apparently automatic disdain for all that is not original. Our ancestors were wiser, and had only admiration for the author who chooses patiently to rethink and explore the thoughts of a mind he recognizes as greater and richer than his own.) Colet had an earnest and effective desire to understand Paul correctly and deeply. As he works his way through the Epistle, his mind shows little tendency toward either recklessness or oversimplification. One finds here none of the intellectual impatience that craves new truths rather because they are new than because they are true; nor does one find the partisan theological or philosophical bias that turns all into grist for the mills that tediously and triumphantly grind ever new confirmations for positions already *ex aliunde* embraced. Colet cannot come to Paul as a newborn infant; he cannot erase from his mind what he already knows, and would not want to if he could, but he does approach Paul with very great candor and honesty.

With the integrity of mind Colet shows in seeking to understand Paul as honestly and truly as a human mind can, is joined an intensely earnest desire to make Paul's thought accessible to others, and a more than scholarly sense of responsibility in this regard. Consequently the style is more often didactic than anything else, as I have remarked above; but here I must add an important qualification. The character and quality of Colet's exegesis are such that the treatise as a whole can be called a didactic work only in a special sense. It is a painstaking exploration of truths to be known, understood, and shared with others, not an instruction in truths previously known by the author and now magisterially communicated to others.

In his exploration, Colet illustrates (according to his lights) as well as any Christian writer has, that to be single-hearted is not the same thing as to be simple-minded. He shows his own awareness of this truth in his clear-eyed recognition that to believe in Revelation is not to believe that the Divine Intellect will necessarily choose for inspiration men who are weak in their wits. His position is that while a false and darksome wisdom is displeasing in the extreme to the Godhead, as are minds "divided, dispersed, and wavering," the highest truths and "purest principles" can be grasped only by men strong in mind, "who are extremely powerful in soul, who are concentrated into oneness . . . and stand firm on the loftiest part of their minds. . . . To this group of men," Colet writes, "Paul also belonged" (p. 109 below). Here it is important to understand the distinction Colet draws between uninformed men like "Peter, John, James, and the rest of their sort," on the one hand, and "men endowed with secular wisdom," like Paul and "his disciple, Dionysius the Areopagite, and not a few others" (p. 89). Both kinds of chosen men are to be recognized as intellectually strong men, wise (i.e., possessing the excellence of the intellect) and powerful (possessing the ex-

cellence of the will). The difference lies then in something extra possessed by
the second group, and this is really only an apparent possession—indeed, a non-
thing—because secular wisdom without God's revelation, Colet argues, is by
its nature at enmity with God. (Paul, when he followed his secular wisdom,
persecuted the servants of God. When his mind was illuminated by God, he
gladly joined the ranks of the persecuted himself, preaching "only Christ crucified," which was "to the Greeks"—men endowed with secular wisdom only—
"foolishness."

Men of Paul's sort, Colet continues, "in undertaking to tell others what they
had learned from God, were of nothing more careful than that men should see
that they were not drawing any of their wisdom from the world; they thought
it an unworthy thing that human reason should mix with divine revelation, and
they wanted no one to think the truth was to be believed because of human
persuasiveness instead of the power of God" (p. 89). The irrelevance (and worse)
of secular wisdom, then, is at least theoretically clear in Colet's mind. But here,
as in several other crucial matters, we must remember that Colet is dealing in
abstractions, and holding an idealized position that is delicate in the extreme.
I shall have occasion below to speak of this position again. Here I wish to draw
attention to only three implications relevant to Colet's exegetical methods.

First, Colet postulates (theoretically, at least) an impassable gulf between the
wisdom of God and the wisdom of men unenlightened by God, between the
truths of revelation and whatever else men can know or think they know. It
is of the utmost importance that the two wisdoms be clearly understood as pertaining to the world of intelligibles: to know the speed of light or the number
of reindeer in Lapland or the principles of combustion is irrelevant, Colet would
have to say; there is no wisdom of either sort in such matters, although presumably
scientia of this sort, too, can inflate and thus fill men's minds to the point where
they cannot care about wisdom. The relation between the two wisdoms can be
seen as one of opposites. Formulated as propositions, then, secular (or false) wisdom
and divine (or true) wisdom will be necessarily antithetical. Hence the principles
of men and those of God are spoken of as being at war. There can be for Colet
no real relation at all between human and divine wisdom. The latter is transcendent in the most integral sense. There is no analogy, intrinsic or extrinsic, between the two. There can be no comparison: one *is*, and the other is not, has
no real existence, and cannot be denominated with respect to the first. There
is no room in Colet's mind for any such distinction as that by which principles
of knowledge and wisdom without divine revelation are (or can be) relative,
or approximate, or partial, while the divinely revealed truths are absolute, and
real, and integral. As a consequence, revelation, as Scripture, cannot strictly be
compared to (or even denominated with respect to) any other sort of writing.

Secondly, Colet stresses a corresponding distinction (which we have already

seen) between men strong in mind and will, and therefore capable of receiving the divine truths, and men who are weak either in will or in mind, and so not apt for the divine truths, however much they may seem to be endowed with the wisdom of the other sort. This distinction raises further difficulties of its own, from which Colet does not altogether satisfactorily extricate himself. As an intellectual conviction, however, it at once reinforces the very great esteem in which he holds Paul for other reasons, and leads him to postulate prior dispositions in any man who is the instrument of divine inspiration or the recipient of any divine gift whatsoever. So far is Colet from a Pelagian position that he insists explicitly with regard to this latter point that the prior dispositions are themselves entirely God's work. Indeed, in an interesting passage (p. 267), Colet recognizes that "sometimes God wishes to give things of worth in unworthy vessels." Yet he does not deny in these matters the role of human responsibility, indicating clearly his belief that dispositions and graces themselves can be merited *ex congruo*, if in no sense absolutely. Certainly a man's acts and thoughts and omissions—his willed darkness and coldness, Colet would say—can make him incapable of receiving them.

A third implication is latent in all this. It is all very well for Colet to draw abstract distinctions that exclude considerations of means and ends in the phenomenological order as they exclude considerations of relative and absolute, approximate and ultimate; in the phenomenological order, in which also willy-nilly we act, a man cannot without *particular* supernatural intervention understand Scripture or anything else unless he knows the meaning of words, unless he has some insight into the historical circumstances and causes that led the inspired writer to set down this truth rather than that, and in this way rather than in some other way, and unless he is able to relate what is written here in one specific context with relevant things written elsewhere in other contexts, or not written at all.

Colet's own premises and methods stand as a very significant qualification to the oft-quoted paragraphs at the close of Chapter X of this Commentary. There Colet puts himself within the militantly antipagan tradition of Christian thought. He argues intransigently that it is a delusion, and perhaps too a self-deception, for a man to maintain that the reading of pagan books helps him to understand Sacred Scripture. "When you act thus, you show distrust of your ability to understand Holy Writ through grace alone and prayer, through the help of Christ and of faith. Instead you put your trust in the principles and the assistance of the pagans." Then, in a manner recalling a legendary Islamic dilemma about the burning of a library, he goes on: "All that belongs to the truth is contained in the splendid, the plentiful table of Holy Scripture. The mind craving for something to feed on beyond the truth is surely far from healthy, and a Christless mind." He reaffirms that "the truth is understood by grace. Grace is provided

when our prayers are heard. Our prayers are heard when they are sharpened by whole-hearted devotion, and made strong by fasting. If you turn to any other course, your conduct is madness" (p. 219).

The intransigence toward pagan books is clearly directed toward what in them is "beyond the truth," or false: their *mythos*. Colet's homely metaphor throughout this passage — he starts from an allegorical reading of Paul's words about a man's not being able to share the Lord's table and the table of demons — deserves attention. The dishes in which the food is set forth may be not only unobjectionable; they may be delightful, pleasing in the extreme, and worthy of all praise. (Colet appreciated beauties of style.) What they contain is another matter altogether, and the content, the "principles of the pagans," is what Colet objects to. The pagans he had particularly in mind were no doubt those who expressed a belief that the High Ruler of Gods and men was a rare seducer of innocent girls, or that self-castration in honor of Cybele was virtuous, or that pederasty was natural, and normal, and proper too; probably he would have included those teachers who delineated for their faithful a Paradise of raki and houris. A mind that has known the Judeo-Christian revelation about the oneness, the holiness, the great and awesome mystery of God, and the calling of men to be perfect "as their Father in Heaven is perfect," might well seem to Colet necessarily unhealthy and Christless if it craved such intellectual food, and something near to blasphemous if it piously asserted that all was directed toward a better understanding of Scripture. In Colet's time there were such men, and not a few of them carried their syncretizing mythography, with however much sincerity, to absurd and staggering limits.

The end of Chapter X must still seem remarkably heedless in the universality of its exclusivism, especially coming as it does from the pen of a man who clearly owes so much, directly or indirectly, to Plato, to Plotinus, to Aristotle, and to other writers outside the Judeo-Christian tradition. Whether or not Colet would reply that none of these is really a pagan philosopher, he must of course admit that their works are not part of Sacred Scripture. Perhaps the fascination of a linguistic preoccupation is here influencing his good sense, as it has influenced that of others. What is not *dominicum* is *demonicum*; a little less impatience with the careful distinctions of Aquinas and other Schoolmen would have helped Colet here.

As I have indicated, however much Colet insists that grace, provided to us when our prayers are heard because of our single-hearted devotion and fasting, is the only means that will enable us to understand Sacred Scripture, in point of fact he does not seek mainly or primarily to help his readers to understand I Corinthians by urging them to be prayerful, devout, and self-denying. The principal aids to understanding he offers them are of a different order, although no doubt they presuppose grace for their correct and profitable use. They are

intellectual disciplines and methodologies proper to the right scrutiny of any written text, whether scriptural or not: linguistic analysis, inquiry about historical circumstances, certain inductive procedures for the weighing of one possible interpretation against another, and so on.

In all these mental operations Colet demonstrates learning, insight, and judgment. He invokes what is relevant and known to him about the culture, the circumstances, and the attitudes of the young Christian community in Corinth, and so leaves the company of those who have treated Scripture as something to be read without regard to the circumstances of its composition. The reader will notice that Colet is very much more realistic about the "Primitive Church" than are many in his century. Indeed, he is as free from the insidious assumption that an earlier Golden Age saw only giants of heroic intelligence and virtue upon the earth as he is from the equally distorting historical perspective in which the past is seen only as a series of causes and occasions for the culmination that is the present. Sometimes he compares the condition of the Corinthian Christians in Paul's time to that of the Christians of Western Europe in his own; but this is either for the better understanding of the former or for some homiletic application that Colet wishes his readers to make to their own lives. The past remains autonomous. There is no attitude of superiority latent in such passages; at the same time, there is no attribution of unreal glories or supernatural clarities to the members or the institutions of the early Christian communities.

Colet has, of course, a philosophy of history, one that could be considered as inclusive and as dogmatic as that of Marx. He sees the universe, *sub specie temporis*, as an Incarnational and a Christocentric phenomenon. There is the time before Christ, and the time after (or, more properly, *with*) Christ. The former time he does not here present as being in its successive parts significantly ordered toward the Incarnation, but rather (for humanity, at least) as a hapless chaos in which men, apart from the holy theologian-prophets of Judaism, are lost in the dark and the cold, unable to find and not caring to seek the light of truth and the warmth of love; the world of intelligibles is closed to them.

With the beginning of the second time there is also the beginning of the ordered universe of men (see below, p. 55). This is our time, as it was that also of Paul and his Corinthian converts. It is not, of course, cyclic, but there is a real and an important sense in which it is progressive: inexorably it is moving (but not, perhaps, in ways that men can see) toward its fulfillment, which should be viewed, no doubt, as a third time. The fulfillment will come, Colet says, when what Christ taught us to pray for every day has been achieved: that God's Kingdom come, and that His will be done on earth as it is in heaven. Then all men will have found their place in the intelligible universe of men, with Christ as the tenth of their order, all sharing in the light and the warmth, in a dynamic balance of beauty and usefulness (p. 253). The rest of the universe is already ordered.

Colet shows no signs, incidentally, of believing that the third time is near.

This transcending view of history does not color the particular historical details Colet uses as relevant background for the understanding of Paul's Epistle. These are either expanded or inferred from the New Testament itself, or drawn from the commonplaces of history rather than from specific secular authors.[31] The Corinthians and the Greek world in general, Colet tells us, in the first century esteemed natural wisdom and intellectual resourcefulness; they had "abundant leisure and learning"; they were skilfully trained in eloquence; they had great faith in their rhetoric as a solvent in which all philosophical questions could be made clear; they did not readily take to the Christian virtue of humility; the converts of Corinth had difficulty abandoning deeply rooted ways and convictions incompatible with Christianity; and so on.

Colet's use of a historical perspective, as these examples show, is not notable for its erudition of detail or distinguished by any evidence of extensive scholarly research. It is the consistency with which the historical perspective is maintained, and the relative emphasis given to it, that set his Commentary off from the main current of exegesis in the centuries preceding his own, and add to it a dimension of significance. Nowhere does Colet lose his awareness of the *Then* and the *Now*, or allow his readers to forget that Paul's letter, while its truths transcend time, was written at a particular time to real men and women in real and altogether particular circumstances. Colet does, in a different sense, what he praises Paul for having done (p. 75): he always takes into account the persons, places, and times.

Colet's linguistic analysis is of two main varieties: he explains Paul's figurative and symbolic language (see, e.g., pp. 83–85 for his rather idiosyncratic explanation of *scandalum*), and he defines terms used literally, when he believes them to require clarification (e.g., pp. 141–89 for extended definitions of *preceptum*, *consilium*, and *indulgentia*). The use of Greek words (some of them in Latin spellings) and allusions to the Greek may be seen on pages 71, 91, 239, 257, 259, 265, 281. In these matters, as in those historical, there is no particular evidence of great specialized learning, but again there is a notable consistency in the use of scholarly aids to understanding.

In textual study of another sort, Colet demonstrates his scholarship more directly and more impressively. Paul's letter is set in a larger context by the very frequent relating of passages in it to other writings that will either clarify or deepen understanding, and these are both scriptural and nonscriptural. With scriptural allusions and references, Colet's method is quite unlike that of the medieval *catenae*; the intrinsic continuity and coherence of Paul's letter are always primary, although sometimes the reader may lose sight of them when Colet pauses for topical elaboration or for preliminary definition. When he draws on either Testament, he does so almost exclusively for the elucidation of the text under consideration.

In his use of the Old Testament, Colet draws more often on the Psalms than on any other book, and in this may be discerned the principal relation he estab-

lishes between the two Scriptures. The Old Testament is seen here not primarily as a *corpus* of direct revelation in itself, or as a history of the Chosen People and of God's dealings with them, or as a collection of explicitly Messianic prophecies and of events that are to be viewed as preparing for the advent of the Messiah. Instead, the relation between the two Testaments is of a more mystical sort. The Old Testament is not to be considered really pre-Christian: it is rather the repository of truths that are most often veiled, figurative, or symbolic; and in the New Testament these truths are unveiled and made literal. Colet explains this explicitly (although in figurative language) in Chapter X of the Commentary: in all parts of Holy Scripture "there is the savor and the solid nourishment of Christ the Life-Giver. The Old Testament (as Paul explains in the Epistle to the Romans) David called a table, when he said: 'Let their table be turned to a trap for them before their eyes' [Rom. XI: 9; Ps. LXVIII: 23]. There, however, the dishes are concealed and covered, and all is sealed. The setting aside of the covers is in the New Testament, with the revealing of the rich banquet of truth and an invitation to eat. The Master of the Feast has opened all. He first in magnificent fashion piled the table high — through the ministry of Moses — with the covered dishes, and he was present there as Ruler of the Banquet, but unseen. And afterwards he himself struck off the covers, offering himself, Truth itself, for the plentiful banqueting of his chosen guests" (p. 217). As for the nature of the allegory by which the truths of Christ are veiled in the Old Testament, this is in itself deep and mystical (pp. 54, 249, 251).

Colet thus establishes a unity between the two Testaments, and throughout the Commentary his practice confirms and expands this unity.

In his use of texts from other parts of the New Testament, one may discern a parallel effect. Colet draws heavily from the Gospel narratives, and intentionally or not, his exegesis affirms and emphasizes throughout a total identity between "the mind of Paul" and "the mind of Christ." The frequent relations he establishes between Paul's letters and the Evangelists preclude altogether any such distinction as that sometimes made between an ethical Christ of the Gospels and a theological, Pauline Christ. "The teaching of Paul [he writes] is in harmony also with that of Christ and with the Gospels (since one and the same Spirit is the author)" (p. 79).

In his use of nonscriptural writings, Colet draws from many complexly interdependent sources, as I have said, and rarely quotes individual authors directly or cites them by name as authorities for particular ideas or concepts. His debt to Aristotle and Plato, the Fathers of the Church, the Pseudo-Dionysius, Plotinus and Philo, the Schoolmen, contemporaries like Pico and Ficino, astrological and alchemical writers, e.g., is to be found in a vast philosophical and theological context, an eclectic world vision, rather than in specific borrowings from their works. (See below, pp. 39–57.) Thus Colet implicitly affirms throughout his Commentary a third unity, parallel to those already mentioned and even more

far-reaching in its implications for his exegetical methods: all that is true, whatever its source, is at one with Paul's letter, and can be used to deepen or clarify our understanding of that letter.

In what may be called his psychological conjectures, Colet shows in this treatise both insight and fearlessness, and a reader might well find this part of Colet's exegesis the most interesting and engaging of all. His delvings into the mind and motivations of Paul are surely the best key to his own mind and motivations; perhaps we ought to call him a Pauline philosopher, as other men are called Platonists or Kantians. Next to Christ, Colet was devoted to no man as he was to Paul, and all through the Commentary are to be found appraisals of Paul that are never injudicious, however enthusiastic. Colet is sensitive to Paul's intelligence, his irony, his selfless love of truth, his consideration for others, his resourcefulness of learning and experience, his insight and thoughtfulness in judging other men, his unerring instinct for the values that Colet also (like all Christians) believes paramount, his horror of false and pretentious standards, his patient idealism, and his clear-headed sense of responsibility. These are qualities Colet not only found in Paul but wished for himself. There is more, then, to his admiration for Paul than the scholar's respect for another thinker or the Christian's devotion to a saintly apostle and missionary, a writer inspired by God. The reader will find himself constantly reminded that, to Colet, Paul is not a name or an author or an object of piety, but a man to be known, understood deeply, loved, and imitated.

The intensely personal character of Colet's relationship to Paul and to Paul's thought distinguishes in several important respects his exegesis from that representative of his age, and from that of the centuries preceding. It contributes to the autonomy of his Pauline commentaries, and can render them interesting even to those to whom Colet could not say, as he said to the good and learned man he describes in his letter to the Abbot of Winchcombe, "I love you, brother, if you love Saint Paul."

From the beginning of the treatise this part of Colet's exegetical method is dominant. Paul praises and congratulates the Corinthians, we are told, *with the intent* that he may make them want to "show themselves worthy of congratulation." He wishes "to draw them on by this gentle and easy beginning to read the rest of the letter, and bring them to hear more readily what he is going to reprehend in their conduct. For if he had been more severe at the beginning, and had at once brought his rather heavy charges against them, surely he would have disaffected from himself and his exhortations their minds, which were still young and little and new in religion" (p. 75). In several other places, Colet draws our attention to Paul's thoughtfulness and prudence in adapting his truths to the weakness of those to whom his letter was originally addressed.

This adaptation of lofty truths to the ability of weak and lowly minds has

sometimes been referred to as *accommodation*.[32] Colet explicitly affirms and describes this operation, finding his authority for it in the words of Paul himself: "Paul means that he did not give to the Corinthians the highest principles of reality and of the Christian religion, but matters more fit for their minds, which clung still to the world more than to God" (p. 111). Colet's assumptions in this matter should perhaps be related to the "principle of divine condescension," as it is called by contemporary writers on the subject, or συγκατάβασις, as the Greek Fathers described it. By this principle of exegesis, the Holy Spirit is assumed to allow the inspired writer latitude, so to speak, in the expression of divine truths.[33]

In one place, Colet's speculation about Paul's intention in a text is based on a faulty copy of the Vulgate. I find this difficult to explain, since he had surely read I Corinthians in more than one manuscript, and he could at will have consulted other copies while writing the present work (see p. 107). Presumably, he could easily have noted that he was following a wrong text.

Since Colet so frequently invokes analysis of Paul's motives and intentions, and emphasizes so consistently the personal qualities of mind that led Paul to write this rather than that, and in this way rather than that, one may well ask whether he is not tacitly abandoning or at least diminishing the role of divine inspiration in these letters. It would be a delicate matter to derive from this Commentary an implicit definition of inspiration in any technical, theological sense. But Colet clearly assumes that while the Holy Spirit guarantees the truth of Paul's words and is in every respect responsible for that truth, at the same time it is Paul's judgment that performs the immediate operations with the results of which our minds must cope. There will be less to tease and puzzle the mind in the maintaining of such a double consciousness if the reader will advert to Colet's conception of the Mystical Body of Christ, and of the direct role of the Holy Spirit in informing it and its members and in providing always the ultimate agent causality in everything attributed to it.

E. *Colet's Philosophy and Theology*

Colet does not simply set Paul's letter within a philosophical and theological context already established from other sources, and interpret it by its relations to that context; on the contrary, he frequently represents the Epistle itself as a primary source, and no negligible one, of harmonious theological and philosophical truths. Such is the disposition of his mind that in many instances it is impossible to discern whether or not he recognizes his interpretations as dependent on categories of thought altogether extrinsic to and independent of Paul and Scripture in general. This can be more easily understood if one recalls Colet's assumption (referred to above) of the three fundamental identities in

substance: between this letter of Paul and the rest of the New Testament; between the New Testament and the Old; and between Scripture and all that is true, from whatever proximate source it may be known.

Further, in practice there is for Colet — as for many minds in all centuries — no really operative distinction between theology and philosophy, since "truth" is for him ontologically identical with "reality" (God being the ultimate reality in what must be represented as a unified and, at least in one important sense, a continuous *systema*), and epistemologically identical with the human mind's accurate perception and understanding of that reality (or "wisdom"). Without misrepresentation, then, we may speak of the structure of his thought simply as his philosophy, provided we bear in mind at once its primarily eclectic nature and its dependence on Revelation. Moreover, Colet's general approach to questions and answers concerning the nature of reality and the nature of wisdom is not unlike that of one of his great teachers, the Pseudo-Dionysius: it is at once a metaphysic, including a cosmology, and a soteriology, with related elements of a rational psychology and a moral philosophy.

In both these characters, Colet's philosophy is concerned with the intelligible world, and only secondarily and indirectly (and not very coherently) with phenomena. He assumes the distinction between the two orders, but does not systematically or explicitly attempt to clarify the relations between them, or even to define what belongs to one or the other, although there are indications of what he assumes in this regard. The elements and structure of his thought are, therefore, speculative and intrinsically logical, not experiential. Further, they are, as I have said, very much dependent on both the fact and the content of the Judeo-Christian Revelation.

1) *Soteriology*

For a closer analysis of this element in Colet's philosophy, we must first establish a distinction between "soteriology" and "moral philosophy" or a system of ethics. Such a distinction is essential in the reading of an author like Colet or the Pseudo-Dionysius; there has certainly been misunderstanding and misrepresentation of Colet because of failure to observe it, and Seebohm might not have had to apologize so often for the "froth" in the works of the Pseudo-Dionysius if he had been familiar with it.

An ethic or a moral philosophy may be defined as some sort of propositional account of human behavior, a coherent set of formulated principles of conduct, interrelated, determined with respect to a teleology of some kind, and resting necessarily on more or less fixed notions about the nature of reality and of man in particular, and of the interrelations between existent things. Whether explicitly normative or (in the intent of its systematizer) purely descriptive, it is always

primarily concerned with ways of behaving, with action, passion, and abstention. A soteriology, on the other hand, is primarily concerned with becoming, and with a "Way" of becoming. It is less susceptible of conceptualization, and can be known, properly speaking, only in its being experienced. Most often it finds its expression in metaphor, analogy, or allegory, rather than in definition and proposition.

In Colet's work, therefore, as in soteriological philosophies generally, metaphor, analogy, and allegory are not merely figures of speech. One need only reflect on the degree of literal intent, the degree to which the symbol and the symbolized coincide, in the idea of progressive "purification," for example, or in the concept of man's passing from darkness to light, from coldness to warmth, or in that of the "ascent to truth," or in the Pauline concept of putting off the old man and putting on the new. In Colet's writings, whether or not they rest on the direct assumption of an analogical or otherwise nonunivocal conception of the nature of being, such modes of expression seem always to carry the latent affirmation that the spiritual or ideal or intelligible realities are, so to speak, more *real* as well as more important than the sensible phenomena to which language is directly fitted. A man climbing a mountain is, to such a way of thought, less truly making an ascent than is the mind rising to God; a man looking for a mislaid book is less really engaged in a search or a quest than is the spirit seeking truth or beauty; the cup from which leavings and stains are washed is only analogically being purified in comparison with the soul from which, by the cathartic working of sacrament or mortification or divine enlightenment, the darkness and kinship with darkness are in process of being expunged. Instead of linguistic metaphor, we are here confronted with a way of thinking to which sensible phenomena are themselves metaphors for an intelligible reality that is the true concern of the mind and will.

The central preoccupation of Colet's soteriology is (as is usual in such structures of thought) the Way itself: the "Road of Truth," the "Path of Life," the "Way of Eternity." The journey man undertakes is variously described by Colet as the *systema*, the *recta vivendi forma*, and the *ratio vivendi* which Christ, God and man, came to teach men during his life on earth. These three terms themselves indicate the eclectic nature of Colet's philosophical terminology; more important, the philosophical background of each term contributes to the correct understanding of the concept itself. That is to say, the pattern or way of being a human being that Christ set forth is an entelechy, a μορφή with respect to the *materia prima* of human existence; it is a rational procedure, a method, an art, a series of judgments; finally, it is an inclusive totality, an intelligible whole or system consisting of intelligible parts, outside of which there is (in the order of human existence) nothing.

These terms must not be understood, however, as pertaining to a Gnosis only;

they involve a Praxis equally. There is perhaps a danger in using these two words, but they are in context natural, and they can be helpful. Before limiting or qualifying them, therefore, I shall develop the extent of their applicability to Colet's soteriology in the present work. Gnosis and Praxis stand in obvious relationship to what Colet accepts as the two distinctly and essentially human determinations, mind and will. "Man's soul consists of intellect and will. By our intellect we are wise, by our will we have strength to do things" (p. 79). The primary modes of expression by which Colet refers to the *forma* or *ratio* or *systema vivendi* as this pertains to the intellect are wisdom and light; as it pertains to the will, they are love and warmth.

The human mind is adequate to know and in varying measure to comprehend intelligible realities—indeed, it was made for this—but man's mixed nature, his involvement in matter, the dispersal of his being, his proneness to torpor of mind and will, his susceptibility to influences that mislead, and his shortsighted instinct for immediate gratification can keep his mind from finding, or even seeking, any personal engagement with the ultimate, the truly meaningful reality. Trivialities and worse can absorb the conscious activities of a human intelligence for its entire duration. Indeed, they will, unless the intellect is possessed of wisdom, and there is no wisdom outside of God, the Father of Wisdom (p. 87). Christ, Colet says, *is* the wisdom of God (p. 79). Participation in Christ (of a kind that indicates Colet's debt to Plato) is the conceptual key to the manner by which minds share in the wisdom of God. Without this participation, there is only darkness of mind, stupidity, ignorance, by whatever other names men may please themselves to call it. Moreover, the true Gnosis is "on high, far above reasoning," and it "can be perceived by no eye but the piercing eye of faith" (p. 83). It cannot be brought down to the level of human reasoning.

In Colet's world view, the common, somewhat dramatized image of man's life as an arduous and a quasi-adventurous quest for truth has really no place. Christ is the great reality of human existence, as the Sun is the great terrestrial source of light. Unless a man is very far underground indeed—or, in Colet's more striking image, under water—he will have no great trouble recognizing the Sun.

On the other hand, many men are very far under water, and the true Gnosis is not one to which a man attains by his own choice and effort:

> Now all this no man sees and apprehends unless he is drawn and lifted by the teaching of the Gospels, like a fish, from the waters of this world into the Spirit; from the darkness into the light; from fragmentation into unity; from falsehood into truth; from wickedness into goodness, into hope, faith, and charity; so that made one in God, and having faith in God, and loving God, from God alone he has fixed being, clear wisdom, and good conduct.   (p. 93)

The admission to the true wisdom is, then, a "leaving" or a being taken out of the sea of this world, which Colet describes as "fluctuating," and in which men have "minds clouded and almost made lightless by the black darkness." Those who refuse to be drawn from it he describes as "living (or rather, dying) in the sea of this world, swimming about like the little fishes, with unfirm flesh and hard eyes and weak strength," and he affirms that they are "unfit to experience anything of the Spirit and of the Light." What might be called the intrinsic substance of the Gnosis, the "divine principles" of truth, are "simple, pure, beautiful, and good," and those things that oppose and hinder their reception, Colet argues, "must have a contrary disposition, and must lie in multiplicity, impurity, meanness, and malice" (p. 95).

Even in the passages I have isolated here as particularly relevant to Colet's soteriology as it pertains to the mind, the reader will notice that references to the will are frequent. He almost never mentions the one faculty without the other, and this indicates his conviction of their inseparability and reciprocal functions. Where there is darkness, there will be cold; where there is stupidity, there will be malice; where there is blindness, there will be powerlessness.

On the other hand, where there is light, there is warmth; where there is wisdom, there is goodness; where there is true vision, there is strength. Gnosis and Praxis cannot be separated, Colet consistently maintains, although he concedes some sort of theoretical priority, at least, to the Gnosis. Recognition of Christ and faith in all that pertains to Him constitute the entering upon the Way, the starting off: "These are the things on the first threshold, and, as it were, in the anteroom of salvation" (pp. 143–45). No man, though, can truly see the good and the true without willing them as well. Basing himself principally on Luke vi: 46, Gal. v: 6, James ii, and I John ii, Colet develops this point with strong emphasis on the ontological impossibility of faith without works: "True faith in Jesus Christ, then, and knowledge of him, can in no wise exist unaccompanied by good conduct, which is an advancing, so to speak, in the journey one has begun by faith, and is the means by which one wins through to the goal" (pp. 145–47). The same point is made in reverse, as it were, at the beginning of the long section in Chapter I in which he characterizes those of the Gentiles and Jews who did not become Christians (p. 81).

Just as there is no wisdom outside of God, so there is no strength. Christ is the incarnate strength of God. Through participation in Christ the wills of men are "straightened," and "by love they take strong hold of his power" (p. 81). Strength and power are not denominated with respect to action only. *Patientia* and *constantia*, firm endurance and steadfastness, are equally the marks of the will that is right. Feebleness, inability, unsteadfastness, restlessness, impatience— these are the principles of the will that are "at enmity with God," the characteristics of the man who has no participation in Christ, and the disposi-

tions that impede and hinder "the warmth-giving rays of the Sun" that would dispel man's coldness.

Strength is, moreover, "freedom of choice, a freedom by nature tending to the good" (p. 189), and its opposite is bondage. Strength is also virtue, and Colet probably always uses the term *virtue* with the double meaning of strength and goodness. The absence of strength, therefore, is characterized as wickedness. Goodness is benevolence, or the willing of good, and as such its opposite is malice or malevolence. Finally, Colet identifies the state of the will in conformity with the *ratio vivendi* as one in which the will possesses and is possessed by love. This denomination is in every respect analogous to that by which the true wisdom of the mind is identified with the supernatural gift of faith. The absence of supernatural love or charity is not merely lovelessness (which is bad enough), but hatred (p. 83).

If faith (or wisdom) has a chronological priority, love (or strength) has a priority of another sort. On this point Colet is clearly taking Paul as his primary source of reasonings for a position that voluntarists (and others) reach by other paths. In Chapter XIII of the Commentary, he develops and expands the relevant texts of Paul (I Cor. XIII) as follows: charity, the grace of love, is that by which only we can please God; this is because charity "completes and consummates all things," and a work "is not held in esteem, however beautifully and felicitously begun, unless it be perfected" (pp. 257–59). "Perfection is, indeed, charity" (p. 259). If there are good deeds and good dispositions in a man, or wisdom, or any other gift from God through participation in Christ, and the man does not have charity, then, Colet explains, those gifts are *in* the man (provided, of course, they are not simply illusory) but not *of* the man. He has no share in them, and they do him no good. He is simply a lifeless instrument, and the Holy Spirit must be understood to be directing those gifts through the man for His own purposes. The man "does no works," but the Spirit does them through him. In another image, such a man is an implement, "moved by God's Spirit as a knife is moved, or a broom" (p. 265). Where there are good works, then, there is always charity, but not always the charity of the apparent doer; the charity of God is operating wherever there is any good.

In clarifying this matter, Colet relies on traditional Aristotelian concepts of principal and instrumental agent causes, but these concepts will not serve so well for the man who has the *forma vivendi*, and whose will is therefore possessed of charity. Colet turns to Platonic concepts (here apparently derived mainly from Pico and Ficino), and explains that an object formed or disposed into a form by an agent "at length acts *per se*. All right action of a perfect object," he goes on, "is by its own form, and from the form action is derived" (p. 259). The Holy Spirit can thus transform a man into an efficient cause in his own right, so to speak, and the form by which the man has this new existence is charity;

it is the "intrinsic and essential form of the spiritual man." It comes into being in "a single instant," after a "slow preparation" (p. 261).

Still, Colet will not have his readers think that the man informed by charity is an agent cause in any ultimate or autonomous sense. He is not the primary cause of his own operations, "but is now a living and perfect instrument" (p. 261). He is an organic and instrumental cause, a living stone in the house. He is a hand, or an eye, of the Builder, not an implement. This last mode of expression is perhaps not, in Colet's intention, primarily metaphorical, but literal (if mystical), since the metaphor here coincides with the Pauline statements concerning the Mystical Body of Christ (see below, pp. 46f).

Finally, Colet introduces the notion of exemplar causality, ascribing this also to the Holy Spirit. "All that is done by perfect men, Christ's members, in the Spirit of God working with them, and by the Spirit of God, is done according to this exemplar" (p. 263). Colet does not explicitly draw from this any of the inferences that might suggest themselves, but implicit in what he says here, it seems to me, there is another philosophical reason for a quasi-voluntarist primacy of the will over the intellect. Even enlightened by God's wisdom, the mind of man comes to conformity with the Divine Intellect in varying and finite degrees; a man's will, on the other hand, becomes the effective coagent of the Deity, bringing to realization (in ways perhaps unknown to the man's intellect) the purposes of the Deity. To put it very baldly, no human mind can do more than learn, according to God's grace, its little part of the infinite wisdom of God — the thought of *adding* to that wisdom is, of course, preposterous. But human wills can, in and through the Spirit, bring to actual realization the infinitely wise plans of God, and so effect a real change in reality. Human wills are, moreover, free not to do so; they can refuse their cooperation. The intellect, on the other hand, must necessarily assent to what it sees to be true.

In what has been said of Colet's account of the effects in the human intellect and will when once they are in the Way, when they are brought into conformity with the *systema* or *forma* or *ratio vivendi*, the qualifications one must add to the terms *Gnosis* and *Praxis* will perhaps be sufficiently clear. The Gnosis, the enlightening of the intellect, is really *Sapientia*, a participation (through Christ, the God-Man) of the Divine Wisdom; it is the supernatural gift of Faith. The Praxis is not a "doing" at all, but really an *esse*, a state of being, the possession of an intrinsic and essential form (the supernatural gift of Charity), with regard to which a man's prior state is that of unformed matter.

Given the symmetry of Colet's thought, in which light and darkness, truth and falsehood, knowledge and ignorance, wisdom and stupidity (the conditions of the human intellect with and without Faith, respectively) are analogous to and in necessary relationship with warmth and coldness, strength and weakness, goodness and wickedness, love and hate (the conditions of the human will with

and without Charity) we should be surprised if there were no third set of opposites related to the third theological virtue, Hope. (*A priori*, we should in any event expect a structure of thought like Colet's to be fundamentally triadic rather than dichotomistic.)

The third set of opposites may be perhaps best understood in Colet's figure of the rays of the sun communicating its own qualities to men. The Godhead in Christ, according to Colet, "shone at length like a good, powerful, and bright-shining sun amid the darkness, and cast Its rays upon darksome and earthbound men, first setting loose and freeing those whom It touched deeply from every principle hostile and contrary to Itself, and then fully purifying them into the simplicity and truth of Its own nature, utterly dispelling the fragmentary and untrue state of wickedness into which men had wrongfully and wretchedly degenerated" (p. 149).

The change in man's essential being is, then, logically ulterior to the changes in his intellect and will. It is a transformation from fragmentation into unity, from division to simplicity, from multiplicity into oneness, from dispersal into self-consistency or integrity. The result of this change is "fixed being." Without it, man remains afflicted by a divided soul and scattered thoughts. Indeed, the difference is between life and death, between being and not being: "The deifying ray of Christ begets anew us who were (in our hopelessness) nothing, so that we hope in God, and by hope have being. . . . Nor did we begin to be, until by grace we began to hope in God, to look to Him for everything, to have our being from Him, so that begotten into being, we might next have true wisdom from Him, and then from Him also have love of the good" (p. 151).

Here one may find the suggestion of a further ontological relationship. The Persons of the Trinity "are equal in power, wisdom, and goodness," but "power and generation are considered to belong properly to the Father." Life, being, oneness, self-consistency, hope come to a man, therefore, in a particular way from the Father. Wisdom, light, truth, faith are similarly attributed to the Son, the Logos. Goodness, warmth, love are attributed to the Holy Spirit. It is always, however, through his participation in Christ that a man has being, wisdom, and goodness.

In all that we have said so far, Colet's categories of thought apply to individual man. Transcending such application, however, there is at the center of his thought a concept of unity of another sort. His soteriological vision of human existence is really much more basically concerned with the species, the human race, than it is with individual men and women.

The collectivity, the race as a whole, has a purpose, a goal, and this is, to put it as baldly as Colet does, to become Christ. There is no question here of "alter Christus": all those who are joined with Christ and through him participate in God constitute "one unity under God," and "rightly may be called, from their common anointing [i.e., christening] one Christ" (p. 73). "This com-

posite being of God and men called to God Paul calls not only Christ, as when he says in this letter to the Corinthians, 'All the members of the body, although they are many, are still one body: so is it with Christ,' [I Cor. XII: 12] but also, in the Letter to the Ephesians, 'the perfect man' [Eph. IV: 13]. And the body of this being is clearly the men who have been taken hold of by God, and the spirit is God, who takes hold of, unites, gives light, warmth, and life to, and sustains within itself His own body. The head of this body is Jesus, in whom is truly God Himself, and therefore he is called Christ above the other members, since the whole man is in the head. . . . All who are in this mystical composite are in God, who, beginning His deification in the Manhood taken from Mary, through Him thence as through the head has distributed to the rest for the fashioning of the whole" (pp. 73–75).

Sometimes, Colet speaks of Christ's Mystical Body as though it were metaphorical, but in so doing he clearly cannot intend to imply that it is not an actual reality. The Body is real, he maintains, now; but it is incomplete, imperfect, and will remain so until all men (except those who deliberately exercise their freedom of will to choose damnation) receive life and become members of it. "Then there will be the end. Wickedness will be vanquished, and darkness, and death" (p. 279). In their every thought, word, deed, and volition, men are either helping toward or delaying the "fullness" of Christ. The outcome, however, is not in doubt. There is no trace of theological dualism in Colet's thought, for all his dichotomizing, and while "principles at enmity with God" can delay, they cannot prevent the eventual realization of the destiny of the human race. The inimical principles are not real in any ultimate sense: cold is the absence of warmth, darkness is the absence of light, and multiplicity is the absence of oneness. All will be overcome. "As long as it finds something to give life to, this force of life that makes things good, bright, and alive will press on with its vivifying gift" (p. 277).

2) Moral Principles

These are related more or less successfully to the soteriological structure of Colet's thought. There are several passages in which Colet writes as any moralist might, setting forth clear-cut and dogmatic propositions about human conduct. Men must not act selfishly or avariciously; they must not contend with others or undertake litigation; they must not be lustful or profligate; they must not read pagan authors; they must avoid sexual pleasures as much as they can; the Church as a whole should surrender her legal rights to any and all temporal things rather than set a bad example to individual Christians, or provide occasion for "outsiders and pagans" to suspect greed in her.

Obviously these moral prohibitions are not all of the same sort, nor are they

all derived specifically from Paul. They cannot all be related in the same way to the *ratio vivendi*, nor are they even all accepted by orthodox moralists of Colet's church.

Such things as profligacy, vainglory, and envy pertain directly, as it were, to the Anti-Way. They are, for Colet, the fruits of multiplicity, stupidity, and weakness, the signs of a dispersed and fragmentary being, a dark mind, and a cold heart. Thus prohibitions against them are really commands to enter upon the *ratio vivendi* in simplicity and in wholeness of heart and mind, or at least to dispose oneself to enter upon it. The force of such commands is, of course, absolute, since all men are obliged to enter upon the Way.

In certain other ethical matters there is an element of apparent contingency. That is, some acts may be in and of themselves morally indifferent. These are to be judged by the principle of usefulness to others and to the Church. If a morally indifferent act conduces to the "building of the whole Christ," then a man must perform it; if not, he must avoid it. Once a man is truly in the Way, he will see and obey this sort of contingent injunction, which pertains to the perfection of the whole Mystical Body, the destiny of the race. The overbold Corinthians, for example, who rightly judged idols to be nothing and the eating of sacrifice-foods morally indifferent, were guilty of a moral fault in a matter of this sort when they had so little charity that they did not respect the scruples of their weaker brothers (pp. 201–203).

A third sort of moral principle might be described as conditional. Certain acts may be free from moral evil—i.e., may have, in Colet's terms, no part of darkness or cold or multiplicity—but still be inconsistent with an earnest following of the Way. Colet follows Paul's analogy: "It is lawful for runners to eat; but if they wish to attain the prize, it is not lawful." For the individual Christian, therefore, such matters take on an absolute quality, since Colet maintains that everyone is altogether obliged to do all he can to advance in the Way, once he has begun in it. But if a man fails in such matters because of weakness, not defect of will, and if he earnestly desires to do better, he is not guilty of evil, although weakness itself is objectively an evil (see Chapter VII, *passim*).

Thus Colet adds two governing and inclusive principles to those of orthodox Christian morality: "That only is lawful which is conducive to the building of the Church"; and "A man is bound to do all the good that he can do." But these are principles that entail a rather alarming rigorism.

Not even they will serve to explain Colet's extremism in matters pertaining to sexual morality. Here, certain metaphysical assumptions lead him to a position of incontrovertible heterodoxy, as well as one so little humanistic as to be virtually inhuman. Arguing that the carnal act is that human activity in which the body is not the instrument of the soul, but is "itself rather the author and performer," Colet states that illicit sexual pleasures not only drag the soul

downward, but constitute "a dissolving of the body into everlasting death" (p. 135).

Colet cannot restrict this reasoning process to those sexual pleasures that are illicit. Here and in other passages it is clear that he considers sexual activity to be by its nature antispiritual, destructive, and evil. Metaphysical dualism is at work in his thought: "One way, then, or the other, upward or downward, whichever direction you have taken, you become entirely of that nature which belongs to the part of yourself whose inclination you follow. The soul becomes like the body, if led by the body; the body like the soul, if drawn by the soul" (p. 133).

He goes on to use a still more particular argument for his position. The carnal act is that in which "the sense and desire and finally the act of touching" reign supreme, and the sense of touch is of all bodily senses the lowest, the basest, and the "least refined"; in short, the most bodily. The soul has, therefore, no part in the carnal act.

With such premises established, we need not be surprised to find that in Chapter VII, where Colet discusses Paul's instructions to the Corinthians on marriage, all thought of marriage as a sacrament is firmly excluded. It is purely an indulgence for weakness, a concession to those who without it would be promiscuous, or worse. "Marriage has no goodness in it except insofar as it is a necessary remedy for evil," Colet writes, and if we were to marry without being forced to do so by irresistible fires of passion, "we should absurdly and damnably act the part of a sick man from choice more than from need, and with the intention, not of curing ourselves when ill, but of deliberately making sickness of our health by the use of an unnecessary medicine. Nothing can be done more wretched, nor more unworthy a man who makes the Christian profession" (p. 191). Even when marriage is genuinely necessary, it ought to be as free from conjugal intercourse as the strength of the partners will permit; otherwise, presumably, they are "practicing harlotry in foul and infamous fashion."

Colet's apologists have made what excuses they could for his extravagance, pointing out the palliating circumstance that prevailing attitudes and practices might well account for so severe a reaction on his part. Indeed, in Colet's time high rank in the Church was perhaps infrequently a sure outward sign of chastity, and we can understand that a man with Colet's high soteriological vision of human existence might turn against all things connected with sex (in the primary sense of the word). It may be useful to recall too that the widely esteemed Dame Christian, Colet's mother, bore the astonishing number of twenty-one brothers and sisters for John after him, and that none of them seems to have lived very long. We do not know how many died at birth or in early infancy. Even if Dame Christian was cheerful and philosophical about this long and tragic succession of lyings-in, John can scarcely have been favorably impressed, during his

formative years, by his own direct observation of the nature and the fruits of marriage; he dearly loved his mother, too. Perhaps his own experience at home fostered what Lupton charmingly calls "the strong preference he often expresses for the celibate life."[34]

Nevertheless, the strong preference made in this treatise rests on grounds more relative than the emotional attitudes acquired in boyhood and adolescence, or disgust at the shameless carryings-on of contemporaries. Metaphysical dualism, identifying the body with matter and the soul with spirit, and postulating a radical incompatibility between the two, together with an Aristotelian assumption about the place and the role of the sense of touch in a hierarchy of the senses, provide the premises that permit Colet to come to his severe conclusions.

Neither premise is much operative elsewhere in the Commentary, if at all. Colet's exposition of the Mystical Body has as one of its postulates that while there is a hierarchy of dignity and beauty in the parts of the body, there is a corresponding inverse hierarchy of usefulness, so that there can be, strictly speaking, no more or less good in the body, but only equality (see pp. 56f).

In this matter, as in that of the pagan philosophers (see above, pp. 33f), Colet does not satisfactorily integrate with the general structure of his thought abstract positions derived from particular and idiosyncratic premises. Such an integration would be, as far as I can judge, impossible. He is much more successful in integrating with his soteriology the two abstract master-principles described above: "A man must do all the good he can," and "Only the useful is lawful." Still, even in his exposition of these principles, he does not by any means altogether satisfy the mind as to the relation between normative principles of conduct with regard to sensible phenomena, and a mysticism of being and becoming in an intelligible order of existence.

3) Principles of Rational Psychology

Certain difficulties also arise with the assumptions Colet makes about the nature of the human intellect and will, especially in what other writers might call the natural state of these faculties. In a philosophy like Colet's, the responsibility and the spontaneity (or quasi-spontaneity) of the will are not, of course, as clearly defined as they are in the inquiries of Aquinas or of Scotus, although they are assumed. The will is the principle of volition, of choice, and it is free, but the degree and nature of its autonomy cannot be with clarity discerned. The nature of its relationship with the intellect is similarly elusive. The nature and operations of the intellect are also left unexplained, although Colet postulates that the intellect is adequate and apt with regard to its object, truth.

It is not enough to point out Colet's frequent assertions that all beings and acts that really exist are to be attributed to God as primary agent cause, and

that no truth can be in the intellect except what God communicates to it by His free gift. The emphasis on grace does not exclude intermediary and secondary causes, and it makes possible the concept of co-causality. Paul, for instance, is an immediate cause of right knowledge concerning charity in the minds of the Corinthians, and each man and woman in the human hierarchy has a comparable role with regard to the building of the Mystical Body. Moreover, even men who are not themselves sincere can be the causes of right knowledge in other intellects. The question naturally arises whether the intermediary causes of truth in the human intellect need be themselves human (or other intelligent beings), and there seems no reason at all to believe that Colet would assert that they have to be (although of course only beings with intellect and will can be co-causes with God). This leaves us with the further question whether the individual intellect itself, in its normal operations on sensory data, could not be considered, together with those data, as an intermediary cause of the truth existing within itself. Colet does not face the question, and we can only conjecture that to be consistent, he would have to answer it affirmatively, in spite of his fulminations against the intellect and everything else human in a state deprived of any grace from God, or refusing to cooperate with grace.

With regard to the will, the principle "agere sequitur esse" takes on a special meaning in Colet's writings. A man's acts and his being are—or must become— one, insofar as this is possible; and his acts are commensurate with his being. He cannot, that is to say, do what is above his nature, and if he does what is beneath his nature, he becomes by this very choice less than what he was. What he is, however—his being—is a becoming, as soon as he has begun in the Way. Even when a man has reached that point of life, wisdom, and power beyond which it is ontologically impossible for him to advance, still he must not rest; his existence remains a dynamic activity, because he must maintain the constant will to advance. Colet speaks of this rather as an activity than as a disposition or habit of willing.

What a man is (or becomes) thus depends on his willing, and what he wills depends on what he is (or becomes). Direct and immediate action of God's freely-given grace will not, I think, solve the dilemma of ontological priority here, let alone that of chronological priority. We must infer again that intermediary causes—or, in some instances, co-causes, or perhaps the will itself, specifically— must be postulated. I think there is no reason why Colet would not go this far, but one must presume also that then such intermediary causes would themselves have to be considered graces in some sense, with the result that the entire universe would have to be seen as a sacramental phenomenon.

Here, as in several other points, it is the tenuity or absence of conceptual links between an intelligible order of reality and the experiential order that leaves the mind of Colet's reader dissatisfied and perplexed. The mystical, soteriological .

vision of human existence, and of reality as a whole, cannot, perhaps, be satisfactorily integrated with those elements of the Aristotelian, Scholastic, and other conceptual structures of rational psychology that Colet's eclectic mind accepted as valid.

On one point, however, there is a striking coincidence of the soteriological vision with an ancient theory of intellection. The concept of the νοῦς *universalis*, the universal intellect, is fascinating enough to have won many fine minds beside Avicenna's to assent to it, and difficult enough to have perplexed many others, long before Colet's time. We find it quietly reappearing in Colet, as "God Himself, the Blessed Trinity," the soul and the "entelechy" of the Mystical Body of Christ, in which all men are meant to be members (p. 239). Furthermore, God the Holy Spirit is in some ways a *Weltgeist*. But Colet leaves unexplored the nature of the relations between the individual human mind and the universal Mind.

4) *Metaphysics and Cosmology*

In these aspects of his work, Colet is greatly indebted to Plato, to the Pseudo-Dionysius, and no doubt to Neoplatonists of various schools, as well as to contemporaries like Pico and Ficino. In this Commentary, however, there is much that would appear to be autonomous, if syncretistic rather than strictly original.

The basic categories of Colet's thought in these matters are order, correspondence, composition, balance, and hierarchy, with the concomitant and fundamental concept of the more and the less.

The Cosmos, the totality of existent things about which there can be predication, consists of four Worlds, four primary intelligible systems: the Spiritual; the Physical World of the heavens; the Sublunary; and the Human. The reader may be puzzled to see that where he affirms most explicitly the oneness of the universe, Colet states that it consists of "three worlds" (p. 249); here he is abstracting from the Human World, which is, since the Incarnation, *in fieri* as well as *in esse*. It is not complete, since there are still some people who are not within it, and whose condition is, therefore, one of chaos and confusion. On the other hand, one must infer that it cannot be reduced to a part merely of the Sublunary World, because that would be to exclude from it those who are part of it, but dead (in the physical sense), and therefore no longer sublunary. Since it is identical with the Mystical Body of Christ, clearly it must transcend the Sublunary World in other ways too.

In each of the four Worlds there is a tenfold hierarchy of being, nine orders with a progressive continuity of qualities, and at the head of each nine a tenth, the pattern, perfection, fullness, and exemplar of the whole.

In the Spiritual World, the highest of the four, God is, of course, the tenth.

The nine orders are the Angelic, from the Seraphim in the highest rank to the Angels in the lowest.

In the Human World, Christ is the tenth, the most spiritual men are in the highest order, and the most "earthy" men constitute the lowest. In spite of the antithesis of spirit and matter here, it must be noted that all are perfect (p. 243).

In the Physical World of the heavens, the tenth sphere is, in Colet's phrase, "God of the orbs," and the lowest order is that of the sphere of the moon. The sun has to play a double role in the system, since he denominates the fourth sphere by it (counting, that is, from the bottom), and at the same time somewhat tentatively assigns to the sun the role of tenth and perfection in the eighth sphere, that of the stars: "Moreover, in the heaven where dwell the stars you can assign nine orders following a certain leader and differing among themselves both in magnitude and in brightness. The Sun can be their tenth and the source of their light" (p. 249).

In the Sublunary World, the first sublunary region is tenth of the hierarchy and "God of the elements," the ninth order is the region of fire, and the lowest is the region that is "altogether earthy." The intervening orders belong to the other two elements and to composites of the four.

Within the Sublunary World, among the things that are "of a mixed sort," Colet maintains that parallel hierarchies can be discerned both in substances and in accidents. "For example, in metals you can discern nine ranks in series from the best in that genus down to the least good; in stones, nine; in plants, nine . . . in colors, sounds, odors, tastes, shapes; in the habits of things also, and in all the other qualities and quantities" (p. 249). To each of these ninefold series in the Sublunary World must be assigned "a leader by which all are governed and measured," and this leader should be "traced back [referatur] to God, since in each class it is absolute perfection itself, and constitutes the tenth in each order, the measure, center, and unity, to be compared to the Unity of unities" (p. 249).

Everywhere, then, and in all that exists, by nature there is order and hierarchy. Equally universal is correspondence; the tenths of each hierarchy are comparable one to another not only in the natural affinity arising from their dignity and perfection — "Every tenth perfection of a ninefold order is an image of God" — but "in their remaining attributes also, in their nature, powers, offices, activities, and names" (p. 249). In the same way, each sixth order corresponds in all respects to every other sixth order in the other hierarchies; each fourth corresponds to every other fourth; and so on.

There is further correspondence and analogy within each hierarchy, since "these ninefold orders in each kind are images one of another, the lower of the higher" (p. 249). The relationships between the orders of one hierarchy, moreover, "agree and accord most accurately" with the relationships between the orders of another.

Each ninefold hierarchy can be considered also as a progression of three triads.

The primary characteristics of the highest triad in any series are love, wisdom, and steadfastness; the medial orders are marked by warmth, light, and steady movement; the lowest show heat, moisture, and some degree of dispersal. In this triadic correspondence of natural qualities can be found an insight into Colet's interchangeable use of love and warmth, wisdom and light; the "steady movement" of a human soul would be, presumably, a mark of its hope or steadfastness: for Colet, as we have seen, true being is a becoming and a forward movement. On the other hand, it is hard to see how there can be any degree of dispersal in the lowest order of the human hierarchy, since all in it must be perfect. Colet does not develop the triadic correspondences beyond what has been sketched here.

With regard to a higher ninefold series, the lower hierarchy stands in the relation of feminine to masculine. "For there is nothing masculine in a higher order without its feminine in a lower. All things in the higher are masculine; in the lower feminine" (p. 251). The perception of this ontological relationship provides a key to the Old Testament, since "Moses and the theologian-prophets betokened it all [i.e., the affinities and sympathies of the universe] by allegory, using interchangeably the names of things that agree by resemblance, and symbolizing by feminine things those that are masculine" (p. 251).

Having delineated this view of the correspondences, Colet does something that seems in context very unusual. One would have expected the terms "masculine" and "feminine" to have validity only in a symbolic way, and to a point in Colet's exposition it would seem that they have. But suddenly, and without transition, they become first literal and adequate terms, and then very literal indeed: "If anyone had known how to gather the beings of the same rank in each series, and bring them the right way to unity, the feminine would have been impregnated by the masculine, and miracles would have been brought forth. This would be to bring the world into marriage . . ." (p. 251). Here is the ancient dream of the Marriage of the World, and in its clearly thaumaturgic quality it comes rather oddly from a Christian author who so far rejects human marriage as to deny it, once the Christian dispensation has begun, even the status of a figure of Christ's relationship with his Church.

The absence of hierarchy, order, and correspondence will necessarily be chaos and confusion, disorder and disharmony: no love, wisdom, steadfastness, warmth, light, etc. but total disintegration in every respect. This will come about if there is no tenth for a series, or if it is not followed by the creatures that should be within the hierarchy it heads, and the pattern of the universe is to that extent disrupted. Apart from the fallen angels, whom Colet does not consider here, only among human beings is there such absence of hierarchy. The order that should exist is broken and destroyed by the unwillingness or the inability of some men to orient themselves toward the perfection of their humanity, the ideal tenth and exemplar of their system. Before the Incarnation, of course, no

man could find his place in the ranks that follow and participate in the perfection of the Human Tenth, except, perhaps, by some special and anticipatory
dispensation of grace.

To restore men to the ninefold order, to intelligibility, to harmony, to true
existence, "the Orderer Himself of all things willed to be a man, and to be the
head, and the center, and the idea, the firmament, the first principle, and the
perfection, and the God of men, so that by imitating Him — each one according
to the strength given him — men might depend on Him by a beautiful succession
in a ninefold order" (p. 251).

This matter is crucial. Without a proper understanding of the necessity, so
to speak, of the Incarnation, one cannot understand the essential structure of
Colet's thought. Here we may validly infer, I think, what he leaves unstated:
had there been no Original Sin, no grave disorder at the beginning of our race,
the original harmony and order in which God created men would have remained
perfect. It was to restore order that Christ, the God-Man, existed and exists,
the human race having been incapable of producing from and of itself its own
tenth. God could provide special graces and interventions for this or that human
being, even for a whole people; but the race, the totality of mankind, had until
Christ no "World" in which to exist, no order or harmony or place in the universe.

The fact that after Christ's earthly existence some men remain outside this
ordered Human World can be attributed only to the enduring consequences of
Original Sin, and to the continued existence of that which made the Original
Sin possible: man's unique privilege of free choice.

Yet all men are called to the truly Human World, and for all, Colet firmly
maintains, it is possible. Only within it can human beings exist as men in a meaningful and intelligible manner. Perhaps this explains why Colet is so emphatic
in his rejection of anything unrelated to Christ. However approximate it may
be, it cannot be more than that; the gulf between what is and what is not within
the Human World is such that once this world exists (after the Incarnation)
all that is "human" outside it is something less than parody. It cannot be said
to *be* in the same way as that which is within the Human World.

The human person is himself a microcosm, "an epitome of the entire universe."
The powers of his soul reflect and correspond to the nine Angelic orders; the
"more lightsome part of his body" similarly reflects the Physical Celestial World;
the "lowest part," itself possessed of a ninefold gradation of the solid humor,
the bones holding the place of lowest earth, reflects the Sublunary World. The
powers of the soul corresponding to the nine orders of angels are those "graces,"
"ministries," and "operations" enumerated in Chapter XII (vv. 8–10) of I Corinthians. Thus Wisdom, in the highest order, is in correspondence with the
Seraphim; Knowledge, with the Cherubim; Faith, with the Thrones; and so
on. Colet's principal intention in introducing the concept of man as microcosm

is to allege a ninefold hierarchy in the dissimilar parts of the body, "in the feet, hands, eyes, and head."

In some instances, the regular, coherent order in the universe is discerned only with difficulty, and the Human World, the hierarchy of men, is one such instance. For this reason, according to Colet, Paul uses the body as a simile to illustrate the existence and nature of the human hierarchy. At this point in his exposition, Colet is clearly shifting his ground temporarily, speaking of the Mystical Body as though it were not a reality, but a fictive concept devised by Paul to assist the understanding. Within a few sentences, however, Colet is again making predications that incontrovertibly affirm the Mystical Body as a reality in and of itself, the same reality as that set forth in his schematic representations in Chapter XII. Apparently we are not confronted here with the use of the linguistic corollary to the hierarchical world structure; that is to say, a man is not to be called an arm or an eye in the Mystical Body simply because the rank he holds in the Human World corresponds to the rank held by the arm or the eye in the hierarchy of the mixed parts of the human body (as he might, for instance, be called a Cherub or a Principality, or the Stellar or Mercurial Sphere, because these also occupy corresponding ranks in their hierarchies). In a way that the intellect can recognize only as a mystery, the Human World *is* the Body of Christ.

The concepts of the more and the less and of progressive deterioration are ulterior to that of hierarchy. The highest of any ninefold series participates most in the perfection of the tenth of that hierarchy, and the lowest participates least, by way of the intermediaries that exist between it and the tenth. Thus, by analogy with the Sublunary World, the men in the lowest rank of the Human World are to be considered "altogether earthy." At the same time they must be in some real sense perfect, or they could not belong to the Mystical Body at all. Using the analogy of the Physical Celestial World, Colet writes: "In this new world, then, this Christian world, no one exists unless he be of form and figure perfect and round and heavenly in Christ" (p. 243). How can a man be this and at the same time altogether earthy?

The answer lies partly in the concept of earthiness, which Colet does not use univocally. Men outside the Human World are said to be earthy in a sense different from that of the paragraph above. They are the earth, Colet says, of Isaiah's sentence, "The Heaven of Heavens is His throne, and the Earth His footstool" (Isa. LXVI: 6). They are therefore below the feet, the lowest part of the Mystical Body of Christ.

More important, however, is the principle of balance and compensation, which serves almost as an antithesis to the principles of hierarchy and progressive deterioration. Colet applies this principle to the Human World only, where the terms are Beauty and Usefulness; presumably the same terms could be extended to the other Worlds and systems as well, because of the principles of affinity and cor-

respondence. The higher and more excellent orders of the Human World possess beauty and loveliness, and from them "there is a manner of progressive degeneration down (if I may so put it) to the worst," the "unlovelier members" (p. 253). This progressive degeneration and lessening of beauty is balanced, however, by a corresponding reverse progression of usefulness, so that the lowest and least beautiful order is the most useful. Thus "in degeneration there is compensation, and . . . an impartial equality, a balanced scale, inclining to neither side, so that there may be an equal respect of all for all, and a recognition of equality" (pp. 253–55).

As a consequence, there is in all the members of the Human World "agreement, mutual love, shared joy and shared sorrow." Further, there can be in this Christian community, the Mystical Body of Christ, no division, no disharmony, no schism, "but only oneness arising from charity and charity arising from oneness. For likeness and equality are the mother of love" (p. 255).

After Colet's insistence on and elaboration of the concepts of hierarchy and progression as master principles governing all reality, this affirmation of equality in unlikeness, of oneness in diversity, and of equal respect of all for all may strike the reader as paradoxical to a degree. Yet it is evidently not just an afterthought, an *ad hoc* improvisation for the reconciling of the hierarchical world vision with Christ's injunction that each of his followers love all his fellow men as he loves himself. In the Commentary it comes as a powerfully climactic conclusion to what has gone before, and one senses that it is at the very heart of Colet's humanism. Here, then, is at once the reason for man's self-respect and for his humility. Reciprocal love and respect rest not on reciprocal dependence merely, but on the recognition of equal worth, not only in the eyes of God, as some would say, but in the eyes of men, when these are capable of seeing rightly.

III
Problems and Perspectives

Order, hierarchy, composition, correspondence, affinity, balance, and compensation — these are the central concepts governing Colet's ontological view of the universe. They are closely related to the master concepts of his soteriological vision: hope, faith, charity; being, wisdom, love; oneness, light, warmth. The structure of Colet's thought, with regard to God, to the universe as a whole, and to man who is both microcosm and image and likeness of God, is profoundly trinitarian and triadistic. The operations of Colet's mind, on the other hand, in making judgments on reality (whether perceived ontologically or soteriolo-

gically) are ordinarily just as profoundly dualistic and dichotomizing. Perhaps the regular imposition of dichotomistic judgments on triadic realities will sometimes lead to incompatible and perplexing results. Disjunctive reasonings, for instance, made separately on each of three elements or principles that are essentially and closely interrelated must slight in some measure the significance of the relations, and so deprive the concept of each co-principle of something ·essential to true understanding. The hierarchical and triadic structure of Colet's conceptualization of the universe in Chapter XII, for example, clearly precludes any even semi-Manichaean view of reality; but some of the disjunctive ethical judgments in Chapter VII just as clearly assume polarities of good and evil, as though evil were a reality in the same univocal sense as good.

Other perplexities arise from three principal causes: Colet's unconcern to establish clearly essential distinctions between the intelligible and phenomenological orders of reality; his apparent impatience with any subtlety or refinement of distinction; and the quality of his eclecticism, which has a reasoned assumption behind it (see above, pp. 37f), but does not question the compatibility of categories and structures of thought drawn from intellectual systems conceived independently of one another.

Over and above these considerations, for most readers since, say, the mid-eighteenth century there will perhaps be some more or less intense degree of general dissatisfaction, even impatience, with Colet's thought in its metaphysical aspects, because so little of it is in the ordinary sense experientially verifiable.

Unless he is intensely partisan, however, the reader need not allow these things to keep him from evaluating justly the structure, patterns, and operations of Colet's mind. The vigor and scope of that mind would be remarkable in any age; they are doubly so in an age like Colet's. Here we do not find the originality of intellectual revolt opening new doors by nailing the old fast shut, or the universalism of the eclectic who makes a patchwork quilt out of wide reading. On the contrary, there is the calm, earnest, and painstaking exploration of a unified cosmic vision and interpretation. Colet would not be satisfied with a metaphysic that seemed to catalogue a more or less static reality, or with a logic that probed the more or less static terms and categories of thought by which men designate reality. The philosophy he built had to cope with Being itself, as directly as possible, and with as true an insight as he could sustain into those sometimes awesome attributes of being, change and activity and relationship. Those who think of a hierarchical world vision as an essentially comfortable habit of mind that assuages a deep human desire for order and security will find in reading Colet that they must modify this concept. He shows that our relationship with the rest of reality is a vigorous and an almost infinitely complex engagement with it; to clarify our mind's understanding of this relationship and of its terms is not to put an arbitrary end to the mind's inquiries. The doors Colet

opens lead the mind into corridors that stretch endlessly — but they are not dark corridors.

Notes

1. Only one copy is known: MS Laud. 193 in the Bodleian. Printed editions of the English translation seem to date from no earlier than 1530. Pynson's edition gives the date 1511 on two pages, but the evidence indicates that this probably refers to the date of the convocation instead of the printing. There is an English translation, presumably by Thomas Lupset, c. 1530, and one by Thomas Smith in 1661.

2. "Nihil autem quod extet in scriptis reliquit; nec multa eum scripsisse constat. Sed purissimam *Latinæ* linguæ Elocutionem, eandem; *Laconica* Brevitate compositam, ex aliquot ejus ad Erasmum familiaribus Epistolis colligere licet." *Virorum aliquot in* Britannia *Elogia* (ed. 1559), quoted by Samuel Knight, *The Life of Dr. John Colet* (London, 1724), p. 252 n. Knight translates rather freely: "He left not behind him any thing that is published; nor probably many Manuscripts. But by what appears in these *Epistles* which he writ to *Erasmus*, he was Master of a pure Latine Style; though chiefly in the *Lackonick* Way" (p. 255).

3. Erasmus, *The Lives of Johan Vitrier . . . and John Colet*, trans. J. H. Lupton (London, 1883), pp. 38–39.

4. *Rejoinder to M. Jewel's Replie* (1566), fol. 44, cited by J. H. Lupton in his introduction to Colet's *Opus de sacramentis ecclesiæ* (London, 1867), p. 5n. The point at issue here between the disputants was whether Colet had rejected the authenticity of the Pseudo-Areopagite. Harding adds: "If he said it at his table, or in a sermon, as M. Jewel perhappes hath heard saye, the proufe is of small auctoritee. We admit not the trial of hearesaies."

5. John Bale, *Illustrium maioris Britanniæ scriptorum summarium* (1548), fol. 214v. Bishop Tunstal records: "Supersunt multa ab eodem Joanne Colet Scripta in D. Paulum, sed puerorum incuria perierunt." Cf. Knight, *Life*, p. viii.

6. *Joannis Coleti enarratio in primam epistolam S. Pauli ad Corinthios*, ed. and trans. J. H. Lupton (London, 1874), p. xxxi.

7. Frederic Seebohm, *The Oxford Reformers*, 3rd ed. (London, 1887).

8. *Erasmus* (N. Y. and London, 1923), p. 162.

9. Some recent discussions of this influence are H. C. Porter and D. F. S. Thomson, eds., *Erasmus and Cambridge* (Univ. of Toronto Press, 1963), pp. 14–22; D. F. S. Thomson and H. Mynors, eds., *The Correspondence of Erasmus*, vol. 1, Intro. (Univ. of Toronto Press, 1974). Roland Bainton in *Erasmus of Christendom* (London: Collins, 1970), says that "if Colet brought about any change it may have been to turn him [Erasmus] from patristic to biblical studies . . ." p. 83 and p. 346, n. 27. James Tracy in *Erasmus, the Growth of a Mind* (Geneva: Librairie Droz, 1972) stresses Colet's example: "In Colet he at last found a practitioner of that theology after the manner of the 'ancients' to which he professed allegiance. Colet belongs with Nicholas Werner and Robert Gaguin

in the sequence of sober and thoughtful men who showed some understanding for the centrifugal tendencies of Erasmus' nature but at the same time reminded him of his promises about theology" (p. 84; see also n. 4, p. 84, disclaiming the notion, suggested by Seebohm, that Colet first sparked Erasmus' interest in theology).

10. Erasmus, *Opus Epistolarum*, ed. P. S. Allen (Oxford: Clarendon Press, 1910), vol. 2, Ep. 423, p. 258. Apparently it was written on June 20, 1516. Translated R. A. B. Mynors and D. F. S. Thomson, *The Correspondence of Erasmus*, vol. 3 (Univ. of Toronto Press, 1976), p. 313.

11. Allen, vol. 2, Ep. 593, p. 599; trans. Bernard O'Kelly.

12. See, for example, Eugene Rice, "John Colet and the Annihilation of the Natural," *Harvard Theological Review* 45 (July, 1952), 141–63. He sets out to demolish the "mythical" humanism and liberalism of Colet, relating him instead to the antinaturalist currents of previous Christian theology and philosophy, and to the ascetic reformers of his own time such as the Brothers of the Common Life. Leland Miles, *John Colet and the Platonic Tradition* (London: Allen, 1962), presents a one-sided and tendentious view; readers may be surprised to find in Colet's writings much that is in direct contradiction to many of Miles' assertions. Donald J. Parsons, "John Colet's Stature as an Exegete," *Anglican Theological Review*, 40 (Jan., 1958), 36–42, adds little to what has been said before, but does recognize that Colet, whatever his formal professions on the matter, uses typological interpretations of Scripture, even allegorical interpretations. Parsons draws attention also to Colet's insistence that no Pauline statement be interpreted without reference to other passages on the same topic. Sidney Dark, "John Colet," in *Five Deans* (New York, 1928), pp. 15–53, takes a different view and identifies Colet as a liberal Catholic. William A. Clebsch, "John Colet and the Reformation," *Anglican Theological Review*, 37 (July, 1955), 167–77, stresses Colet's "genuinely humanistic approach to the Pauline writings as human documents" and his adherence to the Church; he suggests that a better term for Colet than *Reformer* might be *repristinator*. Edward Surtz, "The Oxford Reformers and Scholasticism," *Studies in Philology*, 47 (Oct., 1950), 547–56, discusses Colet's commentaries on Paul with reference to the great theological and philosophical revival of Scholasticism that came after him in the sixteenth century. P. Albert Duhamel, "The Oxford Lectures of John Colet: An Essay in Defining the English Renaissance," *Journal of the History of Ideas*, 14 (Oct., 1953), 493–510, shows the contrast between Colet's exegetical method and that of his contemporaries, and offers a useful historical perspective. Perhaps the best restatement of the general lines of interpretation set down by Seebohm and Lupton is to be found in a very short essay by Kathleen MacKenzie, "John Colet of Oxford," *The Dalhousie Review*, 21 (April, 1941), 15–28; she stresses that the center of Colet's thought is Christ, not Plato or even Paul. Ficino's Platonism could not satisfy Colet's heart, she says, any more than it could satisfy Pico's, however much it might please their minds; as Pico turned from Plato to Christ, so Colet moved on from Paul to Christ. The chronological implications here are, of course, questionable, but this emphasis on "Christian" as a name for Colet counterbalances the too rigorous and too highly exclusivist identification of him as a Platonist. Sears Jayne, *John Colet and Marsilio Ficino* (Oxford, 1963), provides a fascinating glimpse of Colet at work on one of his favorite authors. This work is an edition and translation of Colet's marginalia on Ficino's *Epistolae*, from a MS in All Souls College, Oxford. Jayne's introduction presents a useful assessment of Colet in relation to his contemporaries, and some persuasive con-

jectures on the possible chronology of his works. See also Giovanni Santinello, *Studi sull' umanesimo europeo: Cusano e Petrarca, Lefebvre, Erasmo, Colet, Moro* (Padua: Antenore, 1969), and *A Bibliography of John Colet*, compiled by Carl Meyer, in *Foundation for Reformation Research: Bulletin of the Library*, 5 (1970), pp. 23–28.

13. See *Ioannis Coleti enarratio in epistolam S. Pauli ad Romanos*, ed. and trans. J. H. Lupton (London, 1873), pp. 155–57.

14. *Ioannis Coleti opuscula quaedam theologica*, ed. and trans. J. H. Lupton (London, 1876), pp. 66–68.

15. Some might object to the names of Ockham and Bacon in a list of Scholastic thinkers, depending on whether one is accustomed to thinking of Scholasticism as a univocal conceptual term, or a complex historical one. Certainly there are sound objections against using a generic name—even one of purely chronological intent—for any two of the major thinkers whom we call Scholastics.

16. See Paul Oskar Kristeller, *The Philosophy of Marsilio Ficino* (N.Y., Columbia Univ. Press, 1943), pp. 130–33.

17. *Oeuvres complètes du Pseudo-Denys l'Aréopagite*, trans. Maurice de Gandillac (Paris, 1942), pp. 53–57.

18. *Renaissance News*, 17 (1964), p. 109.

19. *John Colet and Marsilio Ficino*, pp. 28–33.

20. Knight, *Life*, p. ix.

21. Lupton, *Corinthians*, p. vii.

22. The frequency of these changes indicates that Meghen knew Latin rather well, but not all the changes are for the better.

23. In speaking of the prose of the Authorized Version, Lewis says that it "haunts our prose not as Mr. Eliot haunts modern poetry or as Macaulay used to haunt journalists, but much more as Homer haunts the prose of Plato; that is, as something set apart, like plums in a cake or lace on a frock, not like wine mixing with water."

24. John Colet, "Statutes of St. Paul's School." See J. H. Lupton, *A Life of John Colet, D. D.* (London, 1887), p. 279.

25. Erasmus, *The Lives of Jehan Vitrier and John Colet*, trans. J. H. Lupton (London, 1883), pp. 38–39.

26. *Dean Colet and His Theology*, p. 7. Hunt is quoting the Nichols translations (*The Epistles of Erasmus*, trans. Francis M. Nichols [London, 1901]), Eps. 411, 457, 459, respectively (Allen, Eps. 423, 468, 471).

27. The following muddled but memorable anecdote in Spence may have given rise to the hypothesis that Colet did not know Greek: "Dr. Collet upon mistaking ψυχη αιολος in his author, wrote in his notes, fifteen reasons to prove why the soul was like a flute.—*Derham, of St. John's*." Joseph Spence, *Anecdotes* (2nd ed., London, 1858), p. 251. Derham of St. John's was probably misremembering his story from Knight's *Life*, where it is told in the middle of a section of anti-Scholastic diatribe (p. 57) as a "pleasant Passage of one of the Clan of 'Scholastical Divines' " in Colet's time, and not, of course, of Colet at all. The mistake was over ἄϋλος (immaterial) and αὐλός (an oboe-like wind instrument). One can imagine Colet and his friends chuckling over the story, and it is ironic to think that it came to be told of him.

28. J. de Ghellinck, "Peter Lombard," *Catholic Encyclopedia* (1907), 11:769.

29. *Doctoris Angelici Divi Thomae Aquinatis Opera Omnia* (Paris: Vives, 1876), "In

epistolam ad Corinthios I," 20:603–752; 21:1–57.

30. *Ecc. Hier.*, 5:107; Lupton's translation. See also Lupton's rather lengthy discussion of this point (p. 105, n. 1) and his apt citation of Erasmus: "Sensus enim Historicus, veluti substratum fundamentum, non excludit, sed sustinet sensum mysticum." *Exposit. in Psal.* lxxxvi.

31. In the commentary on Romans, however, Colet cites Suetonius (Lupton's edition, p. 201), if not with complete accuracy. See Hunt, *op. cit.*, pp. 92–93 and n.

32. More customarily, *accommodation* is used in exegetical literature to designate the application of a scriptural text to a subject with which it has no intrinsic connection, but toward which it bears some particular aptness, either substantive or verbal. Colet seems to assume the validity of this process, but it is hard in any given instance to say whether one is confronted by accommodation in this sense, or some sort of typological reading.

33. See Encyclical *Divino afflante Spiritu* (Sept. 30, 1943), par. 41; article on "Inspiration and Inerrancy," *Jerome Biblical Commentary*, 2:494–98.

34. Lupton, *Life*, p. 14.

John Colet

Enarratio in Primam S. Pauli Epistolam ad Corinthios

The Latin Text

An English Translation

Summaria quedam° commemoratio eorum que aguntur in prima Pauli epistola ad Corinthios, in octo partes divisa; quibus agnitis et anima⟨d⟩versis, lecta epistola facilius intelligitur

Prima pars

In prima parte arrogantiam et superbiam Corinthiorum premit, et eos revocat ad subiectionem Deo et ad imitationem sui ipsius, ut expectent revelationem desuper, et ex Deo solo sapiant; utque quicquid sit hominum, id contemna⟨n⟩t, et in solo Deo glorientur.

Secunda

In secunda arguit asperius negligentiam Corinthiorum in corrigendis vitiis et tollendis morbis a corpore christiano, que est ecclesia; quod facit maxime propter quemdam qui sibi in uxorem accepit suam novercam, quod facinus valde detestatur Apostolus.

Tertia

In tercia improbat in illis Corinthiis quod contentiones et iudicia habent et ex⟨er⟩cent foris apud infideles de rebus secularibus; de quibus nugis certe sentit Paulus christiano viro nullo modo nec apud quemquam contendendum esse, sed potius omnes iniurias perp⟨e⟩tiendas.

Quarta

In quarta respondet litteris et interogatis Corinthiorum de matrimonio et usu feminarum, ubi Paulus concedit matrimonium et legittimum cum mulieribus coitum, sed plurimum extollit et exortatur virginitatem, que est coniugali copule longe anteponenda. Item de idolatitis, i.e. idolis immolatis, quorum degusta-

---

See above, p. 21, for the procedures followed with respect to spelling in this reproduction of Colet's MS.

The Matters Treated in St. Paul's
First Epistle to the Corinthians Are Recalled
in a Summary, Divided into Eight Parts;
Recognized and Heeded, These Divisions Make the
Epistle Easier to Understand When It Is Read

I

In the first part, Paul curbs the arrogance and the pride of the Corinthians; he calls them back to submission to God and to imitation of himself, so that they may look for revelation from on high, and may be wise only by the wisdom of God, and may moreover despise whatever is of men, and glory in God alone.

II

In the second, he rebukes with considerable severity the negligence of the Corinthians in correcting vices and in removing diseases from the Christian body, which is the Church. The principal occasion for this rebuke is a man who has married his own stepmother, a misdeed which the Apostle finds deeply abhorrent.

III

In the third, he reproaches the Corinthians because they engage in disputes and trials, and conduct lawsuits about worldly matters before unbelievers. These are surely trifles, Paul believes; the Christian should altogether avoid wranglings in any court, preferring to be entirely submissive to all injuries.

IV

In the fourth, he answers the letters and questions of the Corinthians about matrimony and the frequenting of women; he permits matrimony and legitimate intercourse with women, but strongly praises virginity, exhorting them to it, as much to be preferred to conjugal intercourse. Concerning idol-meats, moreover, i.e., things sacrificed to idols, Paul does not forbid the eating of them, but warns

tionem non vetat Paulus, sed in eo genere vitandum scandalum et lesionem infirmorum fratrum omnino admonet.

Quinta

In quintta de se ipso Apostolus non nihil loquitur, asserens sibi |75r| multa licere que non facit, et ex evangelio vivere posse, quamquam apud Corinthios consulto id noluit facere ne videatur victus causa docuisse. Item in ea parte est etiam de velatione capitis mulierum in ecclesia, et ut viri detectis sint capitibus. In quo sermone de re parva alta misteria reconduntur. Preterea de conventu Corinthiorum ad dominicam cenam et cominicatione eiusdem, quod velit Paulus sancte, sobrie, et cum charitate esse.

Sexta

In sexta parte surgit sermo Apostoli ad Spiritum et spirituales operationes in christiana societate, que quasi corpus constat ex multis et variis membris, omnibus tamen necessariis, que debent una conuniri charitate. De qua charitate deinde multa et magna loquitur, eius mirificam vim ostendens, et exhortatur Corinthios ut eam enixius sectentur, atque ut plurimum laborent in acquis⟨it⟩ione Spiritus Sancti et possessione, ut ex Divino Spiritu omnia agant et loquantur. Laudat multitudinem et peritiam linguarum, sed multo magis velit ut contendant in Spiritum cognitionemque divinorum sentium ex revelatione, ut tandam prophete evadere possint.

Septima

In septima disserit de resurrectione mortuorum, probans exemplo Christi resurrecturos homines immortalibus corporibus et spiritalibus.

Ultima

In octava iubet prompti sint Corinthii ad liberalitatem in sanctos fratres qui fuerunt Hierosolime, et symbolum faciant. Postremo concludit epistolam suo more commendationibus et salutationibus.

Finis |75v|

that in this sort of thing scandal and the offending of the weak brethren must be altogether avoided.

V

In the fifth, the Apostle says something about himself, pointing out that many things are allowed him which he does not do: he can live by the Gospel, but among the Corinthians he has expressly wished not to do so, lest he should seem to have taught them for the sake of earning a living. In this part also he takes up the veiling of women's heads in church, and the fact that men ought to be bareheaded. Lofty mysteries are hidden in this discussion of a small matter. In addition, Paul speaks of the assembling of the Corinthians for the Lord's Supper: he would like it to take place with holiness, sobriety, and charity.

VI

In the sixth part, the Apostle's discourse rises to the Spirit and to spiritual operations in the Christian society. Like a body, this society is composed of members which are all necessary, though many and different, and which ought to be bound into oneness by the one charity. Of this charity he then speaks many and great things, showing its wonderful power, and he urges the Corinthians to seek it more vigorously, and to strive especially for the obtaining and the keeping of the Holy Spirit, so that by the Divine Spirit they may speak and perform all things. He praises diversity and skill in tongues, but would wish much more that they vie in seeking the Spirit and the understanding of divine meanings from revelation, so that at length they may be able to become prophets.

VII

In the seventh, Paul discourses about the resurrection of the dead, proving by the example of Christ that men will rise with bodies immortal and spiritual.

VIII

In the eighth, he commands the Corinthians to be ready in their generosity toward the holy brethren who were at Jerusalem, and to take up a collection. Finally, he ends the Epistle, in his usual manner, with commendations and greetings.

Hic latius tractantur ea que in prima parte continentur prime epistole ad Corinthios

Caput primum°

Salutatio

Paulus, quem Deus voluit Apostolum Iesu Christi esse, salutans Corinthios simul et omnes ubique locorum qui invocant Dominum Iesum, eis optat gratiam et pacem a Deo Patre et Domino Iesu.

Sermo Epistolaris

Gaudet deinde et gratulatur Corinthiis ac agit gratias Deo fideli a quo est misericordia et gratia in homines per Iesum Christum, a quoque Corinthii sunt vocati in sanctam illam societatem que est electorum apud Patrem cum Iesu, ut simul cum eo filii Dei aliquando in celo correg-

Gratulatio Corinthiis exhortatoria: ut digni se gratulatione prestent.

nent. Gaudet (inquam) et Deo gratias agit quod illi in Christo Corinthii sub radiis diffuse a Deo gratie sic fide et charitate abundant ut quicquid dispensavit Deus de Christo suo, id et fortiter et sapienter profiteantur, videlicet quod ad constitutionem unius Christi in terris ex delectis hominibus Filius Dei et Verbum caro factum est, qui Iesus est Christus.

Qui Deus et homo apparuit in hominibus tandem ut rectam vivendi formam edoceret, utque quos velit sue divinitatis radiis ad se iusticiamque attraheret. Qui

---

Caput primum *Ed.*] *om. C M*

A Fuller Treatment of the Matters Contained in the First Part of I Corinthians

Chapter I

The Greeting

Paul, whom God has willed to be an Apostle of Jesus Christ, greeting the Corinthians and at the same time all men everywhere who call upon the Lord Jesus, wishes them grace and peace from God the Father and from the Lord Jesus [I Cor. I. 1–3].

The Text of the Epistle

Next he expresses joy, and congratulates the Corinthians,[1] and offers thanks to the faithful God, from whom there is mercy and grace to men through Jesus Christ and by whom the Corinthians have been called to that holy society of those chosen with Jesus in the Father's presence, that they may together with him at last reign in Heaven as sons of God. He rejoices, I say, and he offers thanks to God, because those Corinthians who are in Christ under the rays of grace diffused by God[2] have such a plenty of faith and charity, that whatever God has determined concerning his Christ, this they profess both with strength and with wisdom. They hold, I mean, that for the establishment from chosen men of one Christ[3] on earth, the Son of God, the Word, was made flesh, and this is Jesus the Christ.

Hortatory congratulations of the Corinthians, with the intent that they may show themselves worthy of congratulation.

God and man, he at last appeared among men to teach them the right form of living,[4] and to draw to himself and to justice[5] by the rays of his divinity those whom he would.[6] For the redemption of his own and their reconciliation to

pro redemptione suorum reconciliationeque Deo sponte necatus interiit. Qui resurrexit ad consolationem suorum. Qui ascen-
dit ad Patrem. Qui denique suo tempore *Gaudet quod Corinthii tenent totam*
redibit°. Qui etiam interea per suos *rationem et formam fidei; quamquam*
Apostolos ipse constructionem sue ecclesie *enim in reliqua superedificatione fuit*
nonnulla labefactio, tamen
in terris et Christi Dei, cuius idem ille est *se res bonam habuit quod adhuc*
capud, sedulo agit, donec ex se et sibi *saltem fundamenta erant salva.*
vocatis tandem quidem plenus et perfec-
tus Christus conficiatur in terris, qui sit, huius mundi cursu finito, apud Deum
et in Deo feliciter quieturus.

Id totum misterium et salutare sacramentum est quod hic vocat Paulus
testimonium Christi |76r| ac dicit in Corinthiis confirmatum esse, cuius pars
preteriit, pars adhuc restat eventura, reditus scilicet et
revelatio Iesu Christi, quando veniet iudicare vivos et *Exorditur a bono eorum et*
laude, ut eos in lectionem
mortuos, quod etiam Corinthii expectarunt. Quaprop- *epistole alliciat. Si carpsisset*
ter ait *nihil eis deesse in ulla gratia ad summam fidei* et *prius, discussisset animos.*
eorum que vel credenda sunt preterita vel exspectanda
futura. Iccirco gratias agit Deo quod apprehensi gratia, ii sic in Christo sunt
iam ut totam Christi rationem et teneant et profiteantur.

Memento ex mente Pauli esse, ex homine quem Deus assumpsit ex Maria
Virgine, quo voluit ipse incarnari, et ex reliquis simul vocatis ac electis hominibus, in quibus etiam vult idem Deus in-
habitare, unum quiddam componi omnino,   *Deo*
ac quasi quadam communi anima animari.   *Ex* ⟨ *unum: Christus.*
Anima autem copulans homines coactos   *hominibus*
in unum quasi membra (ut Paulus philosophatur) Divinus est Spiritus Deusque
ipse, qui in principali membro huius compositi et capite, *Deus anima,*
i.e. homine a Virgine sumpto, plene residet; in quo est om- *filius Virginis capud.*
nis plenitudo divinitatis corporaliter°. Deinde ab illo diriva-
tur in reliqua membra que adherent capiti ac cuique ut iusta exigit proportio
impartitur. Hec impartitio gratie in Sacris Litteris spiritalis *Reliqua membra*
unctio intelligitur. Uncti autem a Grecis christi vocantur. *hominum filii.*
Unde Ioannes in epistola scribit: *Vos unctionem habetis a*
Sancto et nostis° omnia, et paulo post, eandem unctionem dicit *Spiritualis unctio.*

---

redibit *C L*] rediet *M*   corporaliter *M L*] corporalitur *C*   nostis *Vulg.*] noscis
C M, noscitis *L*

God, he died, allowing himself to be killed. For the comfort of his own, he rose again. He ascended to the Father. In his own time at last he will return. And in the meantime, by his Apostles he himself is constantly working the establishment of his Church on earth and of the Christ of God, of which he is himself the head, un- til at last there shall be completed on earth,

He rejoices because the Corinthians hold the whole meaning and form of faith; for although in the rest of the superstructure there has been some falling away, still there is the good circumstance that as yet the foundations are intact.

from himself and those called by him, the full and perfect[7] Christ, destined to repose in happiness, when the course of this world is ended, with God and in God.

This entire mystery and saving sacrament[8] it is that Paul here calls the testimony of Christ, and he says it has been confirmed among the Corinthians, part of it being in the past, part still to be accomplished in the future, the return, namely, and the revelation of Jesus Christ, when he shall come to judge the living and the dead. And this latter also the Corinthians looked forward to. For this reason he says that they lack no grace toward the fullness of faith, either about things past and to be believed or about things to come and to be looked for- ward to. So he offers thanks to God that those whom

He begins with what is good in them and with praise, that he may draw them to read on. If he had first scolded, he would have discouraged their souls.

grace has taken hold of are already to such an extent in Christ that they both hold and profess the whole system of Christ.[9]

Remember that according to the mind of Paul, from the manhood which God took to himself from the Virgin Mary and in which he wished himself to be incarnate, and from the rest of men who are called and chosen with him, in whom also the same God wished to dwell, there should be constituted one unity, and that

this should be animated, as it were, by a common spirit. Now the spirit joining men, brought together into one as members (as Paul reasons it), is the Divine Spirit and God Himself, who resides fully in the principal member and head of this

God is the soul; the Son of the Virgin is the head.

composite body, i.e., in the manhood taken from the Virgin. In him is em- bodied all fullness of the Godhead [Col. II. 9]. From him it is then derived into the other members which are joined to the head, and to each it is shared as due proportion requires.[10] This sharing of grace is what is understood in Holy Scripture by "Spiritual anointing."[11] The anointed are called by the Greeks "Christs," and this is why John writes in his epistle: "You have been anointed by the Holy One, and have all knowledge" [I John II. 20], and a

The other members are the sons of men.

Spiritual anointing.

little further on he says that this anointing teaches those who have it [II. 27].

docere eos qui ea inunguntur. Huic consonat quod hic dicitur: *Divites facti estis in illo in omni verbo et in omni scientia;* quod dicit quia velit Corinthios sapere omnia et loqui ex Spirito Sancto.

Sed ad rem redeo. Omnes ergo participes huius gratie Divinique Spiritus et Dei, ut cum eo copulentur quem Maria peperit, qui primus extitit in hac gratia totamque gratiam in se possidet, quem Ioannes vocat *plenum gratie* |76v| *et veritatis,* sunt a spirituali unctione participationeque Dei quidam christi. Qui cum primo illo uncto quem, ut cecinit David, *unxit Deus oleo letitie pre consortibus suis,* unum quiddam sub Deo ex multis et variis membris constituunt. Qui ab una commune unctione unus Christus rite potest appellari°. *Ex omnibus Christianis unus Christus.* Quod hoc compositum ex Deo et hominibus in Deum vocatis Paulus non modo Christum ut in hac epistola ad Corinthios, quum dicit *omnia membra corporis quum sint multa unum tamen corpus sunt: ita et Christus,* sed etiam in epistola ad Ephesios *virum perfectum* vocat. Cuius quidem corpus sane homines apprehensi a Deo sunt, anima vero Deus ipse est apprehendens uniens, illuminans, calificiens, vivificans, et sustinens in se suum corpus. *Deus / Vir perfectus: Christus. / Homines.* Cuius capud est Iesus, in quo est vere Deus ipse: ideo hoc membrorum maxime vocatur Christus, siquidem totus homo in capite est. Cetera autem corporis membra sunt ceteri homines qui in Divini eius Spiritus vivificationem asciscuntur, qui inter se ita censentur differre, ut vel propius vel remotius a capite videntur distare.

Deus autem ipse animi inster totus in toto est et totus in qualibet parte. Verumtamen non omnes partes similiter deificat (Dei enim animare deificare est) *Deus anima deificans homines.* sed varie, videlicet ut convenit ad constructionem eius quod est in eo unum ex pluribus.

Hoc compositum etiam ex Deo et hominibus modo templum Dei, modo ecclesia, modo domus, modo civitas, modo regnum a Dei prophetis appellatur°. Item (ut modo dixi) in epistola ad Ephesios vocat idem Paulus *virum perfectum,* in illo loco ubi hec verba scribuntur: *Et ipse* *Templum. Ecclesia. / Domus. Civitas. / Regnum. Vir perfectus.* *dedit quosdam apostolos, quosdam prophetas, alios evangelistas, alios pastores et doctores, ad consummationem sanctorum in opus ministerii in edificationem* |77r| *corporis Christi donec occurramus omnes in unitatem fidei* *Caput IV.*

---

appellari *M L*] appellarari *C*   appellatur *M L*] appellantur *C*

What is said here is in agreement: "You have become rich in him, in all utterance and in all knowledge" [I Cor. I. 5]. Paul says this because he would wish the Corinthians to have all wisdom and utterance from the Holy Spirit.

But I return to the subject. All who share, then, this grace and participate in the Divine Spirit and God, so that they may be joined with him whom Mary bore—who stood forth as the first in this grace and possesses in himself all grace, who is said by John to be "full of grace and truth" [John I. 14]—are, as it were, Christs, by reason of their spiritual anointing and the communication from God. These constitute, with that first anointed whom, as David sings, "God anointed with the oil of gladness above his fellows" [Ps. XLIV. 8], one unity under God, from many and varied members. These rightly may be called, from their one common anointing, one Christ.

From all Christian men, one Christ.

And this composite being of God and men[12] called to God Paul calls not only Christ, as when he says in this letter to the Corinthians, "All the members of the body, although they are many, are still one body: so is it with Christ" [I Cor. XII. 12], but also, in the Letter to the Ephesians, "the perfect man"

*God
The Perfect Man: Christ.
Men*

[Eph. IV. 13]. And the body of this being is clearly the men who have been taken hold of by God,[13] and the spirit is God, who takes hold of, unites, gives light, warmth, and life[14] to, and sustains within itself His own body. The head of this body is Jesus, in whom is truly God Himself, and therefore he is called Christ above the other members, since the whole man is in the head. And the other members of the body are the rest of men who are gathered into the giving of life from his Divine Spirit.[15] These are judged to differ one from another according as they are seen to be more or less distant from the head.

God, however, as the soul, is all in the whole, and all in every part. Not all the parts, however, does He in the same way make godlike[16] (for God, to dwell within as spirit is to make godlike) but in different ways, as is appropriate for the fashioning from many of that which in Him is one.

God is the soul, making men godlike.

Further, this composite being of God and men is called by God's prophets[17] sometimes the Temple of God, sometimes His Church, sometimes His House, sometimes His City, sometimes His Kingdom. Similarly (as I remarked just now) Paul

Temple, Church, House, City, Kingdom, the Perfect Man.

calls it "the perfect man" in his Epistle to the Ephesians, in that passage where these words are found: "Some he has appointed to be apostles, others to be prophets, others to be evangelists, others pastors and teachers, for the perfecting of the saints, for the working of the ministry, for the building of the body of Christ, until we all meet in the unity of faith and of the knowledge of the Son

et agnitionis° Filii Dei in virum perfectum in mensuram etatis plenitudinis Christi.

Quum itaque eiusmodi quiddam unum compositum ex Deo et hominibus constans divina mens Pauli cogitat qui ex quam plurimis unctis unus est Christus, ex hoc facile licet cernere quid sibi velint illi loquendi modi qui sunt crebri apud Paulum: per Christum, in Christo, cum Christo, per ipsum, ex ipso, in ipso, in Deo cum Christo, in Deo per Christum. Nam omnes qui sunt in hoc mistico composito sunt in Deo, qui incipiens suam deificationem in homine a Maria sumpto, per eum deinceps tamquam per capud distribuit in reliquos ad constructionem totius. In quo composito viroque perfecto et Christo qui est, is in Deo quasi anima vivificante est, per Christum capud: in eo scilicet Christo qui constat ex Deo et hominibus.

Christus capud.
Christus compositum.

In quo quum Corinthii erant, ut videri voluerunt et professi sunt, sapienter sane Paulus, anima⟨d⟩vertens si quid laude dignum in illis erat, inde exorditur, et gratias agit de eo quod pre se ferunt boni, quodque adhuc fidei et ecclesie fundamentum tenent, ut hoc leni et molli principio alliciat eos in lectionem relique epistole, faciatque quod reprehendet in moribus eorum facilius audiant. Nam si statim in initio asperior° fuisset graviusque accusasset, profecto teneros adhuc animos et novellos in religione, presertim in gente illa greca arrogante et superba ac prona in dedignationem, a se et suis exhortationibus discussisset. Prudenter igitur et caute agendum fuit pro ratione personarum, locorum, et temporum. In quibus observandis fuit Paulus certe unus omnium consideratissimus, qui proposito fini ita novit media accom-

Consideratio Pauli.

modare ut quum nihil aliud quesierat nisi |77v| gloriam Iesu Christi in terris, et amplificationem fidei ac charitatis, homo divina usus solertia nihil nec agit nec omisit unquam apud aliquos quod eiusmodi propositum vel impediret vel retardaret.

Itaque iam necessario correcturus quam plurima per litteras in Corinthiis, qui post eius ab eis discessum obliqua acciderant, acceptiore utitur principio, et quasi quemdam aditum facit ad reliqua que non nihil amara cogitur adhibere, ut salutaris medicine poculum, modo eius os saccharo illiniatur, Corinthii libenter admittant et hauriant.

Quamquam vero Corinthii omnes qui fuerunt ex ecclesia Christum professi sunt, in illiusque doctrina et nomine gloriati sunt, tamen super hoc fundamento nonnullorum erant male et prave edificationes, partim ignorantia, partim malitia superintroducte.

---

agnitionis M] *agnisionis C L*   *asperior M*] *aspirior C L*

of God, unto the perfect man, unto the full measure of the completed growth of Christ" [Eph. IV. 11–13].

Since, then, the divine mind of Paul is thinking of this sort of composite unity consisting of God and men, one Christ from a very great number of anointed, we may therefore easily understand what is meant by those forms of expression frequently found in Paul: through Christ, in Christ, with Christ, through him, from him, in him, in God with Christ, in God through Christ. For all who are in this mystical composite are in God, who, beginning His deification in the manhood taken

Christ the head.
Christ the composite.

from Mary, through him thence as through the head has distributed to the rest for the fashioning of the whole. And whoever is in this composite and perfect man and Christ, whoever is in that Christ which consists of God and men, is also in God, the life-giving soul, as it were.

And since the Corinthians were thus in him — as they desired to be thought to be, and professed — wisely does Paul begin by drawing attention to whatever is praiseworthy in them, and offer thanks because of the good they manifest and because they continue to hold to the foundation of the faith and of the Church, so that he may draw them on by this gentle and easy beginning to read the rest of the letter, and bring them to hear more readily what he is going to reprehend in their conduct. For if he had been more severe at the outset, and had at once brought his rather heavy charges against them, surely he would have disaffected from himself and his exhortations their minds, which were still young and little and new in religion. This was all the more sure because he was dealing with Greeks, a race haughty and proud and prompt to feel disdain. Prudently then and carefully he had to manage the affair, taking into account the persons, places, and times.[18] And in taking these

Paul's thoughtfulness.

things into account, Paul was surely of all men the most considerate, knowing so well how to adjust the means for the desired end that although he sought nothing other than the glory of Jesus Christ on earth and the increase of faith and charity, he used a godlike tact with all men, never doing anything that might be a hindrance or an obstacle to the gaining of his purpose, never omitting anything that might further it.

And so now, when by letter he must correct in the Corinthians a great many things which had gone awry since his departure, he begins with what will be more acceptable, and makes as it were an easy approach to the other and rather bitter words he is forced to use, so that the Corinthians may willingly accept and drink down the cup of saving medicine, its rim being coated with sugar.

For although all the Corinthians who belonged to the Church professed Christ, and gloried in his teaching and name, still upon this foundation had been raised by way of addition the wicked and wrong fabrications of many others, partly through ignorance and partly through malice.

Fuerunt enim quidam parum modesti, idemque non parum arrogantes, qui Deo et Christo et Christi Apostolis nonnihil posthabitis, ceperunt de lucro suo cogitare, ac freti sapientia seculari, que semper plurimum potuit apud Grecos, in plebe sibi autoritatem querere, simulque apostolorum opinionem, maxime Pauli, derogare, cuius tamen adhuc apud Corinthios (ut debuit) nomen plurimum valuit. At illi nescio qui, invidi et impatientes laudis Pauli, et suam laudem ac gloriam amantes, attemptaverunt aliquid institutionis in ecclesia, ut eis venerat in mentem utque sua sapientia et opibus probare potuerint, volueruntque in populo videri multa scire et posse, ac quid exposcit° christiana religio nihil ignorare, facileque° quid venerat in dubium posse solvere et sententiam ferre.

Qua insolentia |78r| nimirum in molli adhuc et nascente ecclesia molliti sunt multa. Multa passi etiam sunt que ab institutis Pauli abhorruere. Item magna pars populi iamdudum et vix a mundo tracti in eam religionem que mundi contemptum edocet et imperat, facile retrospexit ad mundanos mores, et oculos in opes, potentiam, et sapientiam secularem coniecit.

Unde nihil reluctati sunt quin qui opibus valuerunt apud eos iidem autoritate valeant. Immo ab illis illecti, prompti illorum nomina sectati sunt. Quo factum fuit ut partes nascerentur et factiones° ac constitutiones sibi diversorum capitum, ut queque conventicula suum capud sequeretur. Ex quo dissidio contentiose altercationes proruperunt, et omnia simul misere corruerunt in deterius.

Quam calamitatem Corinthiensis ecclesie, quorumdam improbitate inductam, illius primus parens Paulus molestissime tulit, non tam quod conati sunt infringere suam autoritatem, quam quod sub malis suasoribus qui bene ceperint navigare in Christi archa periclitarentur.

Itaque quantum est ausus et licuit, insectatur eos qui volunt videri sapientes quique in christiana re publica plus suis ingeniis quam ex Deo moliuntur. Quod tamen facit ubique modestissime homo piissimus, magis querens refirmationem malorum quam aliquoram reprehensionem. Itaque docet omnem et sapientiam et potentiam a Deo esse hominibus, per Iesum Christum, qui Dei sui eterni Patris virtus et sapientia est, cuius virtute oportet sapiat et possit quisque qui vere sapiat aliquid et recte possit.

---

exposcit *M L*] expossit *C*   facileque *M L*] faceleque *C*   factiones *M*] faciones *C L*

For there were some of little humility but much arrogance who began to think of profit for themselves, setting this well ahead of God, and Christ, and his Apostles. Reassured by their natural wisdom, which has always been of great influence among the Greeks, they began to seek for themselves authority among the people, and at the same time to belittle the prestige of the Apostles, and especially of Paul, whose name was still, however, a great one among the Corinthians, as indeed it deserved to be. These men—their identity is uncertain[19]—were jealous and impatient of the praise given Paul, and they were in love with their own praise and glory. They tried to bring new things into the Church, as these occurred to their minds, testing them by their own wisdom and intellectual resources; and they wanted to seem to the populace to have much learning and power, to know all the precepts of the Christian religion, to be able with ease to solve and judge whatever was doubtful.

Since this was a Church still in its infancy and not yet firmly formed, quite naturally because of their arrogance many relaxations came to exist in it. Things were permitted, moreover, that were altogether repugnant to the institutions of Paul. Further, since the greater part of the people had only very recently been withdrawn from the world—and at that, not very far from it—into that religion which teaches and enjoins contempt of the world, they readily looked back to their worldly ways and wistfully turned their eyes to wealth, power, and secular wisdom.

And so they had no hesitation in esteeming as most authoritative those among them who were most richly endowed. Indeed, when these men encouraged them, they eagerly enrolled under their names. And so it came about that parties and factions arose,[20] and a variety of heads took to themselves organized systems, with the result that each little conventicle followed its own head. From this dissidence there broke forth strident wranglings, and everything was rushing at once from bad to worse.

This grievous misfortune of the Corinthian Church,[21] brought on by the wickedness of a few, afflicted Paul, the first father of that Church, not so much because those responsible tried to slight his authority, but because under wicked counsellors those who had begun well their voyage in the bark of Christ were in peril of shipwreck.

So he attacks, within the limits of prudence and propriety, those who wish to appear wise and who within the Christian commonwealth are building rather on their own native endowments than on God. Most unassumingly, however, does he, the kindest of men, do this, seeking to restore the wicked to soundness rather than to blame anyone. He instructs them, therefore, that all wisdom and power come to men from God, through Jesus Christ, who is the might and wisdom of God, his eternal Father. By his power must a man be wise and strong, if he would have either true wisdom or the strength to do what is right.

Hominum autem sapientiam inanem et |78v| falsam affirmat, item potentiam vel quamquumque quamdam enervationem et infirmitatem; atque hec utraque Deo odiosa et detestabilia, ut nihil possit fieri nec stultius nec impotentius, neque vero quod magis Deo displiceat, quam quempiam suis ipsius viribus conari aliquid in ecclesia christiana, quam totam suam solius opus esse vult Deus, atque quemquam in eo ex se solo suoque Spiritu sapere, ut nulla sit in hominibus prorsus neque quod possunt bonitate neque quod sapiunt fide neque denique quod sunt quidem spe, nisi ex Deo in Christo, gloriatio; per quem sumus in ipso et in Deo, a quo sane solo possumus°, et sapimus, et sumus denique quicquid sumus.

Hoc in tota hac epistola contendit Paulus asserere, verum maxime et apertissime in prima parte, in qua nititur eradicare et funditus tollere falsam illam opinionem, qua homines suis viribus se aliquid posse arbitrantur, qua sibi confisi, tum Deo diffidunt, tum Deum negligunt.

Alta de se opinio.

Que hominum arrogantia et opinio de se ipsis fons est malorum et pestis, ut imposibile sit eam societatem sanam et incolumem esse, in qua possunt aliquid qui suis se viribus aliquid posse arbitrantur. Secundum vero Pauli doctrinam, que est Christi doctrine et evangeliis consona (siquidem unus est Autor et idem Spiritus) nihil quisquam ad se ipsum sed dumtaxat ad Deum spectare debet, ei se subi⟨i⟩cere totum, illi soli inservire, postremo ab illo expectare omnia, et ex illo solo pendere, ut quicquid in christiana re publica, que Dei est civitas, vel vere sentiat, vel recte agat, ab illo id totum credat proficisci et acceptum |79r| Deum referat.

Sed ut clarius Apostoli sermo intelligatur, qui in hoc loco artificiosissimus est, que ad rem pertinent paulo altius repetamus.

Hominis anima constat intellectu et voluntate. Intellectu sapimus: voluntate possumus. Intellectus sapientia fides est: voluntatis potentia charitas. Christus autem Dei virtus (i.e. potentia) est et Dei sapientia. Per Christum illuminantur mentes ad fidem, qui illuminat omnem hominem venientem in hunc mundum, et dat potestatem filios Dei fieri iis qui credunt in nomine eius: per Christum etiam incenduntur voluntates in charitatem, ut Deum homines et proximum ament; in quibus est completio legis. A Deo ergo solo per Christum et sapimus et possumus, eo quod in Christo sumus. Homines autem ex se intellectum habent cecum et voluntatem depravatam, in tenebrisque ambulant et nesciunt quid faciunt.

---

possumus *Ed.*] possimus *C M L*

The wisdom of men, however, is foolish and false, he affirms, and their power of whatever sort is a lack of vigor and a state of helplessness.[22] To God, both of these are hateful and abhorrent, so that one can do nothing more unwise or more unavailing, or indeed more displeasing to God, than to attempt anything of one's own strength in the Christian Church. For God wishes it to be altogether His own work, and everyone in it to have wisdom only from Him and from His Spirit, so that there may be in men no sort of glorying, either because they are strong in goodness, or because they are wise in faith, or, finally, because they have their being in hope, unless this glorying be from God in Christ. Through him it is that we exist in him and in God; in him alone are we strong and wise, and are whatever we are.

Throughout all the letter Paul endeavors to affirm this, but especially and most explicitly in the first part, in which he strives to root out and banish entirely that wrong opinion by which men believe they can do something by their own strength. Trusting *A high opinion of oneself.* this opinion they not only fail to put their trust in God, but disregard him altogether.

This insolent presumption and self-esteem in men is a wellspring of evils and a disease, so that a society in which those have power who think they can do things by their own strength cannot have health and wholeness. But according to the teaching of Paul, which is in harmony also with that of Christ and with the Gospels (since one and the same Spirit is the author), no one should look to himself, but only to God. To Him he must submit himself wholly, and Him alone must he serve. And he must look to Him for all that is to come, and depend upon Him only, so that whatever in the Christian commonwealth — which is the City of God — he either knows truly or does rightly, he will believe to proceed entirely from God, and will assign to God as something received from Him.

But to understand more clearly the words of the Apostle, whose reasoning here is most skilfully refined, let us review a little more deeply some relevant truths.

Man's soul consists of intellect and will.[23] By our intellect we are wise, by our will we have strength to do things. The wisdom of the intellect is faith, the power of the will is charity. Now Christ is the strength of God — i.e., the power — and the wisdom of God [I Cor. 1. 24]. Minds are enlightened to faith through Christ, who enlightens every man coming into this world, and gives to those who believe in his name the power to become sons of God [John 1. 9, 12]. Through Christ also are wills enkindled to charity, that men may love God and their neighbor, thereby fulfilling the law. From God alone, then, through Christ, do we have both wisdom and strength, by reason of our being in Christ. Of themselves, men have a sightless mind and a twisted will, and they walk in the shadows, and know not what they do.

Tria apud Paulum sunt hominum genera: Iudei, gentes, et ex hiis vocati Christiani. In Iudeis fuit cecitas ex depravatione voluntatis: in gentibus pravitas ex ignorantia. In hiis ex sapientia eorum invaluit stulticia, unde male Christo voluerunt: in illis ex malitia surrepsit atra et misera cecitas. Quod *Christiani.* *Gentes.* *Iudei.* si Dominum glorie cognovissent, numquam illum crucifixissent.

Christus autem (ut modo dixi) Dei virtus et Dei sapientia est. Qui sunt calidis radiis illius divinitatis acciti ut illi in societate adhereant, hii quidem sunt tercii illi quos Paulus vocatos et electos in illam gloriam appellat, quorum mentes presentia divinitatis illustrantur, volu⟨n⟩tates *Electi.* corriguntur; |79v| qui fide cernunt clare sapientiam Christi, et amore eiusdem potentiam fortiter apprehendunt.

Qua luce destituti gentiles ad bonum Christi nuncium stulti fuerunt idque stultum iudicarunt, siquidem est quodque ut is qui recipit, omniaque sunt stulta stultis. Iudei autem, potenti amore carentes, infirmi, offenderunt se ad lapidem offensionis et petram scandali, et ad fortitudinem et invictam Christi patientiam passionemque impotentes fuerunt, sane° motantes se in necem Christi, quem experti sunt constantem in virtute usque ad mortem, mortem autem crucis. Habuit se in Christum ille Iudeorum° impetus perinde ac fluctus in saxum, quod suo loco herens conantes illidere illiduntur; ita similiter fluxa Iudeorum impacientia et importuna actio a stabili Christi et immota impatientia diffringitur, ut ignaviter agentes repati et relidi potiusquam agere aliquid, alte rem considerantibus, videantur, ac interficientes Christum non tam vicisse quam victos esse, quando quidem illorum impatientia non potuit facere quo minus Christus forti patientia pateretur. Quod Christum pati *Christus patiens* *vicit actionem.* agere fuit et in patientia vincere, quod voluit facere ex dispensatione, ut fortis et invicte patientie exemplum suis sequacibus relinqueret, qui nulla virtute victoriosius pugnare possunt quam patientia. In qua re perstare usque ad mortem est finem imponere motui impatientium cum trophea constantie.

Itaque fluctuantes Iudeos et impetuosius irruentes in mortem Dei fortis et patientis, Dei potentis in prelio, saxeus et secum constans ingens Christus ipsa patientia et sua morte defregit, et de victa impatientia imbecilium passus fortiter et mo |80r| riens gloriose triumphavit. Verumtamen Iudei, ex odio et malivolentia

---

sane *C M*] Vane *L*   Iudeorum *M*] iudiorum *C*] Iudiorum *L*]; impetus *M*] impitus *C L*

Paul recognizes three kinds of men: the Jews, the Gentiles, and those called from among these to be Christians. In the Jews there was blindness from perversity of their wills; in the Gentiles there was wickedness arising from their ignorance. *Christians, Gentiles, Jews.* Stupidity prevailed over the Gentiles, arising from their own wisdom, and they wished Christ ill. Over the Jews there crept from malice a dark and wretched blindness. For if they had known the Lord of glory, they would never have crucified him [I Cor. II. 8].

But Christ (as I remarked just now) is the strength of God and the wisdom of God. Those who have been summoned by the warm rays of his divinity to cling to him in fellowship are that third class, whom Paul speaks of as those called and chosen into that glory. Their *The Chosen.* minds are enlightened by the presence of the divinity, and their wills straightened. By faith they behold clearly the wisdom of Christ, and by love they take strong hold of his power.

Bereft of this light, the Gentiles were stupid toward the good news of Christ, and judged it to be stupidity, since that which is received is received according to the measure of the receiver, and to the fool all things are folly. And the Jews, weak, and lacking a strong love, stumbled at the stumblingstone and the rock of scandal [Rom. IX. 32],[24] and were powerless against the strength and the unconquered patience and the suffering of Christ. They stirred themselves, indeed, to the killing of Christ, but found him steadfast in virtue even to death, even to death on the cross [Phil. II. 8]. The onslaught of the Jews on Christ was like the waves against a rock, which holds its place and breaks the would-be breakers. Just so were the turbulent impatience and heedless activity of the Jews shattered by the fixed and unwavering patience of Christ. Men who use insight will see that, acting basely, they were not really doing anything, but rather being acted on[25] and dispersed, and when they killed Christ, they were the vanquished, not the victors, since their impatience could do nothing to the strong patience with which Christ suffered. And the suffering of Christ was a doing, and a victory in patience, and he willed *The patient Christ overcame action.* it according to God's dispensation so that he might leave an example of steadfast and unconquered patience to his followers. With no virtue can these war more victoriously than with patience. To remain steadfast in it to death is to set an end to the activity of the impatient with the trophy of constancy.[26]

And so the Jews, in their restless activity and their headlong rush to the death of the God who is strong and patient, the God who is mighty in battle [Ps. XXIII. 8], were broken by the great Christ, rocklike and inwardly constant. He broke them by patience itself and by his own death. Suffering in strength, dying in glory, he triumphed over the vanquished impatience of the weak. But the

ceci, potens quiddam facinus se egisse crediderunt quando Christum de medio
sustulerunt illumque et infirmum et offensum censuerunt, ac suis viribus victum
et sublatum. Quapropter, audientes necem Iesu et Christum crucifixum, infirmi
ipsi, non potuerunt aliter de Christo quam de infirmo et scandoloso, i.e. offenso
et leso, iudicare. In quo quamquam innumerabilia et manifestissima argumenta
viderint potentie et divinitatis, tamen frigens odium in eis nihil potuit admittere
et in bonam partem coquere. In Belsabub demoniorum principe dixerunt illum
eiecisse demonia; ac cotidie cernentes in eo testimonia mirifice virtutis, tamen
interea signa et potentificum aliquod opus flagitarunt; impotentes illi sane, infirma
invidia et odio, ut aliquid potens et mirificum agnoscant. Atque ut refert Matheus,
similiter principes sacerdotum illudentes cum scribis et senioribus dicebant, Alios salvos
fecit: seipsum non potest salvum facere. Si rex Israel est, descendat nunc de cruce et
credimus ei.

Itaque manifestationem alicuius virtutis potentieque in Iesu quesierunt Iudei,
invalidi ipsi et nequiuntes experiri in alio quid forte et potens est. Unde est factum ut patientiam passionemque Iesu Christi, illam mirificam et voluntariam
mortem, mortem ipsam vincentem, infirmitati darent; Christumque crucifixum,
Christum infirmum, offensum, fractumque suis viribus iud⟨i⟩carunt, tam impotentes odio et malivolentia ut virtutem potentiamque cognoscant, quam gentes
ignorantie tenebris ut lucem veritatemque videant.

Quibus cecis, omnia sunt ceca, et falsis, falsa. |80v| Qui non emergentes ex
caliginosa° sapientia eorum senserunt nihil habuisse saporem sapientie nisi quod
ad eorum rationem descenderat. Quod vero longe supra rationem in alto se tenet,
quodque nullo alio oculo quam per⟨s⟩picacis fidei cerni potest, utpote divinum
quiddam revelatum cui credatur, id homines fide non prediti et ratione carere
et stultum esse statuerunt.

Quorum vero animi agitati divina gratia ut filii Dei sint, et affulserint fide,
ut Deo veritatem docenti credant, et simul concaluerint amore, ut bonitatem
Dei in eos et misericordiam redament, ii nimirum facile et Christi crucifixi ac
totius illius rei misteriique de Verbo Dei incarnato sapientiam veritatemque
credentes perspexerunt, et eiusdem etiam magnificam vim potentiamque omni
charitate ac cultu amplexi sunt.

Quapropter a Paulo est illud scriptum hic ad Corinthios, *Quoniam et Iudei signa*
petunt et Greci sapientiam querunt: nos autem predicamus Christum crucifixum, Iudeis
quidem scandalum, i.e. Iudeis visam offensionem Christi et lesionem infirmi ac

---

caliginosa *M L*] caliginasa *C*

Jews, blind in their hatred and ill-will, believed that they had worked some mighty crime when they took Christ from their midst. They judged him both weak and rejected, and they thought him conquered and cut off by their own strength. And so, hearing that Jesus was killed, that Christ was crucified, in their weakness they could not judge Christ to be other than weak and an occasion of scandal, i.e., rejected and lacerated. For although they had seen proofs without number and most clear of his power and divinity, still the freezing hatred[27] within them kept them from understanding. They said that he cast out demons through Beelzebub, the prince of demons [Matt. XII. 24], and although every day they saw in him manifestations of his wondrous power, still they constantly clamored for signs and for some extraordinarily mighty accomplishment. In the weakness of their envy and hatred, they were, indeed, powerless to recognize what was powerful and marvellous. As Matthew reports: "The chief priests, with the scribes and elders, mocked him in the same way. He saved others, they said, himself he cannot save. If he is the King of Israel, he has but to come down from the cross, here and now, and we will believe in him" [XXVII. 42].

Thus the Jews sought always a demonstration of some strength and might in Jesus, being themselves feeble and simply unable to recognize in another what was truly strong and mighty. So they decided that the patience and the passion of Jesus Christ, that wonderful and willingly accepted death which conquered death itself, was due to weakness, and they judged that Christ crucified was Christ weak, and spurned, and broken by their strength. Their hatred and ill-will made them as powerless to recognize power and strength as the darkness of ignorance made the Gentiles to see light and truth.

To the blind,[28] all things are blind, and to the false, all things are false. The Gentiles, failing to rise above their own darksome wisdom, were conscious of no taste of wisdom in anything that had not been brought down to their own reasoning. But that which is on high, far above reasoning, and which can be perceived by no eye but the piercing eye of faith—and such is anything divine revealed for belief—this they decided, since they were men not endowed with faith, to be unreasonable and stupid.

On the other hand, those whose souls were moved by divine grace to be sons of God, and enlightened by faith to believe in God when He taught them truth, those whose souls were at the same time warmed by love, so that in return they loved God's goodness to them and His mercy, these without difficulty saw rightly and believed the wisdom and truth of Christ crucified and of that whole mystery of the incarnate Word of God, and with all love and devotion they embraced his splendid strength and power.

So Paul writes here to the Corinthians: "For the Jews seek signs, and the Greeks ask after wisdom. But we preach Christ crucified, to the Jews a stumbling-block,"—to the Jews, i.e., something seen as a spurning of Christ and a hurting

impotentis supplicium et interitum: *gentibus autem stulticiam,* qui iudicaverunt illam rem omnino carere ratione; *nobis autem vocatis Iudeis atque Grecis Christum
Dei virtutem*, i.e. potentiam, *et Dei sapientiam*.

Nam ii benigna Dei gratia quadam arbitraria electione a tenebris gentilium
in lucem fidei et a Iudeorum frigore in calorem amoris attolluntur ut in Iesu
Christo et veritatem Dei videant et de eius bonitate ac potentia gaudeant.

Attolluntur iidem etiam in id prestantie ut omni humana stultitia et infirmitate
discussa, in Christo quum sint, longe supra homines ipsi et divinitus sapiant et
operibus admirabiles exstent. Nam quid mirum |81r| est qui ad ipsam Dei vir-
tutem et sapientiam accedunt si ipsi protenus sapientes et virtute potentes eva-
dant, tametsi a stultis et invidis insipientes et infirmi censeantur. Etenim (ut apud
Paulum sequitur) *quod stultum est Dei sapientius est hominibus, et quod infirmum est
Dei fortius est hominibus*.

Quod ita scriptum est ab Apostolo genere ambiguo et ancipite, et hoc quidem
(ut mihi videtur) consulto et ex proposito, ut utram in partem velis, id vel in
antecedentem vel in subinsequentem comode trahas. Antecedunt hoc quod modo
dixi que significant que acta fuerant cum Christo, ea a Iudeis et gentibus stulta
et infirma haberi. Subsequuntur que narrant habitos in mundo stultos et infirmos
potius ad Dei virtutem et sapientiam esse attractos.

Quod si ad superiora referas, tum Paulus stultum et infirmum Dei vocat, quod
dicit fortius et sapientius esse hominibus, illud quod actum fuit de Christo inter
Iudeos, in quo gentes stultitiam et Iudei infirmitatem esse cogitarunt. Quod ipsum quamquam calumniati sunt homines, tamen tum *sapientius* tum *fortius fuit
hominibus*, i.e., quoquam quod ab hominibus fieri potest.

Quod si ad ea trahas (uti potes) que subsequuntur, in quibus est vocari eos
maxime a Deo qui in mundo minimi estimantur, ut ostendatur qui magni habentur
in hoc mundo sapientia vel opibus, eos Dei iudicio indignos esse suis misteriis
et a sua virtute ac sapientia repudiari—ad hoc ergo si vis illud Pauli spectare,
quod inquit infirmum et stultum Dei sapientius et fortius esse hominibus, tum
significat eos habitos stultos et imbecilles in mundo, dummodo nunc in Deum
tracti in Deo maneant, ex Deoque et sapiant et agant omnia, sapientiores in Deo
et potentiores esse hominibus, quos vocat Apostolus stultos et |81v| infirmos
Dei, propterea quod quos mundus reputavit stultos et infirmos, viles et nihil,
eos sibi Deus elegit; ut ex nihilo aliquid, ex stultis sapientes, ex infirmis potentes
efficiat, construatque quiddam opus ex hominibus vocatis quod totum esset suum;

of one without strength, and the torment and death of one without power—
"and stupidity to the Gentiles," who judged the whole thing altogether unreasonable; "but to us who have been called, both Jews and Greeks, Christ the strength
of God," i.e., the power, "and the wisdom of God" [I Cor. 1. 22–24].

For these in the free choice of God are lifted by His gracious gift from the
darkness of the Gentiles into the light of faith, from the cold of the Jews into
the warmth of love, so that they may see in Jesus Christ the truth of God, and
may be joyful in His goodness and power.

To such an excellence are they raised that being now in Christ, and having
shaken off all human stupidity and weakness, they are themselves divinely wise
far beyond things human, and in their works they are seen to be a cause for
wonder. For it is not strange that those who approach God's power itself and
His wisdom should themselves forthwith become wise and strong in power,
though the stupid and the envious may judge them to lack wisdom and strength.
For (as Paul continues) "The foolishness of God is wiser than men, and the
weakness of God is stronger than men" [1. 25].

The Apostle writes here in this ambiguous and obscure manner, it seems to
me, with deliberate intent, so that you may properly interpret what he says in
either of two ways, by choosing to refer it either to what goes before or to
what follows. What precedes I have just said. The meaning was that what happened concerning Christ was held by the Jews and the Gentiles to be folly and
weakness. In what follows, we are told that those accounted stupid and weak
in the world were drawn rather than others to the strength and wisdom of God.

Now if you relate the doubtful passage[29] to what goes before, then what Paul
means by the foolishness and weakness of God, which he says is stronger and
wiser than men, is what happened to Christ among the Jews, in which the Gentiles saw folly and the Jews weakness. No matter how much men spoke ill of
it, still it was both wiser and stronger than men, i.e., than anything men could do.

But in what follows, we are told that those especially are called by God who
are least thought of in the world, so that it may be shown that those considered
mighty for wisdom or wealth in this world are, in the judgment of God, unworthy of His mysteries, and are turned away from His power and wisdom.
So if you wish that saying of Paul's about the weakness and foolishness of God
being wiser and stronger than men to refer to this, then it means that those
who are thought to be stupid and weak in the world are wiser and more powerful in God than men, provided that once drawn to God they remain in God
and have their wisdom and activity in God alone. The Apostle calls them the
foolish and weak ones of God, because God has chosen for Himself those whom
the world has rated foolish and weak, mean and worth nothing. Thus He would
make something of nothing,[30] wise men of the foolish, and strong men of the
weak, and build up from the men He had chosen a work altogether His own,

ut in eo quicquid sit, id non habeat nisi ex Deo de quo glorietur, ut ubique
in suo opere et civitate fulgeat sola Dei gloria, utque homines ex quibus con-
struitur nihil in se sed in solo Deo glorientur.

In hac parte etiam didicimus a Paulo, quando Christum Dei Filium virtutem
et sapientiam Dei vocat, Deum ipsum parentem esse sapientie et virtutis, cuius
Filius est potens sapientia et sapiens potentia; qui voluit infirmus quodammodo
et stultus videri in humana carne infirma et caliginosa, descendereque in humilitatem
nostram et quasi misericorditer manum porrigere iacentibus in infirmitate et
tenebris, ut nos ad se in lucem et robor ad sapientiam et potentiam traheret,
ut in eo redempti, sanctificati, iusti, sapientes, sati in agro Dei, plantati in illius
vinea, adolescamus illius virtute qui solus incrementum dat, in eam perfectionem
quam in messione, in vindimia, in seperatione bonorum a malis, in retributione
cuique secundum opera sua, dominus frugum sibi assumet et reponet in horreo suo.

Sunt homines suapte natura mali, insipientes, impuri, nihili. Deus autem ipse
ipsum est esse, ipsa puritas, ipsa sapientia, ipsa bonitas. Mediator vero Dei et
hominum Iesus est Christus, qui in se complexus est simul mirifice divinitatem
et humanitatem, qui Deus hominem deificavit, in quo regeneramur ut simus,
purificamur, illustramur, iustificamur, ut sancti, sapientes, et boni simus, utque
Deo assimilati, dii evadamus.

Is a nobis omni amore |82r| amandus et excolendus Iesus Christus, ineffabili
Dei bonitate, benignitate, et misericordia, stupendo in terris et adorando miraculo
quidem, factus est nobis (ut scribit Paulus) sapientia et iusticia, sanctificatio et
redemptio, in quo eodem ex Deo sumus quicquid sumus, ut, sicut Divino Spiritu
preditus cecinit Hieremias, *non glorietur homo in sapientia*, fortitudine, divitiis suis,
sed in hoc glorietur quod scit et novit Deum, qui facit misericordiam, iudicium,
et iusticiam in terra. Quod oraculum Paulus brevius commemorat dicens, *Qui
gloriatur, in Domino glorietur*°.

---

glorietur *Vulg. L*] gloriatur *C M*

so that whatever is done in it can glory in nothing except God, and everywhere throughout His work and His City shines God's glory alone, and the men of whom it is built find no glorying in themselves, but only in God.

When Paul in this part calls Christ, the Son of God, the power and wisdom of God, we learn also that God is Himself the Father of wisdom and strength, His Son being powerful wisdom and wise power.[31] Christ wished to appear in a manner weak and foolish, in the weakness and darkness of human flesh, and to come down into our lowliness and stretch out his hand in mercy, so to speak, to those lying in weakness and darkness, so that he might draw us to himself into light and robust health, might draw us to wisdom and power; so that ransomed in this way and made holy in him, made just and wise, sown in the field of God and planted in His vineyard, we might grow by His power who alone gives growth, into that perfection which in the harvest, and the gathering of the grapes, and the separation of the good from the bad, and the rewarding of each according to his works, the Lord of harvests may take to Himself and gather into His granary.

In their own nature, men are wicked, unwise, impure, nothing.[32] God, on the other hand, is Being itself, Purity itself, Wisdom itself, Goodness itself. There is, however, between God and men a Mediator, Jesus Christ, who united wondrously within himself Godhead and manhood. Being God himself, he made man Godlike. In him takes place our rebirth, so that we may exist, may be made pure, may be enlightened and justified, to the end that we may be holy, wise, and good, and being made like God, may become gods.

This Jesus Christ, whom we must love and worship with all our love, became, in the ineffable goodness and kindness and mercy of God, by a miracle to be adored on earth and marvelled at, our wisdom (as Paul writes) and justice, our sanctification and redemption [I Cor. i. 30]. Whatever we are, our being is in him from God, so that, as Jeremiah prophesied by the inspiration of the Holy Spirit, "man may not glory in his own wisdom, strength, or riches, but in this may he glory, that he has knowledge and understanding of God, who works mercy, judgment, and justice on earth" [Jer. ix. 23, 24]. This prophecy Paul more briefly recalls when he says, "He who glories, let him glory in the Lord" [I Cor. i. 31].

Caput secundum°

Quam invisa et odiosa est potentia et sapientia huius mundi Deo, quam divine sapientie adversa et contraria, iccirco etiam quam despecta et reprobata, vel ex hoc licet cernere quod mysteria sapientie sue et bonitatis Deus neque voluit plurimum a sapientibus et potentibus audiri, neque a talibus predicari, sed accipi° ab illis et tradi qui erant huius tenebricose sapientie, que humana ratione constat, penitus expertes.

Quod si quando voluerit quempiam preditum sapientia seculari, cuiusmodi Paulus et eius discipulus Dionisius Ariopagita ac nonnulli alii, veritates sapientie sue et accipere° et ad alios deferre, profecto hii, nunciaturi aliis quod a Deo didicerint°, dedita opera nihil magis curarunt quam ut ex seculo nihil sapere viderentur, existimantes indignum esse ut cum divinis revelatis humana ratio comisceatur, nolentes etiam id comittere quo putetur veritati credi magis suasione hominum quam virtute Dei.

Hinc Paulus, in docta et erudita Grecia, nihil veritus est ex se videri stultus et impotens, ac profiteri se nihil scire nisi Iesum Christum et eundem crucifixum, |82v| nec posse quicquam nisi per eundem, ut per stultitiam predicationis salvos faciat credentes et ratio⟨ci⟩nantes confundat°.

Hoc enim placitum fuit Deo ut ita fiat, quod testatur Salvator apud Matheum: *Confiteor*, inquit, *tibi, Pater, Domine celi et terre, quia abscondisti hec a sapientibus et prudentibus, et revelasti ea parvulis*. Que misteria Dei profecto sunt eiusmodi, ut qui non abnegat semetipsum prorsus, qui non stultus fit ut sit sapiens, qui non desinet esse homo ut sit deus, is Deum, divinam sapientiam, et Spiritum nunquam sentiet. Agitatus omnino oportet sit Spiritu Dei, et regenitus factusque novus in formam spiritalem, ut totus spiritalis, spiritualia Dei spiritaliter

---

Caput secundum *Ed.*] cap:2. *C*] om. *M*   accipi *M*] accepi *C L*   accipere *M L*] accepere *L*   didicerint *M*] dedicerint *C L*   confundat *L*] confundet *C M*

Chapter II

We can see how displeasing and hateful to God are this world's power and wisdom,[1] how opposed and hostile to the divine wisdom, and therefore also how much disdained and rejected, even from this fact, that God willed the mysteries of His wisdom and goodness neither to be heard principally by the wise and powerful nor to be preached by them, but to be received and passed on by those who were profoundly inexperienced in this darksome wisdom that takes its stand on human reason.

At times, however, He willed that certain men endowed with secular wisdom — and Paul was one such, as was his disciple, Dionysius the Areopagite,[2] and not a few others — should both receive and bring to others the truths of His wisdom. These men, in undertaking to tell others what they had learned from God, were of nothing more careful than that men should see that they were not drawing any of their wisdom from the world; they thought it an unworthy thing that human reason should mix with divine revelation, and they wanted no one to think the truth was to be believed because of human persuasiveness instead of the power of God.

So Paul, even in learned and erudite Greece, did not hesitate to appear foolish and weak in himself, and to profess that he knew nothing but Jesus Christ, and him crucified [I Cor. II. 2], and that he had no power except through him, so that by [what he called] the foolishness of his preaching he might save those who believed [I. 21] and put the reasoners to shame.

For it pleased God that it should be this way, as the Savior testifies in Matthew: "I give Thee praise, Father," he says, "Lord of Heaven and Earth, because Thou hast hidden all this from the wise and the prudent, and revealed it to little children" [Matt. XI. 25]. And truly, the mysteries of God are such that he who does not forthwith deny himself, does not become foolish that he may be wise, does not leave off being a man[3] in order to be a god, will never experience God, or divine wisdom, or the Spirit. A man must be moved entirely by the Spirit of God, and reborn and made new into a spiritual form,[4] so that now, entirely

examinet, exquirat, colligat, percipiat; percipiat, inquam, non suo spiritu sed Spiritu Dei, qui solus novit que sunt Dei, quoque etiam prediti soli que sunt Dei cognoscunt, solique possunt et debent dici sapientes. Idem etiam potentes, non sua quidem potentia et virtute, sed solius Dei, per Iesum Christum Dominum nostrum.

In quo illud venerandum et adorandum miraculum quod Deus ipse coierit cum humana natura, quod quiddam compositum ex Deo et homine, quod Greci vocant theant⟨h⟩ropon, hic vixit in terris et pro hominum salute versatus est cum hominibus, ut eos Deo Patri suo revocatos reconciliaret, quod idem perstitit in probatione et ostensione virtutis defensioneque iusticie usque ad mortem, mortem autem crucis. Quod deinde victa morte, fugato dyabolo, redempto humano genere, ut liberam habeat potestatem, omnino sine adversarii querela, elegendi ad se quos velit, ut quos velit vocet, quos vocet iustificet; quod, inquam, sic victa et prostrata morte mortisque auctore, ex morte idem resurrexit vivens ac |83r| vivum se multis ostendit, multisque argumentis comprobavit. Quod tum postremo cernentibus discipulis sursum ut erat Deus et homo ascendit ad Patrem, illic ex celo progressum sui inchoati operis in terris et perfectionem despecturus, ac quantum sibi videbitur continuo adiuturus. Quod deinde post hec tandem oportuno tempore, rebus maturis, contrariis Deo rationibus discussis longe et a creaturis suis exterminatis, iniustitia videlicet et ignorantia, in quarum profligatione nunc cotidie Dei sapientia et virtus in suis ministris operatur, operabiturque usque in finem, quod tum, inquam, post satis longum conflictum et utrinque pugnam inter lucem et tenebras, Deo et angelis spectantibus, tandem ille idem Dux et Dominus exercituum, qui hic primus bellum induxit adversariis et cum hostibus ipse manum conseruit, patientia et morte vincens, in subsidium suorum prelucens et prepotens rediet, ut fugata malitia et stultitia, illustret et bona faciat omnia, utque postremo resuscitans mortuos ipsam mortem superet sua immortalitate et absorbeat, ac victuros secum rapiet in celum, morituros a se longe in sempiternam mortem discutiet° in tenebras illas exteriores; ut per ipsum in reformato mundo sola vita deinceps in perpetuum, sapientia, et iusticia regnet.

Hoc, inquam, totum magnum admirabile et obstupescendum miraculum in Iesu Christo, per quem Dei Filium incarnatum tota hec dispensatio sapientissime

spiritual, he may spiritually inquire into the spiritual things of God, may seek them out, take them to himself, grasp them firmly; may grasp them, I say, not by his own spirit but by the Spirit of God, who alone knows the things of God [I Cor. II. 11]. Those only who are invested with the Spirit know God, and they alone can be and ought to be called wise. They are the strong also, not by their own strength and power, but by that of God alone, through Jesus Christ our Lord.

In him is that miracle which must be adored and venerated, that God Himself should enter into union with human nature. This Being, composite of God and man, whom the Greeks call[5] the θεάνθρωπος, lived here on earth and dealt with men for their salvation, that he might call them back and reconcile them to his Father. He was steadfast in the testing and showing of virtue and in the defense of justice, even to death, even to death on the cross. Then when he had conquered death, had routed the devil and ransomed mankind, so that he might have free power of choosing for himself, without the adversary's having any grievance,[6] those whom he wished to choose, might summon whom he would,[7] and might justify those he summoned—when he had thus, I say, vanquished and laid low death and the author of death—living he arose from death, and showed himself alive to many, and confirmed the fact with many proofs. Then finally, as his disciples looked on, he ascended on high in his Godhead and manhood to the Father, to watch thence from Heaven the progress and perfection of the work he had begun, and constantly to help it to the extent that it shall seem good to him to do so. And then at last, after all these things, when the right time has come, when all has reached its fullness, when the principles at war with God[8] have been scattered afar and banished from His creatures utterly—injustice, that is to say, and ignorance, for the overthrow of which the wisdom and power of God are even now each day at work in His ministers, and will be to the end— then at last, I say, when the warfare and the battle everywhere between the light and the darkness will have lasted long enough, he shall come again, as God and the angels look on, the same leader and Lord of Hosts who first brought war against the enemy and who was himself the first to meet the foe in hand-to-hand combat, winning victory by his patience and his death. To the aid of his own will he come, in great light and power, so that with wickedness and stupidity driven to flight, he may enlighten all things and make them good, and may at the end of all, by raising the dead to life, conquer death and make it lose its identity in him. Those who are to live he shall carry off with him into Heaven; those who are to die he shall scatter into the darkness outside, into everlasting death, far from himself, so that thenceforward, in a world formed anew, only life may reign forever, only wisdom and justice.

This is that great and wonderful and dazzling miracle in Jesus Christ; through him, the incarnate Son of God, with all wisdom and power is worked this entire

et potentissime peragitur; hoc, iterum inquam, miraculum omne fide credendum, omni amore amandum, miraculum plenum gratie et veritatis, miraculum
in mysterio absconditum, predestinatum ante secula in gloria nostra, temporibus
suis congruis re ipsa et effectu prestitum et exhibitum revelatumque hominibus,
nemo sane perspicit, nisi ad id |83v| trahatur attolaturque tanquam piscis, evangelica
doctrina, ab aquis huius mundi in Spiritum, a caligine in lucem, a divisione in
unitatem, a falso in veritatem, a malicia in bonitatem, in spem, fidem, et caritatem,
ut unitus in Deo, et Deo credens, et Deum amans, ex Deo solo stabiliter sit,
sapiat clare, et bene agat.

Ad quam gratiam felicitatemque qui manent in hoc fluctuanti mundo, divisi
animis et cogitationibus dissipati, qui caligine et atritate huius secularis sapientie
obfuscatas habent mentes ac pene extinctas, qui malicia et infirmitate depravatas
habent voluntates et appeticiones ad omne malum inclinatas, cuiusmodi habent
procul dubio omnes qui ex more (ut videmus) pisciculorum instar in mundano
hoc mare nantes vivunt — immo potius moriuntur — fluxa carne, duris oculis, debili
virtute, ii profecto sunt ita inepti ut aliquid Spiritus et lucis sentiant ut non aliter
atque ipsi pisces quibus eos assimulavi, qui in aere nequiunt vivere, abstracti aliquousque in Spiritum, mori se arbitrantur; qui nihil minus possunt pati quam
aliquid depromptum ex penu spiritali. Id enim (ut ipsis videtur) necat spiritus
eorum, nec se convalescere putant priusquam rursus in mundo relapsi fluctibus
mundi obruantur.

O misera° hominum et perdita condicio. Sed quodque est ut providetur fore,
ac novit Deus probe qui sunt ad sua mysteria magis idonii. Qui quidem sunt
hii qui minus visco huius mundi tenentur, qui minus plagis huius seculi nequam
irretiuntur, vita scilicet, sapientia, et potentia seculari. Que revera non est sapientia, potentia, et vita, sed mors, stulticia, et infirmitas, falsis nominibus ex-
ornata. A quibus qui longius abfuerint, quique fuerint impotentes et stulti ap-
pellati ac nullius precii estimati, ii nimirum vero Dei iudicio iudi |84r| cati fuerunt
magis apti quibus sua misteria commendentur, quique ipsi formentur divina sapientia et voluntate, ut ex Deo solo sciant omnia et velint.

Quapropter prisca nostra ecclesia, que° Dei attractu constitit, ex contemptis
et abiectis huius mundi exorta et aucta est. In qua nemo ingressus est nisi qui
vel nihil habuit huius secularis sapientie et potentie, vel habitam deposuerit, ut,
stultus factus, sapiat ex Deo.

Quocirca Pa⟨u⟩lus huius rei admonet Corinthios, et iubet videant vocationem
suam intelligantque in ipsis ecclesiaque eorum non multos sapientes secundum

---

discutiet *Ed.*] discutiat *C M L*   O misera *L*] O miseria *C? with i heavily cancelled*]
O miseria *M*   que *Ed.*] qui *C M L*

economy of God. This is the miracle we must believe with all faith and love
with all love, the miracle full of grace and truth, the miracle hidden in a mystery,
predestined before time in our glory,[9] and at the appropriate times brought into
reality and effectual being, made manifest and revealed to men. Now all this
no one sees and apprehends unless he is drawn and lifted by the teaching of the
Gospels, like a fish from the waters of this world, into the Spirit; from the darkness
into the light; from fragmentation into unity;[10] from falsehood into truth; from
wickedness into goodness, into hope,[11] faith, and charity; so that made one in
God, and having faith in God, and loving God, from God alone he has fixed
being,[12] clear wisdom, and good conduct.

Those, however, who remain in this fluctuating world, with divided souls
and scattered thoughts, who have minds clouded and almost made lightless by
the black darkness of this world's wisdom, have wills and appetites twisted by
malice and weakness and prone to all evil—and there is no doubt that such wills
and such minds are possessed by all those whom we see living (or rather, dying)
in the sea of this world, swimming about like little fishes,[13] with unfirm flesh
and hard eyes and weak strength—such as these, surely, are unfit for this grace,
this happiness of God, unfit to experience anything of the Spirit and of the light.
Just like the fishes to which I have compared them, which cannot live in the
air, they think they are dying if they are drawn away a little into the Spirit,
and there is nothing they are less well able to support than something brought
down from the store of the Spirit. For that, it seems to them, kills their own
spirits; and they think they cannot get well again until they slip back into the
world and are washed over by the waves of the world.

O wretchedness and lost state of men![14] Still, everything is as foreknowledge
knows it will be, and God knows which men are the more fit for His mysteries.
These are the men who are not held so fast by the sticky snares of this world,
not so much entangled in the nets of this wicked world, i.e., the worldly life,
wisdom, and power. In truth, these are not wisdom, power, and life; they are
death, stupidity, and weakness, decked out with false names. Those, then, who
have been farther removed from them, those who have been called powerless
and weak, and considered worthless, will be judged the more suited, in the true
judgment of God, to be entrusted with His mysteries and to be formed by the
divine wisdom and will, so that all their knowing and willing may be from God
alone.

Our early Church, therefore, set up by God's drawing, had its origin and
increase from the despised and the lowly. No one entered unless he either had
no share of this world's power and wisdom, or laid down what he had to become
foolish and have wisdom from God.

To the Corinthians, then, Paul recalls this fact, and he bids them look to their
calling and understand that among them and in their Church[15] there have been

carnem, potentes, nobiles, vocatos et electos a Deo in societatem cum Christo;
sed infirmos, stultos, humiles, et abiectos, ut ipso Dei delectu manifeste pateret
eo gratiorem Deo quemque esse, quo mundo minus acceptus est vilipensosque
ad se accivisse ut magni qui habentur in mundo minimi a Deo estimare osten-
dantur, qui revera habent in se rationes et dispositiones longe contrarias divine
formationi, quas suasu inductuque demonico, in quem facile labuntur homines,
contraxerint; que si non eluantur, sique animus ab ipsis penitus non purgetur,
divinarum rerum rationes et imagines excipere referreque non potest.

Que quum simplices, pure, pulcre, et bone sint, necesse est que adversantur
et impediunt harum impressionem naturam et nominationem habeant contrariam,
sintque locate in multitudine, impuritate, turpitudine, et malitia, hominesque
ipsi talibus rationibus non prestant (ut ipsi falso putant) sed subsunt, nec in alto
sed in imo, nec liberi vagantur supra in luce et calore, sed tenebrecoso frigore
et maliciosa ignorantia deorsum in inferiori loco, longe a regione claritatis et
vite detenentur; hoc ipso miseri quod carent veritate et bonitate, verum eo
miseriores quo |84v| hiisce se carere non intelligunt, quoque in ignorantia et
infirmitate se sapientes et potentes esse putant. Quorum sapientia malicia est,
potentia impatientia, nobilitas et altitudo revera ignobilitas et in imum depressio
est, atque ut apud Lucam inquit Salvator, *abominatio apud Deum.*

Quamobrem non ab re quidem videtur factum fuisse a Deo ut, illo vulgo
hominum et quasi fece in fundo residente longe a claritate posthabita, qui in
tam altam obscuritatem non fuerint dilapsi prius et facilius a divino lumine attingerentur; qui fuerunt qui minus in vallem mundi miserieque° descenderunt,
qui altius multo extantes quam alii, merito priores exorto iudicie sole illuminati
fuerunt; qui supra multitudinem, varietatem, et pugnam huius mundi simplices,
sui similes, et quieti, extiterunt tanto propiores Deo quanto remotius a mundo
distiterint°.

Quod si Deus ipse est ipsa nobilitas, sapientia, et potentia, quis non videt Petrum,
Ioannem, Iacobum, et id genus reliquos, etiam antequam veritas Dei illuxerat
in terras, tanto aliis sapientia et viribus prestitisse, quanto magis abfuerint ab
eorum illorum stulticia et impotentia. Ut nihil sit mirum si Deus, cuius est bonis
suis meliores eligere et accomodare, eos habitos stultos et impotentes deligerit,
quando quidem revera universi mundi nobiliores fuerunt, a vilitateque mundi
magis seiuncti, altiusque extantes; ut quemadmodum id terre quod altius eminet

---

miserieque *Ed.*] miserique *C M*] miseriæque *L*   distiterint *Unk. Rev., written over*]
distaverint *C M L*

called and chosen by God into fellowship with Christ not many who are wise in the world's fashion, or powerful, or noble, but weak men, the foolish, the lowly, the despised, to the end that by the choice itself of God men might clearly see that the less acceptable some one is to the world, the more pleasing he is to God [I Cor. I. 26, 27]. Those held worthless He had summoned to Himself, to show that those considered mighty in the world are least thought of by God, having in themselves principles and dispositions most inimical to the divine formation[16] and entered upon at the urging and guidance of the Devil, into whose power[17] men easily slip. And if these are not washed away and if the mind is not thoroughly cleansed of them, it cannot receive and reflect the principles and likenesses of things divine.[18]

Since these latter are simple, pure, beautiful, and good, the things that oppose and hinder their reception must have a contrary nature and denomination, and must lie in multiplicity, impurity, meanness, and malice. Nor by such principles do men excel, as they wrongly think, but rather, because of them men are inferior, and such principles are not lofty, but base. Because of them, men do not range in freedom on high in light and warmth, but are imprisoned below by the darksome cold and by malicious ignorance, far from the land of clearness and life. Such men are wretched[19] in their very lack of truth and goodness, but all the more wretched because they are not aware they lack truth and goodness, and because in their ignorance and weakness they think themselves wise and powerful. Their wisdom is malice, their power impatience, their nobility and loftiness really meanness and the lowest degradation, and, as the Savior says in Luke, an abomination in God's sight [Luke XVI. 15].

God's action, then, is seen to be not meaningless, in His setting far behind the common herd of mankind, the lowest dregs, as it were, settled on the bottom far from the light, and in His having those reached sooner and more easily by His divine light who had not slipped into so deep a darkness. Those who had sunk less deeply into the valley of the world and of wretchedness, those who stood out far higher than others, deserved to be the first enlightened by the risen Sun of justice.[20] Above the multiplicity, the diversity, and the strife of this world in their simplicity, their self-consistency, and their repose, they reached the nearer to God the further they stood off from the world.

If God Himself is the essential nobility, wisdom, and strength, surely Peter, John, James, and the rest of their sort,[21] even before God's truth had shed its light upon the earth, were as far above others in wisdom and strength as they were removed from the stupidity and the weakness of those others. So there was nothing strange about it if God, whose way it is to choose and prepare for His good things those who are better, chose men considered to be stupid and weak, since in reality they were more noble than all the world, were further severed from the meanness of the world, had a loftier stature. Just as at sunrise

exorto sole facilius et citius radiis tangitur, ita similiter fuit necesse, prodeunte luce que illuminaret omnem hominem venientem in hunc mundum, prius irradiaret eos qui magis in hominibus eminuerint, et quasi montes ad hominum valles extiterint.

Ad alios autem qui sunt in imo, in regi |85r| one frigoris, nebulosa sapientia obducti, et tardius penetrant divini radii et illic difficilius illuminant et citius destituunt, nisi forte vehementius incumbentes rarifecerint nubem et levifecerint hominem, ut abiectis omnibus que habet, evolet in Christum. Quod si fecerit, tum emergit in conditionem et statum° Petri ac talium parvulorum quos dudum contemserit, ut per eam viam ascendat ad veritatem qui ipse est Christus.

Qui dixit: *Nisi conversi fueritis, et efficiamini sicut parvuli, non intrabitis in regnum celorum.* Qui parvuli sine dubio sunt maiores illis qui magni in mundo reputantur, ac ideo iure a Deo ad sua misteria antepositi, siquidem descendenti Deo in homines, altiores hii aliis in Deum occurrerunt; qui primi illum accipientes, habuerunt in mandatis ut deinde eius nomen, lucem, et bonitatem dirivarent gradatim deorsum ad infimos° quosque, etiam ad illos, si fieri possit°, qui valles terrarum et profunda maris inhabitant.

Nemo ergo dubitet quin Deus, quamquam tales non habebantur, tamen revera elegisse° sibi nobilitatem, et sapientiam, et potentiam humane generationis, ac nubem hominum in sinceriore sua parte illustrare incepisse, ut deinde radii ad spissam atritatem penitrent. In qua atritate fuerunt et sunt sapientes et potentes huius seculi, qui difficulter in se sane lucem admittunt. Verum pergent radii in consummationem illuminandorum.

Deus elegit sibi nobiles, potentes, sapientes.

Quod non est particeps lucis discutietur. Ille qui baptizat in Spiritu et igne, i.e., igne spiritali, ventilabro in manu permundabit aream suam. Et congregabit triticum in horeum suum, paleas autem comburet igne inextinguibili. Palee sunt que arescunt vana sapientia, quique falsa potentia inefficaces sunt, qui iure apud Deum ultimo loco habentur, ne dicam nullo, vel potius in nullo, ne falso dicam |85v| in aliquo. A quorum ratione vivendi et forma qui longius abest differentiusque se gerit, is profecto apud equos iudices et nobilior et sapientior et denique (quod minus stulti vident) etiam potentior debet haberi, quando quidem vera potencia non tam elucet in mobili accione quam in constanti patientia.

Palee.

---

statum *M L*] statim *C*   infimos *Ed.*] infirmos *C M L*, *L with note "Leg. infimos."*
possit *M*] posit *C L*   elegisse *Ed.*] eligisse *C M L*

the higher reaches of the earth are first and more easily touched by the rays of light, so likewise when the light came forth which was to enlighten every man coming into this world [John I. 9], it first had to shine upon those who stood more lofty among men and soared like mountains out of the valleys of mankind.

More slowly, however, do the rays of divine light pierce to the others, who are in the depths, and in the place of coldness, and are wrapped round by their own misty wisdom. There they enlighten men with more difficulty, and they abandon those men more swiftly, unless it should happen that with more vigorous invasion those rays disperse the cloud and so lighten a man[22] that he may cast off all that he has and rise up to Christ. If he does, then he comes out into the condition and state of Peter and the little ones like him, whom lately that man scorned, so that by this path he may go up to the truth which is Christ himself.

Christ said, indeed: "Unless you are turned about and made like little children again, you shall not enter the Kingdom of Heaven" [Matt. XVIII. 3]. And these little ones are doubtless greater than those who are of great repute in the world, and therefore are justly preferred by God for His mysteries. For when God came down to men, these met Him with loftier stature than others. The first to accept Him, they had as one of their commands to diffuse by degrees downwards[23] from themselves His name, His light, and His goodness to all the bottommost; even, if possible,[24] to those who dwell in the earth's valleys and the sea's depths.

No one must doubt, therefore, that God really did choose for Himself the nobility, and the wisdom, and the power of the human race, although they were not considered such, and that *God chose to Himself* He began to enlighten mankind's cloud in its purer *the noble, the powerful,* part, so that thence the rays of light might pierce to *the wise.* thickest blackness. Within this darkness were and are the wise and the powerful of this world, men who not easily, indeed, receive the light into themselves. But the rays of light will hasten on to the perfection of those to be enlightened.

What does not share in the light will be flung away. He who baptizes in the Spirit and in fire, i.e., in spiritual fire, with winnowing-fan in hand will sweep his threshing-floor clean. And the wheat he will gather into his storehouse, but the chaff he will burn up with unquenchable fire [Matt. III. 12]. The chaff are those who grow dry in empty wisdom, and who are *Chaff.* ineffectual in false strength. These in God's sight rightly hold the last place, or rather, no place at all. Indeed, to speak accurately, they do not hold, but *are* in no place at all. Whoever is farther from their method and form of living, whoever behaves more differently from them, ought in the sight of right-minded judges to be deemed at once the more noble, and wise, and finally (although the stupid are slow to see this) even the more powerful. For true strength does not shine so much in restless activity as in steadfast patience.[25]

Corinthii et sua ipsorum opinione et aliorum etiam habiti sapientes, nihil arbitrati sunt venire in sermonem posse de quo non disertissime disputarent, de quoque etiam probabilem sententiam non proferrent. Homines insolenter confisi suis ingeniis et sapientiam sibi arrogantes, in quaque re et veritatem et falsitatem posse suis viribus deprehendere opinati sunt. Gens ingeniosa, abundans et ocio et litteris, ac simul artificiosa quadam eloquentia freta, quicquid in medium venerat, id in utramvis partem et suadere et dissuadere nihil diffisa est.

Fuit illa Greca natio, illis argutiis versatib⟨i⟩lis humani ingenii, semper prompta ad arguendum et redarguendum, sed hiis humane mentis deliramentis miserabiliter decepta, siquidem quo putarunt maxime se videre et veritatem percipere posse, eo maxime excecata fuerat Grecia ne veritatem intueretur.

Quod putaverunt° sibi fuisse subsidio fuit impedimento. Quo valuerunt apud homines, apud Deum impotentes fuerunt. Hinc sapientiam illorum vocat Paulus stulticiam apud Deum, et admonet si volunt veri sapientes esse, stulti fiant ut sapiant. Humanis viribus, facultate° rationis quantum maxime potentis, spiritu huius mundi, adminiculis humane doctrine ac eloquentie quibusquumque et quantisquumque accumulatis°, non valet homo aspirare ad ea que Deus in sua absoluta ratione et voluntate longe supra omnem rationem molitur et prestat. Que solus Divinus Spiritus novit, et qui eodem Spiritu afflati sunt ut fide videant dum hic sint et per speculum in enigmate donec facie sint ad faciem visuri. Qua inhalatione Divini Spiritus qui non tanguntur ii acie qua divina cernant |86r| misteria careant necesse est. Paulus autem arreptus in unum illo benigno° et suavi afflatu egregie claruit perspicuitate Spiritus et liquide vidit mirabilia Dei, et ex eodem Spiritu constanter eadem docuit, maxime Iesum Christum crucifixum°, cuius salutaris rei mysterium unde et quorsum tendit probe novit. Qui ita abnegavit semet ipsum, ita se dedit et vovit Deo, ita totus ex Deo dependit, ut nihil se prorsus nec sapere nec posse nisi ex Deo professus est.

Atque apud Corinthios, qui non parva de se nec parum se sapere et posse cogitarunt, is nuncium Christi afferens vili se pendit ac nihil se scire nisi Iesum Christum et eundem crucifixum, nihilque nisi ex Deo posse presetulit. Cuius spiritum tenuit, quo sapuit, quo docuit, quo egit omnia, ut non ipse homunculus° ins⟨i⟩piens et impotens, sed sapiens et mirificus Deus in eo videatur omnia egisse. Qui operatur in fidelibus ministris suis, et trahit ad fidem mysteriorum

---

putaverunt *Ed.*] putaverint *C M L*   facultate *Ed.*] facultatem *C M L*   accumulatis
Ed.] accumilatis *C M L*   benigno *M L*] beningno *C*   crucifixum *M L*] crucifixium
C   homunculus *M L*] hummunculus *C*

Now the Corinthians were reputed wise, both in their own opinion and also in that of others, and they thought that nothing could be brought up on which they could not most learnedly argue, and even produce a probable verdict. Men who presumptuously trusted their own endowments and arrogantly claimed wisdom for themselves, they thought they could grasp by their own powers truth and falsehood in any matter at all. A talented race, with abundant leisure and learning, and equipped with a highly skillful sort of eloquence, they had no self-distrust about upholding or overthrowing either side of any subject that came up.

In such acuteness of a resourceful human ingenuity that Greek nation was always ready to argue things back and forth. But by these caprices of the human mind they were wretchedly misled, since the ability by which they thought themselves most clearly to see and best to determine the truth was precisely that by which Greece was blinded against looking upon the truth.

What they took for an advantage was a block to them. What made them strong in the eyes of men made them weak in God's eyes. And so Paul says that their wisdom is, with God, folly, and tells them that if they wish to be truly wise, they must become foolish in order to be wise [I Cor. III. 19, 18]. Human strength, the faculty of reason (however great in power), the spirit of this world, the props of human learning and eloquence (of whatever sort and however many) will not make a man strong enough to aspire to those things that God establishes and shows forth in His absolute reason and will, far above all reasoning. These things only the Divine Spirit knows, and those in whom the same Spirit breathes so that they here may see by faith and by a confused reflection in a mirror, until they are to see face to face [XIII. 12]. Those who are not touched by this inbreathing of the Divine Spirit must lack the sharp vision to see the divine mysteries. Paul, however, was carried into the One;[26] he was given extraordinary clarity of vision by that gracious and gentle inspiration, and saw lucidly the wonders of God [II Cor. XII. 2–4]. Drawing on the same Spirit, he taught these constantly, especially Jesus Christ crucified, the saving mystery of which he knew throroughly the beginning and the end. He so denied himself altogether, so gave himself over and vowed himself to God, depended so entirely on God, that he professed thenceforth to have no wisdom nor power except from God.

Before the Corinthians, then, who thought they had no little intrinsic wisdom and power in many things, he belittled himself extremely, when he brought the message of Christ, and boasted that he had no knowledge except of Christ crucified, no power except from God [I Cor. II. 2]. God's Spirit he held, by it he was wise, by it he taught, by it he did everything, so that they might see that the wise God, the worker of wonders, worked all in him, and not he himself, a poor mere man without wisdom and power. For in His faithful ministers

suorum quos ipse vult. Eligit in regnum quos libet Dei, qui cum Christo regnent in monte sancto suo.

Ideo velit Paulus Corinthios non confidere in sapientia sua, que inimica est Deo, sed regenitos extra se ire in Deum et evadere supra se novos, spiritales, et divinos homines, in quo statu sint, sapiant, et ex Spiritu agant omnia, ut vere possint illud dicere, *Nos non spiritum huius mundi accepimus, sed Spiritum qui est ex Deo, ut sciamus que a Deo donata sunt nobis*, i.e., redemptionem per Christum et salutem, i.e., misterium quod Deus abscondit sapientibus et revelavit parvulis, misterium absconditum, predestinatum ante secula in gloriam electorum. Quod voluit notum fieri per stultitiam predicationis ut confundat sapientes. Quod voluit periuntibus esse stulticiam: talibus qui salvi fient, virtutem Dei; Iudeis scandalum, gentibus insipientiam: vocatis et delectis, Dei virtutem et Dei sapientiam. Quod voluit etiam esse thesaurum in vasis fictilibus, propinatum ab Apostolis et habens |86v| odorem, aliis mortis in mortem, aliis vite in vitam.

Est enim quodque ut is qui recipit, et odoriferum Christi evangelium tale sentitur, ut is qui audit divina voluntate vel eligitur vel reprobatur. In quo ut in omnibus est iustus et misericors Deus, cuius ratio, voluntas, et actio omni humilitate veneranda et colenda est, non nostra stulticia attrectanda temere et disputanda.

God operates, drawing to faith in His mysteries those He wishes, choosing whom He pleases for the Kingdom of God, to reign with Christ upon His holy mountain.

Paul, therefore, would wish the Corinthians not to trust in their own wisdom, which is at enmity with God [Rom. VIII. 7], but to be born again and go out of themselves into God, and to become new, spiritual, and divine men, above themselves. He wants them to have their being, their wisdom, and their operations in that state from the Spirit, so that they may say with truth, "We have not received the spirit of this world, but the Spirit which is of God, so that we may know God's gifts to us" [I Cor. II. 12] i.e., redemption through Christ and salvation, the mystery that God has hidden from the wise and revealed to little ones, the mystery hidden and predestined before the ages for the glory of the chosen. This mystery God wished to be made known through "the foolishness of preaching," to confound the wise. He willed that it should be stupidity to those who perish, but the strength of God to those who are saved; to the Jews a stumbling block,[27] to the Gentiles unwisdom, but to those called and chosen, the might and the wisdom of God. He willed further that it be a treasure in earthenware vessels, set out by the Apostles for men to drink, and having the savor of death to some unto death, to others the savor of life unto life [II Cor. IV. 7; II. 16].

For whatever is received is received[28] according to the measure of him who receives it, and the sweet-savored Gospel of Christ is experienced differently, according as he who hears it is chosen or condemned by the Divine Will.[29] And in this as in all things God is just and merciful. His reason, will, and ways are to be worshipped and revered with all humility, not rashly handled[30] and disputed over by our stupidity.

Caput tertium°

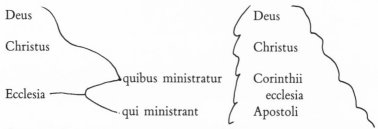

Deus
Christus
Ecclesia — quibus ministratur / qui ministrant

Deus
Christus
Corinthii
ecclesia
Apostoli

Paulus: spiritalis, potens spiritu, escam et solidum cibum habens, spectans
ad Deum, sectans charitatem quam sequitur unitas, potentia, fortitudo.

Corinthii: quasi carnales, infirmi carne, adhuc lacte et fluida potione potiusquam cibo pascendi, spectantes ad humiles homines, non ad summum
Deum, gloriantes in hominibus, non in Deo.

Deus: autor et effector est omnium in hominibus, agricola, architectus°,
pontifex.

Christus: fundamentum est, quo nemo potest aliud ponere.

Corinthii ipsi bona agricultura Dei est, pulcra architectura, sanctum
templum, Divini Spiritus hospicium.

Ministri sunt in duplici genere: alii veri, boni, simplices, sancti, fideles Deo,
pii erga homines, prudentes et diligentes in ecclesia per gratiam, et
adiutores Dei; alii contra fallaces, maliciosi, multiplices, impuri°, perfidi,
iniusti, stulti, temerarii, adiutores diaboli.

Deus ipse iustus et misericors, operis sui et quasi edificii in hominibus auctor
est. Qui altum et solidum fundamentum posuit Iesum Christum. Supra quod
apte et conciniter voluit reliquum opus erigi et consummari, quod assimulatione
ad veritatem et simplicitatem Christi |87r| secum constat firmiter et duret
perenniter.

Caput tertium *Ed.*] Ca.3. *C] om. M*   architectus *M L*] architrectus *C*   impuri
M L] inpuri *C*

Chapter III

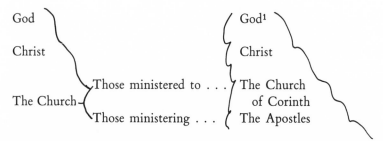

Paul: spiritual, mighty in the Spirit, having nourishment and solid food, looking toward God; pursuing charity, of which the consequences are unity, power, and strength.

The Corinthians: carnal, as it were, and weak in the flesh, still to be fed with milk and easy liquids rather than with food; looking to men low on the ground, not to the highest God; glorying in men, not in God.

God is the author and worker in men of all things, the husbandman, the architect, the High Priest.

Christ is the foundation, and no man can set up any other.

The Corinthians are themselves the good husbandry of God, the fair architecture, the holy temple, the home of the Divine Spirit.

Ministers are of two sorts: the first true, good, simple, holy, faithful to God, right-feeling toward men, prudent and diligent in the Church through Faith, and helpers of God; the others are deceivers, wicked, divided, impure, faithless, unjust, stupid, rash, helpers of the Devil.

God Himself is just and merciful, and He is the author of His work and His building, as it were, among men. He has placed a deep and steadfast foundation, Jesus Christ, and He has willed that the rest of the work be built up and finished fittingly and harmoniously, to stand in steadfast self-consistency by being made like to the truth and simplicity of Christ, and to stand forever.

Ministri humiles, quibus utitur Deus in construendo et perficiendo opere suo, sunt apostoli, ii videlicet qui fideles sunt Deo; qui in eo quod inchoatum est a Deo, ipso Deo duce et eius Spiritu, pergunt, non suis usi ingeniis, sed tractu Divini Spiritus, nec sibi quicquam con- *Caput iii.* fisi, sed soli Deo, ii nimirum in vero et solido Christo, pro ratione fundamenti, concinne edificant in hominibus et sapientiam et bonam actionem, et promovent edificium structura durabili et pulcherima, lapidibus aureis, argenteis, et gemeis coagmentatis, ut sua constantia et patientia non timeat iniuriam adversariorum, sua specie et nitore perplaceat Deo et amicis Dei.

Contra autem qui suis confisi ingeniis arbitrantur ex se ipsi aliquid in ecclesiam bene introducere posse, profecto ii edificationem adhi- *Confisi sibi.* bent fundamento disparem indignamque° Christo, ingra- tam° Deoque et ecclesie dedecorosam; edificationem quasi ligneam, feneam, stipulinam, falsam, fragilem, caducam, quam facile adversari- *Ignis Dei.* orum impitus disperget, et ignis ille examinatorius Dei in die Domini dissipabit.

Ut enim in segitibus zizania usque ad messem, item in rhete ut mali pisces, quam diu in mare sunt, una commiscere sinuntur, in littore° vero facta est seperatio; ita similiter fert Deus omnia et tollerat improborum in sua ecclesia malam edificationem, usque ad consumationem seculi ad diem Domini.

In quo cuiusque opus ignis probabit, ignis quidem ille de quo Esaias: *Excoquam ad purum (inquid) scoriam meam*; ignis quem Christus venit mittere in terram; ignis mala consumens. Qui Spiritus *Ignis purgifaciens* ille bonus et sanctus est, quem Iesus quasi ventilabrum habuit *Spiritus Sanctus.* in manu sua. Qui Spiritus permundabit aream Domini. Qui *Spiritus Sanctus.* etiam idem Spiritus purgatorius unius cuiusque opus quale sit probabit. Cuius potentem presentiam quod quadam spiritali cognatione ferre poterit, id stabit illesum, immo etiam adiutum et conservatum, in foventibus radiis Divini Spiritus, qui quodque spirituale |87v| statim *Sanctus Spiritus* agnoscet et sustinebit ut suum, nec agnoscat quidem *agnoscet spiritale.* quicquid aliud quam suum et spirituale.

Quod si quicquam alienum fuerit a Spiritu, olens magis infirmitatem humani ingenioli quam fortitudinem Divini Spiritus, id potentiam et veritatem Divini Spiritus non sustinens, ut vanum et futile longe propelletur, cum etiam dispen-

---

indignamque *Ed.*] indgnumque *C*] indignumque *M L*   ingratam *Ed.*] ingratum *C M L*   Deoque *M Ed.*] deo *C with abbrev. for* -que *above line, with foll.* et] Deo *L* littore *M*] littere *C L*

The humble ministers whom God uses in building and perfecting His work are the Apostles, the ministers, i.e., who are faithful to God. These press on in what God has begun, with God Himself and His Spirit for their guidance; not using their own resources, but the drawing on of the Divine Spirit; not trusting themselves for anything, but God alone. These, clearly, build up harmoniously among men, on the true and firm Christ, both wisdom and good conduct befitting the foundation, and they advance the building with a lasting and most beautiful structure, with stones that are of gold and silver and precious jewels all cemented together, so that in its patient constancy it will not fear harm from the adversaries, and in its splendid beauty will be altogether pleasing to God and to God's friends.

Those, however, who rely on their own resources, and think they can of themselves to advantage bring some new thing into the Church, are actually setting up a building that is out of proportion to and unworthy of the foundation, Christ, and *Those who rely on themselves.* is displeasing to God, and a disfigurement to the Church. This is a building of wood, of hay, of stubble; a building false, fragile, perishable, easily shattered by the attack of the enemy; and in the day of the Lord that searching fire[2] of God shall sift it away [I Cor. III. 11–15]. *The fire of God.*

For just as the tares are allowed to remain in the wheat until the harvest, and the bad fishes, as long as they are in the water, to mingle with the good in the net, but are separated once on the shore, so likewise God bears with and tolerates the evil constructions of wicked men within His Church, until the end of time and the day of the Lord.

In that day the fire will prove each man's work, that fire of which Isaiah writes: "I shall smelt away my dross" [Isa. I. 25]; the fire which Christ came to spread over the earth [Luke XII. 49]; the fire that burns up evil things. And this *The purifying fire is the Holy Spirit.* is that good and holy Spirit, which Jesus had as a winnowing-fan in his hand, the Spirit who will sweep clean the Lord's threshing-floor. This same cleansing Spirit will also prove the worth of *The Holy Spirit.* each and every man, to see of what sort it is [I Cor. III. 13]. And whatever will be able, by a spiritual affinity, as it were, to bear His mighty presence, shall stand unhurt, shall even stand strengthened and confirmed in the sustaining rays of the Divine Spirit. *The Holy Spirit will recognize the spiritual.* He shall know at once for His own and uphold whatever is of the Spirit, and nothing other than what is spiritual and His own will He acknowledge.

But if there is anything alien to the Spirit, tasting rather of the weakness of man's little intellect than of the might of the Divine Spirit, it will not support the power and truth of the Divine Spirit, but will be driven far away as empty

dio illorum a quibus illa inanitas profecta est, qui volunt in divino opere insolenter plus sapere quam oportet.

Tamen tales salvos fore dicit Paulus, *sed quasi per ignem*; nisi quod adhibet Apostolus *si*—dicit enim *si tamen*—significat Paulum subdubitare salvi erunt eiusmodi necne; vel significat corruptos purgatos fore, corruptores damnatos°. Verum hoc proculdubio certum est, salvi si fuerint illiusmodi violatores templi, per ignem eos purgationemque Spiritus Sancti salvos fore, quamquam quod sequitur talibus salutem non videtur proponere. Nam tales violatores templi Dei dicit Deum disperditurum. At utquumque est, id nequaquam dubitamus velle Paulum: qui impuri sunt inquinatoresque sancti operis Dei, eos si salvi fuerint, non aliter quam purgatione divini ignis et Spiritus Sancti salvos facturos esse.

In eodem capite tertio:

Quod autem scribit Paulus se Corinthiis adhuc carnalibus non potuisse loqui spiritaliter, nec divisis et multiplicibus unita et simplicia, nec infirmis et insipientibus sapientia et fortia, nec denique dare *Caput iii.* languentibus solidum cibum et escam, sed fluentem potum, qui facilius admittitur, citius coquitur, congruentius coaptatur, id a corpore similitudinem trahens dixit.

Nam ut se habet corpus ad cibum suum, ita animus ad suum; utque soluto, diviso, et fluentiori potione aluntur° egriora corpora, ita animi impotentiores tenuius et dimissius et magis quasi fluidum facilius fert, et in eo alitur comodius. Ut enim vires sunt cuiusque vel animi vel |88r| corporis, ita quo reficiantur convenienter oportet sumministrari; ut etiam sanum et robustum corpus solidiores et duriores cibos non recusat, cuiusmodi tamen infirmiorem stomachum debilitarent et frangerent, ita contracta in se sursum et unita anima potentius fortia fert sine offensione, et sublimiora potest intelligere.

Sublimiora vero et difficiliora perspectu in intelligibilibus duro et difficili coctu papulo comparantur. Ab hiis quanto magis deorsum *Sublimia durum.* descendis, reperis divisa, vaga, fluxa, multiplicia, pro qua- *Humilia molle.* rum instabilitate potui et fluenti liquori comparantur.

Est mos medicorum quum vident egrotos solidiores medicinas non posse deglutire, tum easdem soluere in liquorem, ut molliores et fluentiores sorbean-

---

vel . . . damnatos *C in marg. with line, om. M L*]   aluntur *M L*] alunttur *C*

and useless. And those also from whom that folly proceeded shall suffer loss, men who impudently wish to be more wise than is fitting in the divine work.

Yet Paul says that such men will be saved, "but as though by fire"; unless the Apostle's use of the word *if*—for he says, "If, however. . . ."—indicates that Paul doubted whether men of this sort would be saved or not, or means that those corrupted will be cleansed and the corrupters damned.[3] However this may be, it is beyond doubt certain that such spoilers of the temple, if they are saved, will be saved through fire and the cleansing of the Holy Spirit. Still, what follows seems to hold out no salvation to such men. For he says that God will scatter the spoilers of God's temple [III. 17]. In any event, however the matter stands, we can have no doubt that Paul intends this: those who are impure and defilers of God's holy work will be saved, if they are to be saved, only by the cleansing of the divine fire and of the Holy Spirit.

In the same Chapter III:

Now as to Paul's writing that he could not speak spiritually to the Corinthians because they were still carnal; that he could not tell them of things one and simple, because they were divided and complex, nor of wise and strong things, because they were weak and unwise; and, finally, that he could not give them meat and solid food, because they lacked strength, but only the easy liquid, which is more readily taken in, more swiftly digested, and more flexibly adapted—in this, Paul is using a simile taken from the body [III. 1, 2].

For the soul has the same relation to its food as the body has, and just as less robust bodies are nourished by diluted, broken up, and watery substances, in the same way souls that are less strong stand more easily a thinner and an inferior and a more liquid diet, so to speak, and are thereby more aptly nourished. For each one ought to be provided with the fit wherewithal for his sustenance, according to his strength either of soul or of body. And as a healthy and robust body does not refuse the more solid and substantial foods, while these weaken and destroy a less strong stomach, so the soul that is upheld firmly within itself and united hears stronger things with more strength and without hurt, and can understand loftier matters.

To food that is hard and difficult to digest is compared whatever is loftier and more difficult to perceive in the intelligible world.[4]
The farther you come downward from these, the more *Lofty things are hard;* you find things divided, fluid, wavering, and multi- *lowly things, soft.* form; and these, because of their instability, are compared to drink and to running fluids.

Doctors, when they see that their patients cannot swallow the more solid medicines, customarily dissolve these in a liquid, so that they may be taken in in a softer and fluid state. Similarly, good teachers ought to test the consistency

tur. Idem boni magistri facere debent, palpareque animos eorum quos doceant°
ac experiri signis quid° valent quatenusque possunt, atque cibos quos habent
duriores quasi cominuere et emolifacere, apponereque cuique quantum deglutire
et coquere potest, nec gravare quemquam onere et quasi crapula, unde lesio sto-
machi, dedignatio, fastidium, contemptus nascitur.

Maiora illa et solidiora et dura coctu (nisi anime saltem sint excellentiores)
sunt summe ille veritates et simplices rationes, divineque ac spiritales, quas ab-
solutissimi et perfectissimi mores consequuntur. Ad quas non sunt idonii quidem
nisi admodum potentes animis qui sunt toti contracti in unum, quique contempto
mundo et corpore, in summo sue mentis, in unitate, in indivisibili, et in puncto
constant. Ii et tales sunt potentes et habiles ut quicque° ex alto traditur quan-
tumquumque solidum, simplex, et supra rationem, id fortibus animis admittant,
teneant firma fide, coquant efficaci amore, convertant in optimum, colant, et
venerentur.

Tales si quos nactus est Moises ille, profecto non velata facie, sed detecta eos
alloq⟨u⟩utus est; qui ex imbecilitate non exhorruissent |88v| gloriam vultus il-
lius, sed quasi in cognato et simili delectati essent. Talibus Christus ipse noster
dedit nosse mysteria regni Dei. Talibus glorificatus in monte se exhibuit.

In hoc hominum fortium genere fuit etiam Paulus, illuc in illam adimantinam
mentem a Christo raptus et tentus ut intu⟨er⟩etur° veritatem Dei et in absoluta
se bonitate conservaret. Ideo illi nihil durum in mysteriis, nihil incredibile fuit.

Quorum autem mentes adhuc minus collecte° in unum sunt multumque sunt
divise° et in corpus ac mundanas res dissipate°, in hiis inconstantia fluentes, non
supra hec in unum consolidate, atque ideo infirme et caduce, atque idio etiam
ad illa altiora et graviora ferenda inepte et impotentes—cuiusmodi sane fuerunt
Corinthiorum mentes, adhuc a diviso et multiplici corpore ac mundo non satis
solute nec separate—in hiis habenda est ratio condicionis et virium. Ac talia et
ea quoque eo modo quo ferre possunt talibus considerare accomodare debent cum
miseratione eorum infirmitatis, cumque optatione maioris fortitudinis, cumque
spe de die in diem melioris valitudinis.

Ita tradidit Moyses veritatem et iudicium Dei quasi deductum ad res sensibiles
et solutum in fluxa veteribus Hebreis. Ita Christus discipulis que poterant por-

---

quos doceant *Ed.*] que doceantur *C M*] qui doceantur *L*   quid *C? Ed.*] quam *M*]
quantum *L*   quicque *C*] quicquid *M L*   intuetur *C M L*   collecte *Ed.*] col-
lecti *C M*] collectæ *L*   divise *Ed.*] divisi *C M L*   dissipate *Ed.*] dissipati *C M L*

of their pupils' minds, and by the symptoms determine what they are worth and how strong they are; those more solid foods they have they ought to lessen, as it were, and soften, setting before each one as much as he can swallow and digest; and they ought not to weigh anyone down with a heavy and troublesome surfeit, so to speak, from which will arise hurt to the stomach, strong dislike, squeamishness, and loathing.

These foods that are harder and more difficult to digest (except, of course, for the more excellent souls) are those highest truths and purest principles, divine and spiritual, which have as their consequences the freest and most perfect ways of acting.[5] Only those are apt for them who are extremely powerful in soul, who are concentrated altogether into oneness,[6] who despise the world and the body, and stand firm on the loftiest part of their minds, in unity, in singleness, and in the undivided center. These men are powerful and able enough to accept in strength of mind whatever is given from above, however solid and simple it be and however much it surpass reason, and to hold it with firm faith, to digest it with effective love, to turn it to the best, to venerate and worship it.

If Moses had found such men, surely he would have spoken to them with face uncovered instead of veiled [Exod. XXXIV. 5], and they would not because of weakness have shuddered back from the glory of his countenance, but would have rejoiced in it as something akin to them and similar. It was to such men that our Christ himself gave the power to know the mysteries of God's Kingdom. To such he showed himself glorified on the mountain.

To this group of strong men Paul also belonged, and he was carried by Christ to such a point of adamantine firmness of mind—and held there—that he looked upon God's truth, and kept himself in absolute goodness. For him, therefore, there was nothing hard in the mysteries, nothing incredible.

To those, however, whose minds are as yet less gathered into oneness and are divided in many ways and dispersed upon the body and worldly things—wavering among these in inconstancy, instead of being fixed on the One above all these—and are therefore weak and unsteady, and therefore are also unfit and powerless for the bearing of those loftier and weightier matters, must be conceded some consideration of their condition and their strength. This was certainly true of the Corinthians, whose minds were as yet not freed or withdrawn enough from the division and multiplicity of the body and the world. For they [the strong] should take thought how they can adapt to such men things they can bear, and consider also the manner in which they can bear them, with pity for their weakness, with a wish for their greater strength, and with hope for their better health from day to day.

In this way Moses gave the truth to the ancient Hebrews, and a manifestation of God brought down, as it were, to matters of sense and diluted in a solution. In this way Christ gave to his Apostles what they could bear. In this more gen-

tare. Itaque denique Paulus et mollius et parcius Corinthiis et quasi lac potum dedit, non escam.

Superiora illa solida quum deducuntur ad inferiora degenerant quodammodo a simplicitate in multiplicitatem, ab intelligibili condicione prope in sensibilem, et (ut ita dicam) a mastigabili condicione in potabilem, fiuntque pro ratione infirmorum animorum lentiora et coctibiliora.

Summa est quod velit Paulus non altissimas se rationes rerum et christiane religionis tradidisse Corinthiis, sed que conveniebant mentibus eorum, magis adhuc herentibus mundo quam Deo. Sapientiam loq⟨u⟩utus est inter perfectos: |89r| imperfectis quodammodo stulta accomodavit, humiliora et crassiora. Hoc consilio etiam minus perfectos minusque absolutos mores ad tempus tolleravit, indulgentia cum eis agens leniter, quatenus licuit, non tam cogitans quantum ei licuit, quam quantum aliis expediat, nec quantum ipse potest, quam quid Corinthiis conveniat, quantumque deglutire, ferre, coquere, et in bonum animi alimentum vertere poterant, ne quorum salutem quisierat, eosdem inconsiderate° enecaret.

---

inconsiderate *M L*] inconsiderare *C*

tle and more sparing way, finally, Paul gave the Corinthians milk to drink, so to speak, not meat.

Those solid, loftier matters suffer, when they are brought down to lower things, a kind of deterioration from simplicity to multiplicity,[7] from the intelligible state to the sensible, and (to use a figure) from the condition in which the teeth must be used on them to one in which they can be drunk; they become softer and more digestible, to suit weaker souls.

In conclusion, then, Paul means that he did not give to the Corinthians the highest principles of reality and of the Christian religion, but matters more fit for their minds, which clung still to the world more than to God. Among the perfect he spoke wisdom [I Cor. II. 6]: for the imperfect, he accommodated things in a manner foolish, lower, and less refined. With this policy he tolerated also for a time less perfect and less absolute conduct, acting gently with them in indulgence, as far as he could. He looked not to how much he was permitted, but to how much something would benefit others, and he took less into consideration his own power than the appropriateness of the matter for the Corinthians, and the extent to which they could take it in, tolerate it, digest it, and turn it into good nourishment for the soul. This he did lest through lack of consideration he should kill those very persons whose salvation was his goal.

Caput quartum°

Magistratus in Christianitate omnes non magistri sed ministri sunt ecclesie. Ministrorum vero est sedulo agere, et laudem non ab hominibus sed a Deo solo expectare, item non hic, sed post hanc vitam, agnoscere etiam non valere se in ministerio viribus suis, sed facultate a Deo accepta. Ideo homines non in suis ministris sed in Deo solo gloriari oportere.

Apostoli quia despecti devexatique° fuerint a mundo iccirco ceperint apud Corinthios vilescere fortasse, haberique° non alio in loco quam apud paganos damnati illi et addicti morti ad bestiasque in spectaculo proiecti.

Quorum cecitatem dolens, prope irridet Apostolus ac yronice et dissimulanter illos effert anteponitque sibi, ut illi stultitiam et arrogantiam suam, maxime qui voluerunt in Corinthiis magistri videri, agnoscant, pudeatque eos despicere Apostolos et suos parentes in Christo, propter vitam eorum erumnosam, quum potius vitam apostolorum et sui genitoris Pauli debent sibi proponere exemplum, existimareque id in primis faciendum esse quod factitant apostoli, illorumque vestigia sectanda, a quibus in recta semita fuerunt instituti. Quod si perdita apostolorum via deliraverint, quem habent ducem quem sequantur? Oportet ergo intendant sine intermissione oculos in eum qui antegreditur et precursor est, maxime vero si via non sit trita, nec alia cernuntur vestigia quam eius qui unus anteivit. Tunc |89v| solicitius observanda est impressio pedum, ne si aberraris, aut sero aut nunquam in viam redeas.

Erraverunt autem Corinthii a vestigiis Pauli. Ideo misit illuc Timotheum qui eos viam suam monstraret reduceretque ad semitam errantes, *Timotheus.* ut eius presentia digniores essent, ab ipsoque promoveren-

---

Caput quartum *Ed.*] Capite 4 C] *om. M*   devexatique L] devextique C] devecti-
que *M*   haberique L] habereque C M

Chapter IV

The officers in the Christian religion are all ministers, not masters,[1] of the Church. It is the duty of ministers, however, to be diligent in action, and to look for praise not from men but from God alone, and not here, but after this life; it is their duty also to acknowledge that they have no efficacy in their ministry by their own strength, but by a power received from God. Men must boast, therefore, not of their ministers, but only of God.

Because the Apostles were despised and ill-treated by the world, perhaps they began to grow worthless in the eyes of the Corinthians, and to have no more esteem than in the eyes of the pagans had those condemned men who were marked for death and cast to the beasts in the spectacles [I Cor. IV. 9].

Although grieving at their blindness, the Apostle almost laughs at this. With irony he pretends to extol them and to give them a place above his own, so that they may recognize — especially those who wished to seem masters among the Corinthians — their own folly and presumption, and be ashamed of despising the Apostles, their own parents in Christ, for their harsh lives. Indeed, they should rather set the lives of the Apostles and of Paul, their father, before them as an example,[2] and believe that the most important thing for them to do is what the Apostles consistently do; they should believe that they must follow the footsteps of those who set them in the right path. For if they turn aside, losing the way of the Apostles, what leader have they to follow? Unwaveringly, therefore, they must keep their eyes on him who goes before them and is their forerunner. This is especially true when the road is not well-traveled, and no footprints are to be seen except those of the one man who has gone ahead. Then with more care is the trail to be watched, lest if you wander from it, you return to the way either too late or never.

The Corinthians had, however, wandered from the footsteps of Paul; so he sent Timothy there to show them his way and lead the strag- *Timothy.* glers back to the path [IV. 17], so that they might be more fit for his own presence, and might be advanced by him to the better, not sim-

tur in melius, non revocarentur ubi eos locavit. Hoc enim esset agere actum, et discipilo alicui magis convenit quam magistro. Ideo Timotheum misit qui illos revocet, ut ipse revocatos promoveat et aliquando promotos perficiat in re, scilicet virtute et divina actione, que spectanda est, non sermo. In quo non est regnum Dei, sed in virtute.

ply called back to the place where he had set them before. For this would be to do what had already been done, an office more fitting for some disciple than for the teacher. And so he sent Timothy to call them back, so that when this was done he might himself advance them and at last perfect them, when advanced — in deed, that is to say, in strength and in godlike action. One must look to this, rather than to words. The Kingdom of God is not in words, but in power   [IV. 20].

Caput quintum°

Pasca nostrum, agnus ille immaculatus in quo non est inventus dolus, sincera azima omnino sine fermento malicie, immolatus est Christus, qui est a nobis comedendus non solum sacramento sed etiam imitatione, ut illo educati, et illius formam induentes, ei assimulemur, simusque (quoad fieri potest et per gratiam licet) ita sinceri et simplices, sinceritate et puritate iusticie, ut eius contrarii nihil admixtum habeamus.

In vita enim ipsa et actione debet esse omnis candor et simplicitas, ac (quatinus datur) relatio Christi in re et factis. Quod est vere christianum pasca facere, et ab Egipteo hoc mundo, Christo duce, ad celestem Hierusalem proficisci. Quo assidue contendere et in continua hac celebratione pasce esse debent universi Christiani.

In quibus si aliquid sit fermentatius, sitque aliquis deprehensus in vicio, is a pasce sanctimonia societateque cominionis in Christo eiiciendus est, ne in cultu christiane pasce, i.e. in purgata et pura vita in Christo, aliquid fermentatius et homo delinquens agnoscatur, quo toti festi celebritas indigne et nepharie violetur.

Quocirca Paulus dat operam ut ille qui novercam suam duxit uxorem (ut fermentum ab azima) ex sancta communione eiiciatur, ut destitutus gratia foris devex |90r| ationibus diabolicis expurgetur, baptizeturque liquore penitentie, ut spiritus eius salvus fiat.

Servanda est enim societas sancta et integra. Auferendum est malum a nobis ipsis. Inviolatum templum Dei custodiendum est. Nullum flagitium, nullum vicium, nihil iusticie contrarium in iustificata civitate morte Christi et fide hominum ferendum est. Nam modicum fermentum totam massam corrumpit, et parum vicii plurimum iusticie potest labefactare.

Itaque vescamur° sinceritate Christi, imitemur illum et ambulemus sicut ille

---

Caput quintum *Ed.*] Ca.5 *C*] *om. M*   vescamur *M L*] vestamur *C*

Chapter V

Our paschal victim, that spotless lamb in whom there was found no guile, the unleavened bread of sincerity without the leaven of malice,[1] has been offered up in sacrifice [I Cor. v. 7, 8]. And this is Christ, who is to be eaten by us, not only by way of the Sacrament, but also by way of imitation, so that taught by him, and taking upon us his form,[2] we may become like him and may be (as far as is possible and grace permits) so sincere and simple, in the sincerity and purity of justice, as to have no admixture of the opposite.[3]

For in life itself and in action there ought to be all candor and simplicity, and (as far as it is given) an echoing of Christ in deed and in acts. This is the making of a truly Christian Passover, and a setting forth from the Egypt of this world, under Christ's leadership, toward the heavenly Jerusalem.[4] Thither ought the whole of Christendom constantly to strive, and all should be unceasingly engaged in the celebration of this Passover.

If, however, there be corruption among them,[5] if anyone be disclosed in sin, he must be cast out from the holiness of the Passover and from the fellowship of communion in Christ, lest in the rite of the Christian Passover, i.e., in the cleansed and pure life in Christ, there be admitted as belonging something that is spoiled, a man guilty of sin, by whom the celebration of the whole feast would be shamefully and wickedly profaned.

For this reason Paul insists that the man who has married his stepmother be cast out from the holy communion, as yeast from the unleavened bread, so that destitute of grace he may be cleansed outside by the diabolic harassments,[20] and may be baptized in the water of repentance, that his soul may be saved.

For the society is to be preserved in holiness and integrity. Evil must be taken away from our midst. The Temple of God must be kept untainted. No crime, no vice, nothing contrary to justice is to be tolerated in the City made just by the death of Christ and the faith of men. For a little leaven leavens the whole mass [v. 6], and the least part of vice can topple the greatest righteousness.

Let us feed, therefore, upon the sincerity of Christ [v. 8]; let us imitate him

ambulavit, sapienter, simpliciter, iuste, et innocenter, ut illo quo ille pervenit perveniamus, requiescamusque in monte illo, quo nemo ascendit nisi qui ingeditur sine macula et operatur iusticiam. Atque quemadmodum nemo ascendit illuc ad Deum, montem altissimum, nisi verus et iustus, ita ille non descendit° huc nec presens est hominibus ut eos ad se sursum trahat, nisi in hiis sit veritas, sinceritas, et iusticia; quam hominum societatem unus improbus potest labefactare.

Ideo sententia est Pauli in christiana societate et ecclesia ut omnes fornicarii, avari, rapaces, idolatrie°, maledici, ebreosi, ita excominicandi sint, ut ne cibum quidem cum illis sit sumendum.

Fornicatores, Rapaces,
Idolatrie, Maledici, Ebreosi.

Fermentum enim ex azima et malum a iusticia et peccatores ab ecclesia fun-
ditus tollendi sunt et ad Sathanam longe abiiciendi ad interitum carnis, ut in die Domini spiritus salvus fiat.

---

descendit *M L*] descendet *C*   idolatrie *C L*] idolatre *M*

and walk as he walked, wisely, simply, with justice and innocence, so that we may come to where he has come, and may rest on that mountain where no one mounts except the man who approaches without spot and works justice [Ps. XXIII. 3; XIV. 2]. And just as no one mounts there to God, the loftiest peak, unless he be true and just, neither does God come down here nor make Himself present to men in order to draw them on high to Himself, unless there be in them truth, sincerity, and justice. And such a society of men one evildoer can overthrow.

The judgment of Paul, then, is that in the Christian society, the Church, all who fornicate, who are greedy, or grasping, or idolaters, or who are evil-tongued, or drunkards, must be excommu-nicated, in such a way that no one should even take food with them.

The fornicators, the greedy, the idolaters, the evil-tongued, the drunkards.

For from unleavened bread yeast must be altogether removed, and evil must be removed from justice, and sinners from the Church. And these must be cast off afar to Satan[6] for the death of their carnal nature, so that in the day of the Lord their spirits may be saved [I Cor. v. 5].

Caput sextum°

In nomine Domini nostri Iesu Christi et in Spiritu Dei qui est totus in Christo, Spiritus sanctificationis, ecclesia baptizata, sanctificata, et iustificata est, ut peniteat preteritorum, non amplius peccet, semper bene faciat, amore et caritate copuletur, convinciaturque in unum contracta sursum, conspiretque in bonum; que sunt huius mundi, que temporalia, que secularia, despiciat, hec non cupiat, non querat, seorsum non rapiat; pro hiis ipsa ecclesia inter se nullo modo dissideat, litiget, |90v| contendat in iudicio, sed remittat de iure suo, et fraudem ac iniuriam patiatur potius quam oculo ad hec verso, i.e., quam disceptatione° inita coram quoquumque iudice, det occasionem vel externis et paganis de se mala suspicandi iudicandique avariciam in ecclesia esse, vel fratribus christianis malum et perniciosum exemplum altercandi litigandique° de eis que nihil ad rem pertinent, de quibus contentio et pugna° apud iudices quosquumque scandalizat ecclesiam, quorum contemptio conservande pacis gratia magnanimitas, robor, admiratio, et gloria est ecclesie.

Angustis sane et minutis sunt animis qui hoc non vident quique sensiunt de secularibus rebus contendendum esse et in hiisce ius querendum suum; qui ignorant que sit divina iusticia, que iniusticia; quique etiam homunciones quorum stulticia haud scio ridenda ne sit magis quam deflenda, sed certe deflenda, quoniam ex ea ecclesia calamitatem sentit ac pene eversionem.

Sed illi homunciones perditi, quibus hoc nostrum seculum plenum est, in quibusque sunt etiam qui minime debent esse, ecclesiastici viri et qui habentur in ecclesia primarii, illi, inquam, ignari penitus evangelice et apostolice doctrine, ignari divine iusticie, ignari christiane veritatis, soliti sunt dicere causam Dei, ius ecclesie, patrimonium Christi, bona sacerdocii, defendi a se oportere, et sine peccato non posse non defendi.

Caput sextum *Ed.*] *om.* C M   disceptatione *M L*] disseptatione *C*   litigandique *Ed.*] letigandique *C M L*   pugna *M*] pungna *C L*

Chapter VI

In the name of our Lord Jesus Christ, and in the Spirit of God who is entirely in Christ, the Spirit of sanctification, the Church is baptized, and made holy and just, so that it may repent of things past, may sin no longer, may always act rightly, may be linked by love and charity, may be gathered together upward and bound into oneness,[1] may share a common aspiration to goodness; so that it may despise the things that are temporal and of the world, may not desire them nor seek them nor seize them unto itself; so that the Church itself may not be at odds within itself over these things in any way, nor be in legal dispute over them, nor struggle for them in court. But she should abandon her legal rights to them, and suffer trickery and injustice, rather than by turning her attention to them—i.e., by entering into action before any judge whatsoever—either give occasion to outsiders and pagans of suspecting ill of her and of judging that there is greed in the Church, or give to Christian brethren a bad and baneful example of wrangling and going to law over things of no account. For strife over these things and quarrelling before any judges whatever gives scandal to the Church, and contempt of these things for the sake of preserving peace is highmindedness, strength, a cause for admiration, and the glory of the Church.

They are surely small-minded and narrow of soul who do not recognize this, and who are convinced that one must strive over worldly things and seek one's rights in them. These men simply do not know what is divine justice and what is injustice. I do not know whether the stupidity of these little men should move one more to laughter or to tears—surely to tears, since because of it the Church suffers calamity, and almost suffers overthrow.[2]

But these lost little men—and our age is full of them, and among them are those who least ought to be, churchmen, and those who are given first rank in the Church—these men, I say, profoundly ignorant of the teaching of the Gospels and of the Apostles, ignorant of the divine justice,[3] ignorant of Christian truth, have the habit of saying that they must defend the cause of God, the rights of the Church, the heritage of Christ, the property of the priesthood, that they cannot without sin not defend them.

O angustia, o cecitas, o miseria istorum, qui quum ineunt rationem perdendi omnia, non solum hec secularia, sed illa quoque etiam sempiterna, quumque ipsa perdunt, putant se tamen eadem acquirere, defendere, et conservare; qui ipso rerum exitu ubique in ecclesia homines ipsis piscibus oculis durioribus non cernunt que ex contentionibus iudiciisque dispendia religionis, diminitio autoritatis, negligencia Christi, blasphemia° Dei sequitur; ea etiam ipsa denique que ipsi vocant bona ecclesie queque putant se suis litigationibus |91r| vel tenere vel recuperare, quam cotidie paulatim et latentur tum amittunt tum egre custodiunt, si quidem magis vi quam hominum liberalitate et charitate, quo nihil ecclesia indignius esse potest.

In qua proculdubio eadem debet esse ratio conservandi que data fuerint quondam que fuerit comparandi°. Amor Dei et proximi, desiderium celestium, contemptus mundanorum, vera pietas, religio, charitas, benignitas erga homines, simplicitas, patientia, tollerantia malorum, studium semper bene faciendi vel omnibus hominibus ut in consta⟨n⟩ti bono malum vincant, hominum animos concitavit ubique tandem ut de ecclesia Christi bene opinarentur, ei faveant, eam ament, in eam benefici et liberales sint, darentque incessanter, datisque etiam data accumulent, quum viderant in ecclesiasticis viris nullam avariciam, nullum abusum liberalitatis sue.

Quod si qui supremam partem teneant in christiana ecclesia, i.e., sacerdotes, virtutem que acquisivit omnia perpetuo tenuissent adhucve tenerent, profecto si staret causa, effectus sequeretur vel auctus vel conservatus, hominesque eccl⟨es⟩iastici non solum quieti possederent sua, sed plura etiam acciperent possidenda.

Sed quum aque (ut ait David) intraverunt usque animos nostros, quumque cupiditatis et avaricie fluctibus obruimur, nec illud audimus, *si divicie affluant, nolite cor apponere*, quumque neglecta illa virtute et iusticia et studio conservandi amplificandique regni Dei in terris, quod sacerdotio nec exposcenti nec expectanti eiusmodi acquisivit omnia, animos suos (proch° nephas) in illos appendices et pendulas divicias converterint, quod onus est potius ecclesie quam ornamentum, tunc ita illo retrospectu, canes illi et sues ad vomitum et ad volutabrum° luti, infirmaverunt se, amissa pulchra et pla |91v| cida conservatrice rerum virtute, ut quum vident recidere a se cotidie quod virtus comperavit, impotentes dimicant et turpiter sane confligunt inter se et cum laicis, cum sui nominis in-

---

blasphemia *M*] blasphema *C L*   comparandi *M*] comperandi *C L*   proch *M* *L*] proth *C*   volutabrum *M L*] volutubrum *C*

O the narrowness, the blindness, the wretchedness of these fools! Undertaking a course that brings the loss of everything, not only of these worldly things, but of those that are everlasting also, they still think, even while they are losing them, that they are acquiring, defending, and saving them. Even in the manifest outcome everywhere in the Church, these men do not see, their eyes being duller than the very fish,[4] what losses to religion follow from their wranglings and litigations, what lessening of authority, what neglect of Christ, what blasphemy against God. They do not even see, finally, how every day little by little and below the surface they are either losing or scarcely maintaining those very things they call the property of the Church, which they think they are keeping or recovering by their lawsuits. For they are seeking to have them by force rather than because of the generosity and charity of men. Nothing can be more unworthy of the Church than this.

There can be no doubt that the method of preserving in the Church the things once given ought to be the same as that by which they were gained. Love for God and neighbor,[5] the heart set on heavenly things, disdain for what is worldly, true piety, religion, charity, loving kindness toward men, simplicity, forbearance, the acceptance of misfortunes, an eagerness always to do good and to all men, so that evil may be overcome in unfailing goodness—these things at last stirred the hearts of men everywhere to think well of the Church of Christ, to be well disposed to it and love it, to be generous and open-handed toward it, and to give unceasingly, heaping gift upon gift, when once they saw that in churchmen there was no greed, no abuse of their free giving.

And if the men who hold the highest office in the Christian Church, the priests, that is, had always held and still held the virtue that won all things—surely, the cause remaining, the effect would follow either unchanged or increased, and churchmen would not only possess what is theirs in peace, but would also receive more to hold.

Now, however, the waters have come in (as David says) even unto our souls [Ps. LXVIII. 2], now we are engulfed in the waves of greed and covetousness, no longer hearing the words, "If riches increase, set not your hearts upon them" [LXI. 11]; now, neglecting that virtue and righteousness and that ardor to maintain and spread God's Kingdom on earth which gained all things for a priesthood neither asking nor expecting them, priests have turned their hearts (alas! how shameful!) to wealth, the irrelevant appendage, a burden to the Church rather than an adornment. And now, because of that backward look—dogs returning to the vomit, and sows to their filthy wallowing [II Pet. II. 22; Prov. XXVI. 11]—they have enfeebled themselves to such an extent by the loss of the fair and peaceful virtue which preserves, that seeing the things which virtue gained slipping daily from them, they struggle helplessly and engage in shameful warfare among themselves and with the laity, to the infamy of their name and the

famia et ignominia° religionis et eius rei etiam quam maxime querunt indies maiore dispendio ac perdicione, non videntes ceci, si quid acquisiverit aliquid, necessario eius contrarium idem auferre oportere. Contemptus mundi mundanarumque rerum quem docuit Christus comparavit omnia: contra earundem amor amittet et perdet omnia.

Quis non videt quum virtute prestitimus nos tunc bona mundi iure exigere non potuisse nisi quatenus tenuiter ad victum vestitumque pertineat, quo iubet Paulus contenti simus? Quis, inquam, non videt multo minus nunc nos exigere debere quum omnis virtutis expartes sumus, quumque ab ipsis laicis nihil fere nisi tonsa coma et corona, capitio°, et dimissa toga differimus? Nisi hoc dicat quispiam, diridens nos, quum nunc sumus relapsi in mundum, que sunt mundi et partem nostram in mundo nos expostolare posse, ut non amplius dicamus, *Dominus pars hereditatis nostre*, sed nobis dicatur, *Mercedem vestram recepistis°*.

O bone Deus, quam puderet nos huius descensus in mundum si essemus memores amoris Dei erga° nos, exempli Christi, dignitatis religionis christiane, professionis et nominis nostri. Amavit nos Deus ut illum solum redamemus° illique soli studeamus. Iesus Christus ille doctrina nostra certissima contempsit mundum et dixit regnum suum non esse de hoc mundo, et se vicisse mundum. Et fratribus ligantibus noluit esse iudex, sed admonuit caverent ab avaricia, unde omnis nostra nascitur litigatio. Et manum abscindi et oculum erui voluit |92r| potius suorum quam ab hiis quispiam scandalizetur.

Quanto magis contemni debent et abiici longe terrena omnia, quam harum cupiditate scandalizetur et detrimentum patiatur ecclesia, que non constat hiis bonis, ut solent falso dicere isti minutili°, sed (ut verissime sentit Paulus) iusticia, pace, et gaudio in Spiritu Sancto, quod verum est bonum ecclesie, quod iubet Apostolus Romani non blasphement, et habitare fratres in unum, quod bonum et iucundum vocat David.

Cuius unitatis conservande gratia omnia posthabenda sunt, et dare debes omnia fratri potius quam cum eo litiges, ut parva amissione bonorum, magnum amorem — quod verum est bonum — redimes; quod est bonum nullo lucro mundanarum rerum vel minima ex parte amittendum. Quod si tenuerimus, omnia alia sua sponte sequerentur. Querite (inquit Iesus) regnum Dei, et omnia hec adiicientur vobis. Quod si contra evangelicam doctrinam et apostolicam hec in primis querimus, profecto et illa que sunt Dei et hec quoque aliquando simul

---

    ignominia *M L*] ignomina *C*   capitio *C*] caputio *M L*   *recepistis M*] *recipistis C L*
erga *M*] ergo *C L*   redamemus *Ed.*] redememus *C L*] reamemus *M*   minutili
M L] munitili *C*

dishonor of religion, and with daily a greater loss and dispersal of the property which most they seek. In their blindness, they do not see that if one quality has won something, its contrary will necessarily lose it. The contempt of the world and of worldly things that Christ taught gained all: love of these things will lose and disperse all.

Who fails to see that even when we excelled in virtue we had no right to exact the goods of the world, except for the meager needs of food and clothing, with which Paul bids us to be content [I Tim. vi. 8]? Who, then, I say, will fail to see that we are much less able to demand them now that we are devoid of all virtue, and hardly differ from the laymen themselves except by our tonsured hair and crown, our chasuble,[6] and our longer robe? Unless some one should say in mockery of us that now that we have slipped back into the world, we may rightly demand the world's goods and our share in the world, so that we no longer say, "The Lord is the portion of my inheritance," but are told: "You have had your reward" [Ps. xv. 5; Matt. vi. 2].

Good God, what shame we would feel at this descent of ours into the world, if we remembered God's love toward us, the example of Christ, the dignity of the Christian religion and of our profession and of our name. God loved us that we might love Him alone in return, and be zealous only for Him. Jesus Christ—of this doctrine there is no doubt—despised the world, and said that his Kingdom was not of this world, that he had overcome the world [John xviii. 36]. And when the brothers were in dispute, he refused to be judge, and warned them to beware of covetousness, the source of all our lawsuits [Luke xii. 13, 14]. And he wished that his own should have a hand cut off or an eye plucked out, rather than that because of these anyone should stumble [Matt. v. 29, 30].

How much the more should all earthly things be contemned and flung away, rather than that the Church should stumble and take harm because of greed for them? The Church does not stand firm in these "good things," as those little-minded men have the habit of saying it does, but rather (as Paul most truly perceives) in righteousness, in peace, and in joy in the Holy Spirit. This is the true good of the Church, and the Apostle bids the Romans[7] not to bring it into disrepute. And this is for brethren to dwell in unity, which David calls a good and a gracious thing [Rom. xiv. 17, 16; Ps. cxxxii. 1].

For the sake of preserving this unity, everything else must be put in second place. You ought to give all to your brother, rather than go to law with him, purchasing by a small loss of goods great love, which is the true good, a good that must not be lost even in the slightest measure for any gain of worldly possessions. If we have this good in our possession, everything else will follow by itself. Seek, said Jesus, the Kingdom of God, and all these things will be given to you unsought [Matt. vi. 33]. But if we go out of our way to seek them, against the teaching of the Gospels and of the Apostle, then surely we shall sooner

(que nunc magna ex parte amisimus) frigiditate et infirmitate nostra omnia amittemus.

Ideo ut divinitus docet Paulus, omnia in gloriam Dei faciamus, et simus sine offensione Iudeis et gentibus et ecclesie Dei, ac imitati Paulum, per omnia placeamus Deo, non querentes quod utile sit nobis, sed quod multis, ut salvi fiant, emulemurque charismata meliora et illam excellentiorem viam que est concordia et charitas, que sine dubio non querit que sua sunt, immo etiam que sunt sua amittit ut se servet, et damnum lucrum computat quo se contineat°, ac potius quam dissideat a fratre cum eoque litiget, ultro ei concedit omnia.

In quo si stultus reputatur, consolatur se quod in Deo sapit, cuiusmodi sapientia apud mundum stulticia est, gloriosumque |92v| sibi reputet stultum appellari pro charitate Christi, pro qua vitam potius amittat, nedum secularia, quam patiatur eam labefactari.

In lite autem non potest esse ullo modo quin labefactetur. Quocirca Paulus nolit lites in ecclesia omnino apud ullum quidem iudicem, sed in externis bonis fraudem patiatur quisque potius et iniuria, atque hoc quoque etiam in ipso corpore. Alioquin nunquam precipissit Iesus si percusserit te aliquis in una maxilla, prebeas ei alteram, nec Paulus in epistola ad Romanos prohibuisset fratribus defensionem sui, iussissetque ut cedant etiam paganis. Quanto tum magis fratribus id faciendum est amoris tutandi causa et charitatis.

Quocirca plane concludamus non esse Christianorum quaquumque de re vel externa vel corporis apud quemquumque iudicem litigare et ius querere suum, quum christiano viro nulla potest esse maior iusticia, nihil magis equum, quam iniurias pati et tollerare. In qua pacientia possidebimus animas nostras. Quod si velimus agnoscere in hoc mundo aliquid nostrum et id exigere, pro eoque in iudicio contendere, consumereque tempus in litigatione—cum qua sinceritatem charitatis manere est imposibile—quis non videt tunc nos et indignum et iniustum facere, ac in impatientia nostra perdere° animas nostras? Quapropter ait Paulus: Iam quidem omnino delictum est in vobis quod iudicia habetis inter vos, nec litigari sine peccato nullo modo potest, quando lite quasi obnigratur candor charitatis, ad quam integram et inviolatam servandam tamquam ad certissimum signum quo dirigantur omnia spectandum est, omnique pacientia incumbendum.

Quod si quispiam dicat Paulum concedere lites atque ut non apud paganos sed apud suos iudices litigent, suaque si velint querant, is audiat et aliquando

---

contineat *M*] conteneat *C L*   perdere *M*] perdire *C L*

or later lose, by our coldness and weakness, everything, both the things of God and those others, which already we have mostly lost.

Let us do all, therefore, as Paul divinely teaches us, for the glory of God; let us be without offense to Jew and to Gentile and to the Church of God. Imitating Paul, let us please God through all things, seeking what is profitable, not to us, but to many, so that the many may be saved [I Cor. x. 31–33]. Let us be zealous for the better gifts, for that more excellent way which is concord and charity [XII. 31]. For charity doubtless does not seek her own [XIII. 5]; indeed, rather loses her own to save herself, and counts as gain that loss by which she may preserve herself intact; and rather than be at odds with her brother and in lawsuit with him, charity freely yields to him everything.

If a man be held foolish for this, he may console himself that he has wisdom in God, of the sort that to the world is folly; and let him account it glorious to be called foolish for the sake of Christ's charity; and for this he should rather lose his life, let alone worldly goods, than allow it to be overthrown.

In a lawsuit, however, it cannot but be overthrown. And therefore Paul wishes that there be no lawsuits at all in the Church, no matter who the judge, but that each man rather suffer deceit and injustice in his material goods and even in his body itself. Otherwise, Jesus would never have given the precept: "If someone strike you on the cheek, turn the other to him" [Matt. v. 39]; nor would Paul have forbidden the brethren, in the Letter to the Romans, to use self-defense, and ordered them to submit even to pagans [Rom. XII. 19; XIII. 1, 5]. How much more, then, should this be the practice with brothers, to preserve love and charity?

Let us plainly conclude, therefore, that it is not the part of Christians to dispute at law before any judge about any matter, whether of property or of person, or to seek their own rights, since for a Christian man there can be no greater justice, nothing more equitable, than to suffer and put up with wrongs. In this patience we shall possess our souls [Luke XXI. 19]. But if we should wish to recognize something in this world as our own, and demand it, and strive for it in court of law, and waste our time in lawsuits—with which the sincerity of charity cannot abide—can anyone fail to see that then we are acting unworthily and unjustly, and in our impatience losing our souls? For this reason Paul says, "Indeed, it is altogether a defect in you that you have lawsuits among yourselves" [I Cor. VI. 7], and affirms that one cannot go to law[8] in any manner without fault, since by lawsuits is blackened, so to speak, the pure brightness of charity. We must see to it that charity be kept spotless and unstained, and with all patience turn our activities to this end, taking it as the altogether unfailing standard by which all things are to be directed.

Now if someone were to say that Paul allows lawsuits, permitting the Corinthians to contend before their own judges, but not pagans, and to seek what

intelligat Pauli |93r| mentem et voluntatem fuisse, in ecclesia ut omnes essent sicuti ille esset; atque quemadmodum post virginitatem concessit unius mulieris co⟨n⟩cubitum, que nuptie sunt, illis qui sine carne omnino vivere nequiverint; et post continentiam° et abstinentiam ab omni munere concessit ut ministratores spiritualium temporalia acciperent°, saltem quatenus ad tenuem victum sufficeret°, iis scilicet qui manubus non voluerint laborare; ita ex defectu gratie nequiuntibus optime facere ut debent, permisit indulgentius ut ad tempus aliquousque starent ab optimo, si urget necessitas, atque si non possint non male facere, faciant tamen malum quam minime possunt.

Et qui viderat Corinthios, ex avaricia quam statim eradicare non poterat, omnino contendere velle et ita exorbitantes ut paganos sibi iudices quererent, invitus, sed tamen ut vitetur maius malum, modo nolint illi non litigare, litigent tunc et expectent° iudicium a suis et equitatem, potius quam ab iniquis. Qui sui debent esse tales ut vilissimus eorum quisque in temporalibus facile agnoscat ubi sit equitas, ut debeat pudere Corinthios excurrere ad externos paganos pro equitate, quasi apud ipsos non esset quispiam qui quid sit equum poterat cognoscere et recta sententia eorum lites derimere, qui sunt electi in eam prestantiam et sapientiam ut etiam mundum et angelos iudicent, in quibus minimus quisque pro suo dono gracie sit maior maximo paganorum et verius arbiter equitatis.

Summa ergo voluntatis Pauli est ut potius nullo modo contendat quisquam quam contendat°. Quod si nolit non contendere, tum id agat magis apud suos quam externos, ut morbus et malum quod curari *non* potest magis lateat in suis quam |93v| prodatur foras, ne agnita ab externis infirmitate eorum, scandalizetur ecclesia.

Consideratus Paulus solet paterne indulgere aliquousque eis et morem gerere quos videt sue meliori voluntati obsequi non posse, quosque sperat si mollius tractentur° aliquando obsecuturos et ad id quod est perfectius profecturos.

Omnia mihi licent: sed non omnia expediunt. Cor. vi.

Putarunt Corinthii se potuisse sua repetere in iudicio, se sine peccato conviviis

---

continentiam *M*] contenentiam *C L*   acciperent *M*] acceperent *C L*   sufficeret *M*] sufficiret *C L*   expectent *Ed.*] expectant *C M L*   contendat *L*] contendant *C M* tractentur *Ed.*] trectentur *C M L*

is theirs if they wish, let him listen and understand at last what was the mind and will of Paul. This was that in the Church all should be as he was [VII. 7]. But just as he conceded as next best to virginity, for those who could not live altogether without the flesh, relations with one woman (marriage); and that as next best to self-maintenance and the refusing of all gifts he permitted ministers of spiritual things—those, that is, who would not labor with their hands—to accept temporal things, at least to the extent of the bare necessities of life; so, in the same way, to those who were unable from a deficiency of grace to follow the very best course, as they ought, he gave permission with more indulgence to remain for a time some little distance from the best, if this was necessary. He wished that if they could not avoid wrong, they should yet do as little wrong as possible.[9]

He had seen that the Corinthians had their hearts set on their disputes, because of a covetousness which he could not all at once root out, and that they were so far from their calling as to seek out pagans to be their judges. Against his will, then, but still to prevent the greater evil, he let them have their lawsuits (only if they would not abandon them), and told them to look for decisions and equity from their own members, rather than from the unjust.[10] Their own people ought to be such that the least esteemed of them should easily in temporal matters recognize where the right lay; the Corinthians ought, then, to be ashamed to go running abroad to pagan outsiders for equity, as though there were not a soul among themselves who could tell what was just and resolve their disputes with true judgment [VI. 4–6]. They were, after all, chosen out for such a degree of excellence and wisdom that they would judge, indeed, the world and the angels [VI. 2,3]:[11] the least among them would be, because of his individual gift of grace, greater than the greatest of pagans, and more truly a judge of equity.

This, then, is in brief the will of Paul, that a man should under no circumstances decide to enter into a dispute. But if he will not observe this, then let him dispute before his own people rather than pagans, so that the disease and evil which cannot be cured may remain hidden among his own rather than be displayed abroad. Otherwise, their weakness will be known by outsiders, and the Church will take scandal.

In his thoughtfulness, Paul has the habit of making limited fatherly concessions and of observing customs with those whom he sees to be unable to follow out his better wish for them, when there is hope that if they are treated more gently they will at last achieve that better wish and advance to what is more perfect.

"I am free to do what I will; yes, but not everything is advantageous."
[I] Cor. VI. 12[12]

The Corinthians thought they could go to law to claim what was theirs, that

idolatrarum interesse, se audacia conscientie fretos sine formidine etiam idolatita propalam degustare. Sed parum considerati non viderunt quid exposcit° bonus ecclesie status, nec didicerunt id licere solum quod expedire et Rei Publice utile esse possit, nec meminerunt universam Christi ecclesiam unum esse quasi corpus, in quo quisque non sibi sed corpori, non ad suam utilitatem sed ad emolimentum totius comunionis (et hoc longo prospectu in posterum, quid ex presentibus actibus evenire poterit) vivere debet et agere omnia, cogitareque semper ex comuni utilitate suum privatum comodum pendere. Quod quidem cuiusque eo diminutius° esse necesse est, quo publice utilitatis ratio quovisquumque modo diminuatur, que maxime et principalissime in unitate, concordia, charitate, pace, et gaudio in Spiritu Sancto consistit; quam ut integram et solidam conserves in societate, abiice quicquid habes in externis bonis, et a corporis voluptate quantaquumque, maxima minimave, abstine.

Immo in hoc quoque detrementum patere vel maximum, et dominico iussu erue tibi oculum potius quam is te scandalizet; detrimentum, inquam, patere vel maximum in te ipso (etiam si sis in christiano corpore excellentius |94r| membrum aliquod et quasi oculus) prius quam corpus Christi et Christus ipse, qui ex se et sua ecclesia constat, tui unius lucro detrimentum patiatur. Quod lucrum tibi, si longius abs te et amplius circumspicias, nullum esse potest, si inde damnum vel minimum aliquando in ecclesia exoriatur, ex cuius malo in te simul malum, si eius sis membrum, proficisci necesse est°.

Quocirca non modo si ames Rem Publicam et unitatem pulchritudinemque christiane societatis, quam in primis et solam amare debes, sed etiam si te ipsum tuumque comodum ames (quo nihil debes facere minus si verus vis esse Christianus), nil unquam habe antiquius ipso Christo, in quo tamquam membrum vivis, non tua quidem virtute se⟨d⟩ illius.

Quapropter non quere que tua sunt, sed que Iesu Christi, nec utere quaque re nisi ad emolumentum Christi, nec te abutere, quum non ipse iam est tuus, sed Christi, cuius es membrum, in cuius corpus es emptus precio magno, precio sacrosancti sanguinis illius, ut illi inservias soli, ex illo pendeas, ex illo agas omnia, non tibi, inquam, sed illi.

Quod si improbe, avare, libediose, ex te ipso et tibi aliquid attemptaveris, solvis tum te ipse et flagisiose et impie a Christo, violasque corpus Christi, et ipsemet

---

exposcit M] espossit C L]   didicerunt M] dedicerunt C L   diminutius Ed.]
dimunitius C L] divinitus M   est C] es M L

without sin they could take part in the banquets of idolaters, that without fear, relying on the boldness of their consciences, they could openly relish things offered to idols. They were too thoughtless, and were not aware of the demands made by the Church's welfare. They had not learned that nothing is *allowed*, unless it can be of profit and advantage to the commonweal. They did not remember that the whole Church of Christ is, as it were, a body, within which each should live and do all things, not for himself, but for the whole body; not for his own advantage, but for the benefit of the entire communion, and with a far-reaching regard to what may result in the future from present acts. Each must be constantly aware that his own personal advantage hangs on the common good, because the former must needs be lessened to the extent that the degree of common benefit is decreased, however this come about. For this consists chiefly and foremost in unity, concord, charity, peace, and joy in the Holy Spirit. To preserve it unblemished and firm in the community, cast off whatever material goods you have, and keep yourself from bodily pleasures, however great they be, the least as well as the greatest.

More, suffer in your body even the greatest harm, and follow the Lord's command to pluck out your eye rather than let it cause you to stumble [Matt. v. 29]. Suffer, I say, in yourself even the greatest loss—even if you be one of the more excellent members in the Christian body, an eye, for instance—rather than let the body of Christ and Christ himself, who consists of himself and his Church, suffer harm for the sake of your sole advantage. Because if you looked away from yourself with deeper and broader vision, nothing can really be an advantage if from it should arise even the least loss to the Church, since from ill done to her must necessarily proceed simultaneous harm to you, if you are a member of her.

Never place any consideration, then, ahead of Christ, in whom you live as a member, not by your own strength, but by his. This must be your resolve, not only if you love the commonweal and the unity and beauty of the Christian society—which ought to be your first and only love—but even if you love yourself and your own advantage; and if you want to be a true Christian, there is nothing you ought less to do than this.

Do not, then, seek what is yours, but what is Jesus Christ's. Use nothing except for the advantage of Christ. And do not misuse yourself, since that "self" is no longer yours, but Christ's. You are his member; you have been bought at a great price for the body of Christ, at the price of his most sacred and holy blood, to serve him alone, to depend on him, to do all things by him; not for yourself,[13] I say, but for him.

If, however, you should attempt something of yourself and for yourself, in wickedness, greed, or lust, then you cut yourself off criminally and impiously from Christ, you violate the body of Christ, and you destroy yourself in wretch-

tu te, tui ignarus, misere disperdis. Vince ergo avariciam amore Dei et contemtu terrenorum. Vince gulam celestis pabuli aviditate. Ut enim ait: *Esca ventri et venter escis: Deus et hunc et hanc destruet.* Cohibe et extingue libedinem desidereo voluptatis illius, quam defundet aliquando in suos Christus inextinguibilem. Cave adulteres, cave meritricere, cave abutaris corpore tuo, non tuo quidem membro iam, sed Christi, ne fedans |94v| corpus tuum, Christi corpus et Spiritus Sancti templum violes, accipiasque que sunt Christi ad sanctitatem sacrilege, et des eadem meritrici ad feditatem, deturpans et dehonestans corpus tuum, immo corpus Christi in tuo, quum in illo coitu evadit unum et meretricium cum corpore meritricis, sicut antiquum illud testimonium tradit, *Erunt duo in carne una.*

An nescitis (inquid Paulus) quoniam qui adheret meritrici unum corpus efficitur? Tollens ergo membra Christi, facies membra meritricis? Et quod debet inservire Christo et Spiritui, pulcre ac honorifice in immortalitatem, subiicies turpiter meritricationi in eternam damnationem? Nonne quo una pars hominis tendit, illuc totus homo trahitur? Si hec inferior corporea inhere⟨n⟩s meritrici meritricia evadit, nonne necessario simul rapitur et divellitur anima a Deo? Atque etiam si hec superior pars animalis tota sursum adhereat Deo, evadatque cum illo unus spiritus, nonne secum attollit corpus in spiritualitatem?

Huc ergo illucve, sursum deorsumve, quoquumque tenderis, eiusmodi totus evadis cuiusmodi pars est illa altera cuius tractum consequeris; animaque corporea, deducta a corpore: corpus animale, attractum° ab anima; hec quoque divina, inherens Deo: illud meritricium, adherens meritrici, efficitur.

Cuius pecati huius et veneree feditatis origo est ex ultimo et infimo corpore, ex eoque sensu qui omnium est vilissimus et crassissimus et (ut ita dicam) maxime corporalis. Is quidem tactus est, *Tactus.* in quo vis corporis et materie maxime viget, sensusque tangendi et appetitus et denique actus ille, ac precipue venereus, in quo tamquam communi cursu in punctum, universalique iudicio et |95r| sensu, totum simul corpus videtur contingere, complerique appetitu communiter°.

Unde merito illius libidinis et fede titillationis sensus potest maxime vocari opus in corpore et maxime corporale. In quo spiritalis partis vis quam minime potes⟨t⟩. Quod si quicquam preterea in peccatis que omnia quamquam commertium habea⟨n⟩t cum corpore, cum hoc uno tamen si compararis, quodamodo

---

attractum *L*] attracta *C M*   communiter *M*] communitur *C L*

edness, lacking true self-knowledge. By love for God, then, and disdain of earthly things, conquer your greed. By longing for heavenly food, overcome gluttony. For as Paul says, "Food is meant for the belly, and the belly for food:
God will destroy both the one and the other" [I Cor. vi. 13]. Restrain and ex-
tinguish lust by the desire of that inextinguishable delight which Christ will
at last infuse into his own. Beware of adultery; beware of fornication; beware
of misusing your own body, which is no longer your own, but a member of
Christ. For in dishonoring your own body, you violate the body of Christ and
the Temple of the Holy Spirit; you sacrilegiously take what is for holiness and
belongs to Christ, to give it to a harlot for shameful dishonoring, besmirching
and debasing your own body—indeed, Christ's body in yours—since in that union
it is made all one and a harlot with the body of the harlot, as that ancient testimony
teaches: "They shall be two in one flesh" [Matt. xix. 5].

"Do you not know" (says Paul) "that the man who unites himself to a harlot
becomes one body with her? Will you take, then, the members of Christ, and
make them a harlot's members" [I Cor. vi. 15, 16]? Will you shamefully subject to a harlot for everlasting damnation that which should serve Christ and
the Spirit in beauty and honor for life unending? Is not the whole man drawn
in the direction to which one part of him inclines? If then this lower and bodily
part becomes harlotish by being joined to a harlot, must not the soul also at
the same time be torn away and divorced from God? And if, too, this higher,
spiritual part should cling entirely upward to God, and be made one spirit with
Him, will it not raise up with it the body into a spiritual state?[14]

One way, then, or the other, upward or downward, whichever direction you
have taken, you become entirely of that nature which belongs to the part of
yourself whose inclination you follow. The soul becomes like the body, if led
by the body; the body like the soul, if drawn by the soul. The soul, moreover,
is made Godlike, if it clings to God; the body is made harlotish, if it clings to
a harlot.

The origin of this sin, this shame of lust, is in the last and lowest part of
the body, that sense which is of all the basest and the least
refined,[15] and, as it were, the most bodily. For this is the   *Touch.*
touch, in which the power of the body and of matter rules most strongly: the
sense and desire and finally the act of touching—especially the carnal act, in which
as though by a common rushing to one point the whole body at once, with
the total involvement of its powers of discernment and of sense, seems to be
in contact and to be completely filled with desire everywhere.

Rightly then can the sensation of this lustful pleasure and shameful excite-
ment be called especially "a work in the body" and peculiarly corporeal, for in
it the power of the spiritual part is of least avail. And if you compare this one
sin with all other kinds, you will realize that although these have some connec-

extra corpus ea et non a corpore fieri putabis. Sunt enim que neque ita intimum corpus, quod ultimum est hominis et longius a spiritu, neque ita simul totum occupant. Sed aliquatenus remotius se tenent, et in his rationis vis plus valet, animeque assensus maior est. In appetitu veneris, velis nolisve nonnunquam regnat corpus, illudque peccatum in ultimo corpore se iactitat, in illoque est et maxime oritur et impetuosius completur, ac (ut sic dicam) corporalius.

Hinc (ut mihi videtur) scripsit Paulus omne aliud peccatum extra corpus esse: qui fornicatur, in suum corpus peccare. Siquidem hoc peccatum ut est maxime corporis, ita est ipsius corporis maxima aversio ab anima, et eiusdem solutio in interitum sempiternum, ut nihil est quod tam imputetur corpori in delictis quam fornicatio, quum hic proprius est eius actus eiusque a continentia solutio et labefactatio. In aliis autem videtur instrumentum magis peccati: hic in meritricatione ipse auctor magis et effector.

Coherciat ergo quisque Deo deditus et in Christum receptus suum corpus, ac anima adherens Deo id sustineat, ne suapte proclivitate delabatur in facinus, et ex se in violationem sui cum labifactatione et dedecore corporis Christi, cumque etiam ipsius anime solutione a Deo ac totius hominis damnatione. Et (ut iubet Paulus) glorificate et portate Christum in corpore vestro, cuius aliquando gloria in totam ecclesiam |95v| redundabit, non solum in admirabile lumen animarum, sed etiam in corporum immortalitatem, quando qui suscitavit Dominum suscitabit per suam virtutem corpora nostra, quandoque mors a vita assorbebitur, ut qui salvi erunt, et animis et corporibus cum Christo et in Christo felicitate perfruentur sempiterna.

tion with the body, still they are somehow outside the body and are not performed by it; for it is their nature to absorb the body, the lowest part of a man
and the farthest from the spirit, neither so immediately nor so completely and
all at once. They are to some extent removed from it, and the power of reason
is stronger in them and the consent of the soul greater. But in the appetite of
lust, whether you will or no, the body frequently rules; and this sin vaunts itself
in the deepest reaches of the body, has its being there, there finds chiefly its origin,
and is there more unrestrainedly fulfilled and in a more bodily fashion, if I may
so put it.

For this reason, it seems to me, Paul wrote that every other sin is outside
the body, while the fornicator sins against his own body [vi. 18]. And just as
this sin most belongs to the body, at the same time it is the greatest turning
away from the soul, and a dissolving of the body into everlasting death. For
no sin, then, is the body held so much responsible as for fornication, since this
is its own act, its own dissolution and fall from continence. In other sins it seems
rather the instrument: in fornication it is itself rather the author and the performer.

Let, then, whoever has been dedicated to God and taken into Christ restrain
his own body. Let his soul, by clinging to God, strengthen the body, lest by
its natural inclination[16] it slip into vice, slip of its own accord into self–viola-
tion, with a falling away, and a dishonoring of the body of Christ, a separation
of the soul itself from God, and the damnation of the whole man. As Paul commands you, glorify Christ and bear him in your body [vi. 20], and the glory
of Christ will at last be spread abroad through the whole Church, not only as
a wonderful illumination of souls, but for the immortality also of bodies, when
He who raised up the Lord will by His power raise up our bodies also [vi. 14],
and when death will be swallowed up by life, so that those who are to be saved
will enjoy to the full with Christ and in Christ an everlasting happiness both
of the soul and of the body.[17]

Caput septimum°

De quibus autem. . . . Cap. VII.

Bonus et misericors Deus, qui voluit suam voluntatem legemque ostendi hominibus oportuno tempore ad salutem eorum et eamdem predicari per suum ipsius Verbum, hominem factum, qui *Iesus Christus.* ipse est Iesus Christus. Qui os, sapientia, Verbum, et virtus est Dei, et hominum doctrina et salus.

Ille bonus et pius Deus in Christo tunc quesivit hominum ad se reconciliationem°, quando magna erat in terris personarum varietas: Iudei, gentes, domini, servi, celebes, coniugati, *Iudei, Gentes, Domini,* vidui; que persone, quamquam fere semper in humano *Servi, Celebes,* genere fuerint, tamen nunc huius varietatis menti- *Coni⟨u⟩gati, Vidue.* onem facio, ut ostendam in illo mirabili adventu Dei ad homines quo pacto se habuit Deus unus ad multiplicem in hominibus personam; quid etiam Paulus tradidit Spiritu Dei de eiisdem personis, quomodo scilicet in sua queque vocatione ad Deum se gerant tum erga ipsum Deum, tum erga homines.

In illa admirabili illustratione mundi per natum Christum in hominibus, quando sub eius gratiosis° et salutaribus radiis fuerint in terreno humano genere tum Iudei tumque gentes, et in hiis utrisque tum domini tum servi, et in eiisdem ambobus tum celebes, tum coniugati, tum vidui; et preterea coniugatorum in quibus tum ambo coniuges, tum alterutra coniugii |96r| pars sola cessit in lucem; quando, inquam, Christus ad imitationem sui, ad fidem Deo, ad amorem boni, emissa quadam ex se spiritali vertute, primum in Iudeis, sed multo copiosius postea per suos apostolos in gentibus, hanc personarum varietatem accersivit, ille unus multos; ille simplex multiplices; ille sui similis varios et inter se dissimiles,

---

Caput septimum *Ed.*] Capd vii *C with* d *crossed, om. M*   reconciliationem *M*] reconsiliationem *C L*   gratiosis *L*] gratioses *C*] graciosis *M*

Chapter VII

"Concerning those matters. . . ." Ch. VII[1]

Good and merciful is God, who wished His will and His law to be shown to men in the fullness of time for their salvation, and to be preached through His own Word become man. This is Jesus Christ, who is the mouth and the wisdom, the Word and the power of God, the doctrine and salvation of men.

Jesus Christ.

The good and kindly God sought in Christ a reconciliation of men to Himself at a time when there was a great variety of persons on earth: Jews, Gentiles, lords, slaves, the unmarried, the married, the widowed. And although these kinds of persons have almost always existed in

Jews, Gentiles, Lords, Slaves, the Unmarried, the Married, the Widowed.

the human race, still I mention them now to show how, in that wondrous coming of God to men, the One God acted toward the diversity of persons[2] among men, and to show also what Paul taught by the Spirit of God concerning these persons: how, that is, each in his being called to God was to behave himself both toward God and toward men.

In that marvellous enlightening of the world through the birth of Christ among men, there were, then, in the human race under the grace-filled and saving rays of Christ, both Jews and Gentiles. And among both of these groups there were both lords and slaves; and among both these latter were the unwed, the married, and the widowed. Moreover, among the married there were instances in which both parties, others in which only one came within the light.[3] And when Christ summoned this variety of persons to imitation of himself, to faith in God, and to love of the good, by sending forth from himself a certain spiritual power first among the Jews and afterwards, through his Apostles, much more widely among the Gentiles—Christ being one and those summoned many; Christ simple, they diverse; Christ consistent with himself, and they varying and dissimilar among themselves—there was very great and prolonged doubt[4] as to what each

plurimum et diu erat dubitatum quidnam in nova professione quisque cum sua veteri qualitate et statu faceret: abdicaret eamne an teneret; et si teneret, faceret° ex ea sicuti antea fecerit quam Christi observantiam protestatus est.

Ut, exempli gratia, gentes circumciderenturne, et Iudei an ad statum gentium se conferrent? Virgines nubantne? Et si nupserint, exactum debitum reddant? Preterea, quos gratia comprehendit ambos coniugatos, iure nove religionis divortio secedantne? Et si coniugati manserint, exercendusne esset aliquando corporum coitus? Item servi, num occasione nove religionis se venditent in libertatem? Et quorum coniugatorum alterutra pars fidelis fuerit, utrum licuit commanere cum altero coniuge infideli, an eum relinquere?

De hiis quidem apud gentes erant ancipites cogitationes et altercationes° ambigue, maxime apud Corinthios, ac in utramque partem varie sententie. Quapropter epistola magnum Paulum consuluerunt, ut ille lites sua sapientia dirimeret, sententiamque ferret quid sit faciendum.

Hinc homo ille, unus omnium divinissimus et consideratissimus, in quo erat Spiritus Dei et sensus Christi, in quo Christus ipse locutus est, qui habuit potestatem non ad destructionem ecclesie sed ad constructionem, is tantus Paulus sapienter et divinitus respondet Corinthiis; et sic respondet, ut misericordem Dei voluntatem vide⟨a⟩tur exprimere, et agnoscere prudenter |96v| hominum infirmitatem, et vehementer cupere in hominibus perfectionem, et dolere homines omnes tam perfectos esse non posse uti christiana exposcit religio, cuius auctor et exemplar ideaque fuit Christus, in quo divina vivendi ratio fuit discripta ac proposita hominibus tum spectanda tum imitanda; qui fuit continens se a contagione mundi, a corporis libidine; qui venit ut prodesset hominibus; qui una cum hominibus vixit, ut multos sibi similes faceret; qui fuit misericors; qui reiecit neminem; qui voluit omnes homines salvos fieri.

Paulus igitur, spectans ad Christum ex Christoque sentiens et loquens, infirmis hominibus sic dat consilium, ut videatur velle in illis bonum quam maxime possit, et necessarium malum quam minime. Si enim infirmitas est res mala, non potuit quin infirmis infirmum quoddam et aliquid mali concedat, quod ipsum quia congruit infirmo non est malum quidem; tamen id in se, et infirmitas illa etiam cui accomodatur, res mala est. Ille quoque qui infirmus est in malis est, nec potest aliquid expetere, ratione saltem illius infirmitatis, nisi malum. Quid enim suapta natura malum exposcit nisi malum? Quod hoc tamen bene conceditur, ne negato minori malo maius° malum sequatur.

---

faceret M L] facereret C   altercationes L] artercationes C] altricationes M   maius
Unk. Rev. L] magis C M

should do with his former quality and condition: whether to resign it or hold to it; and if he held to it, whether to act in acccordance with it as he had done before he professed the observance of Christ.[5]

Should the Gentiles, for instance, be circumcised?[6] Or should the Jews bring themselves to the condition of the Gentiles? Should virgins marry? And if they married, should they fulfil the marital obligation [I Cor. vii. 3]? Further, when both spouses were embraced by grace, were they to separate or not in divorce, by the law of their new religion? And if they remained wed, were they ever to practice intercourse? Slaves, again—taking advantage of the new religion, were they to promote themselves to freedom? And when one party to a marriage was a believer, was he allowed to remain with the other, the unbelieving spouse, or was the believer to depart?

About these matters there were divided thoughts and unresolved disputes among the Gentiles, especially among the Corinthians, and decisions were made variously, one way or the other. So by letter they consulted the great Paul [vii. 1], that he might decide their disputes by his wisdom and pass judgment as to what they should do.

Hence that man,[7] of all men the most Godlike and the most kindly—in him was the Spirit of God and the mind of Christ; in him Christ himself spoke; he had authority, not for the destruction, but for the edification of the Church [II Cor. xiii. 10]—this Paul, in all his greatness, answers the Corinthians in wise and Godlike fashion, and in such a way as to seem at one and the same time to convey the mercy of God's will, and prudently to recognize the weakness of men, and eagerly to desire perfection among men, and to grieve that all men cannot be as perfect as the Christian religion demands, whose founder and ex- emplar and idea was Christ. For in Christ was portrayed and set forth to men the divine pattern[8] of living, for them to see and imitate. And he kept himself unspotted from the world [James i. 27] and from the lust of the body; he came to do good to men; he lived with men, that he might make many like himself; he was merciful; he rejected no one; he wished all men to be saved [I Tim. ii. 4].

Paul, then, with his eyes on Christ and his mind and his words drawn from Christ, gives his advice to men who are weak in such a way that he is seen to wish for them the greatest good that can be and the least possible amount of unavoidable evil. For if weakness is a bad thing, he could not but concede to the weak something weak, and therefore something evil, but something which at the same time is an evil not because adapted to weakness, but in itself; and the weakness also to which it is adapted is a bad thing. Moreover, he who is weak is in the midst of evils, and can seek for nothing, at least by virtue of that weakness, unless it be evil. For what else can evil ask for of its own nature, except evil? Notwithstanding, it is well that allowance be made, lest from the denying of a lesser evil there should follow a greater.

Itaque bonus Paulus, volens optima, exhorrens pessima, quos videt trahi non posse ad optimum iubet sistant citra pessimum, ut qui non valent esse in primis stent saltem in secundis, et in aliquo potius sint loco gratie quam in nullo.

Sed antequam videamus quid Corinthiis a Paulo respondetur, dicamus primum quid est preceptum, quid consilium, quid denique indulgentia. |97r|

Ante omnia cognoscendum est in rebus, et in expetendis ab hominibus, et in hominis vita, alia bona, alia mala esse; Deum et Christum et Paulum velle, idem etiam omnes homines debere cupere, ut quam maxime possint sequantur meliora, deteriora quam maxime possint fugiant. Non enim est sane mentis qui sponte minus bonum eligit, si maiori bono° potiri potest.

Quid autem hominibus bonum malumve sit, antequam Christus docuit, universo mundo fuit incognitum. Is primus faciem et vultum boni ostendit, non tam ver-bis quam re ipsa, non foris sed in se ipso, in sua ipsius vita in qua bona et vera vivendi ratio describebatur°. Itaque Christus est in hoc genere primum et metrum et mensura omnium aliorum. Is itaque° id exemplum est veritatis ad quod omnes qui illum sectantur contendere debent, cui quanto propius accedis, eo perfectior evades. Fuit enim Christus ipsa humane vite perfectio, qui venit ut perfectionem doceret utque homines ad perfectionem traheret. Quod si susceperis° Christi pro-fessionem, et ad formam illius vite non contenderis, frustra tum est tua pro-fessio. *Quid vocatis me, Domine, Domine* (inquit *apud Lucam) et non facitis que dico*? Quod autem dixit, fecit. Nec fuit in illo aliud dicere, aliud facere.

Quocirca plane constat omnes qui Christiani volunt esse eniti oportere, ut Christum quam maxime possunt referant, nec debere consistere sponte aliquo in loco donec illum adepti sunt. Necessitate autem et infirmitate si hereas in ascensu ad Christum et sistas aliquo loco humiliori, modo hoc invitus facias et doles te non posse altius, et velis altius si possis, ac implores dies noctesque auxilium ut cum Christo sis, hoc animo profecto si heres humilius° in aliqua huius montis parte, tibi non potenti altius ascendere ad Christum, et volenti si posses, datur venia. Atque istud studium tuum ac conatus proficiscendi quoad possis, cum con-tinuo desiderio |97v| pergendi altius, etiam si altius non perrexeris, satis est, etsi non ad summum, tamen ad aliquem salutis gradum et felicitatis.

Verum si sub professione christiani nominis et vite, que iter et continua ascensio° ad Christum est ac renovatio spiritus de die in diem, ut tandem cum ipso Christo et pleno Spiritu Sancto simus, si in hoc itinere° nostra sponte et voluntate eligamus aliquo loco consistere, non desiderantes nec curantes altius progredi, sed, inquam,

---

maiori bono *Unk. Rev. L*] magis bonum *C M*   describebatur *M*] discribibatur *C L*
Is itaque *written above* Id *prob. not by C*] om. *M*   susceperis *M*] susciperis *C L*   humi-
lius *C*] humilimus *M*] humilis *L*   ascensio *M*] assensio *C L*   itinere *M*] itenere *C L*

The good Paul, then, wishing the best and abhorring the worst, orders those whom he sees incapable of being drawn to the best to stop short this side of the worst, so that those who cannot be in the first rank may at least stand in the second, and may be in some place of grace rather than in none at all.

However, before we look at Paul's answers to the Corinthians, first let us define *precept*, *counsel*, and, finally, *indulgence*.[9]

The most important reality to recognize is that in things, and in man's desires and demands, and in man's life, some things are good and some bad. God and Christ and Paul wish — and indeed all men ought to have the same desire — that as much as possible men follow the better, and as much as possible flee the worse. For he cannot be of sound mind who deliberately chooses the lesser good, if he can gain a greater.

Now before the teaching of Christ, the whole world was ignorant as to what was good or evil to men. He was the first to set forth the features and countenance of the good.[10] And this he did not so much in words as in the reality, in himself rather than extrinsically, in his own life, in which the good and true manner of living was portrayed. Christ is, therefore, the first in this kind of being, and the measure, and the standard.[11] He is, consequently, that exemplar of the truth toward which all his followers ought to strive; and the closer you come to him, the more you will become perfect. For Christ, who came to teach perfection and draw men to it, was the perfection itself of human life. If then you take upon yourself the profession of Christ, and do not strive for the form of his life,[12] your profession is in vain. "How is it" (he says in Luke) "that you call me Lord, Lord, and do not do what I say?" [Luke vi. 46]. What he said, he himself did; and it was not his way to say one thing and do another.

Most clearly, therefore, all who wish to be Christians must labor to reproduce Christ as much as they can. They should not willingly stop at any point until they have reached him. If unavoidably, however, you stop because of weakness in the ascent to Christ and stay in some lower rank, provided this be against your will and you grieve that you cannot mount higher, and provided you wish to mount higher if you could and by day and night entreat that you may be with Christ, surely if thus you stop lower on some part of the mountain, unable to climb higher to Christ and wishing to do so if you could, you will be granted mercy. And your zeal and your efforts to advance as far as you can, together with your unfailing desire to push higher (even though you fail to do so) will be enough, if not for the highest, still for some degree of salvation and happiness.

But if under the profession of the Christian name and life, which is a journey, and a continual ascent to Christ, and a renewing of the spirit from day to day, to the end that we may at last be with Christ himself and the fullness of the Holy Spirit; if in this journey we decide by our own deliberate choice to halt somewhere, neither desiring nor making any effort to advance higher, but, as

consistere aliquo loco inferiori volentes et libentes, profecto ut illi quiquam qui aliquo itinerantur, si medio in cursu sistant, non perveniunt ad finem, ita hii qui nec re nec voluntate attingunt Christum, sed sponte et ex voto in gradu aliquo longe ab eo distante quiescunt, nunquam sunt sane ad Christum perventuri. Quo oportet pervenias, antequam ad gloriam venias. Nam per iusticiam que fuit in Christo est via ad gloriam. Ideo dixit se fuisse viam et veritatem. Verum ubi est ardens voluntas perficiendi itineris, etiam si hic non perfeceris, tamen voluntas ea que hic attigit Christum necessario ex Christo post hanc vitam pendebit.

Quisque ergo oportet contendat et certet ac in infirmitate nitatur pro viribus, nec sponte quiescat nisi in summo. Nam hoc est quasi nolle summum, et damnabile. Quod qui summum bonum nolit videtur nihil habere, et qui in bonis aliquid habet, velit omnia.

Verum omnes homines non possunt quantum velint. Debent tamen velle posse et assidue petere ut possint quatenus desiderant, ne distare a Christo magis voluntate quam necessitate videantur. Voluntaria enim a Christo distantia plane damnabilis est, necessaria vero ex infirmitate et invita venialis. Miseretur enim Deus infirmitatis ad deterius |98r| ubi videt promptam voluntatem ad melius. Item proculdubio damnat potentiam ad melius ubi videt perversam ad deterius voluntatem.

Quapropter quod potes facito. Velis posse optima, ut faciens optima sis optimus. Non potes nisi ex Deo. Exigitur° abs te necessario et iure ut velis et facias quatenus possis, ne divina gratia ad posse et dato talento ad multiplicationem abuti videaris. Memento finem itineris quo tendis esse Christum, quem (ut ait Paulus) *si secundum carnem novimus, sed iam non novimus.*

Hoc iter ingredi et pergere incessanter donec ad Christum perveneris consulitur universis. Cui consilio quatenus ad primam eius partem, videlicet ut iter ad Christum ingrediamur, oportet necessario omnes pareant. Alioquin sane salvi non possunt. Ingredi autem ad Christum est illum agnoscere a Deo Patre venisse, et credere Filium Dei incarnatum, et interiisse in ara crucis ut seipso, sacrosancta hostia, et Deum placaret hominibus et homines Deo reconciliaret, ac summatim que spectant ad fidem adhibendam Christo, Dei nuncio et mediatori inter Deum et hominem.

Hec sunt in primo limite et quasi vestibulo salutis, que Christus et Apostoli

---

Exigitur *M L*] Exegitur *C*

I say, willing and accepting our halt in some lower place, surely we shall be just like men journeying somewhere who stop midway and so never reach their goal. In just the same way those who do not reach Christ either in fact or in desire, but deliberately and by choice seek their rest in a rank far distant from him, will never come all the way to Christ. And you must come to him, before you come to glory. For the road to glory is through the justice that was in Christ, and this is why he said he was the way and the truth [John xiv. 6]. But where there is an ardent will to acccomplish the journey, even if you do not accomplish it here, still that will which reaches to Christ here will necessarily be linked to him after this life.

Each must strive, then, and labor and struggle on in his weakness as much as his strength will let him, and not come to rest by choice except at the summit. For to act otherwise would be like not wanting the summit, and would deserve damnation, because we can see that he who does not will the highest good[13] has no good at all. The man who has some part of good must wish all good.

Not all men, however, have the power to match their will. Still, they must wish for that power, and seek unfailingly to be able to do as much as they desire to do, lest they should appear willingly to remain far from Christ rather than unavoidably. For a voluntary separation from Christ is clearly damnable, while one that is inescapable because of weakness, and not willed, is pardonable. For God will have mercy on weakness that leads to ill, where He sees a ready will for the better. So likewise He doubtless damns the power for good where He sees a will perverted to the worse.

Do, therefore, what you can do. And will that you might do the best, so that doing it you might be best. You have no power except of God. And it is required of you by necessity and by law that you will and do to the utmost of your power, or else you will make it clear that you are abusing the divine grace which confers your ability and the talent given you for increase. Keep in mind that the goal of the journey, toward which you are striving, is Christ, "whom" (as Paul says) "even if we used to, we now think of no longer in a human fashion" [II Cor. v. 16].

Now it is counseled to all that they enter upon this way and press on in it unceasingly until they come all the way to Christ. And as to the first part, namely that we enter upon the way to Christ, all must necessarily obey this counsel:[14] otherwise they cannot be saved. To start off toward Christ is to recognize that he came from God the Father, to believe that he is the incarnate Son of God, and that he died upon the altar of the cross to make men pleasing to God and reconcile them to Him, by sacrificing himself as a most holy victim — in short, to believe all that pertains to having faith in Christ, God's messenger and the mediator between God and man.

These are the things on the first threshold and, as it were, in the anteroom

consulerant predicantes, ut universi credant et ad primum ingressum in salutis
domum divertantur, ut deinde pergant.

In hoc recusando nulla est venia, ne impotentie quidem et infirmitati. Nam
sine fide imposibile est placere Deo. Est ergo faciendum omnino ut incipias hoc
iter quod ducit ad celum, credasque in Christum, ac hominibus hoc consulentibus pro tua salute obedias. In hoc nulla potest esse excusatio infirmitatis, quum
id si nolis (ut videtur) infirmitas non est in causa sed malicia. Nam ut |98v| meminit
illud Esaie Paulus ad Romanos, *Prope est verbum in ore tuo et in corde tuo.* Quod
idem Apostolus exponens addit: *Hoc est verbum fidei, quod predicamus. Quia si*
confitearis in ore tuo Dominum Iesum et in corde credideris quod Deus illum suscitavit
a mortuis, saluus eris. Corde enim creditur ad iusticiam, ore autem confessio fit ad salutem.

Et bene inquit *ad iusticiam* et *ad salutem,* ut ostendat illuc tendere fidem, et
inchoamentum esse necessarium quo ad iusticiam salutemque eatur; non tamen
ipsam fidem per se ad iusticiam satis esse, que consistit supra fidem, ex amore
in continua actione bonorum. Quod si credens simul non recte egeris (ut in epistola
ad dispersos Iudeos gravissime disputat divus Iacobus) profecto frustra et vana
est ista tua fides quam profiteris. Nam inquit Apostolus ille: *Quid proderit, fratres*
mei, si fidem quis dicat se habere, opera autem non habeat? Numquid poterit fides salvare
eum? —quasi diceret minime, et addit idem: *Si autem frater aut soror nudi sint, et*
indigeant° victu quotidiano, dicat autem aliquis ex vobis illis, Ite in pace, califacimini
et saturamini, non dederitis autem eis que necessaria sunt corpori, quid proderit? Sic et
fides, si non habet opera, mortua est in semetipsa. Si credis Deum unum, item demones
credunt et contremescunt. Abraam, non solum quia credidit sed quia etiam paratus fuit
re ipsa Isaac filium offerre et immolare, Deo iustificatus est. Unde fit ex operibus iustificatur
homo, non ex fide tantum. Ideo ex hiis concludit Iacobus°, *Sicut corpus sine spiritu*
mortuum est, ita fides sine operibus.

Ioannes autem Apostolus adhuc maius quiddam loquitur in epistola sua prima
canonica, et significat fidem sine operibus non modo vanam, sed etiam plane nullam
esse, |99r| ac eiusmodi homines mendaces esse omnino qui dicunt se nosse Christum
et mandata eius non custodiunt°. *In hoc s⟨c⟩imus* (inquit) *quoniam cognovimus eum,*
i.e., ei credimus, nam nostra cognitio Christi hic est sola credulitas, *si mandata*
eius observamus. Qui dicit se nosse eum et mandata eius non custodit°, mendax est, et
in hoc veritas non est.

---

indigeant *M Vulg.*] indegeant *C L*   Ideo . . . Iacobus *underlined C M*   custodiunt
M L] costodiunt *C; marg.* ca. *C followed by illegible number*   custodit *M L*] costodit *C*

of salvation. Christ and his Apostles counseled them in their preaching for all to believe, so that afterwards they might turn to the first approach into the house of salvation, afterwards to press on therein.

When this [setting out on the way] is rejected, there is no pardon, not even for weakness and lack of strength; for without faith it is impossible to please God [Heb. XI. 6]. So it is an inescapable duty to begin this journey that leads to Heaven, and to believe in Christ, and to obey the men who give you this counsel for your salvation. Weakness cannot be an excuse in this matter, since if you are unwilling, the cause (it is apparent) lies not in weakness but in malice. For, as Paul says to the Romans,[15] recalling the words of Isaiah, "The message is near at hand, in your mouth and in your heart" [Deut. XXX. 14]. And the Apostle adds in explanation, "That is, the message of faith, which we preach. Because if you confess with your mouth the Lord Jesus, and believe in your heart that God has raised him from the dead, you shall be saved. For with the heart a man believes unto justification, and with the mouth he confesses unto salvation" [Rom. X. 8–10].

And he says well "unto justification" and "unto salvation," to show that faith works in that direction, and that it is the necessary beginning for the way to justification and salvation, but not by itself enough for righteousness, which stands above faith in love continually doing good acts.[16] So that if you believe and do not at the same time act well (as the holy James most weightily argues in his letter to the Jews of the Dispersion), that "faith" which you profess is surely vain and empty. For, says that Apostle, "What use will it be, my brothers, if a man claims to have faith, when he has no works? Can faith save him?"—as though he were saying, "Not in the least" and he adds, "But if a brother or a sister goes naked, and is without daily sustenance, and one of you say to them: 'Go in peace, warm yourselves and take your fill,' without providing for their bodily needs, of what use is this? Thus even faith, if it have not works, is dead within itself. If you believe in the one God, so do the demons, and they shrink back in terror. Abraham found justification with God, not only because he believed, but because also he was ready to offer in sacrifice his son Issac. So it happens that a man is made just not by faith alone, but by works." And therefore, James concludes from these facts, "Just as the body without a spirit is dead, so is faith without works" [Jam. II. 14–17, 19, 21, 24, 26].[17]

The Apostle John, moreover, speaks even more strongly in his first Canonical Epistle, to the effect that faith without works is not only empty, but simply no faith at all; and that the sort of men who say they know Christ and do not keep his commandments are altogether liars. "This is how" (he says) "we know whether we have reached knowledge of him"—i.e., believe in him, since here our knowledge of Christ is only believing—"By whether or not we keep his commandments. The man who claims knowledge of him without keeping his commandments is a liar, and there is no truth in him" [I John II. 3, 4].

Vera ergo fides cognitioque Iesu Christi non potest esse ullo modo sine comite bona actione, que est quasi progressio in cepto itinere a fide, qua tandem pervenitur ad finem. Finis autem et felicitas nostra est Christus.
In quo, ut ad Galathas scribit Paulus, nihil valet *nisi fides*   *Gal. v.* [6].
nisi fides que per charitatem operatur.

Credere igitur evangelio bonoque nuncio Christi oportet possis et velis. Operari autem simul velis, quatenus possis. Operari autem, inquam, sicut operatus est Christus, oportet velis omnino quatenus possis. Quod Ioannes Apostolus testatur, dicens, *Qui dicit se in illo manere, debet sicut ille ambulavit et ipse ambulare*, quatenus videlicet possit. Potest autem quisque quatenus ei a potente Deo in Christo datur. *Unusquisque* (inquit Paulus) *proprium donum habet, alius quidem sic, alius quidem sic*. Et sunt a divisione et infirmitate ad unitatem et potentiam varii tractus per unificos Christi radios et prepotentes, qui tamquam a sole veritatis fusi, multiplicatos quasi colligunt et contrahunt ad se in unitatem ut luceant, ut deinde ex luce caleant.

Ut enim potentes, luminosi, et calentes solis radii, profecti in aliquod quod faciant solare, primum agunt ut quod apprehendunt id simplex omnino et sui simile faciant, et (quoad fieri potest) vere sibi unum in se, que rei sua unitas potentia est; tum illustrant; postremo calificaiunt; ut ex unitate lux, ex luce calor enascantur; ita similiter |99v| omnino ab uno, vero, et bono Christo in homines ubi vult proficiscitur quidem quod primum unit infirmos in potentiam, deinde illuminat in veritatem, postremo calefacit in bonitatem, ut ex unitione hominis veritas, ex veritate bonitas sequatur.

Fuit enim et est quoque deitas in Christo nostro, una,
vera, et bona, que admirabili comertio assumpsit hominem   *Christus.*
ex incorrupta virgine coitque cum humana natura ineffabiliter in unitatem, veritatem, et bonitatem divini suppositi, ut homines eo gratioso suffitu deitatis et quasi fermentatione tandem deificati, uni in Deo, veri, et boni fiant; in Deo, inquam, per Iesum Christum, in cuius homine incepit hec divina et salutaris subfumigatio, a quo deinde pergit mirifice sapore deitatis dirivato per massam electam, pergetque continuo sane donec qui salvabuntur omnes oleant deitatem. Que

True faith in Jesus Christ, then, and knowledge of him, can in no wise exist unaccompanied by good conduct, which is an advancing, so to speak, in the journey one has begun by faith, and is the means by which one wins through to the goal. This, our goal and our happiness, is Christ. And nothing, as Paul writes to the Galatians, has value in his eyes "except the faith that finds its expression in love"[18] [Gal. v. 6].

You must, therefore, be able and willing to believe in the Gospel and the good tidings of Christ. But you must also want to do works, as much as you can. You must will, I say, to work to the limits of your resources, just as Christ worked. To this the Apostle John testifies, when he says, "The man who says he abides in him ought to walk in the way he walked" [I John II. 6], as far, that is, as he can. And each one's ability to do so depends on the strong God's gift to him in Christ. "Each one," says Paul, "has his own gift, one of this sort, another of that" [I Cor. VII. 7]. And through the unifying and most powerful rays of Christ there are diverse ways in which men are drawn from division and weakness to unity and power. These rays, pouring from the Sun of truth,[19] gather men from their diversity, as it were, and draw them together to themselves into unity in order to enlighten them, so that next they may draw warmth from the light.

For just as the strong, luminous, and warmth-giving rays of the sun, reaching something and making it sunlit, first act so that what they seize upon they make altogether simple, and self-consistent, and (as much as possible) truly one with itself, since the strength of anything is its oneness; and just as next they enlighten it; and finally they fill it with warmth, so that from oneness[20] comes light, and from light heat; so in exactly the same way, from the one, true, and good Christ there is an emanation into men, wherever he chooses, that first unites them, weak as they are, into strength; then enlightens them into a state of truth; and finally gives them warmth to the point where they are in a state of goodness. From the making of a man one, therefore, follows his truth, and from his truth, his goodness.[21]

For in our Christ was — and is — the Deity, one, true, and good [John XVII. 3, I Cor. VIII. 4-6, Luke XVIII. 19, etc.]. And this Deity by a wondrous intercommunication took to Itself manhood *Christ.* from the untainted Virgin, and joined Itself in a manner beyond words with human nature, into the oneness, truth, and goodness of a Divine *Suppositum,*[22] so that man, at length made Godlike by that grace-filled inhalation and leavening (as it were) of the Godhead, might become one, true, and good in God; in God, I say, through Jesus Christ, in whose manhood began this fragrant purification, divine and saving. From him it spreads wondrously by the diffusion of the Godhead's sweet savor through the mass of chosen men, and will, indeed, continue to spread until all who are to be saved shall have the fragrance of the

cepta in homine Christi, a cuius plenitudine nos homines accepimus, procedit pro voluntate Dei donec compleatur quod predestinatum est ad perfectionem Christi, qui constat ex Deo et hominibus vocatis gratiose.

Hec deitas, cuius plenitudo fuit in Christo corporaliter, tamquam sol bonus, potens, et luculentus, effulsit aliquando in tenebris et tenebricosos terrenosque homines irradiavit, hos quos intime tetigit primum ab omni aliena et contraria sibi ratione solvens et liberans, ac perpurgans in simplicitatem proprie nature et veritatem, multiplici et falsa malicia penitus discussa, in quam homines improbe et misere degenerarunt.

Tum deinde secundo eosdem ad se et suam unitatem restitutos sol ille divinus gratioso suo radio illuminat ut simplices nunc tandem in eo eluceant.

Tertio loco pergit idem radius assidue instans donec simul cum luce ingentem flammam excitavit, ut quod simpliciter lucet in Deo simul simpliciter ardeat.

Hac quidem |100r| simplici potentia, luce, et calore reformatus homo, regignitur hic mirifice vitali Dei Spiritu et renascitur, ut nunc deinceps non hominis sed Dei filius agnoscatur; ut illud Pauli testatur: *Qui aguntur Spiritu Dei, hii sunt filii Dei.*

Simplicitas illa nature, puritas, et unitas, ad quam, omni corruptela depulsa, expurgantur, spes quidem certe est in Deo, iam potens et expectans Deum. Nam ut desperatio quiddam vacillans est *Spes.* ex infirmitate, que infirmitas accidit ex adulteratione et ammixtione contrarii, ita restituta re in simplicitatem et sinceritatem suam, ex potentia tunc est constans et perseverans secum spes, que *Desperatio.* nihil est aliud quam cum desperatione tibi ipsi, certa expectatio omnium ab omnipotente Deo. Quod quidem facit quisque quo est simplicior, et sincerior, et sui similior, atque (ut summatim dicam) quanto est a mundo mundanisque rebus omnibus et a se ipso denique abductior Deoque deditior, ut non amplius in mundo, sed in Deo sit solo, habeatque suum esse et posse totum in Deo, quod revera suum sperare est, et expectare sibi omnia, dependereque a solo Deo.

Hec spes et unitas hominis in se per Deum in Christo est illa spes quam dicit Paulus non confundere, quia ad illam trahimur ab amore et Spiritu Dei, que charitas appellatur; que est diffusa in cordibus nostris per Spiritum Sanctum qui datus est nobis.

Deity. This Godhead, having its start in the manhood of Christ, of whose fulness we men have received [John 1. 16], proceeds according to God's will until there shall be fulfilled that which was foreordained for the perfecting of the Christ that consists of God and of men called by grace.

This Godhead, of which the whole plenitude was embodied in Christ [Col. II. 9], shone at length like a good, powerful, and bright-shining sun amid the darkness [John 1. 5], and cast Its rays upon darksome and earthbound men, first setting loose and freeing those whom It touched deeply from every principle hostile and contrary to Itself, and then fully purifying them into the simplicity and truth of Its own nature, utterly dispelling the fragmentary and untrue state of wickedness into which men have wrongfully and wretchedly degenerated.

Then secondly, that divine Sun by its grace-filled ray enlightens those who have been restored to themselves and to unity, so that being simple they may now at length shine forth in Him.

In the third place, that same ray steadily and unceasingly presses on until together with the light it has kindled a mighty flame, so that what shines in God in simplicity may at the same time be ablaze in simplicity.23

Formed anew in this power of simplicity, this light, and this warmth, man is wondrously regenerated and reborn here by the life-giving Spirit of God, so that henceforth he may be known for a son of God, not of man, as the words of Paul testify: "Those who are led by the Spirit of God are all the sons of God"24 [Rom. VIII. 14].

That simplicity of nature, that purity and unity into which men are purified when every the least corrupting element is driven out, is without doubt hope in God, a hope already strong and *Hope.* looking to God. For just as despair is some sort of wavering thing arising from weakness, weakness that comes from an adulteration and admixture of opposites, so when something has been restored *Despair.* to its simplicity and sincerity, there is then a hope unfailing and perseveringly self-consistent, a hope which is nothing other than a sure expectation of all things from God, with the abandonment of hope in oneself. And this hope a man has to a greater extent, the more he is simple and sincere and self-consistent—the more (in a word) he is withdrawn from the world and from all worldly things, and the more he is removed, finally, from himself and dedicated to God [Heb. VII. 19], in such a way as to be no longer in the world but in God only, and to have his being and his power all in God. This is truly to hope, and to expect for oneself all things, and to be dependent on God alone.

This hope, this oneness of a man within himself through God in Christ, is that hope which Paul says involves no delusion [Rom. v. 5], because we are drawn to it by the Spirit of God and by the love which is called charity. This is diffused in our hearts through the Holy Spirit, whom we have received.

Hanc etiam spem in eadem epistola ad Romanos significat quasi gigni ex hominis probatione et patientia, quam tribulatio operatur. *Caput v.* [5]. Quid autem operatur tribulatio, nisi ut homo hinc extrudatur in se ipsum et Deum? Qui recursus in se ipsum et suam ipsius simplicitatem in Deo, est recursus in fortitudinem et altam patientia⟨m⟩. Patientia enim malorum |100v| fortitudo est. In qua si invictus secum constiterit homo, quod non facit suis viribus, sed expectans subsidium a Deo, tunc patientia illa probat et declarat spem suam in Deo totam fuisse.

Ideo hoc ordine rerum motus, Paulus admonuit Romanos ut in tribulationibus glorientur. Quia tribulatio (inquit) patientiam operatur, patientia probationem, probatio spem. Spe salvi facti sumus. Tribulationibus igitur ex inferiori loco hinc exturbantibus nos, et illinc simul ex superiori loco Spiritu nos sursum trahente — Spiritu illo quem dicit Paulus, *adiuvare infirmitatem nostram et postulare pro nobis gemitibus inenarrabilibus* — ascendimus in nosmetipsos in hanc unitatem nostram, in simplicitate⟨m⟩, in spem, in Deum nostrum, a multiplici et infirmo mundo in unum et potentem Deum. Ex quo nostra condicio divisa, debilis, et caduca unitur in fortem et constantem spem in Deo.

Que spes eum locum tenet in hominibus erga Deum que in Deo ipsius potentia erga homines. Potentia autem est Patris et gignentis°. Tota Trinitas operatur in refectionem et perfectionem nostram: *Pater* (inquit) *meus operatur et ego operor.* Sunt personarum operationes communes, que sunt equipotentes, equisapientes, equibone. Tamen ut habetur Patris proprium posse et gignere°, ita quod regeneratur in nobis, quo possumus esse, que mihi videtur spes, que est ex unitate essentiaque potentia nostra, quum fiimus filii Dei, Deo Patri referenda est.

Ut ergo redeamus ad propositum, deificans Christi radius regignit° nos qui nihil (desperantes) eramus, ut speremus in Deo, speque essemus. Nam desperantes Deo et nobis sperantes, nihil prorsus fuimus. |101r| Nec incepimus esse, donec per gratiam cepimus sperare in Deo, expectareque et esse ex illo: ut geniti in esse, deinde ex eodem sapiamus verum, et ex eodem deinde bonum amemus.

Inicium ergo salutis nostre est spes, qua sumus in Deo et vivimus. Qui quu⟨m⟩ incipimus omnia expectare a Deo, tum simul incipimus sapere ex eodem Deo. Sapientia autem nostra doctrina et fide constat. Nam doceamur oportet et doctis credere: doceamur quidem que sunt Dei divinarumque rerum, quarum cognitio sapientia est. Doceamur, inquam, iis, ut qui cepimus in Deo esse spe, in eodem Deo fide vere vivamus. Omnis enim sapientia instrumentum vite esse debet.

---

gignentis *M*] gingnentis *C L*   gignere *M*] gingnere *C L*   regignit *M*] regingnit *C L*

And in the same letter to the Romans Paul indicates likewise that this hope is born from the proving and the patience that tribulation works in a man [v. 3]. What else does tribulation bring about but that a man be forced from this world into himself and into God? This return into oneself and one's own proper oneness in God is a return to strength and high patience. For patience in ills is strength, and if a man stand firm in it unvanquished within himself—and this he does, not by his own strength, but looking to God for help—then that patience proves and manifests that all his hope has been in God.

Impelled, then, by this interrelationship, Paul exhorted the Romans to glory in tribulations. For tribulation, he says, brings about patience; and patience, the proving of faith; and this proving, hope [v. 3, 4]. By hope we are saved [VIII. 24]. And so with tribulations forcing us out of this lower region, and the Spirit from the higher region at the same time drawing us up from it—that Spirit who, says Paul, "comes to the aid of our weakness and intercedes for us with groans beyond utterance" [VIII. 26]—we mount into ourselves, into this our oneness, into simplicity, into hope, into our God, from the divided and weak world into the one and strong God. In this way, our divided, feeble, and impermanent state is united into a strong and steadfast hope in God.

The role of this hope toward God in men is the same as that of God's power toward men in Him. Now power belongs to the Father and Begetter. The whole Trinity works for our re-making and our perfecting: "My Father" (he says) "works, and I also work" [John v. 17]. There are common operations of the Persons, who are equal in power, wisdom, and goodness. But just as power and generation are considered to belong properly to the Father, so that which is reborn in us, that by which we have the power to be—and this, I believe, is hope—must be attributed to God the Father. It is our power, arising from our oneness and our essence, when we become the sons of God.

To return, then, to the subject: the deifying ray of Christ begets anew us who were (in our hopelessness) nothing, so that we hope in God, and by hope have being.[25] For when we had hope in ourselves and none in God, we were indeed nothing. Nor did we begin to be, until by grace we began to hope in God, to look to Him for everything, to have our being from Him, so that begotten into being, we might next have true wisdom from Him, and then from Him also have love of the good.

The beginning of our salvation, therefore, is hope, by which we are and live in God. And when we begin to look to God for everything, then at once we begin to have wisdom from the same God. Our wisdom consists of teaching and faith, for we must be taught, and we must believe what we are taught. We must be taught the things that belong to God and to divine matters, and the knowledge of these things is wisdom. We must be taught by these things, I say, so that beginning to be in God by hope, we may also truly live in the same God by faith. For all wisdom must be an instrument of life.[26]

At quis novit que sunt Dei nisi Spiritus Dei? Quid faciet nos tandem sapere veritatem Dei nisi vera ipsa Dei sapientia, qui Filius est Dei, quem nemo cognovit nisi Filius, et cui vult Filius revelare? Non omnibus est datum nosse mysteria Dei, sed iis solis qui habent aures audiendi ut audiant. Alii autem videntes non vident, et audientes non audiunt. Cecos videre et surdos audire fecit Dei Sapientia incarnata.

Hic obstupesco, et exclamo illud Pauli mei: O altitudo diviciarum sapientie et scientie Dei! O sapientia admirabiliter bona hominibus et misericors! ut iure tua pia benignitas altitudo divitiarum potest appellari. Qui comendans charitatem tuam in nobis voluisti in nos tam esse liberalis ut temetipsum dares pro nobis, ut tibi et Deo nos redderemur. O pia, o benigna, o benefica sapientia! O os, Verbum, et veritas Dei in homine, Verbum veridicum et verificans, qui voluisti nos docere humanitus, ut nos divinitus sapiamus; qui voluisti esse in homine, ut nos in Deo essemus; |101v| qui denique voluisti in homine humiliari usque ad mortem, mortem autem crucis, ut nos exaltaremur usque ad vitam, vitam autem Dei.

In illo admirabili commercio Creatoris humani generis, animatum corpus sumentis, qui de virgine dignatus est nasci et procedere sine semine, ut nobis suam elargiatur deitatem—in illo, inquam, admirabili et adorando comertio, i.e., in Iesu Christo sacrosancto mediatore Dei et hominum, qui factus est nobis sapientia et iusticia et sanctificatio et redemptio—in illo omnis est cognitio et salus nostra: qui est vera Dei virtus et Dei sapientia.

Que sapientia tandem quasi humanata in persona humana erudivit et edocuit homines voluntatem Patris sui, videlicet quid velit Deus a nobis intelligi et fieri hic, ut nos etiam eum Patrem habeamus et in eius filiis numeremur, adoptemurque in divinam familiam, ut Deum clamemus Abba, Patrem, et simus filii Dei et heredes, confratres Primogenito, et coheredes Christi.

Hec ut doceret et traderet, Verbum Dei homo factus est, ut non aliunde quam a suo ipsius Verbo suum beneplacitum discamus; ut in nobis sibi conplaceat sicut in Christo complacuit. Olim patribus Hebreorum
locutus est in prophetis: nobis locutus est tandem in Filio   *Hebreos.*
suo, qui splendor et gloria est Patris et exacta atque expressa imago et figura substantie illius; qui portavit omnia verbo virtutis sue, et in hominibus fecit purgationem peccatorum.

Hoc Verbum mirificum, humanatum, ratio Dei in homine, Iesus Christus,

But who knows the things of God, except the Spirit of God [I Cor. ii. 11]? What will make us come at last to wisdom in the truth of God, except God's true wisdom itself? And this is the Son of God, of the God whom no one has known except the Son, and those to whom the Son chooses to reveal Him [Matt. xi. 27]. Not to all is it given to know God's mysteries, but to those only who have ears to hear with. Others, seeing, do not see, and hearing, do not hear [xi. 15; xiii. 13]. But the incarnate Wisdom of God makes the blind to see and the deaf to hear.

At this point I repeat in utter amazement the exclamation of my beloved Paul: "O the depths of the riches of the wisdom and knowledge of God!" [Rom. xi. 33]. O wisdom most wonderfully good and merciful to men! Rightly may Your faithful kindness be called a depth of riches. To show Your love for us, You willed to be generous to the point of giving Yourself for us, so that we might be restored to You, to God. O loving, O kind, O beneficent Wisdom! O Mouth, Word, and Truth incarnate of God, Word uttering truth and making true, who willed to teach us in human fashion that we might be wise in divine fashion; who willed to be in man, that we might be in God; who willed, finally, to be abased in man even unto death, even unto death on the cross, that we might be exalted unto life, even unto the life of God.

In that wonderful communicating of the Creator of the human race, when He took a living body, deigning to be born of a virgin and to come into life without human procreation, in order to bestow upon us His own Godhead — in that wonderful and adorable communicating, I say, i.e., in Christ Jesus, the most holy mediator of God and men, who became our wisdom and justice, our sanctification and our redemption — is all our knowledge and our salvation, the true power and wisdom of God [I Cor. i. 30, 24].

This Wisdom, at last humanized, as it were, in a human person, instructed and taught men his Father's will, i.e., what God wants us to know and do here, that we also may have Him as Father and be numbered among His sons; may be adopted into the divine family and so call upon God as Abba, Father; may be sons and heirs of God, brothers with the First-Born, joint-heirs with Christ [Rom. viii. 15–17].[27]

To teach these things, to communicate them, the Word of God became man, so that we might learn God's will from no other source than His own Word, to the end that He might find in us the same pleasure for *The Hebrews.* Himself as in Christ. Of old He spoke in the prophets to the fathers of the Hebrews: to us at length He has spoken in His own Son, the splendor and the glory of the Father, the exact image and full expression[28] of His substance, who upheld all creation by the Word of His power, and worked among men the cleansing from sins [Heb. i. 1–3].

This wondrously humanized Word, the Reason of God in man, Jesus Christ,

homo de celo celestis, extitit tempestive et apparuit in terra, ut homines de terra
terrenos ad celestia instrueret, promoveret, raperet, |102r| denique secum et cum
Deo suo et communi Patre deificaret, primum animas nostras, quas significavit
et quibus dedit pignus Spiritus sui, tum deinde tandem etiam corpora. Nam si
anima, spiritus noster vitalis, lucidus, bonus, eternus, et immortalis, potest esse
in hoc corpusculo nostro finito, temporali, malo, tenebrecoso, et moribundo,
idque sua vi finita ad longum tempus sustinere, multo tunc magis potest esse
in immortali anima vera illa ipsa et benigna eternitas,
ac eam apud se ete⟨r⟩nam felicissime sustinere. Que   *Immortales sumus.*
anima etiam quum viribus nature sue potuit sustinere caducum corpus ad tempus, tunc necessario quum in eternitate fuerit, eternitatis illius viribus sine fine
beatissime poterit vel multo facilius sustentare.

Sapientia illa Dei luculenta, quam tenebre ulle non comprehenderunt, voluit
tamen quodammodo obumbrata esse, et quasi peccatum pro nobis facere, um-
bramque hominis in se assumere, et inter tenebras et ipsam
lucem quiddam medium constitui, ut extinctam lucernam   *II Cor. v. [21]*
accenderet in terris, illustraretque tenebras illuminaretque omnem° hominem
venientem in hu⟨n⟩c mundum, daretque   *Dei filii.*
eis potestatem filios Dei fieri et lucis, iis   *Hominis filius Christus.*
qui credunt in nomine eius; ut ex Deo nati   *Hominum filii.*
non hominum deinceps filii sed per hominis filium Dei filii essent.

Nam hominum filii per Dei et hominis Filium habent accessum et facultatem
ut renascantur filii Dei, non ex sanguinibus sed ex ipso Deo parente, per eum
qui factus est ex semine David secundum carnem, qui predestinatus est Filius
Dei in virtute secundum Spiritum sanctificationis, per quem
homines revivificavit, ut resurgant a mortuis toti aliquando   *Ad Rom. i. [3, 4].*
et sint Iesu Christi.

Fuerunt autem homines uniti in quamdam spem a Deo Patre, cuius est precipue
|102v| potens unitas, longe ante Christum, expectaruntque salutem a Deo iugiter,
quam sibi a Deo promissam habuerint. Nam veteres Hebrei Christum, qui salus
est hominum, expectarunt tam diu scilicet ut in Davidis hymno est, Defecerunt
oculi a salutari tuo. Hinc Salvator apud Lucam, Dico vobis quod prophete et
reges voluerunt videre quod vos videtis et non viderunt, et audire et non
audierunt°. Quod salutare datum tandem, Iesum Marie filium, quum Simion

---

omnem *M L*] omninem *C*   Hinc ... audierunt *C in marg. with lines, om. M L*

the Man from Heaven who was Heavenly [I Cor. xv. 47], came forth in due time and appeared on earth, that he might instruct toward heavenly things men of the earth, earthy [xv. 48]; might advance them and carry them off; might at last deify with himself and with his God and the common Father, first our souls, which he anointed and to which he gave a foretaste of his Spirit [II Cor. i. 22], and then at length our bodies also. For if our soul, our vital spirit,[29] lightsome, good, eternal,[30] and immortal, can exist in this our poor finite body, which is time-bound, wicked, dark, and prone to death, and can sustain it for a long time by its own finite power, then much more fully in our immortal soul[31] can that true and kindly Eternity exist, much better able is It to sustain the soul everlasting in the greatest bliss. The soul itself, just with the powers of nature, has been able to sustain a per-

We are immortal.

ishable body in time;[32] necessarily, then, when the soul is in eternity, it will be able by the powers of that eternity to support forever the body in the greatest blessedness—much more easily, even.

Still, that shining Wisdom of God, which no darkness could absorb [John i. 5], willed to be in a manner obscured; and to commit sin for us, as it were, and to take unto Itself man's dark-

II Cor. v. [21.]

ness, and to become a middle ground[33] between the shadows and the light itself, so that It might light on earth the lamp that was dead, might illumine the dark places [Ps. xvii. 29] and enlighten every man coming into this world, might give them—those who believe in His name—the power to become sons of God and of the light; so that thenceforth born of God, not sons of men but through the

The sons of God.
Christ, the Son of Man.
The sons of men.

Son of man, they might be the sons of God [John i. 9–13].

For through the Son of God and of man the sons of men have a way and the means to be born anew as sons of God, not from human blood, but from the very God the Father, through Him who according to the flesh was made from the seed of David, and who was foreordained the Son of God in power according to the Spirit of sanctification,

Rom. i. [3,4.]

through whom He renewed life in men, so that they might at last rise altogether from the dead, and belong to Jesus Christ.

Men were, indeed, bound together in some sort of hope by God the Father, to whom especially belongs powerful unity, long before Christ; and unfailingly they awaited from God the salvation promised them by God. For the Hebrews of old were waiting for Christ, who is man's salvation, for as long as David's hymn suggests: "My eyes have failed for Thy salvation" [Ps. cxviii. 123].[34] Hence the Savior in Luke: "I say to you that prophets and kings have wished to see what you see, and have not seen it; to hear, and have not heard it" [Luke x. 24].[35] And when Simeon had taken into his arms that salvation, Jesus, the Son

in ulnas acceperit, Nunc (inquit) dimittis servum tuum, Domine, secundum verbum tuum in pace, quia viderunt oculi salutare tuum.

Sed ceca Iudeorum turba quem venturum certo expectarunt, quum venerit non agnoverunt. Itaque expectarunt a Deo Patre quod promissum fuerat, datum promissum Filium non viderunt. Erat ergo in illis spes futuri,
sed in presenti defectus fidei. Constituti fuerunt a Deo *Spes in. . . .*
Patre ut essent in spe supra gentes, que sine spe nihil fuerunt. Sed illuminati non fuerunt omnes a Filio ut viderent quod presens fuit; ut fide et Filii beneficio gentibus sint inferiores; ut deinde etiam Sancti Spiritus munere qui amor est careant; ut qui ceperant esse aliquid spe, odio et stult⟨it⟩ia sua propria nihil fiant.

Spes est expectatio hominum sibi omnium a Deo. Quod expectatum fuit, qui hominibus presens esset omnia, omnipotens fuit Iesus
Christus, gentium expectatio. Non est faciendum solum ut *Spes.*
expectemus futurum aliquod, sed etiam quum is venerit qui venturus erat, credamus venisse et eundem peramemus, ut per illum Deo credere a quo expectavimus et Deum amare |103r| possimus.

Spes igitur et expectatio fuit Christi venturi, fides et amor venti eiusdem. Is talibus qui in nomine eius crediderunt dedit potestatem filios Dei fieri, nova fide et spe et charitate, videlicet si credant nunciis suis, si nunciata expectent, si expectata desiderent°. Ut enim Hebrei audientes Deum expectarunt Christum, quem ventum non amaverunt, ita vocati ad Christum, audientes ipsum, expectant Deum quem iam desiderant aliquatenus, sed aliquando plene et feliciter amaturi.

A fide ergo indubia Christo nuncianti veritatem futuram, et a firma spe expectationeque illius quod erit, et denique ab amore tum eius quod iam agnoscimus fide per speculum in enigmate, tum eius quod plene agnoscemus posthac facie ad faciem°, quum apparuerit quod erimus quando videbimus Deum, ut Ioannes testatur, sicuti est — ab hiis tribus et hoc triplici fune tracti hinc ex hac regione mala, tenebrosa, mortifera, rapimur Dei gratia, modo sequi volumus, ut in regno bonitatis et lucis sine fine vivamus. Interea quidem dum hic vivitur, si damus operam inservientes christianis, evangelicis, et apostolicis preceptis quoad possumus,

---

marg. Spes in . . . *word illeg.*   desiderent *Ed.*] desiderant *C M L*   ad *M L*] ad ad *C*

of Mary, he said, "Now thou dost dismiss Thy servant, O Lord, according to Thy word, in peace, because my eyes have seen Thy salvation" [Luke II. 28–30].

But after having looked for him with all conviction when he was yet to come, the blind multitude of the Jews did not recognize him when he came. And so they awaited from God the Father what had been promised; His Son, the promise fulfilled, they did not see. There was in them, then, hope of the future. In the present there was failure of faith. They had been established by God the Father to be above the Gentiles in *Hope in. . . .*[36] hope, the Gentiles without hope being nothing. But not all were enlightened by the Son to see what was present, so that by faith and in the favor of the Son they were less than the Gentiles, with the result that they lacked also the gift of the Holy Spirit, which is love; they who had begun to be something, therefore, by hope, became by their hatred and their own stupidity nothing.

Hope is an expectation on the part of men of all things for themselves from God. And the object of expectation, who was to be every-thing to men, when present, was the all-powerful Jesus *Hope.* Christ, the expectation of the nations [Gen. XLIX. 10].[37] We are to do more, however, than look forward to something that is to be. When he has come who was to come, we must also believe that he has come, and love him altogether, so that we may through him be able to believe in God from whom we had our hope, and to love God.

Hope and expectation, then, were directed toward Christ while he was still to come; faith and love are directed to him after he has come. To such as have believed in his name he has given the power to become sons of God [John I. 12], with a new faith and hope and love; if, that is, they believe his messengers, if they look for what has been revealed, if they long for what they look for. For as the Hebrews, hearing God, looked for Christ, but did not love him when he came, so those called to Christ, hearing him, look for God, to whom already to some extent their hearts go out, but whom at last they will love with the full perfection of happiness.

Drawn, then, by an undoubting faith in Christ as he reveals truth that is to be, and by a steadfast faith and expectation of what will be, and finally by love[38] both of Him whom by faith we already know as through a glass, darkly [I Cor. XII. 12], and of Him whom we shall hereafter know fully, face to face, when it will appear what we are to be, when (as John declares) we shall see God as He is [I John III. 2]—drawn by these three and by this threefold cord from this wicked, darksome, and killing region, we are swept up by God's grace, if only we wish to obey it, so that we may forever live in the Kingdom of goodness and of light; and if meanwhile, while our life is here, we apply ourselves as much as we can to the service of the precepts of Christ, of his Gospels, and of his

ut virtute scilicet et justicia gradatim proficiamus propinquemusque idee iusticie nostre Iesu Christo cotidie magis atque magis, ut tracti a claritate in claritatem a Domini Spiritu demum in eandem imaginem transformemur.

Quod autem credamus Christo nuncianti est, et in primis, ut credamus eum verum Dei nuncium fuisse et que nunciavit omnia vera esse, partim hic agenda dum hic vivitur, partim expectanda futura. Que hic |103v| aguntur est ex amore boni contentio et ad eam rectam vivendi rationem, piam et iustam, quam in se ipso iustus Christus tamquam exemplar nobis representavit; quod autem expectatur futurum est supra modum illud in sublimitate eternum glorie pondus quod talis imitatio Christi operatur in nobis non contemplantibus que videntur sed que non videntur.

Desiderio illius tanti et tam beatifici premii, anhelo cursu in Christi vestigiis illum sectari debemus antecedentem, ut quo ille pervenerit nos perveniamus; et hoc quadrupedis inster, ut mihi videtur, pedibus quatuor pernicibus: id est, patientia boni ex superiori; patientia mali ex inferiori; actione boni erga superos, que pietas dicitur; actione etiam continua boni erga inferos homines et equales, que iusticia appellatur. Nam hac quadrata forma incedendum est in hac vita, ut firmius nobiscum constemus. Per hec arma iusticie a dextris et a sinistris eundum est in hac perigrina terra, ut tuti ab iniusticie periculis evadamus. Eundum est primum ad Christum, ut deinde eamus ad gloriam.

Consulitur° autem et precipitur universis quibus triplex ille aureus funis est iniectus, ut ad Deum trahantur, ut quatenus maxime possunt assidue querant Deum fide, petant spe, pulsent charitate; currant in Christi semita ut inveniant quod quesierint, accipiant quod petierint, aperta sibi habeant pro quibus pulsaverint.

Omnes autem |104r| istam vestigationem accincti totis viribus et alacriter ingredi debent. Alioqui nullo modo salvi esse possunt. Ingredi autem debent non solum, sed etiam velle perficere. Alioquin censentur non ingressi quidem. Promoventur autem in melius, quatenus a Deo propius atque propius Christo attrahuntur. Attrahitur autem quisque quanto magis et ardentius amatur. Amor enim inflammat hominem in cursum et actionem.

Erat ante Christum in Iudeis multa spes sed parum fidei. Sub ipsa Christi luce multa fides sed modicus amor. Nam instante passione omnes illius discipuli eum deseruerunt, ita ut etiam Petrus accessit ad ignem ut se califaceret. At post illius

---

Consulitur *M L*] Consulutur *C*

Apostles, so that in virtue and justice we may advance step by step and approach daily nearer and nearer to our ideal of righteousness, Jesus Christ, to the end that drawn from clearness to clearness by the Spirit of the Lord we may at last be changed into the same image [II Cor. III. 18].[39]

Now to believe in Christ as he announces his tidings is, above all, to believe that he was the true messenger of God, and that all his message is true: part of it to be accomplished while our life is here, part to be looked for in the future. What is to be done here is a striving from love of the good to that right, devout, and just way of living which the just Christ showed us in himself as exemplar. And what is looked for in the future is that unending weight of glory above all measures in loftiness which such a following of Christ works in us, as we contemplate not the things that are seen but those that are not seen [II Cor. IV. 17, 18].

In our desire of so great and so blessed a reward we ought to follow after Christ in his footsteps with breathless pace as he goes before us, so that we may arrive where he has arrived. And this we should do, it seems to me, like a four-footed beast with four swift feet: the patience, i.e., of good from above; the patience of ill from beneath; the doing of good toward those above, which is called piety; the constant doing also of good toward men who are our equals and inferiors, which is called justice.[40] For in this four-square form[41] we must press on in this life, so that we may be the more steadfastly self-consistent. By means of this armor of righteousness on the right hand and on the left [II Cor. VI. 7] we must go on in this land of our homelessness, so that we may escape safely from the perils of injustice. First we must go to Christ, that from him we may go to glory.

Now all to whom this threefold cord of gold is thrown down to draw them to God are given the counsel and the precept to seek God constantly by faith as much as they can, to entreat for Him by hope, to knock at His door in love; to run in the way of Christ that they may find what they sought, may receive what they have entreated, may have opened to them the things for which they knocked.

And all must set out upon this following eagerly, and armed with all their strength. Otherwise they cannot in any manner be saved. They must not only set out, however, but have as well the will to finish. Otherwise they are judged not to have set out. And they are advanced to the better according as they are drawn by God nearer and nearer to Christ. Now a man is drawn the more, the more he is loved,[42] and the more ardently. For love fires a man to the race and to doing.

Before Christ there was in the Jews much hope, but little faith. Under the light itself of Christ there was much faith, but little love. For on the brink of his Passion, all his disciples deserted him; even Peter drew near to a fire to warm

discessum in celum, venit amoris effectus in Christi discipulos qui⟨n⟩quagesimo die per amorem ipsum, benignum Dei Spiritum, qui incendens credentium corda, fecit inflammatos et indubitantius credere, et certius quam ceperint omnia expectare.

Hoc Spiritu Christi Paraclito, quem hinc abiturus suis se promisit missurum, et misit largius absens quam presens ipse dederat, qui presens suos afflans iussit accipiant Spiritum Sanctum: absens autem omnes una eodem Spiritu replevit ut igniti ignita loquerentur que alios essent ignitura, hoc (inquam) Spiritu et igne quo baptizavit Iesus, quem venit ut mittat in terram ut spinas et vepres adurat, ut purgata terra viciis ex conceptis divinis seminibus proferat multiplicem fructum, alia tricesimum, alia sexagesimum, alia centesimum; hoc (iam tercio dico) Spiritu califiimus ut luceamus in Christo, lucemus deinde ut in eodem vivamus.

Nam calor |104v| ad lumen, lumen perducit ad vitam. Ex vita Dei lux pendet Christi, ex luce calor spiritalis. Per Spiritum ergo amoris credimus Christo, per hanc fidem in vitam imus eternam. Spiritu aguntur omnia, quo emisso recreantur omnia et renovatur facies terre, frigida recalescunt in lucem, et relucescunt in vitam; aversi, et abeuntes, sedentes tandem in cathedra pestilentie, revocantur sursum in thronum vite, et benigniter reducuntur in celum ad maiestatem Dei, ut illic filii dulcem Patrem patriamque revisant.

Qui ergo Spiritus ductum sequi velint, qui sunt quidem qui incalescunt amore optimi, toti versi in optimum persequi debent, conantes quoad maxime possunt ut in se quod est optimum assequantur, ut ipsi facti optimi, saltem in genere suo, optimo habeantur non indigni.

Exemplar autem optimi in humana vita, uti sepe diximus, fuit optimus Iesus Christus, qui et vita et verbis invitavit ad optimum; qui iussit ut sui tollant crucem suam cotidie et sequantur ipsum. Ratio sue optime et verissime condicionis fuit in se, abducto a mundo quam longissime et tradito Deo quam coniu⟨n⟩ctissime; qui confessus est mundum odisse se et se mundum, et suos a mundo odio habitos esse propter se, alioquin eos suos esse non potuisse.

himself.[43] But after his departure into Heaven, there came on the fiftieth day into the disciples of Christ the effect of love through Love itself, the kindly Spirit of God. Firing the hearts of the believers, He made those He had enkindled both believe more unwaveringly and hope for all things more firmly than they had begun to.

By this Spirit of Christ, the Paraclete, whom Christ promised to send to his own when he was about to depart from them [John xiv. 16, 17, 26; xv. 26; xvi. 27], and whom he sent more fully when he had departed than he had in person given when present — Christ while among his own breathed on them and bade them receive the Holy Spirit [John xx. 22]: but when he was departed he filled them all at once with the same Spirit so that enkindled themselves, they might speak words of fire to inflame others — by this Spirit, I say, and this fire by which Jesus baptized, which he came to set upon the earth [Luke xii. 49] to burn up the thorns and brambles, so that cleansed of blemishes the earth might bring forth abundant fruit of the divine seeds with which it was impregnated, some thirtyfold, some sixtyfold, some a hundredfold [Matt. xiii. 8]; by this Spirit (for the third time I say it) we are given warmth that we may have light in Christ, and we have light so that we may then have life in him also.

For warmth leads to light, light to life. On the life of God depends the light of Christ; on this light depends spiritual warmth. Through the Spirit of Love, then, we have faith in Christ, and through this faith we pass into life everlasting. By the Spirit are all things accomplished — at His sending forth all is created again, and the face of the earth is renewed [Ps. ciii. 30]; the cold things, growing warm again, come into light, and regaining the light, they come into life; those who had turned away, and those who were wandering apart, and those finally who were seated in the chair of pestilence [Ps. i. 1][44] are called back on high to the throne of life, and led back in kindness into Heaven, to the majesty of God, that there as children they may come to see again their dear Father and their Fatherland.

Those, then, who would follow the guidance of the Spirit — and these are the men who are warmed by a love of the best — must turn all their being to the reaching of the best, trying to the utmost of their power to achieve within themselves what is best; so that having themselves become best, at least within their own order of being,[45] they may be judged not unworthy of the Best.

Now the exemplar of the best in human life was, as we have often said, Christ Jesus, who is the Best. By his life and his words he invited us to the best. His own he ordered to take up their cross daily and follow him. The cause of his best and truest state was in himself, most completely withdrawn as he was from the world, and most intimately given over to God. He acknowledged that the world hated him and he the world, that his own were held in hatred by the world because of him, or else they could not be his [John xv. 19].

Mundus autem est ratio vivendi in mundo ea tota que fuit ante Christum, que tota inimica est Deo. In quo Ioannes° contestatus est nihil esse nisi concupiscentiam carnis et oculorum et superbiam vite. Et Ioannes Apostolus sepe malignum vocat ac totum mundum in maligno positum esse asserit.

In quem |105r| quanto quis magis descendit, eo miser magis malignis spiritibus qui sunt principes (ut loquitur Paulus) harum tenebrarum se subiicit in fedissimam et perniciosissimam servitutem. Unde nulla est alia exeundi ratio quidem, quam abstrahi et per gratiam sequi Christum, qui se omnino supra mundum tenuit ab eius contagione intactum°. Quo‧quanto propius accedis, eo sordes mundi eluis magis. Omnino autem purgatus esse no⟨n⟩ potes donec ad eum ipsum perveneris representarisque eundem ipsum in te ipso.

Quod dum hic vivitur, perquam difficile est sane, ne dicam imposibile. Nam in homine assumpto ad utilitatem nostram et doctrinam videtur Deus exemplum impossibilitatis non proposuisse: id enim discussisset magis infirmos a vita quam ad vitam conciliasset. At in Deo, qui inclinavit celos et descendit, qui comendavit charitatem suam in redemptione hominum, illiusmodi cogitare nepharie impietatis est. Onus dixit suum Christus suave et iugum leve, relevans sane et in altum homines elevans subiiciensque Deo, in quo est dulcis iucundaque libertas. Quocirca vocans ad se Iesus, Venite (inquit) ad me omnes *[Matt. xi. 28, 29.]* qui° laboratis et onerati estis, et° ego reficiam vos. Tollite iugum meum super vos et discite a me, quia mittis sum et humilis corde, et invenietis requiem animabus vestris.

Is Filius Dei, qui solus novit Patrem, docuit imitationem Patris, et iussit sui perfecti essent sicuti Pater in celis. Cuiusmodi autem perfectio illa celestis in hominibus sit docuit ipse Iesus, homo celestis, sua ipsa vita |105v| quasi loquens expressius et instruens homines. Quam profecto est omnium totis conatibus imitari qui illius tam re quam nomine haberi volunt, et tamquam ad commune signum propositum omnibus, illuc dirigere vitam, ut prope quasi sagittantes ad vitam, ipsam vitam lucrentur, qua mensurabuntur omnia.

Atque ut quisque hic in terris ad illud signum se habet vel propinquius vel distantius, sic et talis profecto ille et ad damnationem et ad salutem censebitur. Quocirca Simeon, qui accepit non se moriturum priusquam Christum viderit, quando illud signum et exemplar humane vite in templo est ulnis amplexus, tum

---

Ioannes *L in note*] Iacobus *C M*   intactum *M L*] intactus *C*   qui *M L*] qui qui *C*   *marg.* Matt. xi.28,29 *L Ed.*] Luc. 11 *C*   et *M L*] et et *C*

Now the world is that whole system of life on earth that existed before Christ, a system altogether at enmity with God. In it, testifies [John], there is nothing but the lust of the flesh, and of the eyes, and the pride of life [I John II. 16]. And the Apostle John often declares that it is evil, and that the whole world lies in evil [I John v. 19].

Now the more a man descends into it, the more wretchedly does he enslave himself into an utterly abominable and ruinous serfdom to the wicked spirits who are the princes (as Paul says) of this darkness [Eph. VI. 12]. Nor is there any other way to escape from it than to be disentangled from it, and through grace to follow Christ, who kept himself altogether above the world, unspotted by its infection. The nearer you approach to him, the more you wash away the filth of the world. But you cannot be altogether cleansed until you really reach him, and reproduce him in yourself.

Now this, while our life is here, is of the very utmost difficulty, not to say impossible. Not impossible, because in the manhood taken for our profit and teaching, God does not seem to have set before us an example of the impossible, since this would have shattered the weak rather than brought them together into life. And to think this sort of thing of God, who bowed the heavens and came down [Ps. XVII. 10], who commended His love in the redemption of men [Rom. v. 8, 9], is execrably impious. Christ said that his burden was easy, and his yoke light [Matt. XI. 30], a burden and a yoke, indeed, to raise men when they had fallen, and lift them on high, and place them under God, in whom there is a sweet and delightful freedom.[46] And so Jesus, calling men to himself, said "Come to me all you that labor and are burdened, and I will give you rest. Take my yoke upon yourselves, and learn from me, for I am gentle and humble of heart; and you shall find rest for your souls" [XI. 28, 29].

This Son of God, who alone knows the Father, taught the imitation of the Father, and bade his own be perfect, as the Father in Heaven is perfect [Matt. XI. 27 etc.; v. 48]. But speaking, as it were, even more clearly by his life itself, the same Jesus, the Man of Heaven, instructed men and taught them what that heavenly perfection in men would be. And surely it belongs to all who wish to be considered his in fact as well as in name to imitate that life[47] with all their efforts, to direct their own lives to it as to a common mark set before all, so that almost as if aiming arrows[48] at life, they may win the prize of Life itself, the standard by which all things shall be judged.

And as each here on earth is nearer that mark or farther from it, surely so also will he be judged to be with respect to damnation and salvation. For this reason Simeon (who had learned that he was not to die until he had seen Christ), having held in his arms that mark and exemplar of human life, in the Temple,

eius matri Marie virgini dixit: *Ecce positus est hic in ruinam et in resurrectionem multorum in Israel, et in signum cui contradicetur.* Nam quam plurimi fuerunt qui illuc suum cursum dirigere recusarunt. Qui autem eum ludum ingressi sunt, tracti gratia ut experiantur, adiuti eadem gratia, quid assequi possunt, quique in eo vite curriculo ad vitam Christum ipsum vitale bravium possint consequi, in hiis quisque ut contenderit et voluerit perfectus esse (secundum eum certe gradum quem adeptus est), modo voluerit altiorem si possit et dedit operam assidue ut altius aspiraret et simul doluit continuo quod non erat in altissimo, profecto bona voluntas illa hominis et conatus ad melius quatenus poterat satis acceptus est Deo ut et laudetur et pro ratione meriti remuneretur.

Sed ipsius optimi ratio et perfecta figura vivendi, cuius fuerit in Christo videamus, ut ex contrario quid quodque ab illo differat clarius possimus discernere.

Quum vero ille ex alto venit, |106r| ut que in imo sunt illuc unde venerat traheret, quumque non venit nisi ut rediret, nec descendit nisi ut ascenderet, nec denique venit ascensurus nisi ut multi secum conscenderent quos° regnum tradat Patri suo, proculdubio est necesse ut ille totus spectaret sursum, nec aliud hic ageret quam ut viam in celum monstraret. Quam ille ingressus primus aliis formam illuc eundi ostendit, ut illum secuti, qui velint scandant montem, montem (inquam) sanctum° Domini, ubi post exantlatos labores cum eodem duce dulciter requiescant.

Tota quidem vita hic Iesu Christi nihil aliud fuit quam ex hoc loco ascensus in celum, quum tota non huc sed illuc spectavit. Anima enim illius tota erat dedita Deo, nihil curans nisi voluntatem Patris in terris, ut quam plurimi hinc decedant propere ut illum sequantur. Unde nisi qui fecerit voluntatem Patris sui in cognatione et sanguine agnovit neminem, nec voluit audire illam mulierem de turba clamantem, Beatus venter qui te portavit et ubera que suxisti, sed corrigens dixit, Quinimmo, beati qui audiunt verbum Dei et custodiunt illum.

Erat totus pius, benignus, mansuetus, misericors, patiens malorum, ferens iniurias; pro sua veritate exhorrens vanam fumam popularem, ut et hominibus et demonibus imperarit ne suam magnificam virtutem devulgarent; pro sua bonitate semper bene faciens, etiam malis, ut Patrem referret suum qui facit solem suum oriri super iustos et iniustos.

---

quos *C but* s *cancelled*] quos *M L*   sanctum *M L*] sanctam *C*

said to his mother, Mary the Virgin, "Behold, this child is set for the fall and for the resurrection of many in Israel, and for a sign that will be contradicted" [Luke II. 26, 34]. For there were a very great number who refused to direct their course to that sign. Those, however, who have been drawn by grace to enter the contest so as to make trial—with the help of the same grace—of what they can achieve, to see who can succeed in that race of life to Life, to Christ himself, the trophy of life—among these, to the extent that each has striven and wished to be perfect (according to the degree, of course, that he has reached), provided he has desired to reach a higher degree if he could, and has unflagging-ly applied himself to draw near the higher, and has at the same time constantly grieved at his not being in the highest, surely that good will of a man and his utmost efforts toward the better are sufficiently acceptable to God for him to win praise and reward in proportion to his merits.[49]

But let us see what it was like in Christ, that system of the best, that perfect type of life, so that we may discern more clearly, by contrast, how anything differs from it.

He came, then, from on high, to draw up the things in the depths to the point from which he had come, and he came for no other reason than to return; he descended only to ascend; he came, finally, with the intention of ascending, only that many might ascend with him to be handed over by him, a Kingdom, to his Father. Beyond doubt, then, he had necessarily to look wholly above, to do nothing else here than to show the way into Heaven. The first to enter upon it, he pointed out to others the way of going there, so that, following him, those who wished might scale the mountain—the holy mountain, I mean, of the Lord [Zach. VIII. 3]—where they might rest in delight, when their labors had been endured, with the same leader.

Indeed, the whole life of Jesus Christ here was nothing other than an ascent from this place into Heaven, since its regard was wholly there, not here. For all his soul was given to God, with no concern except for the will of the Father on earth [Heb. x. 5–10], so that as many as possible might leave here swiftly and follow him. And so he acknowledged no one as belonging to his kinship or blood except those who did his Father's will. And he did not wish to listen to that woman crying from the crowd, "Blessed is the womb that bore thee, the breast that thou hast sucked." But correcting her, he said, "Nay, rather, blessed are those who hear the world of God and keep it" [Luke XI. 27, 28].

He was altogether devout, kindly, gentle, merciful, patient of evils, long-suffer-ing; because of his truth, he shrank from empty popular fame, to the extent of commanding men and demons not to make public his wondrous power [Matt. VIII. 4 etc.; Luke IV. 41; Mark I. 34]; because of his goodness, he always did good, even to the wicked, so that he might reproduce his Father, who makes His sun rise on the just and the unjust [Matt. v. 45].

Quod si in omnibus hiis imitatus est Patrem qui in alto |106v| est, hiis vir-
tutibus perseverare nihil aliud fuit quam in altum ad Patrem ascendere. Corpus
habuit omnino obediens et inserviens beate anime, sensus omnes sursumversus
spectantes, ex inferiori loco nihil appetentes nisi quod ad summam necessitatem
pertinuit. Post longa enim jeiunia esuriit, post longas vigilias dormivit. Ab omnibus sensuum delenimentis° abstinens, a venere castus, ab illis denique que in
mundo sunt, que in fortune bonis numerantur, totus alienus. Erat oculus eius
penitus simplex, ut totum corpus eius lucidum esset. Unde invidia, ira, odium,
emulatio, rixa, avaritia, ambitio, contentio, iniuria, deceptio, dolus, rapina, super-
bia, contemptus Dei et hominum, plurimi factio sui, gula, luxuria, desidia, vanitas,
bellum, homicidium, eversio rerum, que duplex et divisus oculus deorsum spectans spisse in mundo parit cotidie, non modo in Christo, sed et in suis sequacibus
ne ullo quidem modo esse possunt.

Itaque Christus, abductus a mundo, abductus a corpore, adductus et inductus
in Deum intime, omnia illuc sursum et animi et corporis versa habuit. Qua forma precessit dux, convocans et contrahens secum quam plurimos qui prorsus
aversi a mundo et conversi in Deum, semper sursum et simpliciter intentis oculis,
sollicito gradu illum sequerentur.

Talem ergo habuimus in celum itineris ducem, qui mortuus est mundo, qui
resurrexit Deo, qui ascendit in celum, |107r| qui sedit ad dextram Patris et orat
pro nobis; quem absque dubio si amplis viribus quoad possumus non sequamur,
in celum nunquam veniemus.

Oportet abneges omnino temetipsum, ut Deum affirmes. Oportet moriare ut
renascare; stultus fias ut sis sapiens; malus et miser non dico sis, sed a malis et
miseris talis habeare in mundo, ut bonus tandem et felix fias. Si discedens a mundo non moriaris mundo, Deo vivere non potes. Hoc est, non potes accedens
ad vitam vite vivere, nisi discedens a morte morti moriaris. Oportet crucifigare
mundo, ut gloriere in Deo; et mundus omnino crucifigatur tibi, ut tibi Deus
gloria sit. Nemo enim potest duobus ⟨dominis servire⟩°. Nemo simul sursum
et deorsum, nisi distractus dirumpatur. Illuc si vis ubi est ipsa simplicitas, est
necesse tunc sis omnino integer et simplex ipse et in unam dumtaxat partem
latus, contendasque solummodo sursum, nec queras a tergo quicquam nisi quod
valde necessarium est ad tenuem corporis sustentationem, et hoc quoque non
quod velis hic libenter vivere, sed ne sis inobediens Deo et onus anime, quod est cor-

---

delenimentis *Ed.*] delinimentis *C L*] delimentis *M*   dominis servire *om. C*] *suppl. M L*

Now if in all these things he imitated his Father, who is on high, to persevere in these virtues was nothing other than to ascend to the Father. He kept his body completely obedient and subservient to his blessed soul; he kept all his senses turned to the sight of things on high, desiring nothing from below except what pertained to the very necessities. For he was hungry after long fasts; after long watchings, he slept. He kept himself free from all blandishments of the senses,[50] pure from lust, and altogether a stranger to those things, finally, which are in the world and are numbered among the goods of fortune. His eye was wholly single, and consequently his whole body was lightsome [Luke XI. 34]. Envy, therefore, and wrath, hatred, jealousy, strife, greed, ambition, contentiousness, hurt to others, deceit, guile, robbery, haughtiness, contempt of God and men, self-glorification, gluttony, wantonness, sloth, vanity, war, murder, destruction and overthrow—all the crowd of evils that a double and divided eye, fixed below, is daily bringing forth in profusion—not only could not exist in Christ, but in his followers also can in no way have place.

Christ, then, withdrawn from the world, withdrawn from the body, drawn to and into God in close union, had all that was his soul and body turned upward to Him. In this form he went ahead as leader, calling and drawing together with him as many as possible, men who would turn completely from the world and toward God, men who would follow him with heedfulness of step, their eyes fixed forever above in singleness.

Such, therefore, is the leader we have had for our journey into Heaven: one who died to the world and rose to God, who ascended into Heaven, who sits at the right hand of the Father and entreats Him for us. And doubtless, if we do not follow him with the fullness of our strength to the limit of our ability, we shall never enter into Heaven.

You must deny yourself altogether, to affirm God. You must die, to be born anew. You must become foolish, to be wise. I do not say you must be bad and wretched, but in the world you must be considered such, that you may at length become good and happy. If, withdrawing from the world, you do not die to the world, you cannot live unto God. That is, drawing near to life, you cannot live to life unless, withdrawing from death, you die to death. You must be crucified to the world, to glory in God; and the world must be altogether crucified to you, that God may be your glory. For no one can serve two masters. No one can go at once upward and downward,[51] without being broken and torn asunder. If you wish to reach the point where simplicity itself exists, you must then be altogether whole and simple yourself, and moved in only one direction; you must strive upward only, seeking nothing from behind you except what is absolutely necessary for the bare maintenance of the body, and this too, not because you would wish gladly to go on living here, but so as not to disobey God by seeming to cast off in your weariness the soul's burden, which is the body.[52] For

pus, tuo tedio abiecisse videare. Vanitati enim (ut ait Paulus) creatura subiecta
est non volens, sed propter eum qui subiecit eam in spe. Et nemo debet habere
odio carnem suam, sed exercere, ut simul cum anima possit promereri immortalitatem, et facere ut in hoc mundo mundo careat in vitam anime, ut extra mun-
dum corpus in vitam suam |107v| animam habeat.

Huius veritatis et vie bellum exemplum proposuit Christus, veritas ipsa et via
et hostium in celum, ut per eius vivendi formam, tamquam per hostiam°, in
celum ingrediamus. Quod tibi aperietur, si ardenti charitate illius continuo
pulsaveris. Pulsate, inquit, et aperietur vobis.

Sed ut iam propius ad rem nostram accedamus de quo incepimus, ut videamus quid inter preceptum, consilium, et *Quid inter preceptum,*
indulgentiam interest. Quum agnovimus *consilium, indulgentiam interest.*
modo optimum quiddam et perfectissi-
mum in Christo propositum fuisse in terris et hominibus, est intelligendum pro
salute omnium consultum esse universis, ut se in illum statum qui erat Christi
reforment. Nec aliud quesivit vel illius vel post illum Apostolorum evangelizatio,
nisi ut ad exemplar Christi omnium vite reformentur.

Hinc Paulus scribit: *Imitatores° mei estote, sicut ego Christi,* et: Vellem vos omnes
esse sicut ego sum. Vis autem infertur nemini, sed consulitur cuique et precipitur,
si salvi esse volunt, Salvatorem Christum sequantur quatenus valent, bono animo
et spe, in ea vivendi ratione qua ille vixerit; ut illum secuti, ubi ille prior ingressus est, ipsi quoque per eundem ingrediantur. Qui huic consilio et precepto
Dei non obedit ullatenus, is in salvandis numerari non potest. Qui vero quatenus
valet paret huic precepto, de eo certe est spes salutem eum Dei misericordia
assecuturum.

Ut autem quisque habeat fidem Christo credatque bono nuncio suo, utque
eundem amet illiusque vivendi formam ardenter desideret, utque simul que pro-
miserat Christus sequacibus suis firmiter expectet |108r| —hec, inquam, ita sunt
necessaria ut qui hec recusant, sicuti recusaverunt innumerabiles, ii omnino salutem
censentur recusare, nec talibus ulla indulgentia et venia esse potest. Nam ipsum
Spiritum Sanctum qui eos vivificet recusant, in quem qui peccat non remittetur
ei neque in hoc seculo neque in futuro.

Fides ergo doctrine Christi, et amans imitatio vite illius, cum expectatione
finis eius quo proficiscitur, oportet necessario in quoque sit qui se sperat aliquando salvum fore. Atque hominibus id consulentibus est necesse ut sponte obe-

---

hostiam *C*] hostium *M L*   *Imitatores M L*] *Imitamini C*

the creature (as Paul says) has been subjected to vanity, not willingly, but because of him who in hope has made it subject [Rom. VIII. 20]. And no one ought to hold hatred toward his own flesh [Eph. v. 29], but occupy it in such a way that it can deserve to have immortality at the same time as the soul. He ought so to act that in this world he may do without the world for the life of his soul, so that beyond the world the body may have the soul for its life.

A beautiful example of this truth and of this way was set before us by Christ, the Truth itself and the Way and the Door into Heaven [John XIV. 6; X. 9], so that through his form of living, as though by means of a sacrificial victim,[53] we might enter into Heaven. If you knock at that door constantly with burning love of him, it will be opened to you. "Knock," he says, "and it will be opened to you" [Matt. VII. 7].

But now to come nearer to our subject,[54] the one we began with, to see the difference between precept, counsel, and indulgence. Since we have just recognized that in Christ has been set forth a determined form of the best and the most perfect on earth and among men, we must under-

The difference between Precept, Counsel, Indulgence.

stand that for the salvation of all, all are counselled to reform themselves to the state that was Christ's. His teaching, and after him that of his Apostles, was aimed at nothing other than that everyone's life should be refashioned to Christ's example.

So Paul writes, "Be imitators of me, as I am of Christ," and, "I would wish all to be as I am" [I Cor. IV. 16; VII. 7]. But force is used against no one. The counsel and the precept are given to all, if they wish to be saved, to follow to their utmost Christ the Savior, with courage and hope, in that manner of living in which he lived, so that having followed him, they also may enter, through him, into the place wherein he first has entered. And he cannot be numbered among those to be saved who fails in any degree to obey this counsel and precept. But there is surely hope for anyone who obeys the precept as far as he can, hope that he will attain salvation through the mercy of God.

For a man, then, to have faith in Christ, and to believe his good tidings, to love him and long ardently for his form of living, and at the same time to look forward confidently to the fulfilment of Christ's promises to his followers—these things are, I say, so necessary that men who refuse them (as men without number have refused) are judged to reject salvation altogether. For such there can be neither indulgence nor pardon. For they are refusing the Holy Spirit Himself, who would give them life. And whoever sins against Him will be forgiven neither in this life nor in the life to come [Matt. XII. 32].

In everyone, then, who hopes eventually to be saved, there must necessarily be faith in Christ's teaching, and loving imitation of his life, with an expectation of that end to which the journey is made. And all must needs obey willing-

diant omnes, inserviantque illorum consilio. Hoc autem consulitur universis, ut universi salvi fiant. Quod consilium versus optimum, propterea quod oportet° audiant omnino qui salvi esse volunt omnes, et id necessario quod consulitur sponte agant, propter eam, inquam, necessitatem rei, peculiari verbo vocatur preceptum. Quod potest diffiniri consilium *Preceptum.* cui necessario pareas si salvus esse velis; in quo non est excusatio impotentie, sed si nolis, tue infirmitatis damnatio.

Ut autem postquam ceperis credere veritati Christi, et illius bonitatem amare, et expectare denique que promiserat; ut, inquam, in hoc incepto salutari pergas, insinuesque te intus magis atque magis in ipsam veritatem et bonitatem Christi, ut quoad possis assimilatus illi, ipse quoque verus et bonus fias; ut deinde expectatam veram bonitatem quo tendis tandem habeas; in hac quidem provectione ulteriori ad perfectionem Christi, unum certum et commune |108v| consilium, cui necesse est omnes pareant, nullo modo dari potest propter hominum varietatem et differentiam virium. Quibus nihil debet consuli ultra vires; sed ut quisque valet viribus et facultate ad cursum, ita ei consilium adhibendum est. Cui consilio eidem accomodato cui arbitratur se parere posse, si non paruerit, profecto tunc, tamquam inobediens in eo ubi potest obedire, indignus salute censetur. Nam non solum oportet incipiat aliquis, sed etiam pergat pro viribus quatenus potest; ut si audierit consilium cui estimat se obedire posse, tunc ei saltem id consilium preceptum est, cui est necesse pareat si salvus esse velit. Est enim necesse faciat quisque quatenus potest, si *Facere quantum potest.°* salutem assequatur.

Quocirca semper ubi agnoscitur posse consilium preceptum est, quando quidem precipitur cuique ut faciat quoad maxime potest ut in salvatorum numero habeatur. Nam non sunt condigne passiones, ut scribit Paulus, ad futuram gloriam. Quatenus autem quisque potest et ad optima consilia que valens est, ipse audiens consilium optimi maxime novit, qui se ipsum maxime agnoscit. Qui inceperunt proficisci ad optimum, illis omnibus consulitur ad optimum eant, quia a consulente singulorum vires non cognoscuntur. Quod si suam cuiusque potentiam ad bonum consiliarius ille quisque sit cognitam et perspectam |109r| habuisset, tum proportionaliter singulis propria daret consilia et ex perpensis viribus quid quisque ferre potest; quod suum cuique consilium ei potenti obedire proculdubio preceptum est, cui oportet omnino pareat, ne minus faciens quam° possit, magis recusetur a Deo quam velit, condemneturque de abusu talenti quod ignaviter datis viribus ad maximum sibi emolimentum non est usus sicuti debuerat necessario si voluerit

---

oportet *M L*] opertet *C*   *marg.* Facere . . . potest *C but perhaps in another hand* quam *Ed.*] quod *C M L*

ly the men who give this counsel, and submit to it. And the counsel is given to all, that all may be saved. And therefore this counsel to the best — because all are bound absolutely to hear it, if they wish to be saved, and must of necessity do freely what is counselled — is called a precept in a special sense of the word; because, I repeat, of its intrinsic cogency. Precept can be defined, then, as a counsel that must necessarily be obeyed if you wish to be saved, one that admits of no excuse of inability. If you are unwilling, your "weakness" has damnation in it.

Precept.

But once you have begun to believe in the truth of Christ, to love his goodness, and to hope for all he has promised, then for you thenceforward to speed on in the salvation you have begun, and to become more and more deeply involved in the truth itself and the goodness of Christ, to become yourself true and good by being made as much like him as possible, and finally to have at length the hoped-for true goodness toward which you are drawing — in all this further progress to the perfection of Christ, no one fixed and universal counsel which all are bound to obey can conceivably be given, because of mankind's variety and differing strength. Men are not to be counselled beyond their strength; but counsel is to be directed to each in accordance with the extent of his powers and ability for the race. Now if a man does not obey the counsel adapted to himself, that he thinks he can obey, he is surely judged undeserving of salvation, on the grounds that he has been disobedient in a point in which he can obey. For a man must not only begin, but must also press on as far as he can to the limit of his strength, so that to one who has heard a counsel he judges he can obey, that counsel is (to him, at least) a precept; and he must necessarily obey it if he should wish to be saved. For to gain salvation, each must do as much as he can.

Do as much as you can.

Whenever, therefore, ability is acknowledged, the counsel is a precept, since all have the precept to do as much as they can to be numbered among the saved. For our sufferings, as Paul writes, are not commensurate to the glory that will be [Rom. VIII. 18]. But how much each can do and what best counsels he is strong enough for, the man himself who hears the counsel of the best knows most thoroughly, since he best knows himself. To all who have begun to advance toward the best is given the general counsel to go on to the best, because the counsel-giver does not know the powers of each. But if the counsellor, whoever he be, had the scrutiny and knowledge of each one's power for good, then he would give individually adapted counsels, having weighed each one's strength to see what he could bear. And a counsel is beyond doubt a precept for anyone who can obey it. He must give full obedience, or else doing less than he could, he may be rejected by God more than he would wish. He may be condemned for misuse of the talent, because the strength given him for the greatest gain possible he has not used as he needs must have done if he had wished to be judged

iudicari optimum desiderasse. Quod oportet omnino faciat, tametsi quod optimum est, pre infirmitate, assequi nequeat.

Ab ignorante hominum facultates et quod est in quoque gratie donum, proponitur ratio optimi sicut Christus ipse optime inter omnes vixit; et consulitur omnibus pariter ut aspirent pro viribus ad optimum. Quod consilium potenti obedire preceptum est sane, cui necessario ille obedire obligatur. Impotenti autem consilium est, cui non cogitur obedire nisi quatenus valet. Ad eum vero terminum cogitur, et eousque ei consilium optimi preceptum est, non quod obligatur re efficere optimum, sed quam melius poterit ad optimum, id facere obligatur.

Debet autem quisque et obligatur necessario semper velle facere optimum: cogitur autem |109v| re ipsa ut efficiat non plus quam possit.

Ut breviter ergo diffinitionibus distinguamus consilium et preceptum, possumus *consilium* appellare sententiam optimi propositam ut ei quisque pareat et secundum idem agat pro viribus quatenus potest; *preceptum* autem sententiam dictam cuivis ad bonum, pro ratione virium, cui debet omnino parere is qui estimat se Dei gratia parere posse, saltem si salvari velit.

Consilium quid.°

Preceptum quid.°

Itaque videtur consilium generale preceptum esse optimi, cui debent velle omnes posse parere, preceptum particulare consilium singulo cuique et suum, cui is qui potest debet omnino obedire. Omne ergo preceptum consilium est, sed non omne consilium preceptum, quia omnes debent facere bene quatenus possunt, quod precipitur, sed non obligatur quisque facere optime nisi potest, quod consulitur°.

In consultore est ignorantia quid homines facere possunt: in preceptore cognitio. Quod si consulas accomodate cuique ex cognitis viribus, tunc ex consultore preceptor es° factus et tuum consilium preceptum est. Quia ignoramus vires hominum et potentiam obediendi, ideo consulimus optima omnibus. Quando cognoscimus quod quisque potest—si hoc cognosci potest—tunc ut quisque hoc certum faciat quatenus potest precipimus.

Omnino oportet |110r| quisque incipiat bene, fide, spe, et charitate, aliquousque quoad potest. Nam hoc generale consilium preceptum est cuique generale. Ut vero deinceps pergas et assequare optimum consulitur. Et certe illuc usquequo potes (quod noveris ipse melius quam consultor) ut pergas omnino et agas precipitur.

In generali ergo consilio ad optimum est cuique suum particulare preceptum, ut ex proposito et consulto optimo id estimet quisque sibi preceptum esse quod ipse suas vires agnoscens—immo in se gratiam Dei—sperat se facere posse. Con-

marg. Consilium quid] Preceptum quid *C but perhaps in another hand*   consulitur *M L*] consilitur *C*   es *M L*] est *C*

to have desired the best [Matt. xxv. 14–30 etc.]. This last he must do no matter what, even if in his weakness he cannot attain to what is best.

Now when someone does not know men's abilities and the gift of grace in each, he proposes the system of the best as Christ himself lived it in the midst of all men, and he counsels to all alike that they aspire to that best with all their strength. To one who *can* obey this counsel, it is doubtless a precept that he *must* necessarily obey. But to one who cannot, it is a counsel, and he is not held to obey it except as far as he can. To that point, however, he is obliged, and the counsel of the best is a precept for him to that extent, not because he is actually bound to accomplish the best, but because he is bound to do as well as he can toward the best.

Everyone must always wish to do the best, and is necessarily obliged to that wish, but he is not compelled to accomplish in fact more than he can.

Let us then briefly distinguish counsel and precept by definitions. We can call a *counsel* a judgment as to the best, set before all so that each may obey it and act according to it as far as his own strength permits. And a *precept* is a judgment given to an individual man about the good in accordance with his powers; and whoever deems himself able, by the grace of God, to obey, must wholeheartedly obey, at least if he should wish to be saved.

What a counsel is.

What a precept is.

We see, then, that a counsel is a general precept of the best, which all must wish to be able to obey; a precept is a particular counsel for an individual person, which he must altogether obey who can. Every precept is, therefore, a counsel, but not every counsel is a precept; because all must do as much *good* as they can—this is the precept—but no one is compelled to do the *best*—this is the counsel—unless he is able.

The counsellor does not know what men can do, the preceptor does. If you give a counsel to someone adapted to him from knowledge of his strength, then from a counsellor you have become a preceptor, and your counsel is a precept. It is because we do not know man's strength and power to obey that we counsel the best to all. When we know what each can do—if this, indeed, can be known—then we give him the precept to do this or that precise thing as his strength permits.

It is altogether necessary that each begin well in faith, hope, and charity, advancing as far as he can. For this universal counsel is also a universal precept for everyone. But that you should from that point press on and attain to the best is counselled. And certainly, that you should speed on as far as you can and do all you can (and you will yourself know what this is better than the counsel-giver) is a precept.

In the general counsel to the best, then, each one has his own particular precept, so that in the best set forth and counselled, let each one deem that to be a precept for him which, in the knowledge of his own strength—or rather, of God's grace

sulitur optimum omnibus: precipitur cuique id assequatur quod potest, quam propiusque° potest accedat ad Christum, qui hic fuit optimus. Quisque agnoscit quid potest. Quisque ergo agnoscit ex consilio ad optimum quid sibi preceptum est, quum videt quatenus consilio parere potest.

Consilium videtur esse omne preceptum quum est ad optimum, quia cuique preceptum ad quodvis bonum in se continet. Si dicas te non posse facere optimum, tum precipitur tibi facias quam melius potes. Debes° tamen simul velle optimum. Velle ergo oportet te obedire consilio optimi: facere autem cogeris quantum dictat preceptum accomodatum; ut consilium, etiam si non potes, ad voluntatem spectat: preceptum ad facultatem, quatenus potes.

Consilium itaque videtur indeterminatum preceptum ex ignorantia, preceptum determinatum consilium ex cognitione, quid quisque facere potest. Hinc in doctore tutius est consilium quam preceptum: in hiis quibus consulitur° fructuosius preceptum quam consilium, quanto magis conducit homini id cui potest obedire |110v| quam cui non potest, quamquam id cui non potest melius est multo quam id cui potest. Sed nemo obligatur ultra posse. Obligatur tamen velle semper ultra quod potest, et facere quoad potest que velit.

Ut summatim ergo dicam, precipitur° cuique ut faciat quoad potest. Quod quia ignoratur quantum quisque potest, iccirco quod optimum est in commu⟨n⟩e consulitur. Nam donec cognoscatur cuiusque infirmitas, suspicanda et speranda sunt meliora.

Quando autem deprehenditur aliquis pre defectu virium altius ad Christum non posse, ex hoc nequam mundo et tota ratione eiusdem ad Christum et ad rationem vivendi illius, hic modo velit altius si possit, conceditur ibi stet ubi maxime potest, ex misericordia infirmitatis eius, que permissio indulgentia dicitur. Que est, quum non potes optimum, ut illic stes quo ultimis viris pervenisti concessio; modo doleas te altius non posse, et velis altius se possis.

Indulgentia.

Que indulgentia in communi tractu sursum ad Christum est remissio cuique ut sua exposcit infirmitas, et quedam invita concessio ut habeat ille aliquid ex ratione huius mundi, in bonis corporis et fortune, qui totus spiritu ad rationem Christi reformari non potest. Que indulgentia tendit deorsum, relaxans semper. Ideo invita, et quanto magis laxantur habene, magis invita est. Cuius indulgentie finis est nolle amplius, et vetare omnino ne ulterius cedas, ne decidens sis

---

propiusque *Ed.*] propriusque *C M L*   Debes *L*] Debet *C M*   consulitur *M L*] consulitur *C*   precipitur *M L*] pricipitur *C*

in him — he hopes he can do. The best is counselled to all: to each is given the precept to attain what he can, and to come as near as he can to Christ, who was the best on this earth. Each one knows his own strength. Each one knows, therefore, what is of precept for him in the counsel to the best, since he sees how far he can obey the counsel.

Every precept, when it is to the best, is seen to be a counsel, because the counsel contains within itself each one's precept to a particular good. If you should say that you cannot do the best, you still have the precept to do as well as you can. And you must at the same time wish the best. You must, then, *wish* to obey the counsel of the best, but you are *obliged* to do as much as the precept adapted to you commands. The counsel pertains to your will, even if you lack the ability. The precept looks to your ability, the extent of your power.

A counsel is thus seen to be a precept that is indefinite because of ignorance, while a precept is a counsel made definite by the knowledge of what each one can do. In the teacher, then, the counsel is safer than the precept; but in those who are counselled, the precept is more fruitful than the counsel, to the extent that what a man can obey profits him more than what he cannot, even though what he cannot obey is much better than what he can: no one, however, is obliged to do what is beyond his power. Still, a man is obliged always to wish more than he can do, and to do as much as he can the things he would like to do.

To say it very briefly, everyone is under precept to do all he can. And because what each can do is unknown, the best is counselled to all alike, for until each one's weakness is known, better things are always to be supposed possible and hoped for.

When, however, someone is discovered unable, through lack of strength, to mount higher to Christ, to advance out of this worthless world and all its system to Christ and his system of living, then, provided he wish   *Indulgence.*
to advance further if he could, he is allowed out of mercy
for his weakness to stand at the point of his furthest progress. This permission is called an indulgence. It is the concession of reaching a standstill at the point which you have attained by your utmost efforts, when you cannot manage the best, on the condition that you lament your inability to move higher, and have the will to do so if you could.

In the general drawing upward of all toward Christ, an indulgence is a slackening for each individual, as his weakness requires, and for the man who cannot be altogether refashioned in spirit to Christ's system,[55] some sort of unwilling concession allowing him to retain some element of this world's system, something of the goods of body and of fortune. And the tendency of indulgence is always downward, always loosening; so it is always given unwillingly, and ever the more reluctantly as the reins are slackened more. It is the goal of indulgence that no further evil be wished, and to forbid you altogether from falling farther,

illic tam longe a Christo, ubi tibi indulgere° non potest. |111r|

Nam aliquousque procedit indulgentia et permissio mali quodammodo ne magis malum sequatur, et facile patitur in mundo sit aliquis parumper et quasi caudam intingat aquis, qui totus igneo spiritu siccus esse nequit. Quod quidem non est patiendum ut bonum sed tamquam malum, ut qui non possit esse optimus, fiat quam minime malus potest esse. Nam est boni procuratoris perfectionis in mundo non solum curare ut omnia sint quam optima, sed etiam procurare simul ut quam minime mala extent; atque ubi cernitur voluntas et desiderium optimi, concedere interea distet is aliquo gradu ab optimo, si necesse sit ad tempus; propterea quod ubi bona voluntas est proficiendi in melius, nec est causa cur absit ab optimo nisi infirmitas, ibi non est spes deponenda. Sed propter spem melioris sinenda sunt indulgenter deteriora que gratia Dei in melius trahi possunt, saltem ubi est voluntas semper et desiderium ad optimum perveniendi. Nam quoquumque inferiori gradu sistis, oportet aveas esse in optimo et invitus stes in inferiori, ac doleas te in summo esse non posse.

Nam proposito optimo omnibus, nemo debet eligere sibi aliquid sub optimo, quasi contentus inferiori gradu in quo velit conquiescere et amplius nolit requirere. Is perinde agit (ac ille quisquis sit) qui in stadio inter cursores ad unum propositum bravium et metam sistit sponte antequam ad finem curriculi venerit; qui nullo modo particeps potest esse premii si nolit amplius, prudens saltem et sciens quo esset perventurus. Quod si velit et desiderat amplius, et sistit non voluntatis |111v| defectu sed virium, hic misericordia locum habet et indulgentia. Ut sinas et foveas hominem in gradu suo et in eodem quibus adiumentis potes sustineas, ne infirmius° relabatur et decidat a bonitatis gradu quem adeptus est. Contineas eum sollicite in loco quo est, medendo ei remediis quibus sua egritudo quequumque eget, donec evadat gratia fortior et potest in ascensu altius pergere.

Quod si fieri non poterit (nam unusquisque proprium donum habet, alius quidem sic, alius vero sic) at tunc omni cura et opera agendum ut quem adeptus est in salutis via gradum in eodem sic teneatur ut nullo modo recidat in deterius. Quod a tergo est malum et quasi sub se, a quo decessit modo, vetandum est ei. Quod consecutus est in bono, ut id conservet precipiendum est ei. Quod distat ab optimo, modo id nolit si possit aliter, modo simul velit et desideret optimum continuo, et agit etiam ieiunio et precibus assiduis ut Christo propius

Vetatio mali.

Preceptum boni.

---

indulgere *C M*] indulgeri *L*   infirmius *C? L*] infirmior *M*

lest you should fall back so far from Christ that there no indulgence could exist for you.

For indulgence — in a manner, a concession of evil[56] — goes a certain distance lest a greater evil ensue, and it readily permits that someone be for a time in the world, and that the man who cannot be made wholly dry by the Spirit of fire dip his tail, as it were, in the waters. Only as an evil, however, is this to be tolerated, not as a good, and to the end that he who cannot be best may at least become as little evil as possible.[57] For the good worker of perfection in this world should not only see to it that all things are as good as they can be, but that at the same time there be as few surviving evils as possible. When he sees the will and desire for the best, he permits that a man remain temporarily in some degree removed from the best, if this be necessary for a time; because where there is a good will of advancing to the better, and no reason for not attaining the best except weakness, one must not abandon hope. Rather, because of hope for the better, worse things are to be permitted with indulgence. These the grace of God can draw to the better, at least where there remains always the will and desire to attain the best. For at whatever lower degree you stop, you must long to be in the best, and stay in the lower against your will, and grieve that you cannot be in the highest.

The best is set before all. No one, therefore, ought to choose for himself something beneath the best, as though satisfied with a lower degree and willing to repose there at a full stop, wishing to make no further effort. Such a man — and it does not matter who he is — acts just like the runner in the stadium, when all are racing for the same goal and prize, who stops of his own accord before reaching the end of the course [II Tim. II. 5]. There can be no share of the prize for him if his will stops short, at least when he knows the outcome and how far he was supposed to have gone. If he should want to go on, however, and ardently wish to, and if he should stop from lack of strength, not of will, then in mercy and indulgence he has a place. You should, then, permit the man to stay in his rank and encourage him, and maintain him there with whatever assistance you can, lest in greater weakness still, he relapse and fall back from the degree of goodness he has achieved. Diligently keep him in his own place, applying the remedies required, whatever his illness, until by grace he grows stronger and can go on in the upward climb.

If this is impossible — for each has his proper gift, one in this way, another in that [I Cor. VII. 7] — then you must exert all care and attention to keep him at the point he has reached in the way of salvation, so that he may make no backward slip. You must forbid him *Prohibition of evil.* the evil that he has just left behind and, as it were, beneath him. The good he has attained, by precept you must bind him to maintain. *Precept of good.* His distance from the best, provided he not will it if he could help it, and provided at the same time he constantly wish and desire the

attrahatur°—quod, inquam, tali mente distat ab optimo Christo, non volens
sed invitus et dolens, indulgendum est ei. Quod velit
ante omnia et cupit optimum, et quod tedet se morbi   *Indulgentia infirmitatis.*
sui avetque convalescere ac perfecte sanus esse, quibus   *Consilium ad optimum.*
rationibus hanc perfectionem consequatur, considerate
et prudenter et amanter consulendum est ei.

Sic vetans et iubens, indulgens et consulens, que quatuor semper una concur-
runt, quoad fieri potest et Deus sinet, a spiritali medico querenda° est |112r|
salus cuiusque eorum qui ingressi salutis viam contendunt totis conatibus ut in
Christo salvi fiant, qui est ipsa salus et hominis sanitas. Que consistit in absoluto
et puro statu a malo tum animi tum corporis, ut neutra pars aliquousque deorsum ex appet⟨it⟩ione inferiorum descendat, sed utraque simul ex vehementi desiderio superiorum tota sursum conspiret; ut sicut in epistola
est ad Romanos, Quemadmodum exhibuistis membra vestra   *Rom. vi. [19].*
servire immundicie et iniquitati ad iniquitatem, ita nunc exhibete membra vestra
servire iusticie in sanctificationem.

Quod debent omnes quidem facere qui se in Christo mortuos esse et resurrex-
isse profitentur, et abdicare mundum prorsus et omne malum, atque non exhibere deinceps membra arma iniquitatis peccato, sed quasi ex mortuis viventes
se totos Deo iam et membra eorum arma iusticie eidem Deo; ut veri, iusti, et
quidam Christi in conspectu Dei, et eiusdem etiam ex representatione in se deitatis
filii appareant, simul cum Christo aliquando apud communem Patrem in celis
corregnaturi.

Illuc vero ut homines traheret ex hoc mundo quotquot poterat, egregie navavit
operam Paulus, sequens suum sapientem amorem Dei et proximi, ut divinitatem
generet in hominibus, augeret et conservaret, utque perficeret homines° in Christo
et Deo. Qui voluit omnes homines esse sicut ille esset, et iussit omnes imitarentur se, sicut ille Christum, ut se ducem sectati, ad Christum eant, et per simplicitatis
portam, i.e., Christum, illiusque vitam simplicem, ingrediantur ad vitam sem-
piternam. |112v|

Que quidem porta admodmum angusta est, ipsius salutis testimonio. Et multi
querunt intrare, et non poterant, propterea quod ipsi non
sunt contracti in se sursum in simplicitatem et unitatem et   *Luc. xiii. [24].*
quasi in angustum, ut intrare possint° a divisione, multiplicitate, et latitudine
huius mundi, in quo lata est illa via et spaciosa que ducit ad perdicionem. A

---

attrahatur *M L*] attrahitur *C*?   querenda *M L*] queranda *C*   homines *M L*]
hommines *C*   possint *L*] possunt *C M*

best, and by fasting and unremitting prayers work to be drawn nearer to Christ—
his being, I say, in this state of mind removed from the best, from Christ,
not willing it, but against his will and in sorrow, is
to be met with indulgence. Because he wishes and   *Indulgence of weakness.*
desires the best above all, and because he regrets his disease and wishes to be
healed and to be in perfect health, he must be coun-
selled thoughtfully, and prudently, and lovingly, as   *Counsel to the best.*
to the means of achieving this perfection.

Thus, by prohibition and command, by indulgence and counsel—and the four
always go together—the spiritual physician[58] must seek, as far as he can and God
permits, the salvation of each of those who have entered upon the way of salvation and who are striving with all their power to be saved in Christ, who is
salvation itself, and the health of man. Health consists in being clear and freed
of evil both of soul and of body, so that neither part sinks in the least degree
downward from desire of lower things, but both together, from strong desire
of things above, unite in upward aspiration. As we find in
the Epistle to the Romans: "Just as you once made over   *Rom.* vi. [*19.*]
your members as slaves to impurity and wickedness, unto wickedness, so now
make them over as slaves to justice, unto holiness."

This all must do who profess themselves dead in Christ and risen again. They
must utterly renounce the world and all evil, must not yield henceforth their
members to sin as instruments of wickedness; but as men who live after being
among the dead, they must now give all of themselves to God and their members
to the same God as instruments of justice [vi. 13]; so that then they may appear
in the sight of God true, just, and, as it were, Christs: even—because of the
likeness of the Godhead in them—sons of the same God, who are at last to reign
in fellowship together with Christ in the presence of the Father they share in
Heaven.

It was to draw thither from this world as many men as he could that Paul
acted with such outstanding zeal. His guide was the wisdom-filled love he had
for God and neighbor, in his efforts to engender the Godhead in men, to increase and preserve It, to make men perfect in Christ and God. All men he wished
to be as he was, and he bade all imitate him as he imitated Christ; so that following
his leadership, they might go to Christ, might enter through the gate of
simplicity—Christ and his simple life—into life everlasting.

Now this gate is indeed very narrow—he who is salvation itself has affirmed
it—and many seek to enter, and have not been able, because
they are not themselves drawn close together and upward   *Luke* xiii. [*24.*]
into themselves, into simplicity and oneness, and, as it were, into narrowness,
so as to be able to enter from the division, the multiplicity, the breadth of this
world, in which that way is wide and ample that leads to perdition [Matt. vii.

qua lata, revera angustia potius quam amplitudine, si non contraxeris te in unum
penitus coierisque tecum in simplicitatem Christi, in indivisam quamdam vivendi rationem et divinam, ut quodamm⟨od⟩o quasi angustatus in unum possis foramen
acus penitrare, quod camelum penitrare est imposibile—nisi, inquam, coactus
fueris simpliciter in punctum veritatis, in punctum amplissimum, in angustiam
latitudinis, in servitutem libertatis, ubi in angusto esse in amplo est esse et servire regnare est, hoc est, nisi reformeris totus quoad fieri potest in altam et
simplicem Christi rationem vivendi induasque parvum illius statum et contemp-
tum in terris sed magnum et honorabilem in celis, atque hanc angustissimam
et simul amplissimam portam que est in vita unica nisi ingressus fueris, plane
credas ad Patrem familias et celestis domus thesauros te pervenire non posse.

Hinc rogatus a quodam Christus (ut Lucas refert) si pauci sunt qui salvantur,
non respondit aperte questioni sed iussit, dicens: Contendite intrare per angustam
portam, |113r| significans suam vivendi rationem simplicem, quod exemplar pro-
posuit omnibus, ad quod (innuebat) qui non contendit pro viribus, eum in salvatis
esse non posse.

Nam etsi non perveneris ad Christum, portam celi, tamen oportet pro virili
tuo contendas illuc quoad possis, et quam longius possis in illo progrediare. Quod
si feceris, conatus tuus extra Dei misericordiam non est censendus. Non plus
potes quam tibi datur, nec minus debes quam datur. Datur enim quod datur
tibi non ad interitum sed ad vitam, modo uteris tuo dato donoque ad id ad quod
potes maxime, ut sequaris lubens et alacriter quatenus traheris, in ultimoque tui
tractus fortiter constiteris, petens assidue et expectans et sperans meliora. Si sic
contenderis intrare, sperandum est gratia Dei te angustam portam intraturum,
id est, per Christum salvum fore, per strictum vivendi modum que angusta porta appellatur, qui fuit Christi. Qui ambulavit in semita veritatis, abhorrens longe
a platea falsitatis et trita via sceleribus, in qua regnat scelus et huius mundi ini-
quitas et servit misere ad interitum sempiternum.

Nam regnare in hoc mundo servire est peccato, cuius stipendium mors est.
A quo abire longissime et inire quamdam simplicitatem in Christo gracia certe
est Dei et vita eterna. |113v| Quod quidem sine magna Dei gratia nemo potest,
quia ad illum nemo potest sine illius gratia. Ille dat quo potes. Ille potentem
adiuvat et adiutum perficit, qui operatur in nobis et velle et perficere. Ille suscitat
a terra inopem et de stercore erigit pauperem, ut collocet eum cum principibus,

13]. If from this broad spaciousness—or rather, to be sure, from this broad narrowness[59]—you have not gathered yourself into deep, inner oneness; if you have not unified yourself into the simplicity of Christ, into a certain undivided and Godlike system of living, so that you are narrowed, as it were, into a unity that will permit you to pass through the eye of the needle though which it is impossible for a camel to pass [Matt. xix. 24];—unless, I say, you have been contracted in simplicity into the point of truth, into that broadest of points, the narrowness of fullness, the servitude of freedom, where to be in the strait is to be in the spacious, and to serve is to reign; unless, that is to say, you are entirely re-fashioned, as far as this can be, into Christ's high and simple system of living; and unless you put on his condition, small and disdained on earth, but in Heaven great and honorable; and unless you enter this narrowest and yet most spacious gate which is in the only life, believe it certain that you cannot reach the Master of the House and the treasures of the heavenly home.

So when a man asked him (as Luke recounts) whether the saved were few, Christ did not answer the question directly, but spoke a command: "Strive to enter through the narrow gate," meaning his own system of living, which is the example he set before all [Luke xiii. 23, 24]. The man who does not strive for this with all his strength, he implied, cannot be among the saved.

For even if you do not reach Christ, the gate of Heaven, still you must strive for that goal as far as you can in accordance with your strength, and advance as far as you can. If you do this, your striving must not be thought beyond God's mercy. You cannot do more than you are given strength for: you must not do less. For what is given you is given, not for your ruin, but for your life, provided you use the gift given you to the very best of your ability, so as to follow wherever you are led with eagerness and joy, remaining firm at the furthest point to which you are brought, seeking constantly and expecting and hoping better things. If you labor thus to enter, you must hope that by God's grace you will enter the narrow gate, i.e., that you will be saved through Christ, through the strict manner of living that was Christ's and that is called the narrow gate. Christ walked in the path of truth, drawing far from the broad way of falsehood and the road worn smooth by sins. In that road reigns evil and the wickedness of this world—reigns, and is in wretched slavery for eternal ruin.

For to reign in this world is to be a slave to sin; and sin's payment is death [Rom. vi. 23]. To depart from it as far as possible and enter upon a certain simplicity in Christ is surely the grace of God, and eternal life. And no one can do this without a great grace of God, because without His grace no one can go to Him. He gives the ability. The man so enabled He helps, and He makes perfect the one so helped, working both the will and the perfection in us [Phil. ii. 13]. He raises the poor from the dust, and from the dunghill lifts up the

cum principibus populi sui. Ad quem proculdubio si velis, oportet hinc aversus, totus in illum conversus sis, totus illuc contendas, omnibus viribus ad illum aspires.

Exigit enim illa provincia et conatus ut in regnum Dei te recipias et apud Deum cum Christo regnes, quicquid potes, undequumque contractis auxiliis. Nam quum nihil potest esse maius homini quam ad magnum Deum pervenire in quo magnus efficiatur, profecto ut hoc opus tam arduum et difficile consummat, ab eo nihil potest fieri nimium. Iccirco ut velit parabola Christi ad turbas apud Lucam disserentis, In tantum edificium computandi sunt sumptus, ne incoatum opus derelictum derideatur. In tantum bellum pen-sitande sunt vires, et considerandum quanto cum hoste demicandum est. Hostis *Luc. xiv.* [28]. autem est hic mundus sub duce diabolo, sub vexillo iniquitatis, quem se vicisse apud Ioannem Christus dicit. Cum quo sane nostra fortissima pugna° fuga est, quoad maxime fieri potest. Qui nihil aliud molitur nisi ut suis falsis illecibris nos in se contineat, ac navigantes in hoc mare quasi Syrenorum cantibus sic nos demulceat ut Deum et quietis portum non meditemur. Quod si |114r| tuto vis preterire et evadere, obturande° sunt aures tue et ab hoc falso et fallaci mundo avertendi sunt oculi penitus, et tu ipse totus in ceptum cursum tradendus es, assidue oculis et mente illuc intenta quo velis, ut optatam tamdem terram, terram illam viventium, feliciter potiaris; pro qua sunt relinquenda omnia, divitie, opes, honores, amici, parentes: immo tu ipse quoque a te ipso deserendus. Et tantus sumptus, tante impense sunt necessario pro tanta margarita cuiusmodi est celorum regnum faciende. Quod voluit Iesus Christus Salvator noster computet secum quisque graviter quanti est celestis hereditas et quam magni venditur. Que profecto (veritatis sententia) tanti est precii venditurque tanti ut quicquid hic habes, etiam te ipsum, oportet des si eam tuam velis esse.

Nam quid aliud velint illa verba Christi, nequeuntis mentiri, apud Lucam, quibus ex parabolis de computandis sumptibus et gerendo bello suam sententiam concludit, dicens turbis etiam, nedum discipulis: *Sic ergo omnis ex vobis qui non renunciat omnibus que possidet non potest meus esse discipulus?* Hec, inquam, verba, quid aliud velint quam danda esse omnia ut habeas tibi quod ipsum est omne? Quod si habes, nihilo carere potes. Quocirca apud eundem Lucam est paulo ante quod a Christo fuit dictum: *Si quis venit ad me et non odit patrem suum et matrem et uxorem et filios, fratres et sorores, adhuc autem et animam suam,* |114v| *non potest*

---

pugna *M L*] pungna *C*   obturande *Ed.*] obturandi *C M L*

beggar, to give him a place among princes, among the princes of His people [Ps. CXII. 7, 8]. If you should wish to come to Him, clearly you must be turned from this place and altogether toward Him; you must strive toward Him with your whole being; you must aspire to Him with all your strength.

For this charge and this attempt to get yourself into the Kingdom of God and to reign with Christ in God's sight requires all that you can do, with all the assistance you can marshal from whatever source. For since there is no greater undertaking for man than to attain to the great God in whom he is made great, surely to achieve this so difficult and so lofty a task nothing he does can be too much. As the parable of Christ speaking to the crowds has it (in Luke), in so great a building the costs are to be reckoned up, lest men laugh to scorn the work begun but abandoned. In so great *Luke XIV. [28.]* a war, one must weigh one's own resources, and ponder how great the enemy to be combatted [XIV. 31]. And the enemy is this world under the Devil's command, flying the standard of wickedness: the enemy Christ says in John that he has conquered [John VI. 33]. With it, to be sure, our most courageous action is flight, the most successful flight possible. Its endeavors are aimed at nothing but to entrap us in itself by its false lures, and as we sail on this sea, to soothe us with Sirens' songs[60] so that we will have no thought of God and of the haven of rest. But if you want to pass on safely and to escape, you must stop up your ears and turn your eyes clear away from this false and deceiving world, and you must give yourself wholly to the course you have begun, with your eyes and your mind fixed on the goal you wish to reach, so that at last you may in happiness take possession of the desired land, that land of the living [Ps. XXVI. 13]. For this are all things to be relinquished: riches, possessions, honors, friends, parents—indeed, you must abandon even yourself [Luke XIV. 26]. So great a price, so high a cost, must needs be met for a pearl as great as the Kingdom of Heaven [Matt. XIII. 45, 46]. And our Savior Jesus Christ wished each one to weigh very seriously within himself what the heavenly inheritance is worth, and how much it costs. Indeed, by the judgment of Truth, its worth is so great and its price so high that you must give whatever you have here, even yourself, if you wish it to be yours.

For what else do those words of Christ in Luke mean—those words of the Christ who cannot lie—in which he draws his conclusion from the parables about weighing the expenses and waging the war? He tells the multitude, and not just his disciples: "So, then, none of you can be my disciple who does not take leave of all that he possesses" [XIV. 33]. What else, I say, can these words mean, except that you must give all to have for yourself that which is all? If you have that, you can lack nothing. There is, therefore, a little earlier in the same Luke a saying of Christ: "If any man comes to me, and does not hate his father and mother and wife and children and brothers and sisters, yes, and his own life, too,

meus esse discipulus. Et qui non baiulat crucem suam et venit post me non potest meus esse discipulus.

Itaque oportet necessario versa facie in celum Christi vestigia sequamur. Alioquin in suis non numerabimur. Nec retrospiciendum est ullo modo ad nostros, nisi quatenus eos nobiscum felices fiant. Qui revera non sunt nostri amplius nisi quatenus nobiscum voluntate Dei coniunguntur. *Ille* (inquit) *frater mihi et soror est qui facit voluntatem Patris mei.* Nec in itinerantibus ad Deum est habenda ulla alia cognatio quam coitinerantium, ut qui tecum in tua perfectione sursum ad celestem Hierusalem volunt esse comites, hii sunt soli qui tecum in sanguine coniuncti° sunt reputandi.

Patrem autem et fratres et reliquam cognationem dabis operam ut tibi asciscas ad societatem felicitatis, copulesque tibi hac nova cognatione celesti in Deo, in qua quisque tecum evaserit maior, is profecto tibi vera affinitate et sanguine est cognatior. Nam in Christo omnis vetustas in hoc genere abolenda est. Transierunt vetera (inquit Paulus), ecce nova sunt omnia. Noluit audire Salvator illam de turba mulierem quum acclamavit, Beatus venter qui te portavit; sed dixit, |115r| Beati qui audiunt verbum Dei et custodiunt illud, volens divertere oculos° hominum in aliud, ut non hominum more spectent ad humilia, advertantque cognationes in terris, sed divina gratia suspiciant Deum et illius iusticiam, atque in ea cognationem solum et beatitudinem reponant.

Verum ne hoc disputans videar esse impius in parentes et charitatem eorum quos natura coniunxit dissolvere, hoc dico, te non posse magis amare tuos quam non amare eos nisi tecum Deum ament, nec magis agnoscere quam ignorare eos nisi tecum a Deo cogniti, Deum pie recognoscant, quem regeneratus in Christo solum agnoscit verum Patrem, in quo filius solos habes fratres eos qui tecum filii regignuntur. Nec est nunc alia cognatio quam fraternitas in Deo, in qua omnis cognatio consanguinitasque continetur, longe verior et arctior quam ea que antea in mundo fuerat, vel natura vel hominum affectu constituta. Et hic etiam maior ac amplior charitas et pax exoritur, non contracta in paucos sed diffusa in omnes, quam unquam vel naturalis in mundo vel humana appetitio potuit procreare.

Quamobrem apud Ioannem Salvator noster ita suos alloquitur: Pacem meam do vobis, pacem meam relinquo vobis. Et addit, significans huius charitatis |115v| et pacis prestantiam, *Non quomodo mundus dat, ego do vobis,* sed (illic subaudiamus)

---

coniuncti *M*] coniunctis *C L*   oculos *L*] oculus *C M, but corr. in M by another hand*

he cannot be my disciple. And he who does not bear his cross and come after me cannot be my disciple" [XIV. 26, 27].

It is, therefore, altogether necessary that with our face turned toward Heaven we follow the footsteps of Christ. Otherwise we shall not be numbered among his own. And we must not look back at all to our own, except to the extent that we wish to draw them with us, so that with us they too may be happy. Truly, they are no longer ours, except in so far as they are joined with us by the will of God. Christ said: "He is my brother and my sister who does the will of my Father" [Matt. XII. 50]. Among those, then, who journey to God, no relationship must be acknowledged except that of fellow-wayfarers, so that those only are to be esteemed as joined to you by blood who wish to be comrades with you in your upward journey to the heavenly Jerusalem.

You will take pains, however, to draw to yourself into the fellowship of happiness your father, and your brothers, and the rest of your kin, and to join them to you by this new and heavenly kinship in God, in which whoever becomes with you greater, he surely is the more closely related to you by blood and by true kinship. For in Christ all that was old in this matter must be taken away. The old things (says Paul) have passed away: "Behold, all things are new" [I Cor. v. 17]. Our Savior would not hear that woman in the crowd when she cried out, "Blessed is the womb that bore thee," but said, "Blessed are they who hear the word of God and keep it" [Luke XI. 27, 28], wishing to turn men's eyes elsewhere, so that they would not look in human fashion to earthly things or heed earthly relationships but would look up to God, by the divine grace, and to His justice, and in it alone find place for kinship and for happiness.

Now lest in these arguments I should seem to be unfeeling toward parents, and to dissolve the love of those whom nature has joined together, I make this assertion: You cannot love your own any more than not love them, unless they share your love for God; you cannot recognize their kinship any more than not recognize it, unless they are recognized by God as you are, and in return rightly acknowledge God as their own. The man born anew in Christ acknowledges that God alone as his Father. In Him, the only brothers a son has are those who are reborn with him as sons of God. Nor is there any longer other kinship than that of brotherhood in God, and in this kinship is all relationship, all tie of blood, contained, far truer now and closer than that which formerly existed in the world, whether founded in nature or in human affection. Here arise too a charity and a peace, not narrowed to a few, but extended to all, greater and fuller than ever human or natural inclination was able to engender on earth.

For this reason our Savior spoke thus to his chosen (in John): "My peace I give you, my peace I leave to you" [John XIV. 27]. And he added, indicating the excellence of this charity and this peace: "Not as the world gives do I give unto you," but (let us understand the unspoken words here) "I give you a much

multo excellentiorem charitatem, videlicet illam que diffusa est in cordibus nostris
per Spiritum Sanctum, qui datus est nobis. Ut nemo fuit unquam qui tantopere
tantaque pietate dilexerit° vel suum indulgentissimum patrem matremve quam
quisque vere filius Dei suum fratrem vere in Deo diligit.

Ut quum dicimus te tuum patrem carnalem non agniturum nec amaturum
nisi quatenus tibi idem est regenitus frater in Deo, vere tecum secundum Deum
vivens, significamus tunc te eundem longe plus et verius et vehementius amare
fratrem in Deo quam unquam in mundo patrem amare potuisti.

Quod si contendas in Deo etiam iam eum qui te genuit et agnoscendum patrem
et preamandum, tu hoc intellige in hac° nova regeneratura, in qua Dei gratia
omnes sumus filii Dei et confratres, neminem se ullius filium debere appelare
nisi illius unius Dei, in quo clamamus Abba, Pater, quum nunc non secundum
carnem ambulemus, sed secundum Deum. In quo (iterum dico) quantoquuum-
que amore velis, non potes plus amare patrem quam eundem fratrem, nec sub
patris nomine plus honorare quam debes si eum fratrem voces. Sub quo nomine
convenientius est sane, a quo genitus eras, modo ille regenitus in filium Deo
est, omni amore et honore prosequare, quam patris appellatione; ut hoc magnificum
nomen iure |116r| debite reverentie gratia ab omnibus soli Deo deferatur, a quo
fuimus geniti feliciter et ab eodem deinde postea felicitius regenerati, a quoque
omnis paternitas et in celo et in terra denominatur. Quod   *xxiii.* [9.]
ut fiat, ut in Matthei evangelio est, apertissime precepit Ma-
gister veritatis, dicens suis: *Et patrem nolite vocari° vobis super terram. Unus est enim
Pater vester qui in celis est. Vos autem omnes fratres estis.*

Sed redeamus, aliquando perventuri illuc quo omnis hic superior tam vagus
et tam diffusus sermo spectat, ut quid tum consulens, tum precipiens, tum indulgens, tum prohibens, Corinthios edocet Paulus videamus; hoc tamen premisso
summatim et breviter, quod tot verbis in antecedente sermone tractavimus, et
paucis absoluto quid inter hec quatuor, consulere, iubere,
indulgere, vetare, discriminis est. Quorum duo posteriora   *Consulere.*
ad malum semper, duo priora ad bonum spectant. Consulis   *Iubere.*
                                                                Indulgere.
enim quando suades optimum, quod quisque sequi debet°.   *Vetare.*
Iubes quando precipis ut quisque id et tantum bonum sequa-
tur quantum potest. Indulges vero quando invitus, necessitate quadam, concedis

---

dilexerit *C M*] dilexit *L*   hac *M L*] hoc *C*   vocari *C M L*] *vocare Vulg.*   debet
C L] debeat *M*

more excellent charity," that, namely, which is spread among our hearts through the Holy Spirit, who has been given to us [Rom. v. 5]. The consequence is that there has never been anyone to love even the most tender father or mother so much or with such great piety as each true son of God loves his true brother in God.

When we say, therefore, that you are not to acknowledge or love your physical father except in so far as he has been reborn to you as a brother in God, truly sharing with you a life according to God's will, we mean that then you will love him much more and much more truly and more intensely as your brother in God than you could ever have loved him in the world as your father.

If you should maintain, however, that even then, in God, he who begot you must be acknowledged your father and especially loved, understand this: in the new regeneration, in which by God's grace we are all sons of God and brothers one of the other, no one should call himself the son of anyone except of that one God in whom we cry, Abba, Father; because we no longer walk in the ways of flesh, but in the ways of God [Rom. viii. 15, 4]. And in God, I repeat, however great a love you care to imagine, you cannot love a man as father more than as brother, nor can you honor him more under the name of father than you must if you call him brother. Under this name, surely, it is more fitting for you to pay all honor and love to him who begot you, provided he has been reborn as a son of God, than under that of father; with the result that this magnificent name may be given over by all to God alone, as is right and in accord with the reverence due Him. He begot us in happiness, and subsequently He renewed our begetting in even greater happiness. From Him all fatherhood in Heaven and on earth derives its name [Eph. iii. 15]. And the Teacher of Truth, as we find in Matthew's Gospel, gave us a most clear command in this matter, when he said to his followers: "And *Ch. xxiii 9.* do not call any man on earth your father. For you have only one Father, and He is in Heaven. And you are all brothers."

Let us go back, however, and at last come to the point at which all the above discussion, so rambling and so diffuse, has been aimed: to see what Paul teaches the Corinthians in counsel, precept, indulgence, and prohibition. I shall say in advance, briefly and compendiously—clearing up in a few words what we have treated in the preceding discourse with so many—only what difference exists between these four things: to counsel, to *Counsel,* command, to indulge, to forbid. The latter two are con- *Command,* cerned always with evil, the former two with good. For *Indulgence,* you counsel when you urge the best, which each ought *Prohibition.* to follow. You command when you give each the precept to follow that good, to follow as high a good as he can. You grant indulgence when against your will you concede, because of some necessity, an evil that (through a weakness

malum quod quispiam, dolens, pre infirmitate nequit vitare. Vetas quando pro-
hibes omnino ne ultra id quod indulgetur malum decidat relabaturque extra in-
dulgentie fines |116v| in ea scelera que morti destinantur, quorum non est venia,
nisi resurgentem te decidisse peniteat.

Itaque in consilio spectatur quod debes etiam si non potes; in prohibitione,
quod non debes etiam si posses°; in precepto, quod quisque potest facere bonum;
in indulgentia, quod quisque nequit vitare malum.

Fortitudo a Deo est, infirmitas ex nobis. Potes in malum quatenus velis, quod
posse est non posse. Potes in bonu⟨m⟩ quatenus traheris a bono, tractumque se-
queris, quod est incipere posse et in maiorem potestatem ire. Qui tractus gratie
non rapit violenter, sed naturaliter et dulciter: immo dulcius et molius quam
natura potest, supernaturali suavitate restituit quod trahit in arbitrii libertatem,
que proprie est ad bonum, dumtaxat bona et constans voluntas.

In quam libertatem tendit voluntas suapte natura, sed impotens omnino ut
in eam prodeat, nisi libere gratie subsidio promoveatur. Quod voluit Paulus dicere
quando dixerit, *Velle mihi adiacet: perficere autem° non invenio*; quod est, naturalis
inclinatio est mei animi ad libertatem in bonum, sed in eam ex servitute in malum
non exit, nec perficitur quidem hoc desiderium libertatis ex me ullo modo, sed
ex gratia, que liberat me de corpore mortis huius, gratia Dei per Dominum
nostrum Iesum Christum.

Verum nunc demum, |117r| hiis expositis, vel effusis delatatius, ad Paulum
nostrum propius accedamus. Qui rogatus a Corinthiis quidnam agendum sit in
re uxoria iis qui Christum profitentur, primum velit omnes in hac re sibi similes
esse celebesque vivere, quo castius et quietius Deo, qui ipsa castitas quiesque est,
inserviant.

Nam voluit ut quisque quoad maxime fieri potuit esset quam optimus, unique
Deo in Christo quam simplicissime deditus. Quapropter innuptis suadet, si virgo
sit non nubat; sin vidua, non renubat; ut magis unita et simplex sanctitati et
orationibus se Deo possit devovere.

Verum quamquam id optimum cuique voluit et in primis cupivit, tamen non
agnoscens quorsum et ad quantum bonum sua cuiusque virtus potuit, abstinen-
tiam omnino omnibus a re uxorea non ausus est imperare, ne ultra potentiam
astricti, ru⟨m⟩pant vinculum legis et prescriptum terminum transgrediantur.

Quapropter indulgenter agens cum Corinthiis, illorum infirmitatis habens rationem, permisit facile quisque ducat uxorem, remediumque sui ardoris asciscat

---

posses *C?*] possis *M L*   *autem M L*] *autem autem C*

he regrets) someone cannot avoid. And you forbid when you altogether restrain someone from slipping beneath the indulgence of evil and relapsing beyond the limits of indulgence into those sins that are appointed for death and for which there is no pardon, unless you rise again and repent your fall.

In counsel, then, it is a matter of what you ought to do even if you cannot; in prohibition, of what you ought not do even if you can; in precept, it is a matter of the good that each can do; in indulgence, of the evil that each cannot avoid.

Strength comes from God, weakness from out of ourselves. You have the power for evil as far as you should wish, and this power is a lack of power. You have the power for good to the extent that you are drawn by the good and follow its drawing, and this is the beginning of power and an advance to greater power. This drawing on of grace does not carry you off violently, but naturally and gently. More gently, indeed, and more softly than nature can, does grace with supernatural sweetness restore that which it draws to freedom of choice,[61] a freedom by nature tending to the good, as long as the will is good and firm.

The will by its own nature tends toward this liberty, but it is altogether powerless to reach it, unless it be advanced by the assistance of free grace. This is what Paul meant when he said, "To will is present to me, but I do not find the means to perform" [Rom. vii. 18]. This is to say, the natural inclination of my mind is to freedom for good, but it does not escape to that freedom from its bondage to evil; nor is this longing for freedom fulfilled through me in any way, but through grace, which sets me free from the body of this death: the grace of God,[62] through our Lord Jesus Christ [vii. 24, 25].

But now at last, with these matters set forth—or rather, too generously stretched out—let us draw nearer to our Paul. The Corinthians asked him what those who professed Christ were to do about marriage. His first wish was that in this matter all should be as he was, and live celibate, so that they might with greater chastity and peace serve God, who is Chastity itself and Peace [I Cor. vii. 7].

For he wished everyone, to the limits of his ability, to be as perfect as he could be, and dedicated in Christ to God alone with as much singleness as possible. For the unmarried, therefore, he urges that if a woman be a virgin, she not marry, and if a widow, that she not remarry, so that she may devote herself to God in holiness and prayers more singly and more simply [vii. 8, 34].

But although he wished this perfection for all, and above all things desired it, still, not knowing the strength and the extent of each one's power of virtue, he did not dare to command for all a complete abstinence from marriage, lest this be a constraint beyond their ability, and they break the bonds of the law and transgress the bounds prescribed [vii. 2].

Acting, therefore, with indulgence toward the Corinthians, and taking into account their weakness, he readily allowed that anyone who knew himself too

mulierem unam matrimonio legittimo, qui pre infirmitate agnoscit se celebem vivere non posse; ut qui non possit ab omnibus, ab omnibus tamen preterquam ab una abstineat. Que una conceditur ne sua proclivitas in libidinem carnis prorumpat forsan |117v| in aliquod facinus detestabilius.

Ut ergo malum vitetur quam maxime possit, et bonum quoad fieri potest conservetur, misericorditer conceditur ut qui non possit in primo esse gradu stet in secundo, habeatque unam qui non potest nullam. Ultra quem gradum descensus non conceditur, propter quod quatenus ad rem spectat refrigeriumque morbi, una sufficit. Que hec quoque non conceditur nisi infirmitatis causa et, ut Paulus ait, ob incontinentiam. Ut ubi non sentitur illa infirmitas, ibi illa ad nuptias licentia non est usurpanda, ne ridicule et damnabiliter personam egroti hominis voluntate magis quam necessitate agamus, velimusque non sanare nos egrotos, sed adhibita° medicina non necessaria ex sanis sponte egrotare. Quo nihil miserabilius nec homine christiane professionis indignius fieri potest.

In ipsis quoque nuptiis, veneris petulantia non nostra voluntate contractis, ut semper videamur velle magis caste vivere quam solute, in coniuge profecto quam minime possumus nos exolvemus, ut nuptie nobis, sicuti esse debent, remedium sint involuntarie libidinis, non diversorium spontanee voluptatis. Quocirca detestandi sunt illi profecto qui et proposito et voto se in matrimonio copulant ut in eo mutuo |118r| suas libidines expleant,

Hieronymus [. . .] huic°, Adulter est in suam uxorem amator ardentior.

quandoquidem in coniugio, quod debet esse quatenus concedit infirmitas castum, turpiter et flagitiose meritricantur.

Hic caveat quisque existimet Paulum ob ullam aliam causam permittere nuptias quam ob impotentiam continendi. Ob quam causam non solum primas sed etiam secundas et si

Nuptie ob infirmitatem.

velis etiam tertias concedit. Quod si eiusmodi quidem causa nulla est, tum persuade tibi ne primas esse concessas. Quoniam nuptie nihil habent bonitatis nisi quatenus mali sint remedium necessarium. Sic quidem bone sunt quum vicicitudinario subsidio coniugatos tenent, ne passim per plures mulieres fornicentur.

Olim autem in principio erat in illis utilitas prolis procreande ut multiplici humani generis propagine mundus repleretur, item quedam ratio sacramenti, spectans ad Christum et suam sponsam ecclesiam. Christus fuit ex virgine natus, ut Christiani ex ecclesia, et matre et virgine, enascantur. In secunda epistola in-

---

adhibita *M L*] abhibita *C*   *marg.* Hieronymus . . . *word illeg.*

weak to live celibate should marry and take to himself in legitimate matrimony one woman as a remedy for the fire of passion. In this way, he who could not abstain from all women might still abstain from all but one. And this one is allowed him lest perhaps his proneness to fleshly lust break out in some crime too abominable [VII. 2].

To avoid evil as much as possible, then, and to maintain good as far as possible, it is allowed in mercy that the man who cannot be in the first rank should remain in the second, and that he should have a wife who cannot be without. Beyond this degree no further descent is permitted, since one wife is enough for the purpose, which is to allay the disease. Further, this one is allowed only because of weakness, and, as Paul says, on account of incontinency [VII. 5]. So that where that weakness is not felt, this concession of marriage is not to be taken advantage of, lest we should absurdly and damnably act the part of a sick man from choice more than from need, and with the intention, not of curing ourselves when ill, but of deliberately making sickness of our health by the use of an unnecessary medicine. Nothing can be done more wretched, nor more unworthy of a man who makes the Christian profession.

And even in a marriage contracted because of the wanton insistence of desire, not because of our own wish, we must always manifest the will to live chastely rather than unrestrainedly, and therefore we shall as little as possible[63] indulge ourselves with our spouse. In this way marriage will be for us—as it ought to be—a remedy for involuntary lust, not a resort for sexual delight at will. Those people, then, are surely to be held in abomination who deliberately and intentionally join themselves in matrimony to *Jerome comments to this: "The man too ardent toward his wife is an adulterer."* fulfil in it their mutual lusts, since in wedlock, which ought to be chaste (so far as weakness permits), they are practicing harlotry in foul and infamous fashion.

Let all here beware of thinking that Paul allows marriage for any other reason than one's inability to restrain oneself. And for this reason he permits not only a first marriage, but a sec- *Marriage is because of weakness.* ond also—even a third, if you should wish it. But if there is no reason of this kind, convince yourself that you are not allowed even a first; because marriage has no goodness in it[64] except in so far as it is a necessary remedy for evil. As such, to be sure, it is good, since by means of the exchange of assistance, married men are restrained from fornicating promiscuously with many women.

Of old, however, in the beginning, there was the quality of usefulness in it, for the procreation of descendants so that the world might be filled with the numerous offspring of the human race. And there was likewise a certain sacramental meaning to it, with regard to Christ and his bride, the Church. Christ was born of a virgin, so that Christians might be born of the Church, both virgin and

quit Paulus: Despondi vos uni viro, virginem castam exhibere Christo. Quum
autem nunc sponsus advenerit, veritasque spiritalis matrimonii adimpleta est, nihil
est necesse amplius extet coniugium ut figura futuri. Neque vero |118v| incremen-
tum subolis exposcit in Christianitate coitum in coniugio, quandoquidem nostra
procreatio regenitura est in Deo, non genitura; qui sumus (ut Joannes scribit)
non ex sanguinibus, neque ex voluntate carnis, neque ex voluntate viri, sed ex
Deo nati.

Quod si omnes vocati in fidem virgines permansissent, superfuisset tamen semper
ex gentilitate qui materiam gratie christiano spiritui suppeditasset, et ecclesia in
se integrior atque Christo sponso castior coniux adhesisset. Quod si rogas, Quidnam futurum erat si universa multitudo gentium ad Christi cultum conversa
fuisset? — fuisset profecto tunc futurum quod docuit Christus ut petamus cotidie
et deprecemur aliquando fiat, videlicet, adveniat regnum Dei fiatque voluntas
eius sicut in celo et in terra; fuisset futurum etiam in universo orbe terrarum
quod Paulus Romanos obsecrat ut illi faciant, videlicet, ut exhibeant corpora
sua hostiam viventem, sanctam, Deo placentem, obsequentem rationi, utque ipsi reformentur toti in novitatem sensus, ut probent quid sit voluntas Dei bona,
beneplacens, et perfecta; fuisset denique futurum tunc ut totus mundus sanctus
esset° et animo et corpore, ac in tanta sanctitate interiisset, statim resurrectura
Deo et sine fine victura, quo fine hominibus nihil felicius° et Deo in hominibus
nihil gratius fuisset. Qui misit suum Filium ut perficeret mundum, ut in
perfectione° finem faceret et tradat regnum Deo et Patri (ut ait Paulus) quum
evacuerit omnem principatum, potestatem, et virtutem, subieceritque, omnia sibi
et Deo; quem oportet regnare donec id fecerit donecque tandem mortem ipsam
destruxerit, feceritque ex mortalibus |119r| et terrenis immortalia et divina, ut
Deus sit omnia in omnibus, concludanturque omnia optimo fine cum maxima
misericordia et beatitudine hominum, et cum eorumdem quam minimo dispendio.

Si provincia Christi et bellum quod indixit mundo — qui hostis est celi et
celestium — et milicia Apostolorum quam armis iusticie, sub Christo duce, sub
vexillo veritatis, strenuiter egerint, eum celerem et prosperum exitum habuisset,
ac preterea tantam et tam felicem victoriam in hominibus, ut discussis omnibus
stulticie tenebris et malitie frigore dissipato, ereptis, inquam, a manibus eorum
istis armis infirmitatis, universi ubique gentium victi, subiecti, concaptivitati (ut

---

esset *M L*] essent *C*   felicius *L*] felicicius *C M*   perfectione *M L*] perficti-
one *C*

mother. In his second letter, Paul says: "I have betrothed you to one husband, to present you to Christ as a chaste virgin" [II Cor. xi. 2]. But now that the Bridegroom has come, and the spiritual truth of marriage has been fulfilled, there is no reason why marriage should remain any longer as a figure of what was to come. And in Christianity no increase of offspring demands coition in marriage any longer, since our begetting is not a generation, but a regeneration in God. As John writes, "We are not born of blood, nor of the will of the flesh, nor of the will of men, but of God" [John i. 13].

And if those called into the faith had all remained virgins, there would still always have been a surplus from Heathendom to supply the matter of grace to the Christian spirit, and the Church would have held fast to Christ, her spouse, as a bride of greater intrinsic integrity and greater purity.[65] And if you ask what would have happened if the whole multitude of the Gentiles had been converted to the worship of Christ — surely, the outcome would then have been what Christ taught us to ask for every day and to pray for the eventual realization of, namely, that the Kingdom of God should come and His will be done on earth as it is in Heaven. And the outcome throughout the whole world would have been (further) what Paul beseeches the Romans to do, that they present their bodies as a living sacrifice,[66] holy, pleasing unto God, obedient to reason; and that they be entirely remade into a newness of their mind, so that they might prove what is the good and the acceptable and the perfect will of God [Rom. xii. 1, 2]. The outcome would have been, finally, that all the world would have been holy both in mind and in body, would have died in this great holiness to rise at once to God and to live forever. No outcome could have been happier for men, nor could anything in men have pleased God more. He sent His Son to make perfect the world so that he might make an end in perfection and deliver to God and the Father the Kingdom (as Paul says), having first dispossessed all rule, authority, and power, and subdued all things to himself and to God. Reign he must until he has done this, and until he has destroyed at last death itself, and made of the mortal and the earthly something immortal and divine, so that God may be all in all, and so that all may be concluded in the best ending, with the greatest mercy toward men and their greatest happiness, and with the least possible loss among them [I Cor. xv. 24–28].

If the charge of Christ and the war that he proclaimed against the world (the enemy of Heaven and of the Heavenly), together with the warfare of the Apostles, which they waged so actively with the weapons of justice under Christ's leadership and the standard of truth, had had that swift and happy outcome; if they had, moreover, achieved a victory so great and so propitious that all the darkness of stupidity had been broken and the coldness of malice dispersed, and those weapons had been snatched, I say, from the hands of all of Heathendom everywhere, and all had been conquered, subdued, and brought into common bondage

Pauli more loquar°) in obsequium Christi et servitutem Deo dedidissent se novo
Imperatori, in illiusque victoris potestate se totos posuissent, accepissentque novam
armaturam, arma splendide fidei et ardentis amoris Dei, obligatique fuissent sub
Christo duce omnes sacramento militari, accepto signo crucis, ut totis conatibus
in celestem rempublicam studeant, ac fortes et firmi spe comilicium° christianum
alacriter iniissent, conseruissentque manus cum illis a quibus, adiuti divina gratia,
profugerint, ut ea prorsus a se abigerent, omnem videlicet stulticiam et vanam
appeticionem inferiorum, atque ita pugnantes° confugientesque in Deum, tan-
top⟨er⟩e in celestem quamdam vite rationem contendissent, sursum fide et amore
Dei ascendentes, ut mundo |119v| longe a tergo relicto et corpore in obsequelam
anime intime contracto et ipsa anima penitus in Spiritum ingressa, in omnibus
scilicet hominibus, ut universi, absoluti a mundo, abducti a caduco corporis affectu,
expediti et liberi, nihil desiderassent nisi Deum, nihilque hic viventes nisi ex Deo
egissent, cum omni fide Christo, spe superiorum, charitate Dei et proximi, quasi
eorum conversatio esset in celis ubi nec nubent neque nubentur; si, inquam, ad
hunc felicem statum in hoc mundo universo C⟨h⟩risti et Apostolorum predicatio
perrexisset ut omnes illico C⟨h⟩risti similes soli Deo sancti et casti inserviissent,
ac regenerati ex hominibus defluentibus in libidinem corporis, quasi facti angeli
in terris celebes secum deinceps constitissent, ac sic singulus quisque suo tempore Deo puriter interiisset, mundusque totus sic particulatim defecisset finitus-
que tandem fuisset—quis, te queso, si hec sic fuissent futura, humani generis
in terris et huius hic hominum perigrinationis et vite aut magis oportunus aut
magis optatus finis esse potuisset?

Sed infirmitate hominum factum est—fitque cotidie—ut tardius ad nos redeat
noster Salvator Jesus Christus, finem huius mundi conclusurus, utque nova creatura
in Deo longius gemens hic expectet adoptionem filiorum Dei, qui (ut in secunda
sua epistola scribit Petrus) non tardat promissum |120r| sed patienter agit pro-
pter nos, nolens aliquem periri, sed omnes ad penitentiam reverti.

Que infirmitas etiam ab indulgenti Deo exegit nuptias et feminarum remedium
pro ratione morbi, ut quatenus necessitas cogit, eis ardore libidinis egroti modice
utantur. Debet tamen optare quisque ut tali morbo non afficiatur, utque masculina
castitate Deo (qui ipsa est castitas) magis assimiletur. Omnis enim nostra vita

---

loquar *M L*] loquor *C*   comilicium *C L*] comilitium *M*   pugnantes *M L*]
pungnantes *C*

(to speak in the manner of Paul) to the obedience of Christ and the service of God [II Cor. x. 5]; and if all men had surrendered to the new Emperor and put themselves entirely in that Conqueror's power, and received the new armor, the arms of shining faith and burning love of God, and had bound themselves by the military oath of allegiance—taking the Sign of the Cross—under the leadership of Christ, to apply themselves strenuously in all their undertakings to the Heavenly commonwealth; and if all men had eagerly entered the Christian comradeship, strong and resolute in hope, and had joined battle with those things from which, with the help of divine grace, they had escaped, to drive these from themselves altogether—all stupidity, that is, and all vain desire of lower things; and if fighting thus and taking refuge in God, they had strained forward to a Heavenly system of life, mounting so vigorously on high through faith and love of God as to leave the world far behind them, and concentrate their bodies into compliance to their souls,[67] and bring the soul itself deep into the Spirit; if this had been the outcome among all men, so that all, disengaged from the world, withdrawn from the perishable affection of the body, unimpeded and free, had desired nothing except God, and had done nothing during their lives here except what was of God, with all faith in Christ, hope in things above, love of God and neighbor, as though their abode were already in Heaven, where there is neither marriage nor giving in marriage [Mark xii. 25]; if, I say, the preaching of Christ and of the Apostles had proceeded to this happy state in the whole world so that all men had served God alone, Christlike, holy, and chaste, and being born anew out of men whose being was flowing into bodily lust, had found a life of celibate self-consistency, as though they had become angels on earth; and if each in his own time had thus gone purely to God in death, and the whole world had in this way failed piecemeal and at last been ended—were these things to have happened, what more fitting or more desirable end, I ask you, could there have been to the human race on earth and to this, man's life here and pilgrimage?

But by the weakness of men it was brought about—and still each day is being brought about—that our Savior Jesus Christ returns to us less swiftly to make a closing and an end of this world, and that the new creation in God, sighing here, awaits the longer its adoption into the sonship of God [Rom. viii. 23]. Not, however, that God (as Peter writes in his second Epistle) is being slack about His promise: He is acting patiently, not willing that anyone should perish, but willing that all should turn back to repentance [II Pet. iii. 9].

This same weakness also wrested marriage from an indulgent God, and the remedy of women in accordance with the nature of the disease, so that those ailing from the passion of desire might use them with restraint as far as necessity obliged. But each must wish to be unaffected by such a disease, and in masculine chastity to grow more like God, who is Chastity itself. For all our life and our

et actio eo contendere debet, ut Deum in nobis quoad fieri potest referamus, ea pura et constanti simplicitate, eo in nobis sapienti ordine, ea denique consummata perfectione, ut dum hic vivitur nihil solute et infirmiter, nihil turpiter et stulte, nihil imperfecte et deficienter agamus, sed angelis firmitate, pulchritudine, et unius Dei amore similes simus.

Sed ut Deus misericors et indulgens est, ita in humana hierarchia, i.e., ecclesia, est misericordia et patientia impotentum. Itaque Paulus permittit nuptias et in nuptiis reddicionem mutui debiti°, et post primas nuptias, impotentibus continere, si velint, secundas.

Atque hec omnis indulgentia, ut ipse ait, est vitande fornicationis cause, et propter hominum incontinentiam. Quod si potentia continendi esset, multo melius et quietius ipsis hominibus, et Deo gratius esset, virginibus non nubere, nuptis in ipso coniugio caste et sine coitu vivere, innuptis viduisque non rursum renubere. Verum (ut ait) unusquisque proprium donum habet, alius quidem sic, alius vero sic.

Summa est: et ante nuptias, et in ipsis nuptiis, et post nuptias, contentio quoad maxime° fieri potest tum virorum tum feminarum |120v| christianarum debet esse ad angelicam castitatem, spiritalemque fecunditatem et masculinam, magis spiritu quam corpore, ut spiritalia et invisibilia pariant° magis quam talia que sensiantur, quo officio belluis nihil prestant, a Deo et vita angelica longe precipitantur.

Quamquam autem nolit Paulus — si esse posset — in ecclesia Christi nec nuptias nec coitum in nuptiis, tamen conubii solutionem non patitur eorum qui connupserint, vel si alterutra pars gentilis sit, modo cum fideli parte velit commanere, siquidem converti et reformari potest quod deterius est presentia melioris, et ubi utraque pars fidelis est, mutuo se fovent in obsequio Dei. Ubi autem alterutra pars infidelis sit, nisi hec voluntatem habet commanendi, illa altera fidelis pars non cogetur commanere. Nam ad lites et iurgia non est vocatio. Ubi vero est animus commorandi, iubet Paulus commorentur, propter spem quam habuit fideliorem partem infidelem convertere ad Deum posse. Ubi vero non est animus convivendi, sinit divortium, propter timorem ne pars fidelis importunis iurgiis pervertatur.

Omnia metitur Paulus edificatione et incremento ecclesie Christi in pace et charitate. Idque est proprium Pauli semper in ambiguis° spem bonam habere in parte meliori, confisus Christi gratie que operatur incrementum et ecclesie perfectionem, per predicationem apostolorum, superveniente Dei gratia et solaris

---

debiti *M L*] debeti *C*   maxime *M L*] maxima *C*   pariant *L*] pareant *C M*
ambiguis *M L*] ambuguis *C*

activity ought to strive to the point at which we can reflect God in ourselves as much as possible, with such pure and constant simplicity, such wise interior order, such complete perfection, finally, that while our life is here we may do nothing careless or weak, nothing shameful or stupid, nothing imperfect or defective, but may be like the angels in constancy, in beauty, and in love of the one God.

But just as God is merciful and indulgent, so in the human hierarchy, i.e., the Church, there is mercy for the weak, and forbearance. So Paul permits marriage, and the fulfilment in marriage of the mutual obligation; and after the first marriage, a second, for those who wish it and who cannot be continent.

And as he says himself, this whole indulgence exists for the sake of avoiding fornication, and because of men's incontinence [I Cor. vii. 5, 6]. If there were, however, the power of total restraint, it would be much better and much more peaceful for men themselves, and much more pleasing to God, for virgins not to wed, for the married to live chastely and without intercourse even in wedlock, and for those who have become unwed and for the widowed not to marry again. Each one, however, has (as he says) his own gift, one to live in this way, another in that [vii. 7].

In short, then, both Christian men and women ought to strive as much as they can for angelic chastity, before marriage, in marriage itself, and after marriage. They ought to aim for a masculine and spiritual fecundity,[68] one of the spirit more than of the body, so as to bring forth what is spiritual and invisible, rather than what is of the senses. In the latter function they do not excel the wild beasts, and they fall headlong far beneath God and the angelic life.

Although Paul would wish, however, that there were no more marriage or marital intercourse within Christ's Church, if this could be, still he does not tolerate the dissolving of a marriage already made, even if one party is a pagan, provided he wish to remain with the believing party [vii. 10–16]. The reason for this is the possibility that by the presence of the better the worse may be converted and reformed. And where both are believers, they mutually encourage each other in the service of God. When one of the parties is an unbeliever, however, and does not have the will to remain, the other, the believer, will not be obliged to stay with him. For our calling is not to disputes and quarrels. On the other hand, when there is an inclination to remain, Paul orders that they remain together, because of the hope he has that the believing party may be able to convert the unbeliever to God. But when there is no such wish to live together, he allows divorce, fearing lest the believer may be undone by quarrels that bring discouragement.

Paul measures everything by the edification and increase of Christ's Church, in peace and love. Always, too, it is Paul's way in doubtful matters to have good hope for the better possibility, trusting Christ's grace, which works the increase and the perfecting of the Church through the preaching of the Apostles, while God's favor extends from above everywhere, and the rays of the sunlike Christ

Christi radiis passim homines personis et qualitatibus differentes illustrantibus ad purgationem, illuminationem, et perfectionem eorum.

Interea, inquam, dum benefica vi divine gratie in Christo hominum unitas, ordo, et salus agitur, nolit Paulus ullo modo aliquam turbam et quasi fluctuationem ex personarum discrepantia, ne |121r| hominum instabilitate supracelestes radii impediantur, retardeturque opus Dei in hominibus edificatioque ecclesie. Ut enim placido et tranquillo mari solis radii et altius et firmius imprimuntur°, ita quietis et longe a perturbatione alienis hominibus descendentes divine gratie radii et latius se fundunt et efficacius operantur, ut homines Deo gratificent et citius et copiosius.

Quapropter apud Corinthios, quum multe et varie et dissimiles erant persone, alii celibes, alii coniugati, alie virgines, alii vidui; et horum circumcisi alii, alii incircumcisi, alii domini, alii servi; generatim suadet quietem et tranquilitatem°, atque ut nemo se moveat mutetque statum, sed unusquisque sicut vocatus est ita ambulet ea persona et qualitate qua vocatus est. Quoniam Deus non habet respectum ad personas. Una est ei quidem sola persona que placet, persona videlicet Christi quam sibi construit indifferenter ex omni personarum genere, donec tandem plenus in eo Christus perficiatur.

Velit ergo prudentissimus Paulus quisque eo loci maneat et eo statu perseveret quo accitus est: Iudei, gentes, domini, servi, virgines, nupti, non respicientes humiliter ad personarum differentiam, quod nihil est, sed suspicientes° sublimiter ac conspirantes omnes obedienter in unam personam Christi, ut in eo, omni dissimili vetustate abolita, nova et una et simplex et similis forma Christi ab omnibus induatur, ut in innovatione spiritus et novitate persone convenientes condiligant, |121v| nulla deinceps habita recordatione antecedentis dissimilitudinis qua plurimum dissiderint homines et discrepaverint.

Christus est oblitterator vetustatis, extinctor illius humilis oculi terrenam varietatem discer⟨n⟩entis, innovatio hominum omnium in novam et similem formam sui, reconsiliatio eorumdem inter se in unitatem spiritus, restitutio denique in Deum et perfectio. Quamobrem non quales sed ad quid vocamur considerandum, nec qui eramus dissimiles, sed qui sumus uni futuri, spectantes sursum et expectantes Dominum, facientes ea que hic sunt tamquam non facientes, necessitate semper magis, si quid fiat, quam sponte.

Velle enim debemus nihil nisi innovationem nostram et perfectionem, in Domino nostro Iesu Christo, cui honor et gloria in secula seculorum.

---

imprimuntur *M*] impremuntur *C L*   tranquilitatem *M L*] transquilitatem *C*
suspicientes *C? L*] inspicientes *M*

enlighten all men, differing though they be in their persons and qualities, to their purification, their illumination, and their perfection.

In the meantime, while the unity, order, and salvation of men are being achieved by the kindly strength of the divine grace in Christ, Paul is altogether set against any disordered confusion or any kind of wavering caused by the difference between persons, lest the unsteadiness of men be a hindrance to the celestial rays, and delay God's work among men and the building up of the Church. For just as the sun's rays penetrate more deeply and more surely into the sea when it is calm and tranquil, so when men are at peace and far removed from disturbance, the rays of divine grace, descending, spread more widely and work more effectively, to bring it about that men become more swiftly and more richly pleasing to God.

Among the Corinthians, therefore, since there was great diversity and dissimilarity of persons — some celibate, some married, some virgins, some widows; and again, some circumcised, others not; some masters, others slaves — Paul recommends universally peace and tranquillity, urging that no one become agitated and change his state, but that each according to his calling walk in the person and quality in which he has been called [VII. 20, 24]. For God is no respecter of persons [Acts X. 34]. One person only, in truth, is there who pleases Him, and that is the person of Christ, which He is building up of every kind of person without discrimination, until at last Christ be full and perfect in Him.

In his great thoughtfulness, then, Paul would wish that each remain in that place and persevere in that state in which he has been summoned: Jews, Gentiles, masters, slaves, virgins, the married; not looking downward to the differences between persons, which are nothing, but looking upward and all aspiring together in obedience to the one person of Christ, so that when all the oldness of dissimilarity has been abolished in him, one new and simple and identical form of Christ may be put on by all. Then, coming together in renewal of spirit and in newness of person, they may be united in love, with no remembrance ever again held of that former dissimilarity which was the principal cause of men's being at variance and in disagreement.

Christ is the eraser of all that is old, the darkener of that abject eye that discerns earthly differences. He is the renewing of all men into a new form identical with his own, their reconciling among themselves into unity of spirit, their restoration, finally, to God, and their perfecting. So we must not take account of what sort of persons we are, but of what we are called to; we must not attend to what we were when we were all dissimilar, but to who we shall be when we shall be one; with our eyes turned upward in expectation of the Lord, and doing earthly things as though we did them not, always because of need, if we do anything, rather than by choice [I Cor. VII. 31].

For our only wish ought to be that we may be made new and made perfect, in our Lord Jesus Christ, to whom be honor and glory for ever and ever.

Caput octavum°

Abducti ab idolorum et simulacrorum cultu, Corinthiorum nonnulli, adhuc recentes in fide, non potuerunt omnino simulachra quibus immolare consueverunt contempnere. Ex inveterato usu alte insedit mentibus eorum, in quibus fides adhuc in perfectionem non adolevit, nescio quid quo putaverunt ex immolatis idolis sibi gustare non licuisse. Alii vero fuere ex maiori scientia ea opinione et audacia quod idolatita nihil exhorruerunt, nihilque cum idolatris commedere sunt veriti.

Quo factum fuit ut infirmiores se offensos sentirent, quum persuadere sibi non poterant ullo modo id a quoquam recte factum esse posse. Quapropter quod ipsi sine scrupulo facere non poterant, |122r| alios inoffensi° facere non cecernerunt.

Paulus autem, homo sapientissimus, intelligens propter immolata idolis Corinthios non satis concinne convenire, quum novit morbi causam esse defectum charitatis, sine qua nihil recte, cum qua etiam nihil oblique fieri potest, persuadet hic illis, qui sibi sapientiores videbantur, scientiam eorum unius Dei inutilem esse et periculosam, nisi simul eundem diligunt. In quo proximi dilectio° continetur.

Hoc scitum est, unum esse Deum Patrem, ex quo omnia, et unum Dominum, per quem omnia; item simulachra et ea que a gentibus dii et domini vocantur et creduntur nihili esse; atque etiam immolata iis nihil polutionis accipere. Verum scientia inflat, charitas autem edificat. Oportet quemque scire Deum cum charitate eiusdem.

Si quis diligit Deum (inquit) hic cognitus, i.e., approbatus est ab illo. Qui non diligit, ait Joannes, non novit Deum. Quapropter (Paulus inquit) si quis

---

Caput octavum *Ed.*] Capud viii sequitur *C*] Cap. viii *M*   inoffensi *C L*] inoffensos
M; cecernerunt *C (as past of cerno?) L*] secernerunt *M*   dilectio *M L*] delectio *C*

Chapter VIII

Although they had been divorced from the worship of idols and images, several of the Corinthians who were still young in the faith were unable altogether to despise the images to which they had been accustomed to make sacrifices. From long established custom, there was some sort of deeply rooted conviction, in the minds of those in whom the faith had not yet grown to perfection, that they were not allowed to taste things that had been offered to idols. But others, on the strength of greater knowledge, were of such an opinion (and of such boldness) that they did not shrink from the sacrifice-foods, and had no fear at all of eating with idolaters.

Now because of this it happened that the weaker ones felt themselves offended, since they could not find a way to persuade themselves that anyone could do this unwrongfully. Thus, what they themselves were unable to do without scruple they did not without taking offense watch others do.

Paul, then, wisest of men, learning that this matter of offerings to idols kept the Corinthians from agreeing with the right harmoniousness, and understanding that the cause of this disorder was a lack of charity—without which nothing can be done rightly, and with which nothing can be done amiss—here persuades those who thought themselves wiser that their knowledge of the one God was useless and perilous, unless they also loved Him. And in love of God is contained love for neighbor.

It was of knowledge that there is only one God, the Father, the origin of all things, and one Lord, through whom we all exist; it was of knowledge that images and the things called by the Gentiles "gods" and "lords" and believed to be such are nothing; and further, that what is sacrificed to them receives no contamination [I Cor. VIII. 4–6]. Knowledge, however, inflates, while charity builds [VIII. 1]. It is with love[1] that each one must know God.

If anyone loves God, Paul says, he is known by God, i.e., acknowledged by Him as pleasing [VIII. 3]. And no one, says John, knows God, if he does not love Him [I John IV. 8]. If then, says Paul, anyone thinks he knows some-

existimat se scire aliquid, nondum cognovit quomodo oporteat eum scire. Oportet
eum scire cum charitate. Alioquin sua scientia non est scientia. Ut in epistola
disserit Ioannes: Nemo Deum videt; si diligamus invicem, Deus in nobis manet,
et charitas eius in nobis perfecta est.

Declaratur amor Dei amore proximi. Quod si proximi cum pietate rationem
non habes, Deum ostendis te non diligere; quem si non diligis, ignoras. Unde
sequitur scientiam illam stulticiam esse, que cum charitate non habet rationem
proximi.

Velit ergo |122v| et docet Paulus, sic sapiant illi apud Corinthios in illis in
quibus putant se posse, ut fratrum in Christo infirmitatis rationem habere videantur; sic sibi placeant ut non displiceant aliis; sic denique placeant Deo charitate,
ut et aliis et sibi placere possint. Non enim semper facies quod arbitraris te posse.
Sapientia invisa est, et potentia infirmis intolerabilis°. At bonitas semper grata
et amabilis. Fac ergo semper quod scis, sic scilicet ut non minus bonus esse quam
sapere videare.

Semper habenda est ratio in factis nostris non quid possumus ipsi, sed quid
alii ferre possunt, ut charitate et amore proximi que facias, non scientia et potentia tua, metiaris, maxime in hiis que nihil ad rem pertinent, cuiusmodi est esca
et potus. Que si manducaverimus non abundamus, si non manducaverimus non
deficiemus. Esca enim non comendat hominem Deo, sed charitas proximi, et
accurata ratio ne quempiam insolentia tua offendat, cuius debes misereri ut velis
Christum misertum esse tui. Conmembrum est Christi, cuius conscientiam tua
audacia non percellas, vel ab omnibus abstinens potiusquam tale facinus commit-
tas. Si esca scandalizat fratrem meum, non manducabo carnem (inquit) in eternum, ne fratrem meum scandalizem.

Summa est: reprobam scientiam quantam |123r| quumque° que non est cum
amore Dei. Is agnoscitur in amore proximi, si eos ames ut velis amari, sique,
ut nolis offendi, non offendas.

---

intolerabilis *M L*] intollerabilis *C with first* l *canc.*   quantamquumque *Ed.*] quantum-
quumque *C L*] quantunquumque *M*

thing, he has not recognized yet how he ought to know: his knowledge ought to be with love [I Cor. VIII. 2]. Otherwise his knowledge is not knowledge. As John reasons in his Epistle, "No one sees God; if we love one another, God dwells in us, and His love is perfect in us" [I John IV. 12].

Love of God is made evident by love of neighbor. But if you do not take account of your neighbor, with the right feeling toward him, you show that you do not love God [IV. 20, 21]. And if you do not love God, you do not know Him.[2] It follows that the sort of knowledge which takes no account of one's neighbor, with love, is stupidity.

Paul's wish, then, and his teaching, is that those people among the Corinthians should be wise in the matters in which they think themselves powerful, so as to show that they take into account the weakness of their brethren in Christ; that they should please themselves in such a way as not to displease others; that they should, finally, so please God by their love as to be able to please both themselves and others. For you will not always do what you judge yourself able to do. To the weak, wisdom is hateful, and power is intolerable. But goodness is always welcome and lovable. Act, then, in accordance with your knowledge always, but in such a way that you may show yourself no less good than informed.

In our actions we must always estimate, not what we ourselves can do, but what others can bear; so that you measure your conduct by love and charity for your neighbor, not by your own knowledge and power, especially in irrelevant matters like food and drink. We have no increase if we eat, no deficiency if we abstain. For food does not commend a man to God, but love of neighbor [I Cor. VIII. 8], and a scrupulous care not to offend anyone by your arrogance, since you ought to have the same compassion for another that you would wish Christ to have for you. He is a fellow-member of Christ: do not dishearten his conscience by your presumption. Abstain from everything rather than commit such a crime. "If food scandalize my brother, I shall not eat meat," says Paul, "forever, lest I scandalize my brother" [VIII. 13].

In conclusion, then, knowledge—however great—is condemned if it exists without the love of God. This love is recognized in your love of your neighbor, if you love him as you would be loved, and if, not wishing to be offended yourself, you give no grounds for offense.

Caput nonum°

Velit Paulus Corinthii se imitentur sicut ille Christum, semperque id arbitrentur se posse solum, et licere, quod ecclesie conducat in Christo, incremento videlicet et firmitati illius. Quod autem contra, non licere omnino, tametsi id forsitan liceat simpliciter. Verum homo consideratus non solum spectat quid absolute et simpliciter liceat, sed etiam quid omni loco et tempore et apud quasque personas liceat. Quod enim licet simpliciter, idem sepenumero, adversante aliqua circumstantia, non licet.

Fine metiunda sunt omnia. Finis Christianitatis auctio et stabilitas ecclesie est Christi, quo si referas omnia caritate, errare non potes quidem. Statue ergo tecum hoc tantummodo licere, tantumque te hoc posse, quod prosit ecclesie incremento et stabilitati illius.

Erat Paulus liber, siquidem Apostolus, et Corinthiorum Apostolus; tamen quod simpliciter et per se licuit iudicavit apud Corinthios sibi non licuisse, ne sua potestate abuteretur, que erat non ad destructionem sed ad constructionem ecclesie. Itaque nec ex evangelio |123v| vivere nec feminas ministras circumducere voluit, tametsi per legem Christi et aliorum Apostolorum exempla licuit. Verum homo studens uti debuit emolumento Christi et evangelii, a licitis abstinuit ubi vidit licitis uti non licere, ne quod offendiculum det evangelio Christi.

In hoc enim cursu, in hoc christiano certamine sub Iesu Christo, abstinendum est ab omnibus que adeptionem bravii impedire possunt. Cursoribus quidem licet edere; at si volunt bravium consequi, non licet. Omnia sunt agenda ex re et utilitate ecclesie, fratrumque comodo ex charitate. Quam regulam si sequare, vel agens quippiam vel omittens, peccare non potes. Unusquisque (scribit ad Romanos)

Caput nonum *Ed.*] Capite 9 Nonum *C with numeral canc.*] *om.* M

Chapter IX

Paul would like the Corinthians to imitate him as he imitated Christ, and always to think they can do and are allowed to do only what profits the Church in Christ, i.e., what contributes to its growth and strength. What does not so contribute, they should consider altogether forbidden, even though it perhaps be allowed in the abstract.[1] The thinking man looks not only to what is allowed absolutely and in the abstract, but also to what is allowed in each place and time, and among what persons. For what is lawful in the abstract is often enough unlawful because of some adverse circumstance.

Everything must be measured by its end.[2] Now the end of Christianity[3] is the increase and the stability of Christ's Church, and if with charity you refer all things to this, most surely you cannot err. Make this, then, your personal decision, that only that which furthers the growth and the stability of the Church is, for you, lawful and within your power.

Paul was free, since he was an Apostle, and the Apostle of the Corinthians. Still, he judged that what was in the abstract and *per se* lawful was not lawful for him among the Corinthians, lest he should abuse his power,[4] which was not for the destruction of the Church, but for its construction [II Cor. XIII. 10]. Consequently, he was unwilling either to draw his livelihood from the Gospel, or to take women attendants[5] about with him, although by the law of Christ and the example of the other Apostles these things were lawful. No, he was a man whose concern was, as it had to be, the advantage of Christ and of the Gospel, and so he abstained from lawful things when he saw that, to avoid giving the least offense to the Gospel of Christ, it was not lawful to use lawful things.

For in this race, in this Christian contest under Jesus Christ, we must abstain from everything that can hinder the winning of the prize. It is lawful, to be sure, for runners to eat; but if they wish to win the prize, it is not lawful [I Cor. IX. 24, 25]. All things must be done for the Church's advantage and profit, with gain for the brethren, and with charity as motive. If you follow this rule, whether in acting or in refraining, you cannot sin. "Let every one of you," writes

vestrum proximo suo placeat in bonum ad edificationem. Etenim Christus non sibi placuit. Et Paulus, sequax Christi, hoc voluit solum quod aliis utile esse cognoverit, qui omnibus omnia factus est, ut omnes lucrifaceret.

Corinthii ergo, exemplo Pauli, non tam quid possunt ipsi spectare debent, quam quid socii ferre possunt, iudicantes id nequaquam licere, quod fratribus aliquo modo possit esse inutile. |124r|

Paulus quidem quod potuit, et in circumductione feminarum ministrarum et etiam in accipiendo victu pro evangelio, noluit facere consulto, timens ne consecutio finis et incrementum evangelii impediretur, in quod quam accuratissime statuit secum dirigenda omnia. Quod si non fecisset, caste et legittime non evangelizasset. Que dispensatio non habet mercedem et gloriam nisi sponte et considerate et cum abstinentia ab omnibus que eius cursui obesse possunt agatur.

Ut in stadiis ita in curriculo ad vitam eternam, abstinentia oportet sit penitus a quoque quod vel frustrare vel evangelium retardare possit. Alioquin periculum est ne evangelizator ipse, etiam in evangelii ministerio, inutilis servus periat. *Omnia* (inquit)° *facio propter evangelium, ut particeps eius efficiar.* In quo partem non habuisset si omnia que possit non fecisset. Hinc et illud paulo post sequitur: *Sed castigo corpus meum et in servitutem redigo, ne forte quum aliis predicaverim, ipse reprobus efficiar.*

Faciendum quatenus potes ad salutem.

Non quid ipsi volumus, sed quod aliis prosit solicite et semper agendum est; nec quid corpus appetit ullo modo, sed ad id quod spiritus desiderat enitendum; nec denique quod ipsi possumus, sed quod ecclesie conducat Christi, omnibus aliis posthabitis, omnibus viribus contendendum est, semper existimantes id solum |124v| licere, quod est ecclesie et hominum saluti in Christo perutile.

Quod autem contra se habet, dum navigas in portum quietis sempiterne, tamquam scopulum fuge. Si credis Christo, si speras in Deo, si agis omnia charitate, si oculos habes fixim in finem intentos (finis autem est Christus, et incrementum ac completio salutis hominum in ipso), si (inquam) istuc omni fide, spe, et charitate intendas dirigasque omnia, delirare non potes.

Hoc belle et constanter facies, si aversus a mundo, a corpore, a te ipso, si pauper, castus, humilis, totus sis conversus in Deum, querens in illo solo dives, fecundus, et altus esse, per Dominum nostrum Iesum Christum.

(inquit) *Ed.*] inquit *C with no other punct.*

Paul to the Romans,[6] "give pleasure to his neighbor in the direction of good, for his edification: Christ, after all, did not please himself" [Rom. xv. 2, 3]. And Paul, Christ's follower, who became all things to all men in order to gain them all, wished only what he knew was profitable for others [I Cor. ix. 19-23].

The Corinthians, then, after Paul's example, should look not so much to what they themselves can do, as to what their comrades can bear, judging altogether unlawful whatever might be in any way disadvantageous to their brothers.

Paul, to be sure, deliberately chose not to do what he was able to do, both in the taking about of female attendants and in the receiving of means of support for the Gospel. He feared that the achieving of the end and the spread of the Gospel might be hindered, and he had made it his resolve that everything was to be most rigorously directed to that end. Had he acted otherwise, his preaching of the Gospel would not have been pure and lawful. It is a stewardship without reward and without glory, unless it be performed of one's own free will, and thoughtfully, and with a refraining from all that can hinder its course [ix. 17, 18].

In the race for eternal life, just as in the stadium, there must be full abstinence from whatever can either delay or defeat the Gospel. Otherwise the Evangelist, even in ministering the Gospel, risks perishing himself as an unprofitable servant. "Everything I do," says Paul, "I do because of the Gospel, so that I may be made a sharer in it." And he would have had no share in it, if he had not done all he could. For the same reason the statement follows a little later: "But *You must do all you can toward salvation.* I chastise my own body and make it my slave, lest when I have preached to others, I should perchance myself become a castaway" [ix. 23, 27].

With all care and at all times we must do what profits others, not what we ourselves want. Our efforts must be aimed, not at what the body calls for, but at what the spirit desires. Finally, we must earnestly strive with all our strength, not to do what we can do, but to do what helps Christ's Church, setting aside all other considerations, and always thinking lawful only what is of great profit to the Church and to men's salvation in Christ.

As long as you are sailing to the harbor of everlasting rest, you must escape as you would a rockshelf whatever is of a contrary nature. If you believe in Christ, if you hope in God, if you do everything in charity, if you keep your eyes unwaveringly fixed on the goal — and the goal is Christ, and the increase and perfecting of men's salvation in him — if, I say, with all faith, hope, and charity you aim at that and direct there all things, you cannot lose your way.

All this you will do with beauty and firmness, if turning away from the world, from the body, from yourself, you be turned wholly to God, in poverty, chastity, and humility, seeking to be rich, and prolific, and exalted, only in Him, through our Lord Jesus Christ.

Propositiones ex superioribus excusse

Non quod ipse possis, semper° sed age quod aliis sit utile.

Non sapis, nisi cum aliorum charitate sapis.

Non es nec potens nec sapiens, nisi simul bonus piusque sis fratribus.

In bonitate benefaciendo aliis in Christo est omnis nostra et sapientia et potentia.

Deum nequis alio imitari, nisi benefaciendo misericorditer.

In hoc quod Deum imitamur ex amore, sapimus.

Hoc tibi per tuam libertatem dumtaxat licet, quod aliis et ecclesie sit utile.

Fine et utilitate ecclesie in Christo metiunda sunt omnia.

Is se salvat, qui in salute ecclesie perit. Is se exauget qui in incremento ecclesie se diminuit. Qui perdit animam suam |125r| inveniet eam.

Quod ages, oportet id et sponte et considerate agas. Alioquin nihil remunerabere.

Caute incedas et cave impedimenta omnia, ut comprehendas.

Qui non facit quoad maxime potest, quam minime conprehendet.

Hoc tantum licet, quod utile est ecclesie.

Hoc tantum puta te posse legittime, quod celeritati tui cursus in vitam eternam conducat.

Non oportet curras solum, sed curras ut comprehendas.

Comprehensio est in omnimoda contentione ad finem et in omnium impedimentorum abstinentia.

Imitare Deum bonitate et pietate. Quere salutem hominum in Christo. Exemplum ostende paupertatis, castitatis, et humilitatis in te ipso. Accomoda te aliis, ut eos quosquumque in imitationem tui trahas. Exauge ecclesiam. Conquire gloriam Dei in Christo, et salvus eris.

---

possis, semper *Ed.*] possis: semper *C*] possis semper *L M*

Propositions Derived from the Preceding

Do not do what you yourself have the power to do, but always what may be useful to others.

You are not wise, unless your wisdom exist with a love for others.

You are neither powerful nor wise, unless at the same time you are good and kind to your brothers.

In goodness, in acting kindly toward others in Christ, is all our wisdom and all our power.

You cannot imitate God in any other way than by doing good with mercy.

Our wisdom lies in this, that from love we imitate God.

This only your freedom makes lawful for you: what may be useful for others and for the Church.

All things must be measured by the goal, by the Church's profit in Christ.

He saves himself, who perishes in the salvation of the Church. He increases himself, who makes himself less in the increase of the Church. "He shall find his life who loses it" [Matt. x. 39].

Whatever you do, you must do it both thoughtfully and spontaneously. Otherwise you shall have no reward.

Advance with caution, and beware of all obstacles, so that you may attain.[7]

He who does not do as much as possible, will attain as little as possible.

This only is lawful—what is profitable to the Church.

This only believe you can lawfully do: what contributes to the speed of your race to everlasting life.

You must not only run, but run so that you may attain.

The attaining is in every sort of exertion toward the goal, and in the refraining from all hindrances.

Imitate God in goodness and piety; seek men's salvation in Christ; show in yourself an example of poverty, chastity, and humility; adapt yourself to others, so that you may draw them, whoever they be, to imitation of yourself; increase the Church; seek the glory of God in Christ; then you will be saved.

Caput decimum°

Ab illo capite octavo, cuius inicium est: *De hiis que idolis immolantur*, deinde usque ad illam clausulam: *Imitatores mei estote, sicut ego Christi*, continuato sermone una res agitur, et emendatio Corinthiorum eorum qui, freti quadam audacia, temere egerunt quicquid parum prudentes putarunt se posse sine periculo, maxime in idolothitarum degustatione cum idolatris, ad quod partim solita familiaritate, partim epularum dulcedine tracti fuerint.

Quam impietatem excusare voluerant conscientia et opinione recti facti, quod noverunt |125v| idolum nihili esse, et libertate in Christo, dicentes aliud se non facere quam facere possunt, sapientia et libertate adepta in Christo; homines qui non adhuc cognoverunt quemadmodum oporteat eos scire et in Christo sapere, qui victi solito more et amore dapum, nec charitatis in proximum nec sacrosancte communionis in Christo rationem habuerunt.

Quamobrem Paulus, ut eos revocet in sinceram et castam Christi communionem, atque etiam ut doceat boni, pii, benigni, et misericordes sint maxime, habeantque amabilem et fraternum respectum in omnibus ad fraterculum quemque in Christo infirmiorem, ne opinione sapientie et audacia insolenter illum offendant, tria que ad propositum spectant conatur illis persuadere: primum, in Christo sapientiam non esse que non est cum charitate, in quo proculdubio ex caritate agere solum sapere est; secundum, hoc solum licere quod est ecclesie utile, posseque hoc tantum quemque quod prosit aliis; tertium, castam et integram in Christo communionem non esse, videlicet carnis et sanguinis Christi, in unitatem cum ipso, ubi cum idolatris est communicatio, non quod idolum quidem et simulachrum

---

Caput *Ed.*] Capud *C, om. M*

Chapter X

From Chapter VIII, which begins "About things sacrificed to idols," right through to that conclusion, "Be imitators of me, as I am of Christ" [I Cor. XI. 1], one topic is treated in a sustained discourse, and that is the correction of those Corinthians who rashly, relying on a certain audacity, did whatever in their want of thoughtfulness they thought they had the power to do without danger; especially in the eating with idolaters of foods offered to idols, a practice to which they were drawn partly by an established familiarity, and partly by the delightfulness of the splendid banquets.

This impiety[1] they wished to excuse on the grounds of an awareness of and a belief in the rightness of the deed (because they knew that an idol was nothing whatever) [VIII. 7], and on the grounds of their freedom in Christ, alleging that they were not doing anything they did not have the power to do, by reason of the wisdom and freedom they had gained in Christ. They were men who as yet did not know how they ought to have knowledge and wisdom in Christ [VIII. 2], men who were so swayed by a rooted custom and by love of banquets that they took into account neither love for their neighbor nor their most sacred participation in Christ.

Paul, then, to recall them to a pure and holy participation in Christ,[2] and to teach them that they must be above all good, pious, kind, and compassionate, and have in all things a fraternal respect of the sort that inspires love toward each least weaker brother in Christ, so as not by their hardihood and belief in their own wisdom arrogantly to offend him, tries to convince them of three relevant points. The first is that in Christ there is no wisdom without charity;[3] indeed, in Christ the only wisdom is without a doubt to act from charity [VIII]. Secondly, only what is profitable to the Church is lawful, and a man has power only for that which works to the advantage of others [IX]. Thirdly, there is no pure and perfect participation in Christ—no Communion, that is, of Christ's flesh and blood making one united with him—where there is participation with idolaters; not, indeed, because an idol or image has any real being, or because

est aliquid, quodve epule ille immolate aliquatenus contaminentur, sed propter demonum cultum quibus sacrificant gentes demonice, cum quibus non possunt se commisceri confratres dominici nisi una cum illis quodammodo separati a Christo demones colere videantur.

Quatenus ergo ad hanc partem spectat, reintegrationemque illius communionis que |126r| quam simplicissima et sanctissima debet esse in Christo, commemorat Paulus in umbris illis Veteris Testamenti et mosaicis imaginibus tanti et tam veri mysterii quod est in Christo, quot et quanta dispendia acciderint propter tran⟨s⟩gressiones et peccata populi. Qui quum Moyses illos continere voluit, in quada⟨m⟩ figura significatrice ecclesie, illi tamen delapsi defluxerunt in idolatriam, adulterium, diffidentiam, discordiam.

Quod si illi, in quibus erat dumtaxat figurata per mare et nubem eorum renascitura hominum in Christo ex aqua et Spiritu Sancto; in quibus etiam per manna et liquorem illum qui ex petra percussa emanavit, significatum fuit ipsum corpus et sanguis Christi, quibus ut coalescant in unum vescuntur Christiani — si (inquam) illi qui erant compositi in quodam ordine ut hec nostra significent tanta, peccatores passi sunt, quam timendum est hominibus in Domino, qui in ipsa veritate constituti sunt, ne quid peccent; et Corinthiis ne quid idolatrice, fornicarie, infideliter, et inquiete agant; ne maioris et verioris rei transgressores longe maiorem et veriorem ultionem sensiant.

In illa enim vitia proclivi erant Corinthii, facileque in idolatriam, adulterium, diffidentiam, et murmurationem delapsi sunt. Sed hanc sententiam testatam apud illos relinquit Paulus, cui vult credant omnino, videlicet ut et cum quibus comparticipat homo sponte, cum illis eum socium esse et concultorem; Corinthiosque, si voluntarie commisceant se et coepulentur cum idolatris, eos in Christo cultores Dei non esse. In quo qui sit oportet totus sit, totusque ex Christo oleat, |126v| sapiatque nihil nec agat nisi ex simplicitate et puritate Spiritus Christi in ipso. Non postestis (inquit) calicem Domini bibere et calicem demoniorum, nec mense Domini participes esse et mense demoniorum.

Emulandus et imitandus est Christus, quo non simus fortiores, immo in quo solo sumus fortes. Ideo non debemus quippiam temptare extra ipsum, extra quem infirmi sumus. Christus ipse non usus est sua potestate, nisi quatenus hominibus pro quorum salute mortuus est prosit. Non sibi placuit (inquit in epistola ad Romanos). Hoc est quod Paulus dicit, interrogans: *An emulamur Dominum?* solutius discurrendo in convivia gentium et immisericordius agendo cum

the festive dishes offered to them are defiled, but because of the cult of demons, to whom those Gentiles who are demon-worshippers make their sacrifices. With these the brothers of the Lord[4] cannot mingle, unless they would appear to join them somehow in their demon-worship, and be separated from Christ [x].

With regard to this last part, the re-establishment in purity of that Communion which ought to be as guileless and as holy in Christ as possible, Paul recalls [x. 1–11] how many and how great were the harms that happened because of the transgressions and sins of the people in those shadows of the Old Testament and those Mosaic figures of the mystery[5] that exists in Christ with such splendor and such truth. When Moses wished to set them within bounds, in a figure signifying the Church, they scattered and slipped into idolatry, adultery, faithlessness, and disunion.

Now in them was only prefigured, by their sea and their cloud, the rebirth of men in Christ of water and the Holy Ghost. They had, in the manna and in the water that flowed from the rock when it was struck, only a symbol of the body and blood of Christ, by which Christians are fed so that they may grow into unity. And if they, who were gathered together and set in a fixed order to symbolize these great realities of ours, suffered when they became sinners, how much should men who are in the Lord, who have been established in the truth itself, be afraid of sinning! How afraid should the Corinthians be of acting somehow idolatrously, or impurely, or faithlessly, or disharmoniously, lest as transgressors in a matter both greater and truer they should feel a far greater and a far truer punishment!

For the Corinthians were prone to these vices, readily slipping into idolatry, adultery, disbelief, and grumbling. But Paul affirms this principle, and leaves it with them in the hope that they will believe it with all their hearts: a man is a fellow and a fellow-worshipper of those with whom of his own free will he is a fellow-participator. The Corinthians, then, if they voluntarily mingle with idolaters and share in their banquets, are not worshippers of God in Christ. A man who is in Christ must be wholly in Christ, must have entirely the savor of Christ, must have no wisdom and no activity that does not come from the simplicity and the purity of the Spirit of Christ within him. "You cannot," he says, "drink the Lord's cup and the cup of demons, nor share the Lord's table and that of demons" [x. 21].

We must emulate Christ and imitate him; but we are not stronger than he. Indeed, only in him are we strong at all. So we ought not to attempt anything outside Christ, where we are weak. Christ himself did not use his own power, except in so far as it would help men, for whose salvation he died. In the Epistle to the Romans, Paul says: "He did not please himself" [Rom. xv. 3]. This is what Paul means when he asks, "Do we emulate the Lord"[6] by running about with no restraint to the banquets of the Gentiles, and by behaving without

fratribus? — quasi diceret, sic agendo sane non emulamur Dominum, sed quasi fortiores illo essemus, confisi ipsis ex nobis aliquid attemptamus. Illud plane dominicum est, nihil licitum nisi quod utile ecclesie est; sapientiam esse nullam que non est cum charitate; immo, charitatem ipsam esse sapientiam hominis consummatam.

Sunt iis Pauli docti Corinthii ut se sanctos et inviolatos in Christi societate contineant; cum amore et pietate agant omnia; idque ex Christo solum esse putent quod est factum cum omnium quam maxima utilitate et quoad fieri potest cum nullorum offensione.

Sed nunc ex hoc novo° capite quam insignia proloquia et sentencie erui possunt videamus. Sunt que sequuntur:

> Renascituram electorum in Christo et eorumdem alimoniam in vitam eternam, quod corpus et sanguis est Christi, prefiguratam fuisse apud Moisem in mare et nube, que aqua et Spiritus Sanctus est; in manna et liquore ex petra emanante, quod caro et sanguis est Christi. Christus enim est petra qui constanter passus et percussus cruce, profudit sanguinem vivificum, sitim explentem in eternum. |127r|
>
> Item, ad maiora qui vocantur, si delinquant, graviores sequi ultiones.
>
> Item, in Mo⟨i⟩se et penarum et premiorum umbras spectari posse.
>
> Item, ut profectis in Christum temtationes° vehementiores sunt, siquidem ad militiam deleguntur, ita munitiones in° eodem Christo et resistendi vires maiores sunt. Sed faciet (inquit) etiam cum temptatione proventum, ut possitis sustinere.

In benedicto calice et fracto pane est salutaris communicatio ipsius veri corporis et sanguinis Iesu Christi, quod communicatur a multis ut unum sint in eo, qui multi uniuntur in participatione unius et reformatione in idipsum, certe in hoc conformes Christo, et ipsi in ipso. Hoc est quod dicit: *Unus panis et unum corpus multi sumus, omnes qui de uno pane et uno calice participamus.*

Alimentum est unum quo vescimur, distributum in universam° societatem ut in unum corpus, ut alti omnes homines uno, unum sint in eo quo aluntur, non vertentes alimentum in se, sed ab alimento tanquam a fortiori transformati in ipsum. Inde enim est conformitas omnium et unitas, quod Christus,

---

novo L] nono C] *with two following words erased and blank* M   temtationes C *following second* ut *inserted above line*] ut tentationes M *with* Item ut *omitted*] tentationes L   in M L] in in C   universam M L] univesam C *with* r *written above* e *by another hand than that of Unk. Rev.*

mercy for our brothers? It is as though he said, "In this sort of behavior, surely we do not emulate the Lord, but attempt something of ourselves, trusting to ourselves as though we were stronger than he." What is clearly of the Lord is this: nothing is lawful except that which is useful to the Church; there is no wisdom without charity; and charity is, indeed, itself man's perfect wisdom.[7]

By these instructions of Paul the Corinthians were taught to keep themselves holy and undefiled within the fellowship of Christ; to do everything with love and affection; to consider that only as being of Christ which is done with the greatest profit to all and with as little offense as can be to anyone.

Now let us see what distinctive declarations and principles can be derived from this new chapter. They are the following:

> The rebirth in Christ of the chosen ones and their being nourished for eternal life—the nourishment being the body and blood of Christ—were prefigured in Moses by the sea and the cloud, which are the water and the Holy Spirit, and by the manna and the liquid flowing from the rock, which are the body and blood of Christ. For Christ is the rock which in steadfastness suffered and was struck on the cross, and poured forth his life-giving blood, quenching our thirst forever.
>
> Again, greater retributions follow those who are called to greater things, should they transgress.
>
> Again, in Moses can be seen the shadows both of penalties and of rewards.
>
> Again, just as the trials are more severe for those who have set off toward Christ, since they are men chosen for warfare, so the means of defense and the strength to resist are, in the same Christ, greater. "With the temptation itself," says Paul, "He will ordain the outcome, so that you may be able to bear it" [x. 13].

In the blessed cup and the broken bread is a saving communication of the true body and blood itself of Jesus Christ, shared by many that in it they may be one. These many are united in the sharing of the One, and in the being formed anew into it.[8] In this sharing, to be sure, they are of the same form as Christ, and are in him. This is what is meant by the words: "We are one bread and one body, though many in number; all of us who partake of the one bread and the one chalice" [x. 17].

One is the food by which we are fed, distributed to the whole fellowship as to one body, so that all men, nourished by the One, may be one in that by which they are nourished. Nor do they transform the nourishment into themselves, but they are themselves transformed by the nourishment, as by a stronger thing, into itself. For from this comes the conformity and unity of all: that Christ, when he is shared by the heterogeneous, does not enter into the nature of their

communicatus a diversis, non vadit in naturam diversorum. Nam ii comunicantes non sunt communicato fortiores; sed diversi, reformati a fortiori Christo in unum, in eundem ipsum quo vescuntur feliciter evadunt.

Forsan ad hunc sensum non inepte potest id dictum a Paulo non minus obscure° quam breviter accomodare, quod est: *An emulamur Dominum? Nunquid fortiores illo sumus?* Nam in mensa Domini ita se res habet ut communicantes Christum transformentur in ipsum. In mensa° demoniorum vel transferunt demones in se, vel in demones transferuntur. Si dicant arro |127v| gantius se transferre, tunc emulantur Dominum, et ei invident, attemptantes facere quod illius est°. Reliquum est ergo ut transferantur in demones. Qui homines sine Christo infirmiores sunt, facileque vincuntur. In mensa° ergo demonum evadunt demonici, qui non sunt fortiores Domino.

In quibus communicat aliquis, eiusmodi evadit.

Ex hoc loco etiam elicere possumus, qui consecrantur Deo in Christo, ut Christum epulentur, non debent se conferre nisi ad eam mensam ubi Christus ministratur. Mensa autem constructa multiplici ferculo ciboque Christi Sacra Scriptura est, in cuius omni parte sapor et solidus cibus Christi est vivifici. Vetus Testamentum (sicuti Paulus exponit in epistola ad Romanos) David mensam vocavit, quando dixi⟨t⟩: Fiat mensa eorum coram ipsis in laqueum. Sed ibi operta sunt fercula et tecta, et obsignata etiam omnia. In Novo Testamento operculorum deposi-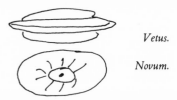

Vetus.

Novum.

depositio est, aperitio et revelatio epularum veritatis, et ad esum invitatio. Aperuit Magister convivii, qui Mo⟨i⟩se ministro primum extruxit mensam magnifice, tectis patenis, in quibus ipse erat architriclinus, sed invisus. Postea idem ipse discussis operculis se ipsum, ipsamque veritatem, affatim delectis conviviis praebuit epulandum.

Cum Christo ergo solo debemus convivere, in lauta mensa Scripturarum, et coepulari largius in Novo Testamento, in quo ab ipso Christo aqua mosaica factum vinum est. In aliis mensis et libris, qui sunt paganorum, in quibus nihil est quod sapit Christum—nihilque est quod non sapit demonem—profecto in illis nemo Christianus |128r| discumbere debet, nisi velit videri magis demonis

---

obscure *C M*] obstare *L*   mensa *M L*] mense *C*   mensa *M L*] mense *C*

diversity; since those who communicate are not stronger than he who is communicated, but being diverse, they are formed anew by the stronger Christ into one, and it is their good fortune to pass from themselves into that by which they are fed.

Perhaps that remark of Paul's, as obscure[9] as it is brief, may be not improperly interpreted in this sense: "Do we emulate the Lord?" he says; "Are we stronger than he?" For at the Lord's table it is thus: those who partake of Christ are transformed into him. But at the table of demons either the partakers translate the demons into themselves, or else they are translated into the demons. Now if over-presumptuously they should say that they do the transforming, then they are emulating the Lord and envying him, attempting to do something that belongs to him. The alternative, then, is that they are translated into the demons. They are men, and without Christ they are too weak, and are easily overcome. Not being stronger than the Lord, then, at the table of demons they become demonic.

Whatever it be that a man partakes of, he becomes that sort of thing.

From this part we can also infer that those who are consecrated to God in Christ, so that they may banquet on Christ, ought not to betake themselves to any table except that where Christ is set forth. Now this table, made up of Christ's many foods and courses, is Holy Scripture,[10] in all the parts of which there is the savor and the solid nourishment of Christ the life-giver. The Old Testament (as Paul explains in the Epistle to the Romans) David called a table, when he said: "Let their table be turned to a trap for them before their eyes" [Rom. xi. 9; Ps. lxviii. 23]. There, however, the dishes are concealed and covered, and all is sealed. The setting aside of the covers is in the New Testament, with the revealing of the rich banquet of truth and an invitation to eat. The Master of the Feast[11] has opened all. He first in magnificent fashion piled the table high—through the ministry of Moses—with the covered dishes, and he was present there as Ruler of the Banquet, but unseen. And afterwards he himself struck off the covers, offering himself, Truth itself, for the plentiful banqueting of his chosen guests.

The Old.

The New.

Only with Christ, then, should we be banqueters, at the splendid table of the Scriptures; and in the New Testament we should feast the more abundantly, since there the water of Moses has been changed by Christ himself into wine [John ii. 1–11].[12] At other tables, in other books—those of the pagans—where there is nothing with the savor of Christ and nothing without the savor of the Demon—in those places, surely, no Christian man ought to seat himself, unless he should wish to appear a guest of the Demon rather than of the Lord. As a

conviva quam Domini. In quibus agris et ut compascit homo, talis evadit. Si queramus vesci sapientia paganorum, que demonica est, non dominica, rationem Domini amittimus. In quorum mensis, i.e., libris, nemo cibum sumit nisi vel diffidens Scripturis vel eas negligens. Quod utrumque nephandum et impium est, et detestabilis Dei temptatio.

Quod si dicant, quod dici solet, paganorum librorum lectiones iuvare ad Sacrarum Litterarum intelligentiam, videant isti si non hoc ipso maxime obsunt, quod eis confisum est. Quod dum facis, diffidis te per gratiam solam et orationes Sacras Litteras intelligere posse, atque per adiumentum Christi et fidei, sed per rationes et auxilium paganorum.

Hiis potest dici: *Que immolant gentes, demoniis immolant et non Deo. Eos cultores librorum gentium non posse calicem Domini bibere et calicem demoniorum, et mense Domini participes esse et mense demoniorum.*

Illi libri legendi sunt solum in quibus est salutaris degustatio Christi, in quibus Christus apponitur epulandus. In quibus vero non est Christus, mensa demoniorum est.

Nolite fieri vos philosophorum lectores, socii demoniorum. In lauta et copiosa mensa Sacrarum Litterarum continentur omnia que sunt veritatis. Animus qui avet aliquid quo vescatur preter veritatem certe parum est sanus et sine Christo. Veritas autem intelligitur gratia. Gratia comparatur audita oratione. Oratio auditur exacuata devotione et fortificata ieiunio. Alio si te devertis, deliratio est. |128v|

Item id excuditur: id tantum licere in ecclesia quod expedit.

Item, quemque in ecclesia alius° comodum debere querere, non suum. Hec charitas est in alios, non in nos: charitas non querit que sua sunt. Et hic dicit: Nemo quod suum est querit°, sed quod alterius. Conqui⟨si⟩tione sui cuiusque proprie utilitatis vel primum interemptio ecclesie est. Aliorum utilitatis studium in primis et omnium habunde, est, tametsi non quesita, utilitas.

In cibis nihil discretionis est. In omnibus habendam considerationem eorum quibuscum vivimus. Offensio vitetur. Gratia prestetur. Omnia in gloriam Dei. Gloria Dei est in bonitate ecclesie, in Christo.

---

alius *C L*] alterius *M*   querit *C M L*] quærat *Vulg.*

man shares his feeding, and in whatever fields, such will he become. If we seek to feed on the wisdom of the pagans, which is demonic, not of the Lord, we lose the principles of the Lord. No one takes his food at their tables, i.e., in their books, unless he either lack faith in Scripture or care not to trouble himself with it. Either is impious and execrable, and an abominable tempting of God.[13]

Now if they should say, as they usually do, that the reading of pagan books helps the understanding of Sacred Scripture, let them look to it themselves whether the placing of confidence in them be not rather the greatest obstacle. When you act thus, you show distrust of your ability to understand Holy Writ through grace alone and prayer, through the help of Christ and of faith. Instead you put your trust in the principles and the assistance of the pagans.

To such men can be said: "What the Gentiles offer in sacrifice, they offer to demons and not to God." The reverencers of the Gentiles' books cannot drink the cup of the Lord and the cup of demons, cannot be partakers of the Lord's table and of the table of demons [I Cor. x. 20, 21].

We must read only those books in which there is the saving taste of Christ; in which Christ is set forth for our feasting. Those in which there is no Christ are the table of demons.

Do not become readers of philosophers and companions of demons. All that belongs to the truth is contained in the splendid, the plentiful table of Holy Scripture. The mind craving for something to feed on beyond the truth is surely far from healthy, and a Christless mind. Now the truth is understood by grace. Grace is provided when our prayers are heard. Our prayers are heard when they are sharpened by whole-hearted devotion, and made strong by fasting. If you turn to any other course, your conduct is madness.

Again, this truth emerges: in the Church, what is profitable is alone lawful.

Again, everyone in the Church should seek another's advantage, not his own. This is charity, toward others, not toward ourselves: charity does not seek its own [XIII. 5]. And here Paul says, "No one seeks his own advantage, but far above all else that of others" [x. 24]. The Church's ruin lies in each one's seeking his own personal advantage. Zeal for achieving first and foremost the profit of others, and of all others, is one's own profit, even when not looked for.

There is no difference in foods: in everything we must be considerate of those with whom we live. Offense must be avoided. Let kindness be shown. All things must be done for the glory of God: the glory of God is in the goodness of the Church, in Christ.

Caput undecimum°

Laudo vos.

Deus.
Christus.
Vir detectus, imago et gloria Dei.
Mulier tecta, gloria viri, creata propter virum, de viro, cui coma decus.

Id maxime convenit, et in rato ac stabili usu haberi debet certe in ecclesia Christi, ut discipuli doctoribus obediant, et a⟨u⟩scultantes precepta magistri, sine contensione omnino et prompte eis acquiescant. Alioquin enim disturbabitur ordo et deformitas extabit. Quapropter Paulus, precepturus et instituturus aliqua apud Corinthios melius quam apud eos in usu erant, quibus illos omnino parere voluit, quo facilius eos inducat ad obedientiam, inquit: *Laudo vos, fratres, quod per omnia mei memores estis, et sicut tradidi vobis precepta mea tenetis,* quiete, non contendentes. Et paulo post quum quiddam quod decuit in ecclesia utrumque sexum docuerat, tum ut sine reluctatione obediant addidit: Si quis videtur |129r| contentiosus esse, nos talem consuetudinem non habemus, neque ecclesia Dei, que est quieta et ordine pulchra, inferioribus superioribus parentibus.

Docet autem Paulus Corinthios quiddam decorum et quod decet in habitu in utroque sexu in ecclesia, videlicet ut in societate que est ex viris et mulieribus, hee° tectis, illi detectis capitibus sint, vel orantes vel prophetantes.

Conans re⟨d⟩dere causam cur tegatur mulier in ecclesia, eam dicit ex viro et propter virum et viri gloriam, et comam decere eam; natura motas feminas ut

---

Caput *Ed.*] Capud *C, om. M*   hee *C?*] (hec?) *M*] heae *L*

Chapter XI

"I praise you. . . ." [I Cor. xi. 2]

God.
· Christ.
The man, uncovered, the image and glory of God.
The woman, covered, the glory of the man, created for man's sake
and from man; whose hair is her ornament.

In Christ's Church it is most especially fitting, and ought, surely, to be kept
as an established and fixed custom, that disciples should obey their teachers, and
that attentively hearing their master's precepts, they should comply with them
forthwith and altogether without dispute. For otherwise order will be upset,
and ugly deformity will show itself. For this reason Paul, prior to establishing
and prescribing among the Corinthians some better points than had been customary
with them, and wishing them to be altogether obedient to these, says (in order
to bring them more readily to obedience), "I praise you, brethren, for being
mindful of me in all things, and for keeping my precepts as I gave them to you"
[I Cor. xi. 2], peacefully, and without dispute.[1] And a little further, when he
has instructed them about a certain matter pertaining to what is proper for both
sexes in church, he adds, so that they will obey without demur: "If anyone shows
himself argumentative, we have no such custom, and neither has God's Church"
[xi. 16], which is peaceful, and shows the beauty of order, with the lower obey-
ing those who are higher.

Now Paul is teaching the Corinthians a point of propriety: what is becoming
in the attirement of both sexes in church. His teaching is that in a society composed of men and women, the latter should have their heads covered, the former
uncovered, when praying or prophesying.

Trying to give a reason[2] why women should be veiled in church, he says that
woman is of the man, and on account of the man, and the glory of the man,

nutriant capillum; mores naturam imitari debere, optimam magistram. Femine industria debent tegere quod natura tectum velit.

Videtur Paulus, quamquam aliud agit, et per ambages circuit sermone, quasi dissimulans se non videre quod vidit, tamen videtur hac accurata ratio⟨ci⟩natione quod maxime vidit in feminis Corinthiis, superbiam videlicet illarum in capellicio, velle extinguere et obruere, inducens ut obvolutis capitibus comam non ostentent, rem in qua facile insolescit femina, in quaque etiam facile, ut quadam illecebra, adolescentes° capiuntur.

Sed hoc tacet consulto, propter causam quam novit ipse, et agit rem ex honestate et decoro in habitu, et ut sit signum in feminis subiectionis, quas vult natura, ut corpus capiti, subiici viris suis: velamen signum est subiectionis.

Vir autem, capud mulieris, presedet mulieri, imago et gloria Dei. Ideo ad mulierem comparatus, sine velamine oportet sit, ut preesse, non subesse, videatur.

Quamquam Christo capiti nostro et Deo omnes in ecclesia sunt quasi femine et quasi corpus, omnesque sub⟨i⟩iciuntur—immo etiam ipse Iesus Christus quatenus homo est, Deo—et omnes etiam velantur, non velamine aliquo, obedientie et subiectionis signo, sed ipsa obedientia, velaminis veritate, quod mentis |129v| verum velamen est. Deus solus, ex quo omnia et qui omnibus preest, Vir est ipse sine velamine; cui universis presedenti omnia sub⟨i⟩iciuntur, in cuiusque conspectu omnia obedientie velamen in capite mentis habere debent, etiam ipse Iesu⟨s⟩, in qua⟨n⟩tum homo; et huic viri, et viris femine, obedientie et subiectionis velamine premi debent.

Sed hic Paulus, in more quodam spectabili, quid decorum sit in virorum et feminarum conventu, animadversa viri prestantia et femine subiectione, in habitu capitis docet. Et iubet tegantur femine in ecclesia, viri detegantur, ut hoc indicetur feminas viris, viros non feminis subesse.

Est animadvertendum hic, quamquam Paulus dicit: *Omnis mulier orans et prophetans non velato capite*, non tamen hiis verbis significat mulierum esse prophetare in ecclesia, quas in eadem epistola postea iubet in ecclesia taceant. Nam inquit: *Mulieres in ecclesiis taceant. Non enim permittitur eis loqui. Si quid autem volunt discere, domi viros suos interrogent. Turpe est mulieri loqui in ecclesia.*

---

adolescentes *M L*] alolescentes *C*

and that her hair is a matter of seemliness for her [XI. 7–9, 15]. He says that women are inclined by nature to take care of their hair, and that human customs ought to imitate nature, the best of teachers. Women should with conscious purpose cover what nature means to be covered [XI. 14, 15].

Although he is making another point, and comes at it circuitously in his words, and in a cryptic manner, as though pretending not to see what he does see, still Paul seems by this careful reasoning to intend the extinction and suppression of something he saw very well in the Corinthian women, their pride in their fine heads of hair. So he induces them to cover their heads up so as not to display their tresses, a matter in which women readily become vainglorious; a matter, too, in which young men are easily captivated as though by a lure.

Of this, however, he deliberately says nothing, for a reason known to himself; he treats the matter from the standpoint of propriety and fittingness in dress, to the effect that it should be a sign of subjection[3] in women, whom nature wishes to be subject to their husbands, as the body is to the head. The veil is a symbol of subjection.

The man, however, as the head of the woman, excels the woman, being the image and glory of God [XI. 7]. Compared with the woman, then, he ought to be without a veil, so that he may be seen to be above, not beneath.

Yet with regard to Christ, our head, and God, all in the Church are, as it were, women; all are, as it were, the body. All too are subject to God—even Jesus Christ himself, indeed, in so far as he is man—and all are also veiled; not with some physical veil as the symbol of obedience and subjection, but with obedience itself, the truth symbolized by the veil, and the mind's true veil. God Himself, from whom are all things and who is above all, is alone the Man, and unveiled. To Him, who is in authority over all things, all things are subject. In His sight all things ought to keep the veil of obedience on the head of their minds, even Jesus himself, as far as he is man. And toward Jesus men ought to be covered by the veil of obedience and subjection; and toward men, women.

But what Paul is teaching here openly is about the question of propriety in the matter of headdress in the assembly of men and women, given man's superiority and woman's subjection. And he commands that in church women be covered, men uncovered, so that thereby it may be signified that women are subject to men, not men to women.

It must be noted here that although Paul says, "Every woman praying and prophesying with head uncovered. . . ." [XI. 5], still he does not mean by these words that to prophesy in church is an office for women. Later in the same Epistle he commands that they be silent in church, for he says: "Women are to be silent in the churches, for to speak is not permitted them." If, however, they wish to learn something, let them ask their husbands at home. It is disgraceful for a woman to speak in church" [XIV. 34, 35].

Prophetare hic docere et interpretari scripturas est et revelationes, quod virorum
est tantum, in ecclesia saltem virorum. In feminarum ecclesia nihil impedit femine
prophetent. Sunt enim sancte moniales omnes viragines. Sed hic Paulus agit solum
ex proposito de tectura et velatione capitis, de oratione et prophitia, que rei,
veritatis, et sensium proloq⟨u⟩utio est per Spiritum, postea suo loco determinatius
loq⟨u⟩uturus. Nunc velamen, postea taciturnitatem mulieribus edicit et imperat.

Sequitur: Hoc autem precipio. |130r|

Heresis manifestatio est probatorum. In divisione et lapsu ostenditur quis secum
stat in veritate. Mirum est quam bonis omnia sunt bona, etiam ipsa mala, quamque pro bonitate Dei ex ipsis malis bona nascuntur. Quid tam mortiferum quam
secta et heresis? At simul quid tam declarans unitatem et constantiam bonorum
in veritate? Propterea ait: *Oportet hereses° esse, ut qui probati sunt manifesti° fiant,
et mala, ut bona appareant.* Ignis aurum probat, et veritas in facibus° falsitatis
secum constat et declaratur. Decidunt et divisim delabuntur defectu sanitatis infirmi.
Sanitas in veritate est; veritas in unitate firma est, in se luculenta, in omnes bona
et benigna. Non vinci, non extingui, non depravari quidem potest.

Ad consolationem verorum apud Corinthios et probatorum, ex falsis heresibus
significat illis bonum esse posse, videlicet exactam examinationem et probationem
eorum, quisnam sit verus et sincerus et sanus in Christo sano. Venti vel vehemen-
tissimi non evertunt nisi eas arbores quarum radices parum alte et firme figuntur
in terra. Terra, fundamentum, petra, et stabilitas nostra Iesus Christus est.

Dominica cena fractus panis est, et distributum suum ipsius sacratissimum corpus. Item una cum pane compotatio sanguinis eiusdem, quo novum Dei cum
hominibus pactum et fedus consecratum° est; sanguine enim sanctarum hostiarum
consecrantur rataque fiunt omnia. Immolati agni, immaculati Christi, sanguine
redimente et sanctificante, cum redemptis et sanctificatis Deo fedus et novum
Dei testamentum consecratur, quod est, si per Christum et in Christo imitantes
illum serviamus Deo, tum ex conventione et pacto sanguine Christi confirmato,
eiusdem Iesu Christi glorie comparticipes erimus. Alioqui pactum irritum est.
|130v|

Habet dominica hec cena manducatioque panis et calicis degustatio commemora-

---

hereses *M*] herises *C L*   manifesti *M L*] manifecti *C*   facibus *C*] faucibus *M L*
consecratum *C? M*] conservatum *L*

To prophesy[4] means here to teach and interpret the scriptures and revelations, and this belongs only to men, at least in a men's church. In a church of women, there is nothing to keep women from prophesying; for holy monastic women are all of them, in this sense, man-like women.[5] In this place, however, Paul intentionally restricts himself to the covering and veiling of the head, intending to speak later more explicitly in their own place of prayer and of prophecy, which is a declaration by the Spirit of reality, truth, and meanings. For women he now ordains and commands the veil; afterwards, he ordains and commands silence.

There follows: "Now I warn you of this. . . ." [XI. 17].

Heresy[6] makes manifest those who have been proved true. When there is division and falling away, it is shown who is constant and self-consistent in the truth. It is wonderful how to the good all things are good, even bad things themselves, and how by the goodness of God good has its birth even from evils. What is so deadly as sects and heresy? Yet at the same time, what declares so well the unity and constancy of the good who are in the truth? For this reason, says Paul, "heresies there needs must be, so that those who have been proved true may be distinguished" [XI. 19], and there must be evils, so that the good may appear. Fire proves gold, and amid the ruinous flames[7] of falsehood truth remains constant and is made clearly apparent. The weak sink down and fall divided, because of their lack of soundness. Soundness is in truth, and the truth is strong in unity, full of light in itself, and kindly and good toward all. It cannot be overpowered, it cannot be extinguished, it cannot be deformed.

For the comfort of the true and the loyal among the Corinthians, Paul points out how from false heresies there can come for them a good: an accurate weighing, namely, and a proving of who is true and sincere and sound in the sound Christ. Even the wildest winds overthrow only those trees whose roots are planted with too little depth and firmness in the earth. And our earth, our base, our rock, our steadfastness is Jesus Christ.

At the Lord's Supper there was a breaking of bread, and his own most sacred body was distributed. Together with the bread there was likewise a shared drinking of his blood, by which a new compact and covenant[8] of God with men was consecrated; for by the blood of victims are made all consecrations and ratifications. By the redeeming and sanctifying blood of the sacrificed Lamb, the immaculate Christ, is consecrated God's new covenant and testament with those who are redeemed and made holy to Him. This covenant[9] is thus: if through Christ, and in Christ, and imitating Christ we serve God, then by the agreement and the compact confirmed by Christ's blood, we shall be sharers in the glory of the same Jesus Christ. If not, the covenant is made null.

Now this Supper of the Lord, the eating of the bread and the drinking from

tionem annunciationemque et representationem mortis Christi, siquidem est fractio corporis et quasi effusio sanguinis. Sed fractio et effusio est, ut ea hostia vescantur electi, ut, Christus moriens in ipsos, ii reviviscant in illo; ut totum habentes in se Iesum, sint toti et penitus in Iesu, iam incorporati et concorporati cum illo, comparticipatione corporis unifici et vivifici illius qui se totum in sua dominica cena impartit nobis, ut nos totos transformet in ipsum, faciatque commembra secum, ut ipso capite, cum suis unum quasi corpus constet, totum habens Deum et totum in Deo, non solum cominicatione Deitatis in animis, sed etiam in corporibus communicatione corporis illius, ut in unum corpus coalescamus in ipso.

Ita ipse (que ecclesia est) vescitur se ipso, nec alio alitur papulo ecclesia quam ipso Christo, omnes in eo sacerdotes et consacrificantes et coepulantes in eadem hostia; ipsa ecclesia, certe ipse Christus, se ipso Christo altus et nutritus in vitam sempiternam.

Mactatus et immolatus et mortuus erat Iesus Christus ut eo vescamur sacrificio donec veniat, utque vescentes recordaremur illius mortui pro nobis, participes mortis illius, ut vivamus in ipso; participes eiusdem vite, ut mortui iam simus in ipso, ex mortuis iam vivi in illo. In templo nunc sumus ut hostia vescamur omnes, omnesque simus participes altaris° Dei, immo, ipsi Dei immolati in ara crucis, ut una cum |131r| illo et in illo crucifixi immolatique, Deo grate simus hostie.

Sic etiam concenatio cum Domino est commori cum illo. Filiis Zebedei dixit: Potestis calicem bibere, quem ego bibiturus sum? Et suam mortem calicem vocavit quando precatus est: *Transeat a me calix iste.* Et Paulus: *Non potestis calicem Domini bibere et calicem demoniorum,* i.e., mori in Christo et vivere cum demonibus.

Dedit corpus suum suis quod pro illis traderetur, quod voluit comparticipent in recordatione mortis illius; et id quoque digne, ne rei sint mortis Domini. Indigne si edant, necant Christum. Digne si edant, vivunt ipsi in mortuo, et commortui in ipso, vivunt in ipso.

Dignitas est in innocentia: ut innocentes sint, sicut Christus innocens; ut innocentes convescentes, innocentissimi Iesu mortem representent. Sontes qui sunt, una cum Iuda rei sunt corporis et sanguinis Domini, necantes id, non vivificati in illo, in eodem commortui ut vivificentur, utque diiudicent decernantque cor-

altaris *M L*] altalis *C*

the cup, contains a commemoration and a proclamation and a making present again of Christ's death, since there is a breaking of his body, and a pouring out, as it were, of his blood. But the breaking and the pouring out exist so that the chosen ones may take that Victim as food; to the end that, Christ dying in them,[10] they may live anew in him; so that having Jesus wholly in themselves, they may be wholly and entirely in him, already embodied in him and with him made one body. This comes about by the joint sharing of the unifying and life-giving body of him who gives himself wholly to us in his own Lord's Supper, to transform us wholly into himself and to make us fellow-members with him, so that with his own he may form one body,[11] so to speak, with himself as head, possessing God wholly and wholly in God; not only by the communication of the Divinity in our souls, but also by the communication of his body in our bodies, to the end that we may grow together into one body in him.

Thus, he—and the Church is he—takes himself as food. By no other food is the Church nourished than by Christ himself. In him, all are priests, together sacrificing and together feasting on the same Victim; the Church itself, assuredly Christ himself, being fed and nourished by Christ himself to everlasting life.

Jesus Christ was sacrificed and immolated and put to death that we might take that sacrifice as food until he comes, and that taking, we might be mindful of his death on our behalf, might be sharers in his death so as to live in him, might be sharers in his life, so as now to be dead in him, now in him alive from among the dead. Our place now is in the Temple, so that we may all take the Victim as food, and may all be partakers of God's altar—more, of God Himself,[12] offered upon the altar of the Cross. Thus, together with him, crucified and sacrificed with him, we too may be victims pleasing to God.

In this way too the sharing of the Supper with the Lord is a dying together with him. To the sons of Zebedee he said: "Can you drink of the cup that I am to drink of?" [Matt. xx. 22]; and he called his own death a cup, when he prayed: "Let this cup pass from me" [xxvi. 39]. Paul, too: "You cannot drink the cup of the Lord and the cup of demons" [I Cor. x. 21], i.e., you cannot die in Christ and live with demons.

He gave to his own his own body to be delivered over for them, and he wished that together they partake of it, in mindfulness of his death. He wished, too, that they do this worthily, lest they be guilty of the Lord's death. If they eat unworthily, they kill Christ. If they eat worthily, they themselves live in him who is dead, and being sharers of death in him, in him they are alive [xi. 23–29].

Worthiness lies in innocence, in their being innocent as Christ was innocent, in their sharing the feast in innocence to make present again the death of the all-innocent Jesus. Those who are not innocent are, with Judas, guilty of the body and blood of the Lord, murdering that body instead of being made alive in it and sharing death in it in order to have life and to distinguish and recog-

pus Domini. Est ille robustus, sollidus, et validus cibus. Mors est egrotis in peccatis, tum animi tum corporis. *Ideo* (inquit) *inter vos multi infirmi et imbecilles,
et dormiunt multi.*

Affligit et castigat Dominus eos qui abutuntur beneficiis suis. Castigare, cor-
ripere, examinare,temptare, probare se ipsum debet quisque sane, ut laude Dei,
non castigatione mereatur°. Experiatur quisque si imitatur |131v| Christum, ante-
quam participet, ne moriatur cibo peccatori intollerabili. Hoc est quod Paulus
iubet: *Probet se ipsum homo, et sic de pane illo edat et de calice bibat. Qui manducat
et bibit indigne, iudicium sibi manducat et bibit.* Unitas, concordia, caritas membrorum,
i.e., hominum innocentium in Christo, facit societatem dignam ut Christum
comparticipent.

Comederunt discipuli Iesum moriturum ipsum, morituri in illo ut cum eodem
resurgant quando veniet. Idem sacramentum deinceps omnes concipiunt, com-
morituri omnes in eodem ut in adventu illius corresurgant.

---

mereatur M] *meriatur C L*

nize the Lord's body for what it is. It is a strong, solid, and powerful food. To men sick in sin it means death, both of soul and body. "That is why," says Paul, "many are unhealthy and weak among you, and many sleep" [XI.30].

Those who abuse his kindnesses the Lord afflicts and punishes. Everyone, then, ought surely to punish himself, to reprove and scrutinize and test and prove himself, so that instead of God's punishment he may merit God's approval. Before he partake, let each put it to the test whether or not he is imitating Christ, lest he should die from that food which the sinner cannot endure. This is Paul's command: "Let a man examine himself, and then let him eat of that bread and drink of that cup. Whoever eats and drinks unworthily is eating and drinking damnation to himself" [XI. 28, 29]. And when a society is worthy to participate together in Christ, it is the unity, concord, and love of its members, i.e., of its innocent men in Christ, that make it so.

When Jesus was about to die, the disciples ate together of him, themselves soon to die in him in order to rise with him when he shall come. And one after another all take this same sacrament, all to die together, so that all may rise again together in his coming.

Caput duodecimum°

De spiritalibus iisque que sunt in hominibus ex Spiritu Dei Sancto, de origine, effectu, et fine eorum, nunc disserit Paulus, ut doceat Corinthios quinam sunt ex Spiritu in Christo et ad quid spiritales facti sunt.

Primum hanc magnam sententiam affirmat, confitentes et credentes in Christo universos spiritales esse, Spiritumque habere, et esse in Spiritu°. Alioquin Christianos non esse, quibus est in Christo per Spiritum Dei et novum esse et operari prorsus spiritale. Sicut extra Christum esse est sine Spiritu Dei esse, ita in Spiritu Dei esse est in Iesu Christo esse, unde profluit in universos Spiritus Dei, ut spiritales sint in eo.

Ad Romanos scribit: Si quis Spiritum Christi non habet, hic non est eius. Et ad Corinthios in secunda epistola: Ex hoc (id est, amodo) neminem cognovimus secundum carnem. |132r| Homo enim quicquid sit oportet cesset in Christo cedatque Spiritui Dei, vivatque non secundum carnem, i.e., hominem, sed secundum Spiritum. Ad Romanos: Si secundum carnem vixeritis, moriemini; si autem Spiritu facta carnis mortificaveritis, vivetis. Et ad eosdem: Vos in carne non estis, sed in Spiritu.

Per carnem fere semper Paulus significat totum hominem, cuius prudentia mors est, sapientia inimica est Deo. Ut ad Corinthios scribit in illa secunda epistola: Si unus pro omnibus mortuus est, omnes ergo mor- *II Cor. v.* [14, 15, 17]. tui sunt; et pro omnibus mortuus est Christus, ut qui vivunt, iam non sibi (i.e. homini) vivant, sed ei qui pro eis mortuus est (i.e., Deo, in Spiritu Dei). *Si qua ergo nova creatura* — toto homine verso in Spiritum — *vetera transierunt; ecce facta sunt omnia nova,* renovatis hominibus Spiritu Christi,

---

Caput *Ed.*] capud *C*

Chapter XII

Paul now speaks of spiritual gifts, the things in men that are from God's Holy Spirit, and of their origin, effects, and end. His purpose is to teach the Corinthians what sort of men they are by the Spirit, in Christ, and to what end they have been made spiritual.

First he gives assurance of this great truth, that all who confess Christ and believe in him are spiritual, and possess the Spirit, and are in the Spirit [I Cor. XII. 3, 11-13]. Otherwise they would not be Christians, since it belongs to Christians to have in Christ through the Spirit of God both a new being[1] and actions exclusively spiritual. Just as to be outside Christ is to be without the Spirit of God, so to be in the Spirit of God is to be in Christ, from whom the Spirit of God flows forth into all men to make them spiritual in him.

Paul writes to the Romans: "A man does not belong to Christ unless he have the Spirit of Christ" [Rom. VIII. 9]. And to the Corinthians, in his second letter: "From this," i.e., henceforward, "we do not know anyone according to the flesh" [II Cor. v. 16]. For in Christ a man must cease to be whatever he is, and must yield to the Spirit of God, and must live, not according to the flesh, i.e., in man's way, but according to the Spirit. To the Romans, then, Paul writes: "If you live according to the flesh,[2] you shall die; but if through the Spirit you mortify the deeds of the flesh, you shall live" [Rom. VIII. 13]. And to the same Romans: "You do not exist in the flesh, but in the Spirit" [VIII. 9].

By "the flesh" Paul almost always means man in his entirety: man, whose knowledge is death, whose wisdom is at war with God. As he writes to the Corinthians, again in the Second Epistle: "If one man died *II Cor. v.* on behalf of all, then all men died; and Christ died for all, so that those who live might live no longer to themselves," i.e., to man, "but to him who died for them" [II Cor. v. 14, 15], i.e., to God, and in the Spirit of God. "If man then is some new creature" — by the whole man's being turned to the Spirit — "the old things are passed away. Lo! everything has been made new" [v. 17], since men by the Spirit of Christ have been renewed in order to

ut sint penitus novi in ipso. Ideo Paulus hic asseverans omnes in Christo, eum confitentes, spiritales esse, ait: *Nemo potest dicere Dominus Iesus nisi in Spiritu Sancto spiritificante.*

Hoc autem pro vero et confesso habito, fideles omnes in Christo in Spiritu Dei esse, ut in eo sint, sapiant, et operentur omnia spiritaliter, nec vocationem hominum in Christum aliud esse quam a falsitate hominum abductionem et eorumdem attractionem in veritatem Spiritus, deinde iam de ortu et progressu, de viribus et facultatibus, de effectu et fine Spiritus Dei in hominibus in Christo disputat; docetque summatim tria: profusionem Spiritus, |132v| in profusione multiplici degenerationem, in graduali degeneratione recompensationem.

De quibus paulo post mentem Pauli secuti fusius explicabimus. Iam interea parumper textum ipsum vel retextum contemplemur.

Spiritus Dei ubi vult spirat, et quatenus vult, et quamdiu vult. In hominibus in Christo hec omnia operatur unus idemque Spiritus Sanctus, dividens si⟨n⟩gulis prout vult, ut Spiritu vivificentur, sapiant, et operentur omnes in Christo aliquid quod sit toti ecclesie, cuius capud° est Christus, utile. Quia unicuique datur manifestatio Spiritus ad utilitatem, ad id quod expedit et quod edificat ecclesiam.

Hic finis est Spiritus, quo quod non tendit non est ex Spiritu Dei. Nec utilitatem in ecclesia |133r| querunt homines suopte ingenio, sed Spiritus Dei in hominibus. Neque vero ipsi homunculi vel sapienter loquuntur vel scienter, vel credunt et confidunt Deo in Christo, vel sanitatem restituunt tum in animo tum in corpore, vel miracula ostentant et opera Dei supra naturam, vel prophetant et vaticinantur et vaticinia oraculaque divina interpretantur, vel discernunt et ponunt differentiam inter spiritus, diiudicantque uter bonus uterque malignus est, vel variis linguis utuntur, vel incognitos sermones recte interpretantur. Qui ipsi homines in se impotentes sunt, et stulti, et mali, et infantes denique. Sed in ipsis gratia vocatis in omnipotentem, omnisapientem, omnibonum Iesum Christum, ipsius Dei Verbum et eloquentiam, hec omnia operatur unus et idem Spiritus, dividens unicuique sicuti vult, ut alii possint mirifice in Christo, alii sapiant splendide, alii benigniter operentur, alii varie loquantur, alii sublimiter a Deo dicta in prophetis interpretentur, alii ipsi quoque ex Deo ex sublimi veritate profentur.

In potentia vero, sapientia, bonitate, operatione, eloquentia, in efficacia, multitudine, varietate, ordine, pulchritudine, in benignitate et beneficiis, in sermone et veritate, in eruditione et doctrina, purgatione, illuminatione, perfec-

---

capud *C but with* d *crossed L*] caput *M*

be altogether new in him. Paul, therefore, asserting here that all who are in Christ and confess him are spiritual, says: "No one can say that Jesus is the Lord, except in the Holy Spirit" [I Cor. XII. 3], who makes spiritual.

But once it has been established as true and acknowledged that all the faithful in Christ are in the Spirit of God, in order to exist in Him, to be wise in Him, and to do all things in Him spiritually; and that the calling of men to Christ is nothing else than the removal of men from falsehood and a drawing of them into the truth of the Spirit, Paul next discusses the origin and the progress, the powers and faculties, the effects and the end of God's Spirit among men in Christ. Briefly, he teaches three things: the outpouring of the Spirit; the lessening in the manifold outpouring;[3] and the compensation in the gradual lessening.

A little further on we shall explain, following the mind of Paul, more at length about these things. But now let us first give our attention for a while to the text itself, or rather, to an analysis of it.

The Spirit of God breathes where He wishes, and as much as He wishes, and as long as He wishes. Among men who are in Christ, one and the same Holy Spirit works all these things, imparting to each as He will, so that all may be given life in the Spirit, may have wisdom in Christ and achieve something that will be useful for the whole Church, of which Christ is the head. For the manifestation of the Spirit is given to every man for profit, for what helps and builds the Church.

This is the end of the Spirit, and whatever does not work toward that end is not of the Spirit of God. Nor do men seek what is profitable in the Church by their own natural disposition, but the Spirit of God in men seeks it. Assuredly, weak little men by themselves speak neither with wisdom nor with knowledge; nor do they believe and trust in God in Christ; nor do they restore soundness either to soul or to body; nor do they proffer miracles and supernatural works of God, or prophesy and predict and interpret prophecies and divine utterances; nor do they discern and mark the difference between spirits, and judge which is good and which is evil; nor do they use divers tongues, or interpret rightly unknown languages. Men of themselves are powerless, and stupid, and wicked, and, in a word, speechless children.[4] But in these same men, when they are called by grace to the almighty, all-wise, all-good Jesus Christ, the Word and the Eloquence of God, one and the same Spirit works all these things. To each He imparts as He will, so that some have wondrous power in Christ, others splendid wisdom; others again are active in kindness; others speak with divers tongues; others sublimely interpret God's words in the prophets; others speak forth themselves from the sublime truth of God's power.

In power, wisdom, goodness, action, eloquence; in efficacy, multitude, variety, order, beauty; in kindness and kindnesses, in speech and truth; in learning, and in the instruction, purification, enlightenment, and perfecting of men in

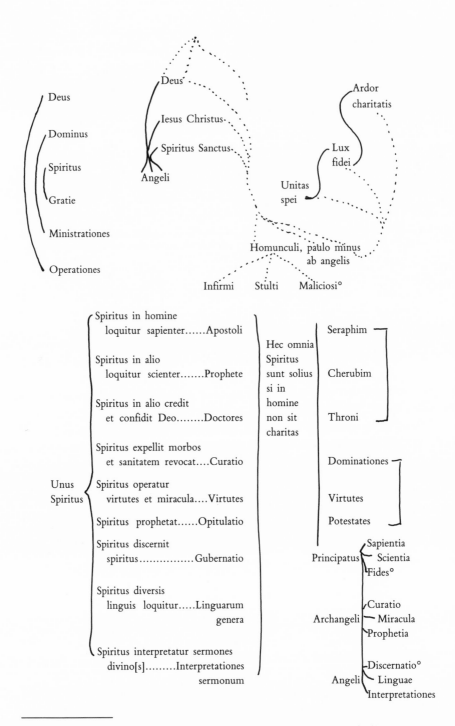

Deus

Dominus

Spiritus

Gratie

Ministrationes

Operationes

Deus

Iesus Christus

Spiritus Sanctus

Angeli

Ardor
charitatis

Lux
fidei

Unitas
spei

Homunculi, paulo minus
ab angelis

Infirmi   Stulti   Maliciosi°

Unus
Spiritus

Spiritus in homine
loquitur sapienter......Apostoli

Spiritus in alio
loquitur scienter.......Prophete

Spiritus in alio credit
et confidit Deo........Doctores

Spiritus expellit morbos
et sanitatem revocat....Curatio

Spiritus operatur
virtutes et miracula....Virtutes

Spiritus prophetat......Opitulatio

Spiritus discernit
spiritus...............Gubernatio

Spiritus diversis
linguis loquitur.....Linguarum
genera

Spiritus interpretatur sermones
divino[s]........Interpretationes
sermonum

Hec omnia
Spiritus
sunt solius
si in
homine
non sit
charitas

Seraphim

Cherubim

Throni

Dominationes

Virtutes

Potestates

Principatus

Sapientia
Scientia
Fides°

Archangeli

Curatio
Miracula
Prophetia

Angeli

Discernatio°
Linguae
Interpretationes

Infirmi   Stulti   Maliciosi] *M L* (Malitiosi), Inf. Stul. Ma.] *C*   Fides] *Ed.*, fi] *C*? (ti?), *om.*
M L   Discernatio] *Ed.*, discern.] *C* (*for* discretio?)

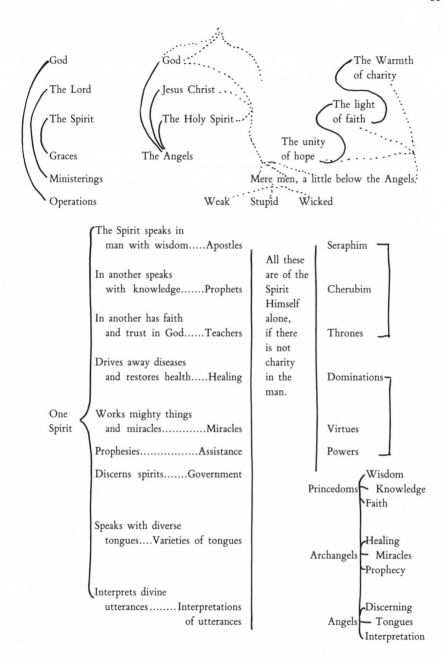

tione hominum in Christo, in constructione et completione Christi in Deo, que
ecclesia est, versatur et se exercet et operatur Spiritus Dei in hominibus.

In quo qui sunt, facta carnis, i.e. humanas operationes ab humana autoritate,
prudentia, et |133v| volun⟨ta⟩te profectas, penitus mortificaverint, quas inven-
tiones hominum vocat David in Spiritu, et sepe *Inventiones hominum.*
detestatur. *Dabit illis* (inquit) *Deus secundum opera eo-*
rum, et secundum nequitiam adinventionum° ipsorum. Et alibi: *Et dimisit eos secun-*
dum desideria cordis eorum; ibunt in adinventionibus suis. Item in alio psalmo: *Et ulciscens*
(inquit) *in omnes adinventiones eorum.* Et illud in psalmo: *Et irritaverunt eum in*
adinventionibus suis, et multiplicata est in eis ruina. Idem alibi: *Deus scit quoniam cogita-*
tiones hominum vane sunt.

Homo ipse per se, et infirmitas eius, stulticia, improbitas, verba, operationes,
effectus—hoc est, quicquid hominis est absolute et ipsius, cuius nihil est nisi
infirmum, stultum, malum, vanum, perditum, nihili, cuius potentia infirmitas
est, sapientia stulticia, voluntas malicia, operatio demolitio, effectus destructio—hic
(inquam) totus homo uno ore et Spiritus sapientia in universa Sacra Scriptura
et divina condemnatur. In religione ergo et in rebus publicis, in institutis eorum
et legibus, in vita hominum et moribus, in artificiis, in exercitiis, in ludis, in
laboribus tum animi tum corporis, hiis ut divitias conquirant, illis ut sapientiam—
quicquid decreverunt et sanctitum° esse voluerunt, vanitas, frustratio, et nihili erat.

Equidem nihil est nisi Spiritus et |134r| quod ex Spiritu est in Domino nostro
Iesu Christo. Virtus, sapientia, bonitas, bona operatio, prophitia, veridicus sermo, eruditio, doctrina, agnitio Dei, confessio Christi, imitatio Iesu, discessus
a mundo, vita in Spiritu, valitudo in visceribus Iesu Christi, operatio assidua
pro mensura Spiritus in eodem, fides, spes, charitas, beneficentia aliis, purgatio,
illuminatio, perfectio, paupertas, castitas, ieiunia, vota, sacrificia, preces, renovatio
in Spiritu de die in diem, transformatio a claritate° in claritatem a Domini Spiritu,
desiderium dissolvi° et esse cum Christo, immortalitas, eternitas, felicitas, re-
quies in beatissimo Iesu in celis—hec sunt revera que sunt in hominibus, et est
quisque°, ipse quatenus in iis est. Quo autem minus in iis est, eo minus in se
ipse°, quisquumque is sit, est. Nec debet quisquam certe desiderare ut vivat hic
longius, nisi ut in iis altius, Dei Spiritu, promoveatur, nec querere que ad hanc
vitam pertinent, nisi ut vivat in aliam vitam, quam nunc incepit vivere in Christo,

---

adinventionum *M L*] *ad inventionum C*   sanctitum *C*] sanxitum *M*] sancitum *C. See*
note.   claritate *M L*] claritatem *C*   dissolvi *M Vulg.*] desolvi *C L*   quisque, *C*
M] quisque *L*   se ipse, *L*] se ipse *C*] seipso *M but by another hand over* se ipse

Christ; in the building and the finishing of the Christ in God which is the Church, the Spirit of God is engaged and active and working in men.

Those men who are in Him will have altogether mortified the deeds of the flesh, those human activities which have their origin in human authority, wisdom, and will. These David *The inventions of men.* in the Spirit calls man's inventions, and often he speaks strongly against them. "God will reward them," he says, "according to their works, and according to the wickedness of their own inventions" [Ps. xxvII. 4]. And elsewhere: "And He let them go according to their heart's desires; they shall walk in their own inventions" [LXXX. 13]. Again, in another psalm: "Taking vengeance," he says, "on all their inventions" [xcvIII. 8]. And those other words in one of the psalms: "And they provoked Him by their inventions, and ruin was multiplied among them" [cv. 29]. Again, elsewhere: "God knows that the thoughts of men are vain" [xcIII. 11].

Man in and of himself, together with his weakness, stupidity, and wickedness, his words, works, and accomplishments — that is to say, whatever belongs as his own and fully to man, who has nothing except what is weak, foolish, evil, vain, lost, and nothing; whose power is weakness, and wisdom stupidity; whose willing is malice, whose working is an undoing, and whose achievements are destruction — this man (I say) in his entirety is with one voice and with the wisdom of the Spirit condemned all through the Sacred and divine Scriptures.[5] And so whatever men have determined and wished to be established[6] in their religion and in their politics, in their institutions and laws, in their life and conduct, in their skills, activities, games, in their labors both of mind and of body (these for the acquisition of wisdom, those for the acquisition of wealth), has been emptiness, frustration, and nothingness.

In truth, nothing *is* except the Spirit,[7] and that which is of the Spirit in our Lord Jesus Christ. Virtue, wisdom, goodness, good works, prophecy, truthful utterance, learning, instruction, knowledge of God, confession of Christ, imitation of Jesus, withdrawal from the world, life in the Spirit, health in the interior of Christ [Phil. I. 8], steadfast activity in him according to the measure of the Spirit, faith, hope, charity, well-doing toward others, purification, enlightenment, perfection, poverty, chastity, fastings, vows, sacrifices, prayers, daily renewal in the Spirit, transformation from glory to glory by the Lord's Spirit [II Cor. III. 18], the desire to be dissolved and to be with Christ [Phil. I. 23], immortality, eternity, bliss, rest in the most blessed Jesus in Heaven — these are the things that truly *are* in man, and any man really exists[8] in so far as he is in them. And the less anyone is in them, the less he is in himself, whoever he is. Nor, surely, should anyone desire to prolong his life here except to be advanced by God's Spirit higher in them, or seek what pertains to this life except to live for the other life, which he has already begun in Christ, in such a way as no longer

ut secundum rationem mundi, secundum desideria carnis et hominis appetitionem, amplius non vivat.

Que hec vita inchoata° in Christo, quia spiritalis est et celestis, terrenorum paucis eget, paucisque et facile sustinetur, siquidem is in Christo, quisquis sit, quasi spiritus est, celestibusque magis |134v| altus et nutritus in vitam eternam quam terrenis ad mortem. Quamobrem que ex terra sunt, et huius temporis ac diei (ut vocat Paulus) mali, petet que necessaria sunt dumtaxat, et ea quam minime et invitus etiam, atque (ut docet supra in hac epistola) quasi non faciens, ut non hic velle vivere libenter, sed vivere hic ut alibi plenius vivat videatur. Spiritum sustineat hic tenuiter, ut altiore spiritu totus et spisse et plene respiret in Deum, in Iesu Christo, qui est ipse in homine, non homo per se in ipso.

Nescio an rideam cum Democrito an cum Heraclito defleam hominum vana et perdita studia in hoc mundo, qui levia, caduca, et momentanea° impensissime sectantur, ignari se, una cum eis quorum tractum sequuntur, in mortem contrahi sempiternam.

A qua deliratione et errabundo cursu ut avocet homines, utque reducat in viam veritatis, in semitam vite, in callem eternitatis, apparuit in hominibus Iesus Christus, veritas ipsa et vita et immortalitas, iussitque ipse ut se sequantur, qui antegressus est, et calvavit et monstravit vestigia, in quibus post eum |135r| sine errore itur in celum.

Quos autem vocavit in iter vitamque celestem, capud, ille Iesus, sui Spiritus vi equabiliter fusa in omnes, eos counivit secum, ut membra ex membro dependeant decenti ordine, et una cum Christo in Deo, perpulchrum et divinum corpus constituant, cuius anima et (ut utar Aristotelis verbo greco) entelechia, i.e., actus, perfectio, et consummatio°, Deus ipse, Trinitas Sancta est, que̜ est plena in capite, in quo est omnis plenitudo divinitatis corporaliter.

A capite deinde impartitur membris *singulis prout vult Deus* (ut loquitur Paulus) *qui posuit membra, unumquodque in corpore sicut vult.* Impartitur eis Deus suam deitatem, ut sint cum Christo in eo, et sapiant, et boni sint, et aliquid utile in corpore agant, aliquidque divinum, cooperatores Dei in hoc mundo ad vincendas malas eius rationes. In quo se ducem prebuit Iesus Christus, ut nos coniuncti cum eo in hoc negotio ancillemur et subserviamus, universa scilicet ecclesia Iesu, ut corpus suo capiti. Quod ipsum certe servire, est in Domino glorie dominari.

---

inchoata *M*] incohata *C L*   momentanea *M*] momentania *C L*   consummatio *M*] comsummatio *C L*

to live according to the world's system, according to the desires of the flesh and man's appetite.

This life begun in Christ, because it is spiritual and Heavenly, needs few earthly things and is by few of them readily sustained, since a man in Christ, whoever he is, is as it were a spirit, and is nourished rather by Heavenly things for eternal life than by earthly things for death. He will seek, therefore, of the things of earth and of this time and this evil day (as Paul calls it [Eph. VI. 13]) only such as are necessary, and even these he will seek unwillingly and as little as possible, and (as he teaches earlier in this Epistle) as though he sought them not [I Cor. VII. 31], so that it may be seen that he does not will to live here contentedly, but wills to live here in order to live more fully[9] elsewhere. Let him barely sustain his spirit here, so as to breathe with the wholeness of a loftier spirit to God, deeply and fully, in Jesus Christ, who is of himself in man, rather than man's being of himself in Christ.

I do not know whether I should laugh with Democritus or weep with Heraclitus[10] at the lost and empty exertions of men in this world. With the utmost intensity they run after things trifling, perishable, and short-lived, unaware that they are being drawn on, together with the objects whose attraction they follow, into never-ending death.

To call men away from this madness and this wayward course, and to lead them back into the road of truth, into the path of life, into the way of eternity, Jesus Christ appeared among men, the Truth itself, and Life, and Immortality. He commanded that men follow him, and he was the one who went before them, marking and showing them his footprints, by which they could go to Heaven behind him, without straying.

Now those whom he called to the journey and to Heavenly life, Jesus, the head, united to himself by the force of his Spirit diffused to all alike, so that they might be, as members, mutually dependent in seemly order, and together with Christ in God, might form a body of utmost beauty, a divine body. The soul of this body and the entelechy[11] (to use Aristotle's Greek term), i.e., the act, perfection, and consummation of it, is God Himself, the Blessed Trinity, which is in the head fully; in the head is embodied all the plenitude of the Godhead [Col. II. 9].

From the head it is imparted in order to the members, "to each," Paul says, "as God wills, who has given each member its own position in the body, as He pleases" [I Cor. XII. 18]. God imparts to them His Godhead, so that they may be in Him with Christ, may be wise and good, may do some useful thing in the body, some divine thing, as cooperators with God in this world for the overthrow of its bad principles. In this work Jesus Christ showed himself as our leader, so that joined with him we—the entire Church of Jesus, that is—might help and serve in the undertaking, as the body serves and is subordinate to the head. And this service is, to be sure, lordship in the Lord of Glory.

Ratio illa et sapientia, qua° regatur tota ecclesia, in Iesu est ut in arce. Cui dum inservit ecclesia, sana est et pulchra, et efficax alicuius utilitatis. Contra vero si accidat, si que humana ratio, ira°, et cupiditas excurrat, et insolentius prescriptos a Spiritu Dei terminos transgrediatur°, tum tumultuantur misere, et fede perturbationibus vexantur omnia in ecclesia Dei quidem.

Quod nunc in hac nostra etate accidit, propterea quod deciderint homines a Spiritu Dei in suas ipsorum rationes, iras, et libidines. Quum autem omnia in se continet et suo quodque ordine conservat Spiritus, contemperatque |135v| sic omnia membra° hominesque in ecclesia, ut omnes vigeant et sentiant et agant omnia Spiritu, tunc in Deo pulchram formam et figuram pre se fert ecclesia, et est tota sana, et integra, et viva, et valens, et divino nitens colore, quando quodque membrum° vere dicat: *Non vivo ego iam, sed vivit in me Christus.*

Christus enim ipsa est vita, in vita Dei. In quo humanitas a Deo, tanquam a magnete, et contrahitur sursum et sustinetur. Que eadem divinitas, magnetis inster qui sunt reliqui homines eiusdem sortis cum Christo, eos simul contractos sursum counitosque cum Iesu, membra cum membro, in alto sustentat, quasi ferreos homines, et suapte natura in terram caducos si a Spiritu Dei deserantur.

Christus magnes.
Ecclesia ferrum.

In illo ergo lapide precioso et petra prepotente, ac celeste° et divino magnete, ecclesia suspensa innititur tota, et supra vallem mundi et miserie in monte extat spectabilis in Christo, suspiciens celum et micantia sidera, despiciens terram et atros caliginosque homines, inter celum et terram in iugo montis excelsi Christi, interea respirans in liquido et vitali aere Spiritus Dei. Pergentes illic cotidie in eodem Christo in purgatione sui a divino igne, qui tamdem in eo quum evaserint penitus simplices, puri, et uni, tunc simul perspicui et illuminantur luce divini solis, et consummato Dei amore perficiuntur in Christo in celis.

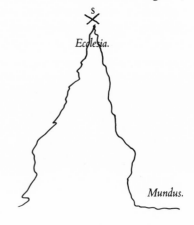

Ecclesia.

Mundus.

Hic finis est fidei nostre, et spei hominum in Christo, et charitatis: ut a claritate in |136r| claritatem in eandem imaginem transformemur a Domini Spiritu.

---

qua *Ed.*] quo *C M L*   ira *C M*] via *L*   transgrediatur *C*?] (trangrediatur?) *M L* membra *M L*] menbra *C*   membrum *M L*] menbrum *C*   membra cum membro *M L*] menbra cum menbro *C*   celeste *C (abl. sing.)*] celesti *M L*

The principle and the wisdom by which the whole Church is directed is in Jesus as the summit. As long as the Church obeys it, the Church is sound, and beautiful, and effectual for some useful action. But if the contrary happen, if any human principle, any human anger or cupidity, should break forth and too presumptuously transgress the bounds[12] set by God's Spirit, then everything in God's Church is wretchedly thrown into confusion and foully beset by disorders.

This is what has happened now, in our own age, because men have fallen away from the Spirit of God into their own principles, impetuosities, and unlawful desires. But when the Spirit keeps all things within Himself and each in its own proper order, and so tempers together all the members, all the men in the Church, that they live, and feel, and act in all things by the Spirit, then the Church displays in God a beautiful form and countenance, and is entirely sound, and pure, and alive, and vigorous, and radiant with a Godly complexion. Then can each member say with truth: "No longer do I live, but Christ lives in me" [Gal. II. 20].

For Christ is Life itself, in the life of God. In him all humanity is both drawn upwards and kept up by God, as by a magnet.[13] And the same Godhead, like a magnet, supports aloft the rest of men who share Christ's lot, keeps them drawn together on high and united together with Jesus as members with a mem-

Christ, the magnet;
the Church, iron.

ber: men being, as it were, of iron, and by their own nature sure to fall to the earth if deserted by the Spirit of God.

On that precious stone, therefore, that most powerful rock, that Heavenly and divine magnet, the whole Church is supported and rests, and above the valley of the world and wretchedness it stands out on the mountain, on Christ, as an object of admiration, looking upward to Heaven and the glittering stars, looking down to earth and to dark men in their mists of gloom. Between Heaven and earth she stands on the summit of Christ, the towering mountain, but breathing in the clear and life-filled air of God's Spirit. Thither she sees men advance onward each day in the same Christ, in their own puri-purification by the Divine Fire. When at

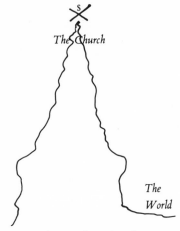

length they become in him altogether simple, pure, and one, then they become at the same time clear, and are filled with light by the light of the Divine Sun; and by the perfect love of God they are made perfect in Heaven, in Christ.

This is the end of our faith, and of men's hope in Christ, and of love: that from glory to glory we may be changed into the same image[14] by the Spirit of the Lord.

Venit Iesus ipse in mundum in subsidium angelorum, ut purget, illuminet, et perficiat mundum. Quos vero primos purgavit, illuminavit, et perfecit in se perfecto, fecitque quasi angelos et spiritus, ut ipsi nunc homines una cum angelis in emendatione mundi elaborent, eos vocavit iam sales et luces, a purgatione et illuminatione; et sunt apostoli, primi in ecclesia, in Christo ample volutantes ac longe lateque caritate delati, potentia efficaces, prestantes luce, bonitate mirabiles. Ii sunt orbes et celici globi, in eo qui omnia continet, Iesu Christo, se in vivificatione mundi volventes, qui per omnes mundi partes decurrere voluerant, ac celestis solis radios Iesu Christi in omnem terram iacere, ut post hyemem et noctem, exorto vere et die Christi, revirescant et luceant omnia.

Id est quod David ait de illis: *Celi enarrant gloriam Dei*, et sub sole veritatis lumen predicando° defundunt; *quorum sonus exivit in omnem terram et in fines orbis terre verba eorum*. In firmamento am-   *Apostoli celi.* biunt omnia. (Firmamentum Iesus est Christus, qui annunciat opera Dei). Sub ipsis ambiunt terram hominum, et ab ipsis constituti, minores orbes et celi angustiores. Atque deinceps sub ipsis contraxio est ad infimos quosque. Omnes tamen sunt orbes, etiam ipsa terra, rotunda et perfecta figura constantes.

Ita in hoc novo et christiano mundo nemo est nisi forma et figura perfecta ac rotunda celestique in Christo, tametsi |136v| alius alio angustior sit et inferior. Quod non facit quominus equalitate necessitatis, in conditione mundi huius et christiane civitatis, amplissimis   *Condire.* et superioribus recompensentur.

Qui christianus mundus conditur et seriatim con-   *Deus, Christus, Caput°.* stituitur ex perfectis in Deo, qui adequat examussim   *Mundus, Ecclesia, Corpus.* alterum mundum, quum capud habet Deum, pedes terrenos homines. *Celum celi sedes eius, terra autem scabellum pedum eius.* Hii sunt qui damnabuntur, qui conculcabuntur ab infimis ec-   *Homo.* clesie. Ut Deus creavit mundum, ita recreavit homines, ut alius ex hominibus et novus mundus condatur a Creatore ipso. In quo sunt que singula singulis illis mundi referre possunt: Deum Verbum Deo Patri (Verbo enim recreatur et conditur hec nova machina humani mundi); spiritibus angelicis homines in Verbo quam maxime spiritales; celestibus orbibus qui deinde sunt

---

predicando C] predicandi M] prædicandi L   Caput Ed.] chapd C with d crossed

Jesus himself came into the world to the aid of the angels,[15] to purify, enlighten, and perfect the world. Those whom first he purified, enlightened, and brought to perfection in his own perfect self, making them, as it were, angels and spirits, so that now men themselves might work with the angels in the betterment of the world, these, he said, were now the salt and the light, naming them from purification and enlightenment. They are the Apostles, the first in the Church, and they revolve fully in Christ, moving far and wide in charity, efficacious in their power, outshining others by their light, wonderful in their goodness. They are orbs and heavenly spheres, in him who contains all things, Jesus Christ, turning themselves in the enlivening of the world.[16] It was their wish to accomplish their course through all parts of the world, and to cast the rays of the Heavenly Sun, Jesus Christ, on all the earth, so that after the winter and the night might arise Christ's spring and Christ's day, and all things be green again and bright.

This is what David affirms of them: "The Heavens proclaim God's glory," and by their preaching pour down their light under the Sun of Truth: "Their sound has gone forth into all the earth, and their words into the ends of the earth" [Ps. XVIII. 2, 4].

The Apostles are the Heavens.

They encompass all things within the firmament. (The firmament is Jesus Christ, who proclaims God's works.) Beneath them, and regulated by them, lesser spheres[17] and narrower heavens encircle the earth of men. And under these in turn there is a progressive lessening to the very lowest. All, however, even the earth itself, are spheres of unchangeably round and perfect figure.

In this new world, then, this Christian world, no one exists unless he be of form and figure perfect and round and heavenly in Christ, although one may be less spacious than another, and lower; the lesser are not by this latter circumstance kept from equality[18] with the most extensive and the highest, since they are necessary in the establishment of this world, this Christian commonwealth.

The establishing.

This Christian world is made up and progressively established from perfect men in God. It corresponds perfectly to the other world, having God as its head, earthly men as its feet. "The Heaven of Heavens is His throne, and the earth His footstool" [Is. LXVI. 6]. These last are they who will be damned, and they will be trodden under foot by the Church's lowest parts. Just as God created the world, so he re-created men that another and a new world might be established from men by the Creator Himself. In it are elements that can be compared, detail for detail,[19] with those of the other world. God the Word corresponds to God the Father (for by the Word is re-created and fashioned this new fabric of the human world); those men who are most spiritual in the Word correspond to the angelic spirits; those who are less spiritual correspond in order to

God, Christ, the head; the World, the Church, the body.

Man.

minus spiritales. Igni deinde et aeri et aque et terre, compara alios inferiores, imaginareque alios terreos esse homines, alios aqueos, alios aereos, alios igneos.

Vel potes ingeniosius et verius spiritalem mundum ex novem angelorum ordinibus constantem cogitare, qui sunt quasi novem orbes, in spiritali circumferentia et firmamento, Deo, se beatissime volventes, ut illius quietem et felicitatem assequantur.

Deus, omnia in omnibus.

In quibus primus est seraphicus ille uti nona spera; secundus cherubicus uti octava°; tercius ut septima Saturni; quartus ut sexta Iovis; quintus ut quinta Martis; sextus ut quarta Solis; septimus ut tertia Mercurii; octavus ut secunda Veneris; nonus ut prima Lune.

Mundus Spiritalis.
Mundus Humanus.
Mundus Corporeus.

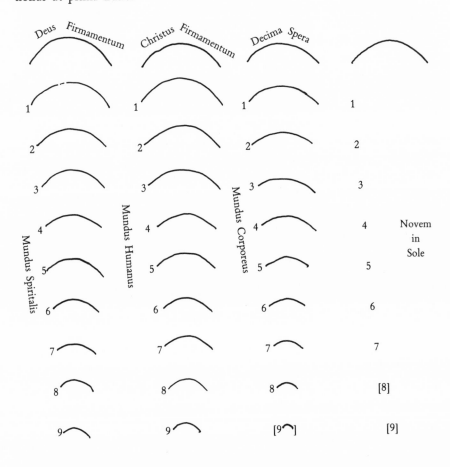

octava *C with schemata immediately following*] tercius fo. 137v

the heavenly spheres. Others, lower still, you may compare to fire, air, water, and earth, imagining some men to be earthy, others watery, others aërial, and others fiery.

Or still more acutely and with more truth, you can think of the spiritual world as consisting of the nine orders of angels, which are, as it were, the nine spheres, evolving in utmost blessedness in the spiritual circumference and firmament that is God, so as to attain
to the tranquillity and happiness that are His.

God, all in all.

The first among these is the Seraphic order, as the ninth sphere; the second is the Cherubic, as the eighth; the third like the
seventh, of Saturn; the fourth like the sixth, of Jupi-
ter; the fifth like the fifth, of Mars; the sixth like the
fourth, of the Sun; the seventh like the third, of Mer-

The Spiritual World.
The Human World.
The Bodily World.

cury; the eighth like the second, of Venus; the ninth like the first, of the Moon.

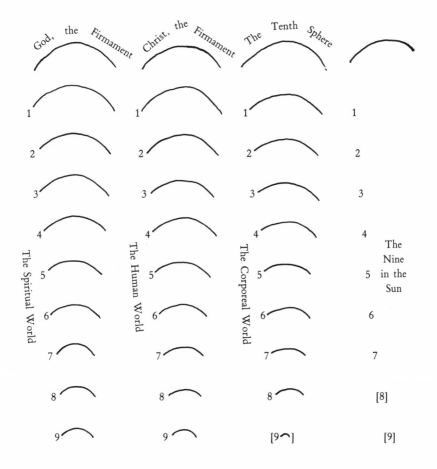

Iesus Christus	Deus	Decima Spera: deus orbium	Sublunaris regio prima: deus elimentorum
Homines primi ordines	Seraphim°	Nona	Nona, ignea regio
Secundi ordinis	Cherubim	Octava, stellarum	Octava, minus ignea
Tercii ordinis	Throni	Septima, Saturni	7, aerea vergens in ignem
Quarti ordinis	Dominationes	Sexta: Iupiter	6, plus aerea
Quinti ordinis	Virtutes	Quinta: Mars	5, aquea et vergens in aerem
Sexti ordinis	Potestates	Quarta: Sol	4, plus aquea
Septimi ordinis	Principales	Tertia, Mercurii°	3, adhuc minus terrea et aquea nonnihil
Octavi [ordinis]	Archangeli	Secunda, Veneris	2, minus terrea
Noni [ordinis]	Angeli	Prima: Luna	1, ipsa terrea

In orbibus spiritalibus illis et celis volutantibus in centro Dei, sunt celestes orbes corporei, item ii novem ordine digesti. Primus quasi seraphicus — quinimmo vocetur ille nonus proximus suo quasi deo stabili, decime spere; octavus quasi cherubicus; septimus throneus, saturnius, et religiosus; sextus, sub ipso, ioveus dominans; quintus marcius, virtute plenus; quartus solaris, potestate prestans; tertius mercurialis, principans; secundus venereus, archangelicus; ultimus lunaris, angelicus.

––––––––––

Seraphim *M L*] Sceraphi *C*   Mercurii *M*] Marcu *C*] Marcurii *L*

Jesus Christ	God	The 10th Sphere, God of the Orbs	First Sublunary Region, God of the Elements
Men of the 1st Order	The Seraphim	The 9th Sphere	The 9th, the Fiery Region
Men of the 2nd Order	The Cherubim	The 8th, of the Stars	The 8th, less Fiery
Men of the 3rd Order	The Thrones	The 7th, of Saturn	The 7th, Aërial inclining to Fire
Men of the 4th Order	The Dominations	The 6th, of Jupiter	The 6th, more Aërial
Men of the 5th Order	The Virtues	The 5th, [of] Mars	The 5th, Watery and inclining to Aërial
Men of the 6th Order	The Powers	The 4th, [of] the Sun	The 4th, more Watery
Men of the 7th Order	The Principalities	The 3rd, [of] Mercury	The 3rd, still less Earthy, and no little Watery
Men of the 8th Order	The Archangels	The 2nd, of Venus	The 2nd, less Earthy
Men of the 9th Order	The Angels	The 1st, [of] the Moon	The 1st, altogether Earthy

Within these spiritual spheres and the heavens that revolve about God as their center are the physical spheres of the heavens, likewise nine in number and arranged in order. Like the Seraphic sphere is the first — or rather, let it be called the ninth, since it is nearest what is, as it were, its own fixed god, the tenth sphere. The eighth is like that of the Cherubim; the seventh like that of the Thrones, belonging to Saturn, and religious;[20] the sixth, next beneath it, is that of Jupiter, the Ruler; the fifth is of Mars, full of strength; the fourth, of the Sun, excels in power; the third, of Mercury, is like that of the Principalities; the second, of Venus, corresponds to that of the Archangels; the last belongs to the Moon, and is like that of the Angels.

In hiis deinde continentur que sub luna sunt, sublunaris orbis, mundusque, et is quoque in decem regiones dispartitus. Que decima regio illa in concavo lune quasi centrum et perfectio est omnium. Sub illa, mera ignea regio est, nona; octava, minus ignea; septima, |137v| magis aerea; sexta, aerea mera; quinta, no⟨n⟩nihil aquea; quarta, aquea tota; tercia, parumper terrea; secunda, magis terrea; prima, ipsa terre crassitas.

> 9. *Ignis summus.*
> 8. *Ignis.*
> 7. *Ignis, Aer.*
> 6. *Aer.*
> 5. *Aer, Aqua.*
> 4. *Aqua.*
> 3. *Aqua, Terra.*
> 2. *Terra.*
> 1. *Terra infima.*

Hiis tribus mundis constat universitas, que una est. Quorum ut se habent duces, atque ut hii inter se duces inter se comparantur, cognationeque et affinitate mutua cognominantur, ita similiter reliqua et in natura, viribus, officiis, actionibus, nominibus communicant. Quoniam omnia sunt in omnibus, sed in primis et melioribus nota meliori, in ultimis degeneratiori et adulterata, in mediis medio modo. Illic stabilitas, sapientia, et amor est. In mediis, stabilis motio, lux, et calor. In infimis et ultimis, corruptio, humor, et ardor.

Potes etiam in celo quod stelle incolunt novem ordines aliquem ducem sequentes, inter se et magnitudine et claritate differentes statuere. Sol fons luminum et decimus ille potest esse.

Potes sub celo, in hiis que incolunt hunc sublunarem mundum, cuiusmodi sunt mixta—utpote in metallis, novem ordines; in lapidibus, novem; in plantis, novem; in piscibus, novem; in brutis, novem, in volucribus, novem; in coloribus, sonis, odoribus, saporibus, figuris, moribus etiam eorum, et in |138r| reliquis qualitatibus et quantitatibus omnibus—ab optimo in eo genere sereatim in deterius, novem gradus discernere.

Tamen semper sis memor ut statuas cuique novenarie seriei ducem quo regantur et mensurentur omnia, qui dux ad Deum referatur, quod sit ipsa in quoque genere absoluta perfectio, quod est decimum in quoque ordine, mensura, centrum, et unitas ad unitatum unitatem referenda.

Id velim significet decimarum oblationum sacramentum ex optimis et perfectissimis in omni genere rerum, quoniam hoc iure Dei, que omnium perfectio, cuius omnis decimaria perfectio imago est.

Atque ut omnis decimaria perfectio cuiusque novemplicis ordinis imago est Dei, ita novemplices illi ordines in quoque genere, alius alius, superioris inferior, imago quidem est. Est enim novinarium ordinum inter se ordo, secundum melius

Within these, in turn, are contained the things that are beneath the Moon: the sublunary sphere, the Earth; and this also is distributed into ten regions. That tenth region, just within the hollow of the [sphere of the] Moon, is, as it were, the center and perfection of all things. Next beneath it is the purely fiery region, the ninth; the eighth is less fiery; the seventh, more aërial; the sixth, purely aërial; the fifth, somewhat watery; the fourth, altogether watery; the third, slightly earthy; the second, more earthy; the first is the thickness of earth itself.

$$\begin{cases} 9. \textit{ Highest Fire.} \\ 8. \textit{ Fire.} \\ 7. \textit{ Fire, Air.} \end{cases}$$
$$\begin{cases} 6. \textit{ Air.} \\ 5. \textit{ Air, Water.} \\ 4. \textit{ Water.} \end{cases}$$
$$\begin{cases} 3. \textit{ Water, Earth.} \\ 2. \textit{ Earth.} \\ 1. \textit{ Lowest Earth.} \end{cases}$$

The whole Universe, which is one, consists of these three worlds. And just as leaders are situated in each, and just as these leaders can be compared to one another, and are named in common because of their mutual relationship, so likewise the leaders have community in their remaining attributes also: in their nature, powers, offices, activities, and names. For all these are in all, but in the first and best they are present with a better quality, in the last with more deterioration and mixture, and in the middle ones they are present in an intermediate way. In the first[21] are steadfastness, wisdom, and love; in the medial are a steady movement, light, and warmth; in the lowest and last are disintegration, moisture, and heat.

Moreover, in the heaven where dwell the stars you can assign nine orders following a certain leader and differing among themselves both in magnitude and in brightness. The Sun can be their tenth and the source of their lights.

Beneath the sky, among the things which inhabit this sublunary world and are of a mixed sort, you can do the same. For example, in metals you can discern nine ranks[22] in series from the best in that genus down to the least good; in stones, nine; in plants, nine; in fishes, nine; in brute animals, nine; in birds, nine; in colors, sounds, odors, tastes, shapes; in the habits of things also, and in all the other qualities and quantities.

Always remember, however, to assign to each ninefold series a leader by which all are governed and measured. This leader should be traced back to God, since in each class it is absolute perfection itself, and constitutes the tenth in each order, the measure, center, and unity, to be compared to the Unity of unities.

This I should like to take as the meaning of the sacred mystery of the offerings of tenths from the best and most perfect things in every class, for this is God's by right, since He is the perfection of all things, and every tenth perfection[23] is an image of Him.

Moreover, as every tenth perfection of a ninefold order is an image of God, so those ninefold orders in each kind are images one of another, the lower of the higher. For there is an order among the ninefold orders, according to the

et deterius. Qui inter se comparatus, singula in ut⟨r⟩isque singulis, examussim quadrant et conveniunt.

Quarum affinitates et amicitias contemplatus, Moises et prophete illi theologi allegoria omnia significarunt, communiter utentes nominibus eorum que similitudine conveniunt, et feminis rebus masculas significantes. Quia nihil est in superiori novemplici masculum, quo⟨d⟩ in inferiori suum feminum non habet°. In superiori omnia |138v| mascula sunt, in inferiori feminea; in infimo feminissima. Quod si quis scivisset in omni serie que eiusdem sunt gradus colligere, atque rite in unum congerere, femine ita masculinis fecundarentur, quod miracula parerent. Hoc esset mundum maritare, et femina masculis substernere.

In serie rerum et novinariis ordinibus, facile suos duces decumanos sequuntur queque, exceptis hominibus. Qui ut redigantur in novemplicem ordinem, ad similitudinem celestium, ad exemplar supracelestium, ad veritatem Dei, Ordinator ipse rerum omnium voluit homo esse, et capud et centrum et idea et firmamentum et primum et perfectio, et Deus hominum; ut illum imitati, quisque pro impartitis viribus pulchra serie° ab illo dependeant° ordine novemplici; cuius primitie° et decima oblatio perfecta hostia erat decimus ille et ordinis capud, Iesus; qui humani ordinis decimus, et quod proprium erat Dei, Deo oblatum fuit in sanctificationem reliquorum. Quo spectant decime Mosaice.

Illo oblato optimo, in eodem omnia quodammodo offeruntur°, qui⟨a⟩ in illo optimo quodque continetur, quicquid est in aliquo minus bono. Ducem ergo Iesu⟨m⟩ Christum, Deum nostrum et solem, sequimur ut angeli Deum, ut orbes decimam speram, ut stelle solem, ut novem regiones id quod optimum est in mundo sublunari, ut preciosissimum lapidem |139r| alii lapides, ut angularem lapidem reliquum edificium, ut radicem reliqua arbor, ut capud corpus, membra de membro°. In qua hominum societate novem ordines distingui possunt, nitentes assimulari se Iesu Christo centro suo, ut in illo quiescant.

Et quia homo, minor mundus, comprehensio est totius universitatis, qui anime potentiis novem angelos refert, luculentiore corpore celum, infimo mundum sublunarem; in quo novinaria distinctio crassi humoris est, in quo ossa infime terre locum habent; in ipsis etiam partibus dissimularibus, pedibus, manibus, oculis, capite, ordo est, sed mutua necessitate recompensa⟨n⟩te. Tanta est simil⟨it⟩udo omnis composite multitudinis dependentis ab aliquo uno, ut que videntur minus

---

habet *M L*] habent *C (contr. mark, prob. by inadvertence)*   serie *M L*] seree *C* dependeant *M*] dependiant *C L*   primitie *M*] premitie *C*] præmitie *L*   offeruntur *M L*] offereruntur *C*   membra de membro *M L*] menbra de menbro *C*

better and the worse. When a reckoning is made of this order within itself, comparing each detail in each ninefold series, they agree and accord most accurately.

Contemplating these their affinities and sympathies, Moses and the theologian-prophets betokened it all by allegory, using interchangeably the names of things that agree by resemblance, and symbolizing by feminine things those that are masculine. For there is nothing masculine in a higher order without its feminine in a lower. All things in the higher are masculine; in the lower, feminine. In the lowest, they are the most feminine. And if anyone had known how to gather the beings of the same rank in each series, and bring them the right way to unity, the feminine would have been impregnated by the masculine, and miracles would have been brought forth. This would be to bring the world into marriage, and to set the female in submission beneath the male.

In the ninefold orders and in any series of things, all the members readily follow their tenth-rank leaders, except for men. To bring them back to a ninefold order like that of things celestial, and patterned after that of the supracelestial, and conformed to the truth of God, the Orderer Himself of all things willed to be a man, and to be the head, and the center, and the idea, and the firmament, the first principle, and the perfection, and the God of men, so that by imitating Him—each one according to the strength given him—men might depend on Him by a beautiful succession in a ninefold order. And the first-fruits and tithe-offering of this order was a perfect victim, that tenth and head of the order, Jesus. The tenth of the human order, and belonging to God by right, he was offered up to God for the sanctification of the rest. The Mosaic tithes were a type of him.

Now that he, the best, has been offered, in him are all things in a manner offered, because in that best is everything—whatever *is* in some less good member. We, therefore, follow our Leader, Jesus Christ, our God and Sun, as the angels follow God, as the spheres the tenth sphere, as the stars the Sun; as the nine regions follow what is best in the sublunary world, as other stones the most precious, as the rest of the building the cornerstone, as the rest of the tree the root, as the body the head, members depending on a member. And in this society of men can be discerned nine orders, striving to become like to Jesus Christ, their center, so that they may come to rest in him.

Now because man, a world in little, is an epitome of the entire universe, reflecting the nine [orders of] angels by the powers of his soul, the heavens by the more lightsome part of his body, and the sublunary world by the lowest (which has itself a ninefold gradation of the solid humor, the bones holding the place of lowest earth), there is also an order even in the dissimilar parts, in the feet, hands, eyes, and head. A mutual necessity makes up for their dissimilarity. And so great is the likeness between all ordered multitudes depending on some one leader that those which seem less well ordered may be shown clearly, by a com-

composita, similitudine sumpta ab eis que magis composita videntur, ordo et compositio declarari potest.

Ita Paulus, similitudine sumpta a corpore humano, humani mundi in Deo et composituram et ordinem et mutuam actionem ad utilitatem in uno Deo ostendit; qui est opifex huius humani mundi et hierarchie; qui vocavit omnes omnium generum, et baptizavit uno Spiritu ut unum sint in eo; qui etiam disposuit membra° hominesque, unumquemque eorum in corpore sicut vult; qui denique dividit singulis Spiritus sui vires et potentias ut vult; ut in ipsis, uti in organis |139v| et instrumentis quibusdam, Divinus Spiritus suam potentiam exerceat.

Est universa ecclesia nihil aliud nisi organum et instrumentum Dei Spiritus, uti corpus anime sue, quam ecclesiam cogit in unum, vivificat et perficit Spiritus, ut in ea suas vires exerceat: in aliquibus sermonem sapientie et visorum mysteriorum; in aliquibus sermonem scientie; in aliquibus fidem dumtaxat; in aliis opitulationem; in aliis opera mirifica; in aliis loquitur variis linguis; in aliis interpretatur ipse Spiritu⟨s⟩ sermones. Ad varias suas vires digerit et disponit diversa membra, homines, et organa, proportione conveniente et concinno ordine, ut in universa ecclesia in ipso resultet pulchra utilitas et utilis pulchritudo, ex hominibus pulchris in ipso et utilibus, in quo nemo nisi pul-

Organum decem cordarum.

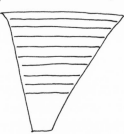

Mortuus sonus
sine vita charitatis.

cher et utilis. Sed in fusione Spiritus in corporis vivificationem, ut est progressus degenerans quodammodo (ut ita dicam) in deterius, ita in ipso progressu simul mirabilis est repensatio; ut quum omnia membra et homines in ecclesia veri spiritales sunt, pulchri et utiles infusione Spiritus, ut pulchritudo degenerat et diminuitur in deformius, ita simul gradatim exoritur et crescit, atque quanto longius procedis ad deformiora membra, in ipsis magis atque magis exaugetur utilitas; ut sicut superiores et prestantiores partes possunt iactare speciem et pulchritudinem, ita contra inferiores |140r| ostentare utilitatem; ut sicut ille pulchriores superant specie et formositate, ita he deformiores excellunt usu et utilitate.

Ita in dissimilitudine est similitudo, et in degeneratione recompensatio, et in vi fusa a Spiritu in ecclesia (si libres omnia) equabilitas quedam° et equa lanx,

---

membra *M L*] menbra *C*

parison drawn from those which seem more regularly ordered, to be an order and a coherent system.

Thus Paul, deriving a comparison from the human body, demonstrates the coherence and order of the human world in its reciprocal activity for advantage in the one God. God is the Framer of this, man's world and hierarchy. He called all from all classes, and baptized them in the one Spirit that they might be one in Him. He it was, too, that arranged in the body each of the members, men, as He wished. And, lastly, He imparts to each the forces and powers of His Spirit, so that in them, as though on organs and instruments, the Divine Spirit may exercise His power.

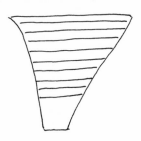

An organ of ten chords.

The whole Church is nothing other than an organ, an instrument, of God the Spirit, as the body is of the soul. The Spirit gathers the Church together into oneness, gives it life and perfects it, so that in it He may exercise His own powers: in some, the speaking of wisdom and of mysteries seen; in some, the utterance of knowledge; in some, faith only; in others, the helping of others; in others, wondrous works; in others again He speaks with divers tongues; in others, the Spirit Himself interprets utterances. The various members — men, the organs — He orders and disposes for His various gifts, with fitting proportion and harmonious order, so that throughout the whole Church in Him there results a beautiful usefulness and a useful beauty, from men who are beautiful and useful in Him. And no one is in Him except such as are useful and beautiful. But in the outpour-

Without the life of charity, the sound is dead.

ing of the Spirit for the enlivening of the body, there is a manner of progressive degeneration down (if I may so put it) to the worst; and parallel with this, in the progression itself there is a wondrous compensating balance; so that while all the members, all mankind in the Church, are truly spiritual, beautiful, and useful, because of the infusion of the Spirit, as beauty degenerates and lessens to the more unlovely, this compensation springs up and increases, and the farther you advance toward the more uncomely members, steadily the more does usefulness wax in them. Just as the higher and more excellent parts, then, can vaunt their fairness and beauty, so for their part the lower can show forth their usefulness; and as the former, the more beautiful, have the advantage in form and loveliness, so the latter, the unlovelier members, excel in usefulness and efficacy.

Hence in unlikeness there is likeness, and in degeneration there is compensation, and in the power diffused through the Church by the Spirit there is, if

in nullam partem magis depressa; ut equus sit respectus omnium in omnes, et agnitio equabilitatis, et ex equabilitate consensus, coamor, et congaudium et condolentia, et denique omnium affectuum mutua coresonantia; ut si patitur unum membrum, compatiantur omnia membra; sive gloriatur unum membrum, congaudeant omnia membra.

Hanc hominum concordiam in ecclesia et concentum armonicum, ad similitudinem humani corporis, preclare describit° Paulus, docens et profusionem unius Spiritus, et convocationem hominum in ecclesiam, et constructuram eorum arbitrario ordine in quoddam corpus, et degenerationem pulchritudinis et recompensationem utilitatis, et partium ubique equabilitatem, unde in ecclesia omnium studiorum, voluntatum, officiorum, actionum in Spiritu debet esse consentio, et omnium hominum in eadem ad communem utilitatem conspiratio.

De qua re sub oculis divina Pauli ipsius contexta verba ponamus. |140v|

Inquit enim primum omnes confitentes Iesum in Spiritu Sancto esse. Neminem posse dicere *Dominus Iesus* nisi in Spiritu Dei. Divisiones gratiarum, ministrationum, et operationum esse, eundem vero Spiritum, Dominum, et Deum, qui est anima ecclesie, et operatur omnia in omnibus. Posuit Deus membra°, unumquodque eorum in corpore sicut vult. Varie operatur in ecclesia, dividens singulis prout vult. Unicuique datur manifestatio Spiritus ad utilitatem. Multa membra°, unum corpus: multi et varii homines, una ecclesia Dei. Nihil in ea non necessarium, saltem si sit a Spiritu Dei. Immo, que viliora sunt membra, multo magis sunt necessaria, et habundantiorem honorem ac curam habent propter necessitatem. Deus temperavit corpus, ei cui deerat abundantiorem honorem tribuendo, ut non sit scisma in corpore.

Ita in ecclesia repensa sunt omnia quadam paritate, ut non sit in ea nisi unitas ex caritate et ex unitate charitas. Sim⟨il⟩itudo enim et equalitas mater est charitatis.

---

quedam *Ed.*] quadam *C M*] quædam *L*   describit *M*] discribit *C L See note.*
membra *M L*] menbra *C*   membra *M L*] menbra *C*

you weigh all, an impartial equality, a balanced scale, inclining to neither side, so that there may be an equal respect of all for all, and a recognition of equality. And, arising from this equality, there is agreement, mutual love, shared joy and shared sorrow, and, in a word, a common echoing of all states of mind and body. If one member suffers, then, all the members share the suffering; if one member is honored, all the members share the rejoicing [I Cor. XII. 26].

By the simile of the human body, Paul admirably describes this concord of mankind in the Church, this harmonious blending of voices. He teaches the outpouring of the one Spirit, and the calling together of mankind into the Church, and their being joined together, in a freely determined order, into a certain body; he teaches the degeneration of beauty with the compensation of usefulness, and the equality of all the parts everywhere; he teaches that because of these things there ought to be in the Church agreement in the Spirit of endeavors, desires, services, and activities, with unanimity of all men in the Church for the common advantage.

Now let us set before our eyes the divine words of Paul himself concerning the matter, restored to their original text.

First he says that all who confess Jesus are in the Holy Spirit: no one can say, "Jesus is the Lord," except in the Spirit of God. There are different kinds of graces, of services, of ministerings, but one and the same Spirit, Lord, and God, who is the soul of the Church, and who performs all in all of us. God set the members, each of them as He would, in the body. He works variously in the Church, imparting to each as He pleases. To each the revelation of the Spirit is given for the best advantage. The members are many, yet the body is one; men are various and many, but God's Church is one. In it is nothing that is not necessary, provided it be from God's Spirit. On the contrary, those members which are the more contemptible-seeming are the much more necessary, and they receive more abundant honor and attention because of their necessity. God has established harmony in the body, giving more abundant honor to that which was deficient, so that there may be no schism in the body.

In this way all in the Church are balanced by a kind of equality, so that in it there may be only oneness arising from charity and charity arising from oneness. For likeness and equality are the mother of love.

Caput tertiumdecimum°

De spiritalibus Paulus agens in superioribus, quum eorum originem a Spiritu, in ecclesia progressum, degenerationem, recompensationem, equabilitatem |141r| ostendebat, cuiusmodi spiritalia et dona Spiritus Sancti sunt loqui linguis multis et preclaris°, prophetare et mysteria ac arcana nosse°, scientiam et scientie sermonem, fidem prepotentem et mirificam, opitulationem et elemosinam°, passionem et gloriosum martyrium, et eiusmodi que tum hic tum supra copiosius commemorat, superioribus iam addit: istiusmodi, quotquumque ea sint et quantaquumque, ipsa tamen sine charitate nihil prorsus valere.

Quod verbum quid significat videamus. Χαρίξο⟨μαι⟩ grecum dono et gratificor significat. Inde χάρις, gratia; et χάρισμα, gratie donum; χαριτόω°, gratia impleo.

Amor est hec charitas. Sed charitas hominum est amor omnium. Charitas est flos fidei, operatio fructus charitatis. Deus homines amat, *Caritas flos.* et gratificatur eis mille modis, charitatisque argumenta ostendit, gratias et gratificationes suas. Sed conferens in nos gratias suas ac donationes gratiarum et charismata, nos tamen ei gratos non facit, nisi aliquando ipsam amoris gratiam nobis dederit, dederitque nobis ut ipsum principium omnis bone operationis in nobis amorem habeamus, et dilectionem Dei ac proximi, amaveritque nos Deus ita, ut nos amati flagremus amore.

Opera multa Spiritus esse possunt sine charitate, que inflant. Charitas autem sine omni bono opere esse quidem non potest. Potest Spiritus donare quam plurima, non addita perfectione charitatis que complet omnia. |141v| Spes purgat in unitatem°, simplicitatem, et stabilitatem. Fides illuminat in scientiam revelatorum. Utreque false, vane, et deceptorie sine consummatione charitatis. Charitas inflammat in perfectionem, ut perfecti grati simus Deo. Non habetur in precio opus,

---

Caput tertiumdecimum *Ed.*] Capud xiii *C, om. M*   preclaris *C? M L*   nosse *L*] nosce *C M*   eleemosinam *Ed.*] elymosinam *C L*] elemosinam *M*   χαριτόω *Ed.*] charistoo *C L, om. and blank L*   unitatem *M L*] unitiatem *C*

Chapter XIII

In what has gone before, Paul was treating of spiritual things, showing their origin from the Spirit, their progress in the Church, and their degeneration, compensation, and equality. These are the kinds of spiritual things and gifts of the Holy Spirit he treated of: to speak with divers and admirable tongues;[1] to prophesy and know mysteries and hidden things; knowledge and the utterance of knowledge; mighty faith that works wonders; help to others and alms-giving; suffering and glorious martyrdom; and the rest of this sort, which he mentions both here [I Cor. XIII. 1–3], and more fully above [XII. 28]. Now to what he has said he adds: "All things of this sort, however many they be and however great, are still themselves of altogether no avail without charity."

Let us see what this word means. The Greek χαρίζο⟨μαι⟩[2] means to give, to bestow favors. Hence χάρις, grace, and χάρισμα, gift of grace; χαριτόω, to fill with grace.

This charity is love.[3] But the charity of men is a love of all. Charity is the flower of faith, activity is the fruit of charity. God loves men, and in a thousand ways bestows favors on *Charity the flower.* them. He shows them proofs of charity, His graces and kindnessess. Still, in conferring on us His graces and gifts of grace—charismata—He does not make us pleasing to Him, unless at length He give us the grace of love itself, and grant us to have within ourselves the principle itself of all good works, love, the grace of loving God and neighbor; unless God has so loved us that we, being loved,[4] are ourselves aflame with love.

Many works of the Spirit can exist without charity, and these puff up. Charity, however, cannot exist without every good work. The Spirit can make gifts in the greatest abundance without adding the perfection of charity, which perfects all: hope purifies to oneness, simplicity, and steadfastness; faith enlightens to the knowledge of revelation; but both are false, vain, and deceptive without the perfection of charity. Charity inflames us to perfection, that being perfect we may be pleasing to God. A work is not held in esteem, however beautifully and

tametsi belle et prospere inchoatum°, nisi perficiatur. Complet et consummat omnia charitas, que approbatur a Deo. Si quis diligit Deum (inquit) hic cognitus est ab eo, i.e., approbatus. Scientia inflat: charitas edificat.

Si amas ut amare a Deo, Deo gratus es. Potes stare in spe ut Spiritus te statuit; potes credere ut Spiritus te facit; potes° operari ut Spiritus movet; potes loqui sapienter et scienter, et prophetare, ut Spiritus te illuminat; potes denique et stare tecum, et credere, et loqui, et operari mirabilia° ex Spiritu Dei—immo in te, figmento et organo suo, hec omnia facere Spiritus ille°, ad eos fines quos novit ipse. Tu tamen adhuc nihilo magis Deo gratus et cognitus et approbatus es; qui ipse sine charitate imperfectus es, perfecto Deo minime gratus, cui non est gratum quicquid nisi perfectum.

Perfectio quidem est charitas. Antequam amaris sic ut redames, tu non hec operaris, sed Spiritus in te. Si melius illud charisma et charismatum forma, ac grata species amoris, etiam ex Dei dono, in te sit, tum profecto perfectus et forma consummatus ac gratus es Deo. Et ipse tum ista omnia agis in Spiritu, nedum in te Spiritus sicuti antea.

Disponit agens |142r| in formam. Res formata denique per se agit. Omnis proba actio rei perfecte est sua forma, unde actio procedit. Homo quasi materia rudis est, spiritalis forme expers, idoneus° tamen ut formetur a Spiritu. Qui ipse homo suapte natura privatur deitate. Causa autem transmutans hunc carnalem hominem in spiritum et efficiens, Spiritus ipse Dei est, qui tractat quasi materiam vi sua, ut fiat demum homo quod potest esse, transformeturque pro arbitrio tractantis Spiritus, qui dividit singulis prout vult, non aliter atque mollis cera manus ductu et tractatu, in aliqua⟨m⟩ figuram spiritalem et divinam, cuius gratia agit Spiritus. Nam finis saltem proximus actionis est consecutio forme et inductio. Nam hoc consilio plane agit Spiritus Dei, et versat materiam carnalemque hominem, ut is ad perfectum forme habitum perducatur. Inter versandum vero afficit hominem prius, et disponit, et preparat congruis qualitatibus que antecedunt, partim ut ordine procedat actio, partim ut experiatur in hiis quam homo humilis et patiens et materie inster est. Postremo species ipsa gratie et decoctionis flos emergit, pulchreque effulget. Hec florens forma charitas est, unde fructus operum procedit, que opera Paulus sepe fructus vocat, quia ex charitatis flore prodeunt.

---

inchoatum *M*] inchoata *C L*   potes *M L*] potest *C*   mirabilia *M L*] miriabilia *C*   ille *C*] ille potes *M*] ille potest *L*   idoneus *M*] idonius *C L*

felicitously begun, unless it be perfected. And charity completes and consummates all things: it is charity that is approved by God. "If anyone loves God," says Paul, "he is known by Him, that is, approved" [VIII. 3].[5] "Knowledge puffs up: charity builds" [VIII. 1].

If you love as you are loved by God, you are pleasing to God. You can stand in hope as the Spirit has stationed you; you can believe as the Spirit makes you; you can do works as the Spirit moves you; you can speak with wisdom and knowledge, and prophesy, as the Spirit enlightens you; you can, in short, stand firm, and believe, and speak and do wonders by the Spirit of God—or rather, all these things can the Spirit do in you, as in the thing He has fashioned, His organ, for ends that He knows Himself—but you are yourself still none the more pleasing to God, or known and approved by Him. Without charity you are yourself imperfect, and so not at all pleasing to the perfect God, to whom nothing is pleasing except what is perfect.

Perfection is, indeed, charity.[6] Until you love as you are loved, it is not you who do these things, but the Spirit in you. If that better charisma also, that form of all charismata, that pleasing fairness of love, be in you by God's gift, then you are indeed perfect, and finished in form, and pleasing to God. Then you perform all those things in the Spirit yourself, and no longer does the Spirit simply do them in you, as before.

The agent disposes into a form.[7] The object, being formed, at length acts *per se*. All right action of a perfect object is by its own form, and from the form action is derived. Now man is, as it were, unformed matter, and destitute of spiritual form, but he is apt for the Spirit to form him. Of his own nature, man is deprived of the divine. But the cause transforming this carnal man into a spirit and an efficient cause is the Spirit of God Himself, who moulds the matter (as it may be called) by His power, so that at length man may become what he is capable of being, may be transformed at the free choice of the moulding Spirit (who imparts to each as He will), no otherwise than soft wax by the shaping and moulding of a hand, into some spiritual and divine shape; and it is for this that the Spirit works. For the proximate end, at least, of action is the achievement and introduction of a form. And clearly, the Spirit of God acts with this intention, treating the matter, carnal man, in such a way that he is brought to a perfect state of form. While treating him thus, however, He first influences, disposes, and prepares him with suitable qualities (which are antecedent), partly so that the work may advance in due order, partly so that He may learn in these [antecedent qualities] how humble a man is, how patient, and how apt as matter. Finally the fair form itself of grace and the flower of the distillation[8] emerges, and shines forth beautifully. This flowering form is charity, and from it proceed the fruits of works: it is because they come forth from the flower of charity that Paul often calls these works fruits.

Itaque post morosam dispositionem tamdem extat premium |142v| individuo momento charitatis, que spiritalis hominis forma intrinseca est et essentialis, effecta in ipso ab opifice et causa, Spiritu Dei; qua homo, ipse iam spiritalis perfectione charitatis, potens est in Dei Spiritu spiritalis actionis et compos, agitque ipse iam perfectus spiritus opera in Spiritu coagente.

Nam sicuti placet Platonicis, tametsi res perfecte in natura, naturalesque agentes cause, nobis appareant ipse sole agere transmutareque et formare in sui similitudinem externas materias, tamen revera ipse primarie non sunt cause eorum que fiunt, sed instrumenta potius divine artis et actionis, cui obediunt et famulantur. Sic eodem modo homo sic amatus a Spiritu Dei ut redamet, redamansque perfectus quum sit, tametsi tunc suapte forma et charitate agit et operatur in ecclesia quam plurima, tamen certe ipse suarum operationum non est primaria causa, sed iam vivum et perfectum est instrumentum, coagens cum eo et in eo qui maxime agit, Spiritu Dei. Qui etiam Spiritus Dei agit in eis qui non vivificantur charitate ut in instrumentis mortuis, qui serviunt Spiritui et voluntati Dei ut cultrum homini, non ut manus et membrum° in corpore.|143r|

Habet Spiritus Dei, anima divini huius compositi et corporis mystici, duo instrumenta et quasi servos: unum mortuum, adhuc sine caritate, id quod non est de corpore; aliud vivum et modulo sue charitatis perfectum, quod hoc intrinsicum est corporis membrum Christi perfecti, in quo nullum membrum esse potest nisi perfectum. Non enim constat perfectus Christus nisi ex hiis quorum quodque suo in genere perfectum est. Christus potest multa agere seorsum ipse

Agit totum in instrumento.
Instrumentum aliquid in agente.

instrumentis et servis mortuis, ad id quod novit ipse, et forsan etiam in edificationem ecclesie parumper. Sed verissime et intrinsece et efficacissime certe agit in edificationem sui eis instrumentis et servis quos ipse sibi vivos fecit et viva membra corporis sui co⟨n⟩calentia in ipso et coagentia cum ipso ex caritate, que edificata edificant, quod maxime edificare est. De quibus Paulus: Charitas edificat.

Alia, mortua organa non edificata ipsa, nonnunquam forsan edificant, vel ipsa inflata. In illis operatur Spiritus solus. In hiis homo, iam vivum° organum et instrumentum et ex corpore, cum Spiritu cooperatur, dono sibi dato, in virtute

---

membrum *M L*] menbrum *C*   vivum *C? L*] unum *M*

At last, then, after a slow preparation, there comes into being in a single instant the reward, charity, which is the intrinsic and essential form of the spiritual man, wrought in him by the Maker and Cause, the Spirit of God. By it man, himself now spiritual in the perfection of charity, has in the Spirit of God the power of and the control over spiritual action, and he now himself performs works as a perfect spirit, in the Spirit working with him.

For as the Platonists hold, although to us perfect things in nature and natural agent causes appear to act of themselves alone and to change and form into their own likeness alien materials, these in truth are not themselves the primary causes of what takes place, but rather the instruments of the Divine skill[9] and action, which they obey and serve. In the same way, although a man who has so been loved by the Spirit of God that he loves in return, and in doing so has become perfect, acts by his own form and charity, and performs by these the greatest number of works in the Church, still it remains certain that he is not the primary cause of his own operations, but is now a living and perfect instrument, working together with Him and in Him who is most properly the agent, the Spirit of God. Further, in those who are not brought to life by charity, this same Spirit of God acts as in dead instruments, which serve the Spirit and the will of God as a knife may serve a man, not as a hand does, not as a member that belongs to the body.

The Spirit of God, the soul of this divine composite and mystical body, has, then, two instruments, two servants, as it were. One of these is dead, being still without charity: a thing that is not of the body. The other lives, and for its little measure of charity it is perfect: an intrinsic member of the body of the perfect Christ, in which there can be no member that is not perfect. For the perfect Christ is made up of *The whole acts in the instrument.* those only who are perfect, each in his own kind. Acting alone, Christ can do many things himself through *The instrument is something in the agent.* lifeless instruments and servants toward an end known to himself; even, it may be, for the building of the Church, at least temporarily. It is certain, however, that he works most truly, works intrinsically and most efficaciously, toward the building-up of himself, when he uses those instruments and servants whom he himself has vivified and made living members of his body, sharing in him because of charity the perfection of warmth, and with him sharing activity. These build, having been builded themselves; and this is most properly to build. Paul says of them: "Charity builds" [I Cor. VIII. 1].

The others, the lifeless organs which have not themselves been builded, perhaps at times build, even if this means their own inflation.[10] In them, the Spirit alone is active. In the former, the man, now a living organ, an instrument and a part of the body, works together with the Spirit by the gift given him and in the

|143v| Spiritus, cause et agentis exemplaris et anime corporis et architecti° domus Dei, i.e., ecclesie. In qua quamquam ut oculi et manus homines, et membra huius corporis, et huius domus quasi lapides vivi, calore charitatis agere, operari, transformare, et effingere omnia videantur, tamen certe tota domus factura accepta referenda est Spiritui Dei. Cuius intima arte in hominibus in architecture fabricam concipiuntur particulatim, digeruntur et explicantur omnia. Cui famulantur, serviunt, et obediunt homines vivificati et perfecti charitate, ut cause organice et instrumentales.

Quod Paulus significavit quum dixit: Sic nos existimet homo ut ministros Christi et dispensatores ministeriorum Dei. Et alibi: Quid est Apollo? Quid Paulus? Ministri eius cui credidistis. Et unicuique sicut Deus dedit; Dei enim sumus adiutores et coedificatores super fundamentum, Iesum Christum. Omnes debent coedificare ad rationem exemplaris in animo architecti°, qui Spiritus est Christi. Alioquin violatum opus detrimentum patietur, violator° ipse disperdetur. Si quis templum |144r| Dei violaverit, disperdet° illum Deus.

I Cor. iv.
Violatus salvabitur per ignem; violator disperdetur.

Quemadmodum certe fabri manus et oculi, in construenda domo, omnem materiam — ligna, lapides, cementa — conquirunt, componu⟨n⟩t, ordinant, transmutant, erigunt, formant, perficiunt, ipse tamen quamquam sole videantur agere, tamen ipsis tota domus factura accepta non referatur, quum operatrices organice sunt dumtaxat, inservientes arti que in architecti animo est constituta; ad eundem modum homines spiritales, qui manuum et oculorum inster operantur in structuram templi Dei, quod ab ipsis fit, tanquam primarie et maxime et *e*xemplari cause totum Spiritui Christi acceptum referatur, ad cuius exemplar in cooperante Spiritu Dei fiunt omnia ab hominibus perfectis, Christi membris, Spiritu Dei.

Perfectio vero est charitas, flos operum, per se in charitate Dei. Que, ut posterior perfectio, non potest esse in homine sine prioribus. Priores autem in homine sine posteriore et charitate hominis, non tamen sine charitate Dei, qui operatur illa in homine, non homo illa in Deo. Homo enim in Deo operatur quando ipse in amore Dei, preditus charitate, ex charitate propria operatur.

---

architecti C *in marg. with* & architectoris *on next line cancelled and above* oris tus *uncancelled*   architecti M L] architecti C   violator C *with* viola *written again more clearly above*   disperdet M L] disperdit C

strength of the Spirit, who is the causal and exemplary agent,[11] the soul of the body, and the architect of God's house, the Church. In it men may seem, as the eyes and the hands and the members of this body, as the living stones, so to speak, of this house, to work everything by the warmth of charity, to perform, change, and fashion everything. Nonetheless, it is certain the entire construction of the house must be assigned to the Spirit of God. By His most profound skill everything for the working out of the architecture is individually conceived in men, set in order, and arranged. The men brought to life and perfected by charity attend upon Him, serve and obey Him, as organic and instrumental causes.

Paul meant this, when he said: "Let men regard us as Christ's servants and stewards of God's ministerings" [I Cor. IV. 1: the Vulgate has *mysteriorum*, not *ministeriorum*.].[12] And elsewhere: "What is Apollo? What is Paul? Ministers of him in whom you have believed, each as God has given to you. For we are God's assistants" [III. 4, 5, 9], and fellow-builders upon the foundation, Jesus Christ.

All must work together in the building, according to the plan of the exemplar in the mind of the Architect,[13] who is the Spirit of Christ. Otherwise the work, being dishonored, will suffer harm, while the man who dishonored it will himself be brought to ruin. "If any man desecrates the Temple of God, God will destroy him" [III. 17].

I. Cor. IV.

The one dishonored[14] will be saved through fire. The one dishonoring will be brought to ruin.

Certainly in the building of a house the workman's hands and eyes gather all the material—the wood, stones, cement—and put them together, arrange them, change them about, set them up in their place, give them form and perfection. But although the hands and eyes may seem to be acting alone, still all the building of the house is not to be set to their credit, since they are merely mechanical effecters, serving the skill which has come to exist in the architect's mind. In the same way, all that is done by spiritual men, who work like hands and eyes toward the building of God's Temple, must be assigned to the Spirit of Christ as the primary and principal and exemplary cause. All that is done by perfect men, Christ's members, in the Spirit of God working with them, and by the Spirit of God, is done according to His exemplar.

Now perfection is charity, the flower of works, and it exists of itself in the charity of God, while in men, since it is a posterior perfection,[15] it cannot exist without what is prior. That which is prior, however, can exist in man without the posterior, without the charity of man; but it cannot exist without the charity of God, who effects the prior in man: man does not effect it in God. For man effects something in God when, already in the love of God, and endowed with charity, he himself operates from his own charity.

Intellige nulla esse opera Spiritus sine charitate, quia non sunt opera Spiritus sine Spiritu: Spiritus autem est charitas. Verumtamen |144v| possunt esse opera Spiritus in homine sine hominis charitate. Que opera sunt bona, et ad finem bonum a Spiritu cognitum pertinentia (qui nihil agit frustra et temere); tamen ipsi homini, modo is sine charitate sit, non sunt bona. Quum autem is sic amatur ut inflammatus et perfectus charitate una cum Spiritu amoris cooperetur, tunc op⟨er⟩a sunt ipsius quoque hominis perfecti in Deo, et illi homini etiam bona et meritoria.

Et hec charitas est que edificat in homine in Deo, ad quamque nunc tanquam ad charismata meliora et omnia alia perficientia Paulus Corinthios exhortatur. Alioquin in omnibus aliis spiritalibus mortua organa et instrumenta Dei, que aguntur a Spiritu Dei ut cultrum, ut scopa. Non agunt ipsi, in quibus agitur, que sunt charitatis. Et cum charitate, non tamen charitate eorum, sed charitate Dei, que est Spiritu.

Ut modo diximus, opera Spiritus non sunt in homine sine charitate; possunt tamen esse in homine sine charitate hominis, quando videlicet homo ipse non inflammatur ut coeat cum Spiritu. Quod si quando coeat cum Spiritu, cumque eo evadat |145r| unum, illi adherens, tunc fecundatus ipse homo quoque in Spiritu, una cum eo parens est bonorum operum, que non solum Spiritui sed homini in Spiritu attribuantur, qui amatus, redamans et adherens Deo, unus est spiritus.

De hac charitate loquitur hic Paulus, que, ut alia, homini excidere et frustrari non potest; que quum adest, omnia deinde reliqua Spiritus sunt hominis in Spiritu; quum vero abest, ne ea quidem que sunt in homine Spiritus, ipsius sunt hominis. Ut iure Paulus dicat: *Si linguis hominum loquar et angelorum, charitatem non habeam, factus° sum velut es sonans et simbalum° tinniens. Et si habuero prophitiam et noverim mysteria omnia et omnem scientiam; et si habuero omnem fidem, ita ut montes transferam, charitatem autem non habeo ipse*—nec ego redamans coago cum Spiritu et charitate *Dei°—nihil sum. Et si distribuero in cibos pauperum omnes facultates meas, et si tradidero° corpus meum ita ut ardeam*—vel quod magis refert Grecum (Hieronimo teste in commentariis ad Galathas) ut *glorier°—nihil mihi prodest.*

Prodest tamen simpliciter, quia temere non agit |145v| Spiritus. Sunt enim hec omnia Spiritus in homine, mortuo organo. Sed ait Paulus: Nihil mihi prodest, si sim sine charitate. Per me tamen prodesse possunt hec omnia aliis, ego

---

factus M L] factum C   simbalum C L] symbalum M] cymbalum Vulg.   nec . . .
Dei *C underlined   tradidero M] tradedero C L*   vel . . . glorier *C underlined*

Understand that there are no works of the Spirit without charity, because there are no works of the Spirit without the Spirit, and the Spirit is charity. Nevertheless, there can be works of the Spirit in man without the charity of man. These works are good, and they are directed to a good end by the Spirit, who does nothing in vain or without design. They are not good, however, for the man himself, as long as he is without charity. But when the man is so loved that he works, inflamed and perfected by charity, together with the Spirit of love, then the works belong also to the man himself, who is now perfect in God, and they are, moreover, good for that man and meritorious.[16]

This is the charity which builds in a man, in God, and to which Paul now urges the Corinthians, as he exhorts them to the gifts that are better and that perfect all the others. Without it, in all other spiritual things they are lifeless implements and instruments of God, which are moved by God's Spirit as a knife is moved, or a broom. Those in whom the action happens do not themselves perform the works of charity, and although all is done by charity, still it is not by their own charity, but by that of God, i.e., by the Spirit.

As we have just said, the Spirit's works are not in a man without charity, but they may be in a man without the charity of the man; to wit, when the man himself is not inflamed so that he joins with the Spirit. But if ever he should join with the Spirit, and become one with Him, clinging to Him, then the man himself is made fruitful in the Spirit, and together with Him he is the parent of good works, which now are assigned not to the Spirit only, but in the Spirit to the man also, who is loved and makes the return of love, and clinging to God, is one spirit.

Paul speaks here of this charity, which cannot slip from a man, as other gifts can, or exist without profit; when it is present, all the Spirit's other gifts belong to the man in the Spirit, and when it is absent, even those of the Spirit's gifts that are in him do not belong to him. Rightly, then, Paul says: "If I should speak with all the tongues of men and angels, and have not charity, I have become like echoing brass or a clashing cymbal. And if I have the power of prophecy, and am acquainted with all mysteries and all knowledge; if I have utter faith, so that I move mountains; yet, if I have not charity in myself"—if I do not share, in my return of love, the activity with the Spirit and with the charity of God—"I am nothing. And if I give away all my resources for the feeding of the poor, if I give over my own body to be burned"—or, as the Greek conveys it more particularly (on Jerome's authority,[17] in his Commentaries on Galatians), so that I may boast of it—"it has no profit for me" [I Cor. XIII. 1–3].

Still, it has profit absolutely and in itself, because the Spirit does not act without design, and these are all things of the Spirit in man, as in a lifeless instrument. But, says Paul, for me it has no profit, if I should be without charity. Through me, however, all these things can profit others, while I, who am without the

interea expers fructus, qui sum° sine vita et flore charitatis; quo tamquam instrumento mortuo utitur Spriritus Dei in spiritalibus suis operibus.

Que Paulus, disserens de spiritalibus, que sunt omnia unius Spiritus Dei, spisse commemorat, que sunt in ecclesia sicut in organo et instrumento mortuo, nisi vivificata° et inter se et cum Christo uniatur charitate, ut in charitate Christi coagant cum eo, sintque ipsi in eo non mortua organa, sed quasi vive manus et coherentia membra conviventia et coagentia in Christo, una Christi charitate in tota ecclesia, et (ut ait in epistola ad Philippenses) unanimes in eodem Spiritu, collaborantes fidei evangelii.

Ut ille meminit in eadem epistola: Erant quidam Rome qui ex contentione Christum annunciarunt, non sincere, exisimantes se pressuram sustinere Paulo. Tamen modo annuncietur Christus, gavisus est, vel a parum sinceris. Qui quamquam tenebrosis suis mentibus obfuscant evangelicum |146r| radium, tamen non possunt facere quin forsan non nihil prosit potentibus lucem ex tenebris eximere et bonum a malo secernere. Ex fedo visu et deformi vasculo suavis liquor hauriri potest. Evangelium vel a peccatore depromptum, si non dispicias peccatorem, sapit. Vult in vasculis indignis digna dare Deus aliquando, ut non homines sed sua spectemus in hominibus, vel indignis quoque.

Charitas autem facit non coadiutores cum Spiritu Christi et cooperatores, ipsos vivos, florentes, et fructificantes iusticiam in Christo, arbore fructifera iusticie. Quod si amati redamamus, non emulamur, non invidemus, gaudemus de bono ubique, de malo dolemus, semper ipsi charitate boni in Spiritu bene facimus, non turgemus, non tumemus, non superbimus, sed humiles et pressi benigniter et sponte inservimus omnibus ad bonum, non ambitiosi et honoris cupidi sumus, sed vilipende⟨n⟩tes nos et alios pre nobis efferentes, in universis honorem et gloriam querentes Dei, nihil nobis sed omnia Deo et bono in omnibus studentes, querentes comodum aliorum, non nostrum, putantes nos magis in aliis quam in nobismetipsis abundare, satis habentes quod benefecimus aliis, hoc Deum |146v| imitati, in quo quum ei assimulamur, satis emolumenti nos quesisse nobis putamus.

Quid enim melius, et nobis melius ac ditius, quam similes fieri Deo? Quod fit in nobis maxime liberalitate et datione aliis largiter, in quo solo videmur Deum posse imitari. Nam alia que sunt in Deo, uti sunt sapientia et potentia, non sunt a nobis imitabiles: bonitatem illius, et amoris Spiritum, in liberalitate et eleemosina° possumus imitari.

---

sum *C M*] sim *L*   vivificata *C M*] vivificatur *L*   eleemosina *Ed.*] elimosima *C*] elimosina *M L*

life and the flower of charity, have no share of the fruit.[18] The Spirit of God in His spiritual workings is using me as a lifeless instrument.

Treating of spiritual gifts, Paul briefly recalls these things, which all belong to the one Spirit of God. They exist in the Church as in a lifeless implement or instrument, unless it has been brought to life[19] and unless it be united by charity within itself and with Christ, so that in the Charity of Christ men themselves share the work with Him, and are in Him, not as dead instruments, but as living hands, so to speak, and as members joined one with another, sharing life and activity in Christ by the one Charity of Christ throughout all the Church, and in the same Spirit (as Paul says in the Letter to the Philippians) one in spirit, fellow-workers of the faith of the Gospel [Phil. 1. 27].

As Paul relates in the same Epistle, there were at Rome certain men who insincerely proclaimed Christ out of rivalry, thinking they were contributing to Paul's distress [1. 17].[20] Still he rejoiced, as long as Christ was proclaimed, even though it were by men with too little sincerity. These, although they cloud the Gospel's ray by their own darksome minds, still cannot prevent it from being of perhaps no little profit to those who are able to free light from the shadows and discern the good from the bad. From a vessel foul and ugly in appearance can be drawn a delightful drink; even drawn forth from a sinner, the Gospel has its savor, if you do not give your attention to the sinner. Sometimes God wishes to give things of worth in unworthy vessels, so that we may look, not to men, but to what is of God in men, even in those who are unworthy.

Charity, however, makes us co-helpers and co-workers with the Spirit of Christ, makes us ourselves the living bearers of the flowers and fruits of justice in Christ, who is the fruitful tree of justice. If, being loved, we love in return, then we are not jealous, we are not envious, we rejoice in the good everywhere and grieve at evil; always by charity good ourselves in the Spirit, we do good; we are not puffed up nor swollen; we are not proud, but in humility and lowliness we willingly and benevolently serve all for good; we are not ambitious and eager for honor, but holding ourselves in slight esteem and elevating others above ourselves, we seek in all things the honor and glory of God; we strive after nothing for ourselves, but after everything for God and for the good in all; we seek others' advantage, not our own, thinking to have abundance in others rather than in ourselves, having enough in that we are doing good to others, and in this imitating God; and when we become like Him in this way, we think that we have sought and found reward enough.

For what could be better, or for us better and richer, than to become like God? And this is brought about in us especially by generosity and bountiful giving to others, in which alone we seem able to imitate God. For the other qualities that are in God, such as wisdom and power, we cannot imitate; His goodness, His Spirit of love, we can imitate in generosity and almsgiving.

Charitas ergo, nitens imitari optimum, larga et liberalis est, non querens que sua sunt. Hillarem datorem diligit Deus. Beatius est dare quam accipere: si accipis, friges tibi in angustius perdite°; dans autem, in amplum cales salutariter tibi et lucrose. Nequit ergo vera charitas non dare omnia.

Homo etiam in amore Dei redamans° Deum et homines, non irritatur provocaturque ullo modo in iram. Ad Ephesios quod est: Irascimini, et nolite peccare; sol non occidat super iracundiam vestram; indulgenter est dictum. Quoniam hic ait: Charitas non irritatur, non cogitat malum.

In vera charitate est etiam semper veritatis amor |147r| et horror falsitatis. Est enim charitas plana imitatio Dei et assimilatio. Qui ille bonus, benignus°, clemens, pius, propitius, liberalis, ignoscens, adiuvans, amplus, dans omnia, accipiens nihil. Que ad imaginem Dei quum omnia nobis in se expressit Iesus Christus, iussit: Estote perfecti sicut Pater vester perfectus est in celis. Charitas perfectio hominis est, completio veritatis, consummatio iustitie, assimilatio Dei. Omnia suffert, ut sincera sit et integra, nihil mali rependens. Omnia credit calore confidentie et luculentia veritatis. Claret mirum in modum animus in charitate, nedum calet. In ea non est aliqua diffidentie nubecula, que ubi est, ibi aerem, spiritum, et animum hominis, discussis nubibus diffidentie omnibus, serenat et penitus sincerum facit, ut nequit liquidior animus in charitate non admittere revelata et credere omnia.

Omnia etiam sperat charitas Dei in homine, siquidem que serenat prius cogit in unum, ut spe stent in Deo, non fluctuantes vacillent |147v| et titubent° in desperatione. Est charitas ipsa in se pura et simplex, sincera et dilucida maxime. Ideo maxime credit et sperat omnia. In qua vera est hominis fides et spes: sine qua si que fides et spes in homine est, ea non hominis sed Spiritus est in homine organico°.

Omnia sustinet ad bonum, agens sedulo ut nihil cadat in deterius, ipsa nunquam cadens. A qua si deciderit homo, flammula illa animi sui redit in Spiritum Dei. Prophitia, lingua⟨e⟩, scientia disperire potest, et perient, que sunt dumtaxat huius vite que finietur. At charitas, qua radicamur in Christo, crescimus, floremus, fructificamus in vitam eternam, qua vivimus uni et simplices, fortes et nitidi fide, qua sumus quasi connaturales et homogenii cum Christo immortali, nunquam excidet. Est perfectio nostra, que non discutietur, qua agnoscemur

---

perdite *M L*] perdide *C*   redamans *M*] redimans *C L*   benignus *M L*] benignis
C   titubent *L*] intubent *C?] over* sperent *cancelled M*   organico *M L*] organigo *C*

Charity, then, in its striving to imitate the best, is generous and bountiful, not seeking its own. God loves a cheerful giver [II Cor. ix. 7]. It is better to give than to receive [Acts xx. 35]: if you receive, you draw coldness to yourself for narrowness[21] and to your ruin; in giving, you derive warmth for yourself and breadth, to your salvation and gain. True charity, then, cannot fail to give all.

Further, the man who, in God's love, loves God and men in return, is not stirred and provoked by any cause to anger. "Be angry, and do not sin; may the sun not go down upon your wrath" [Eph. iv. 26]. These words to the Ephesians were spoken by way of indulgence,[22] because here Paul says: "Charity is not exasperated, does not think upon evil" [I Cor. xiii. 5].

Moreover, in true charity there is always a love of truth and a horror of falsehood, for charity is a distinct imitation of God and a growing like Him. And God is good, kind, merciful, gentle, gracious, bountiful, forgiving, helpful, magnanimous, giving all and receiving nothing. When Jesus Christ had set forth for us in himself all these qualities in the image of God, he commanded: "Be you perfect, as your Father in Heaven is perfect" [Matt. v. 48]. Charity is man's perfection, the fulfilment of truth, the accomplishing of justice,[23] the being made like God. It sustains all things, that it may have purity and integrity, making no return in kind for evil. Its faith is entire, in the warmth of firm trust, in the brilliant light of truth. In charity the mind grows wondrously clear, not to speak of the warmth it receives. In charity there is not the least darkness of mistrust. Wherever charity exists, it disperses all the clouds of faithlessness, making fair and wholly pure the air, the spirit, and the mind of man, with the result that the mind, grown more limpid in charity, cannot fail to accept what is revealed, cannot fail to believe all.

The charity of God in man has all hope, too, since that which it enlightens it first brings into unity, to be steadfast in hope in God, and not to falter and waver, or totter in despair.[24] Charity itself has intrinsic purity and oneness, clarity and the greatest brightness. This is why its faith is most great, its hope entire. In it are man's true faith and hope. Without it, if there be any faith and hope in a man, these are not of the man, but of the Spirit, in the man as an instrument.

Charity sustains all for the sake of good, working constantly that nothing may fall into a less good state, never falling itself. If a man drops away from it, then that little flame of his mind returns into the Spirit of God. Prophecy, tongues, knowledge can perish, and perish they will, belonging as they do only to this life, which shall come to an end. But charity, by which we are rooted in Christ, by which we grow, and bear flower and fruit for life everlasting, by which we are alive in oneness and purity, in the strength and brightness of faith, by which we are of one kind, as it were, of one nature[25] with the undying Christ, this shall never pass away. It is our perfection, and it will not be brought to nothing: by it we shall be recognized and accepted.[26] The other things are par-

et admittemur. Ex parte hic sunt alia, scientia videlicet et prophitia, ut nos quoque ex parte sumus, qui nondum apparet quod erimus. Videmus enim parvuli nunc per speculum in enigmate imaginarium vultum veritatis. Quum autem venerit quod |148r| perfectum est, tunc evacuabitur quod ex parte, et viri cernemus veritatem, facie ad faciem, retinentes charitatem quam habemus pusiones°, sed aversi ab imaginaria scientia et prophicia, ex speculo in verum ipsum vultum veritatis.

Hic nota in scientia, sermone, et prophitia multum gloriatos Corinthios; maxime in scientia et eloquentia; inter quos etiam era⟨n⟩t nonnulli acti spiritu prophitie.

Nunc manent fides, spes, et charitas; maior autem horum charitas. Que non excidet nec transmutabitur quando spes transferetur in possessionem, et fides in veritatem. Etenim charitas que nunc est cum fide et spe eadem tunc erit cum possessione et veritate, quando viri habebimus et cernemus facie ad faciem.

Ut amamur ergo amemus, ne cadamus non amantes. Amore prosimus aliis, ne ipsi deficiamus. In aliorum abundantia per nos abundamus ipsi maxime. Quum alios maxime amas, aliorumque comodum queras in Deo et Christo, tum te amans ipsum maxime, tibi queris maxime.° |148v|

---

pusiones *C over* parvuli *cancelled*   maxime. *M L Ed.*] maxime. finis xiii *C*

tial here—knowledge, i.e., and prophecy—as we also are partial, what we shall be not having yet appeared [I John III. 2]. For now we are little ones, and we see by a mirror in obscurity the imaged countenance of truth. But when that which has been made perfect comes, then shall be laid aside what is partial, and we shall discern the truth as men, face to face, keeping the charity we have as little ones, but turning our backs[27] on the reflection of knowledge and prophecy, from the mirror turning to the true countenance of truth itself [I Cor. XIII. 10–12].

Observe, at this point, that the Corinthians much prided themselves on their knowledge, discourse, and prophecy; it was especially on their knowledge and eloquence, but there were also among them not a few who were moved by the spirit of prophecy.

"Now faith, hope, and charity persist, but the greatest of these is charity" [XIII. 13]. It will not perish, nor will it be transformed, when hope is made over into possession, and faith into truth. For truly, the charity that now exists with faith and hope will then be the same, existing with possession and truth, when we are men, and have, and see face to face.

Let us love, therefore, as we are loved, lest not loving, we fall away. Let us by love benefit others, lest we ourselves fail. In the richness of others through us we are ourselves most rich. When most you love others, and seek in God and Christ the advantage of others, then are you most loving of yourself, and then do you most seek for yourself.

Caput quartumdecimum°

Ab eo loco ubi scribitur: *De spiritalibus*, usque ad finem huius quartidecimi capitis, continua et perpetua est oratio, docens in spiritalibus meliora, et ad meliora exhortans. Optimum est in ecclesia sapientia cum charitate. Corrinthii arrogantes fuerunt, et facultate linguarum gloriati sunt. In superioribus ita exhortatus est ad charitatem, ut sine ea nihil hominibus in spiritalibus prodesse statuit.

Nunc ad spiritalem intellectum eorum in ecclesia que vel leguntur vel dicuntur ita precipit ut homines intendant, ut si non recte intelligunt quod vel eloquentissime loquuntur ex revelatione superne dimissa, omnino taceant, et ecclesie nihil° loquantur; loquantur sibi solis°, et Deo si velint. Linguarum peritia bona est, sed sonus inanis est sine intellectu, et qui loquitur, in aera° loquens et barbarus.

Quocirca velit Paulus vel in hoc quoque munere linguarum Corinthii ad spiritalia contendant. Spiritus loquitur mysteria; prophitia et spiritalis interpretatio docti et sapientis, Spiritu prophetali, et Deo loquitur et hominibus, et ecclesiam edificat, maxime si re ipsa et effectu prestat, exemploque et actione, quod intelligens loquitur.

Ut enim intellectus vita sermonis est, ita actio intellectus. Quapropter intellige quod loqueris; ora ut |149r| intelligas; quod intelligis age; ut actio vivificet intellectum, intellectus illustret sermonem. Tunc, ut scribit Paulus ad Hebreos°, vivus est tuus sermo, et Dei, et efficax, et penitrabilior omni gladio, gladio ancipiti, et pertingens usque ad divisionem anime ac spiritus, compagum quoque

---

Caput quartumdecimum *Ed., om. C M*   nihil *C?* (nihili *but final* i *appears to be cancelled*) *L*] nihili *M*   solis *Ed.*] soli *C M L*   aera *C M L (Gk. accus.?)*   Hebreos *M L*] Habreos *C*

Chapter XIV

From the point at which are written the words, "Concerning spiritual things. . . ." [I Cor. XII. 1], right on to the end of this fourteenth chapter, the discourse is a continuous and an uninterrupted instruction about the better spiritual gifts, and an exhortation to seek them. The best thing of all in the Church is wisdom with charity. Now the Corinthians were vainglorious, and they prided themselves on their skill with languages.[1] In what has gone before, Paul has egged them on to charity, to the point of decreeing that without charity, nothing else can profit men in spiritual matters.

Now he commands that men give their minds to the spiritual understanding of what is read or spoken in church, in such a way that if they do not properly understand what they are saying from the Revelation given from above — even if they are saying it with the utmost eloquence — they should be silent altogether, and say nothing to the assembly. Let them talk to themselves when alone — and to God, if they wish [XIV. 28]. Skill in tongues is good, but without understanding it is an empty noise; the man who speaks thus is one speaking into the air, a speaker of an alien tongue.

Even in the gift of tongues itself, therefore, Paul wishes the Corinthians to strive for the things that are spiritual. The Spirit speaks mysteries [XIV. 2]; and the prophecy and spiritual interpretation of a learned and wise man, by the Spirit of prophecy, speak both to God and to men; and they build up the Church, especially if in fact and effect the speaker displays, by example and by deed, what he says with understanding.

For just as understanding is the life of speech, so action is the life of understanding. Understand, then, what you speak; pray, that you may understand; what you understand, do; so that action may give life[2] to your understanding, and understanding may give light to your speech. Then, as Paul writes to the Hebrews, your speech is living, and of God, and effectual, and more piercing than any sword, than a two-edged sword, reaching the very division between the soul and spirit, between joints and marrow, and it is a discerner of thoughts and

ac medullarum, et discretor cogitationum et intensionum cordis. In epistola ad
Ephesios, gladium spiritus vocat verbum Dei.

Quod si intellectis verbis vita non responderit, tunc barbari sunt concionatores
et in aera loquentes, et tamquam cythera, cuius cytherizatio ignoratur, ut ad
quid saltent homines et tripudiant non intelligant. Audiunt nesciunt quid, sed
non vident. In actione emicant omnia. Hinc David cecinit: *Peccatori dixit Deus,
quare tu ennarras iusticias meas, et sumis testimonium tuum per os meum*°?

Vide alte et perspicaciter. Nolite pueri effici sensibus, sed perfecti. Tum factis
maxime, tum verbis, quod vides eloquere.

Mulieres in ecclesia taceant. |149v|°

Quia, ut ait David, declaratio sermonum Dei illuminat et intellectum dat parvulis, iccirco voluit Paulus Corinthii maxime studeant, ut quod legerint in ecclesia intelligant. Quem intellectum spiritalem vocat mysterium, prophitiam, virtutem, sensum, mentem, interpretationem, eruditionem idiotarum, infidelium
superationem, edificationem denique ecclesie.

Quapropter orationibus et precibus Deo enitendum esse, ut quod dicas in ecclesia rite intellectum edoceas alios. Alioquin taceas, tecumque ipso solo loquare.
Nam sermo populo, nisi audiatur sensus spiritalis, scilicet quidnam sit quod divino
oraculo dicitur, li⟨n⟩gua est solum et aereus spiritus, quiddam sine anima, sine
sensu, verba et spiritus hominis aereus sine Spiritu Divino. Qui Spiritus solus
intelligit verba prophitie.

Admonet ergo Paulus: Conveniant omnes in ecclesia, quisque cum eo quod
habet, consensu et charitate. Prophete, homines spiritales, divino sensu prediti,
que audiuntur lecta particulatim interpretentur, et ubi plures sunt prophete, cedat
quisque iudicio meliori; quia a prophetis prophitie intelliguntur, que rite inter-
pretate mirifice movent et rapiunt in Christum. Mulieres in hiis taceant in ecclesia et cetu sanctorum. Domi discant a viris suis.°

---

tuum . . . *meum* C] meum . . . tuum *M L Vulg.*   finis xiiii C *on following line*]
on first line of 150r In capud xiiii prime epistole ad Corinthios See note   finis xiijj
capitis on following line, the second j in another ink and apparently by another hand

of the heart's intents [Heb. iv. 12]. In his letter to the Ephesians, he calls God's word the sword of the Spirit [Eph. vi. 17].

But if men's lives do not answer the words they have understood, then they are makers of harangues in an alien tongue; they are men speaking to the air; they are like a cithern whose harping goes unheeded, so that men do not understand the air to which they should dance and beat the ground. They hear something—they know not what—but they see nothing. In action, everything shines forth clearly. Hence David sang: "To the sinner[3] God has said, 'Why do you recount my justices, and take your testimony through my mouth?' " [Ps. xlix. 16].

See deeply and clearly. Do not become children to sense,[4] but perfect [I Cor. xiv. 20]. Then you will speak what you see, both in your deeds—above all— and in your words.

Let women be silent in church [xiv. 34].[5]

Because the speaking forth of God's words, as David says, enlightens little ones and gives them understanding [Ps. cxviii. 130], Paul wanted the Corinthians to be particularly industrious about understanding what they read in Church. This spiritual understanding he calls a mystery; he calls it prophecy, strength, mind, interpretation, the instruction of the ignorant, the overcoming of unbelievers, the building, finally, of the Church.

By prayers and entreaties to God, then, you must strive that what you speak in church you may rightly understand as you teach it to others. If you do not, then say nothing, and speak to yourself alone. For discourse to the people is simply language and airy breath, unless the spiritual meaning is heard, i.e., what it is that is being said by divine inspiration; without this, discourse is a thing without soul, without meaning: words and unsubstantial breathings of a man, lacking the Divine Spirit. The Spirit alone understands the words of prophecy.[6]

Paul advises, therefore: Let all come together in church, each with whatever he has, in harmony and love. Let the prophets, the spiritual men who are endowed with divine understanding, interpret on particular points[7] the readings that are heard. Where there are several prophets, let each yield to a judgment that is better. Prophecies, to be sure, are understood by prophets, and rightly interpreted, they move men wondrously and transport them to Christ. In these matters let women be silent in the church and in the assembly of saints. Let them learn at home from their husbands.

Caput quindecimum°

Erit quidem aliquando ab ipsa vita que lux est hominum quedam admirabilis revivificatio rerum et moribundarum creaturarum. Qui creavit ex nihilo, ruinas recreabit, ex nullis omnino meritis. Que erat causa in creatione, mera voluntas et Dei bonitas, eadem erit sola et unica causa recreationis.

Hec vivificatio mortis incipit |150r| ab homine. Angeli prius peccaverunt. Sed quod ex impotentia et inscitia seductum fuit, misericordia et gratia apprehendit. Malus, tenebrecosus, mortuus erat homo. Ex malicia tenebre, ex tenebris mors suborta est. Induit vita ipsa misericorditer malum, tenebras, mortem, ut in ea recalifactus et illuminatus homo spiritaliter reviviscat, adolescatque indies in statum spiritalem, totusque tandem homo spiritalis fiat.

Hec bonifica, clarifica, et vivifica vis vite, incipiens in homine, perget vivificabitque, quatenus reperit quod vivificetur. Invivificabilia vero, quorum peccatum nec impotentia nec ignora⟨n⟩tia excusat, quorumque impia voluntas et gratiam recusans damnat, in quibus sunt angeli illi decidui, et homines item qui Christum repudiarunt, ab ipsa potenti vita longe discutientur, extra omnes vite terminos, in ipsam mortis miseriam sempiternam. Qui autem a vita bonifica et clarificante, incipiente in homine Christi, que ut ignis serpit in mundo vivificans, califacti et illuminati rapiuntur radiis Dei ut in Christo sint; hii boni et sapientes, viventes ex Deo in Christo, ad vitam designantur sempiternam; ut quod assumpsit in se vita, vivificavit id in se in vitam et gloriam immortalem, ita quod deinceps apprehendetur radiis Christi pariter reformabitur spiritali et divino calore et lumine, in eis mirifice transmutationem a morte in vitam et statum spiritalem operante.

Qui vivificator quum vivificavit quod vivificatum erit, simulque quum exter-

---

Caput quindecimum *Ed.*] In Capud xiiij xv *C with* d *crossed,* xiiij *cancelled and* xv *added in another ink, prob. by another hand*

Chapter XV

There will take place hereafter, from that Life itself who is the Light of men, a certain wondrous revivifying of things and of creatures that die. He who from nothing created shall re-create — not because of any merits of theirs whatsoever — the ruins. That which was the cause in creation,[1] the mere will and goodness of God, will be likewise the only and the exclusive cause of the re-creation.

This vivifying of death begins with man. The angels sinned first; but mercy and grace take hold of what was led astray from weakness and ignorance.[2] Man was wicked, darksome, dead. From wickedness there arose darkness; from darkness, death. Life itself in mercy took on the wickedness, the darkness, and the death, so that in life man might be made warm again and enlightened, might begin to live again spiritually, might grow from day to day to spiritual stature, and might become at last an altogether spiritual man.

As long as it finds something to give life to, this force of life that makes things good, bright, and alive will press onward with its vivifying gift, beginning with man. Those things, however, that are not vivifiable,[3] those whose sin neither weakness nor ignorance excuses, but which are damned by their own impious and grace-refusing will (and among them are those fallen angels, and likewise the men who have rejected Christ), by that same mighty life will be cast away beyond all the boundaries of life, into the endless wretchedness itself of death. But those who are carried up to be in Christ by the life that makes good and clear, the life which begins in the manhood of Christ and spreads like a fire, giving life through the world; those who are made warm and lightsome by God's rays;[4] these men are marked for unending life, having goodness, and wisdom, and life from God in Christ. That which life took unto itself it brought to life within itself for deathless life and glory; in the same way, that which will be caught up hereafter by Christ's rays will be equally formed anew[5] by the spiritual, the divine warmth and light, working wondrously in them the change of substance from death to life and to a spiritual state.

Now when this Life-giver has given life to all that is to have it; when at the

minaverit fecem mortem, quumque postremo suo magnifico splendore omnes creaturas illustravit in clarius, tunc finis erit, victa malicia, tenebris, et morte, quum victor tradidit regnum Deo et Patri, et unus ille in orbe vite et obedientie regnabit gloriosus. Cui subiicientur omnia, ut Deus sit omnia in omnibus.[150ᵛ]°

Iesus noster Christus resurrexit et visus est quam plurimis. Homines ergo in illo omnes resurgent. Ille primitie° est, vita iam ipsa vivificans reliquos. Alioquin Christiani miserabiliores sunt omnibus gentibus, quorum professio est mala pati temporalia ut bonum agant regnum eternum.

Seminantur mortales ut suo tempore vivificati emergant novi et immortales, varii pro meritis et claritate et perfectione. Suo tamen in genere perfectum erit quodque, et tale quidem qualis homo ille celestis. Qui, ut scribit ad Philippenses, reformabit corpus humilitatis nostre, configuratum corpori claritatis sue, secundum operationem qua etiam possit subiicere omnia. Mysterium est: resurgent omnes, sed non omnes° immutabuntur. Immutabuntur in melius et in formam Christi soli veri Christiani. Impii non resurgent |151r| in iudicio, nec peccatores in consilio iustorum. Reciperunt enim mercedem suam: bonis temporalibus emerunt sibi mala sempiterna.

Qui veniet tamquam fulgur erumpens ex oriente et pergens raptim in occidentem, is suos corripiet in se et sibi in sui similitudinem couniet, simul fugatis et discussis tenebris morteque exacta et exterminata, ut vita et lux occupet omnia. In qua qui erunt quam beatissimi erunt, in glorioso Domino nostro Iesu Christo. In qua qui non erunt quam infelicissimi erunt, sine Domino nostro Iesu Christo, in frigore, in tenebris, in morte illa sempiterna; in qua potius quam sit homo, prestaret eum omnino non esse, qui erit tunc ut sine fine non sit, infeliciter, in se ipso°. |151v|

---

finis *C after this line*] Capud xvi *C at top of next folio*   primitie *M*] premitie *C*]
primitiæ *L*   omnes immutabuntur *M*] omnes omnes immutabuntur *C L* (*with second*
omnes *set between daggers*)   ipso *M L*] ipso, finis xv *C*

same time He has banished the impurity, death; and when finally He has enlightened all creatures into the more lightsome state by His own splendid brightness, then there will be the end. Wickedness will be vanquished, and darkness, and death. The Vanquisher will deliver the Kingdom to God and to the Father, and He alone will reign in glory throughout a universe of life and of obedience. To Him shall all things submit, that God may be all in all [I Cor. xv. 24, 28].[6]

Jesus our Christ rose and was seen by a very great number. In him, therefore, will all men rise again. He is the first-fruits, life itself, now giving life to the rest. Otherwise Christians are the unhappiest of all peoples [xv. 19], since they profess that the evils of time are to be borne for the achieving of a kingdom of good in eternity.

The seeds are planted in mortal state to come forth when the time is right for them filled with life, and new, and immortal; varying in brightness and perfection according to their merits, each will be nonetheless perfect in his own order, and will resemble, indeed, that Man of Heaven. For he will form anew the body of our lowness, as Paul writes to the Philippians, moulding it into the image of the body of his own brightness, by that action through which he has power also to make all things obedient to himself [Phil. iii. 21]. There is a mystery: All shall rise again, but not all will be changed [I Cor. xv. 51].[7] Only the true Christians will be changed into the better state and into the form of Christ. "The impious will not rise in the judgment, nor sinners in the meeting of the just" [Ps. i. 5]. For they have received their reward [Matt. vi. 2]: with the good things of time they have bought for themselves things ill in eternity.

He who will come like lightning breaking forth from the East and sweeping swiftly into the West [xxiv. 27] will gather in a moment his own to himself and unite them into his own likeness, at the same time scattering and dispersing the darkness, driving death away and banishing it, so that life and light may possess all things. Most blessed will be those who are in that light and that life, in our Lord of Glory, Jesus Christ. Most wretched will be those who are not: they will be without our Lord Jesus Christ, and in cold, in darkness, in death unending. It were better for a man to be altogether without being than to do be in that death. For in it he will be then[8] as though without end, in his wretchedness, he were not in himself.

Caput sextumdecimum°

Habuit in memoria et cura, peragrans regiones Paulus et Christum hominibus ac salutem in eo nuncians, ut egentibus et inopibus Christi sequacibus Hierosolime ex fidelium liberalitate et gratia subsidium victus collectum illis convehetur. Partim enim Iudeorum impietate et iniuriis, quibus Christi nomen erat odiosum, partim frugum inopia et famis quam fore predixit Agabus, extrema penuria cruciati sunt.

Est verisimile Paulum sibimet ipsi nusquam nec petivisse quicquam ne⟨c⟩ si quando quid oblatum fuit ultro et datum accepisse°, preterquam a Macedonibus, ut ipse testatur in secunda epistola ad Corinthios. In Grecia quidem et in Achaia, protestatus est accepturum se nihil. Non quod non licuerit, nam, ut scribit in hac prima ad Corinthios: Dominus ordinavit qui° |152r| evangelium enunciat, de evangelio vivere, sed ne occasio detur ulla malevolis et invidis obtrectandi, utque ex omni parte integerimus sit suus labor, sitque nusquam locus scandali et offensionis vel levissimus. Quam etiam integritatem abstinentiamque manuum apud Ephesios in Asia servavit, sicuti testatur idem ipse Paulus, auctore Luca. Qui ultimo discedens ab Ephesiis, tunc Hierosolimam profectus, cum illis collocutus hec verba habuit: Argentum et aurum aut vestem nullius concupivi, sicut ipsi scitis, quoniam que mihi opus erant et hiis qui mecum sunt ministraverunt manus iste.

Erat tamen ei precipua cura ut sanctis qui erant Hierosolime subveniatur. |152v| Quam eleemosinam° in secu⟨n⟩da ad Corinthios vocat benidictionem, quod Grece εὐλογία° dicitur, que sunt munera que minutili sacerdotes ad sinodum convenientes maioribus sacerdotibus summatibusque deportant.

Marhanatha, Hebreo verbo, asserit Paulus et affirmat Dominum venisse.

Finis Epistole prime ad Corinthios. |153r|

Caput sextumdecimum *Ed.*] In capud xvj & Ultimum *C*] *om. M*   accepisse *M L*] accipisse *C*   qui *M L*] qui qui *C*   eleemosinam *Ed.*] elimosinam *C L*] elemosinam *M*   εὐλογία *Ed.*] Elogia *C M*] *elogia L*

Chapter XVI

As he journeyed through all lands, announcing to men Christ, and in him salvation, Paul kept in his memory and care Christ's needy and resourceless followers in Jerusalem, arranging that assistance in the necessaries of life be collected from the generosity and kindness of the faithful everywhere and brought to them. For in part because of the unbrotherly conduct and the harshness of those Jews to whom the name of Christ was hateful, and in part because of the scarcity of grain and the famine Agabus foretold[1] would come [Acts XI. 27, 28], they were racked by extreme want.

Paul probably asked nowhere on his own behalf, nor did he accept anything that was offered and given voluntarily, except (as he testifies himself in the second letter to the Corinthians) from the Macedonians [II Cor. XI. 9]. Indeed, he formally affirmed that in Greece and in Achaia he would accept nothing. Not that this was forbidden him; for as he writes in this first letter to the Corinthians, "The Lord has decreed that he who preaches the Gospel should live by the Gospel" [I Cor. IX. 14]. Rather, it was to avoid giving to the spiteful and the envious any occasion for carping, and to ensure the perfect integrity of his endeavor, and leave no place anywhere for the least scandal or discredit. This integrity and restraint of the hands he observed also in Asia among the Ephesians, as Paul himself again testifies, this time in what Luke has written. As he set out for Jerusalem, leaving the Ephesians forever, he addressed these words to them: "I have coveted no man's silver or gold or clothing, as you yourselves know, since whatever my companions and I needed, these hands of mine have supplied" [Acts XX. 33, 34].

His foremost concern, however, was that the saints who were in Jerusalem[2] should be assisted. Such almsgiving he calls in the second letter to the Corinthians "a blessing": the Greek word is εὐλογία,[3] and means gifts that the priests of the lowest rank, coming together into the ecclesiastical council, carry to the higher and more distinguished priests.

By the Hebrew term, "*Maran atha*,"[4] Paul proclaims and affirms the coming of the Lord.

The End of the First Epistle to the Corinthians.

Capud XVI

Jesus noster christus resurrexit q̃ visus est ~~xxxxx~~ ē
ãplurimis. homines ergo in illo omnes resurgent
Ille primitiæ est. vita iam ipã viuificans reliquos.
Alioqn christiani miserabiliores sunt omnium genus
quorum ꝓfessio ē mala pati temporalia: ut bonum
agant regnum eternum. Seminamur mortales
ut suo tempore viuificati surgant nomi q̃
immortales. varij ꝓ meritis q̃ claritate q̃
ꝑfectione. Suo tamen in genere ꝑfectum erit quodq̃
et tale qdem. qualis homo ille celestis. qui
ut scribit Ad philippenses/ reformabit corpus
humilitatis nrē configuratum corporis claritatis suæ. secundum operationem qua etiam
possit subijcere omnia. Mysterium est resurgent omnes: sed nõ omnes omnes immutabur
immutabunt in melius q̃ reforma jõ ~~feli~~
soli veri christiani ~~surgent~~ surgunt nõ resurget

Notes on John Colet's *Commentary on I Corinthians*

Chapter I

1. The Christian community in Corinth was flourishing at this time (A.D. 53–57), but as the rest of the letter indicates, some abuses had crept in. Apparently some members of the community had sent letters to Paul asking questions about marriage, celibacy, use of meat sacrificed to idols, etc. Paul wrote this letter from Ephesus in response.

2. Colet frequently describes the operation of grace in this way. Cf. Intro., pp. 42f; *Romans* IX–X, 44; XII, 62 *et passim; Cel. Hier.* IV, where he speaks of the "diffusion of the out-poured Deity," and VIII, 26, where he envisions the "divine ray" transmitted through the hierarchies of angels and then to men. P. O. Kristeller points out that the neoplatonic concept of the genesis of substances underlies such expressions, which are frequent in both Colet and Ficino: "The divine ray which contains all forms descends from God to matter through several degrees, thereby withdrawing farther and farther from its origin. In like measure the derived forms become more and more different from their originals, finally becoming impure instead of pure, dispersed instead of united, particular instead of universal, mutable instead of immutable. The ray must therefore be reduced to its origin, the derived forms to their originals" (*The Philosophy of Marsilio Ficino*, p. 110). In chap. X of *Cel. Hier.*, the "divine ray" is the Gospel, coming from Christ (p. 31); in *Ecc. Hier.* the sun image is more fully developed. The ancient idea of conception by means of the sun's rays underlies the metaphor. Colet brings out this aspect more specifically in his marginalia on Ficino's *Epistolae*: 'Christiani solis radiis humana et fidelis mens gravida quasi seminibus eniti debet solem parere [*sic*] et referre Christum. . . ." ("The human mind, when touched by faith, being pregnant by the Christian sun's rays, as it were with seeds, ought to strive to produce a sun and resemble Christ"—Sears Jayne, *John Colet and Marsilio Ficino*, p. 112).

3. This phrase introduces Colet's concept of the Mystical Body of Christ, of which he will have much to say in this commentary. Cf. Intro., pp. 46f. As he goes on to explain (p. 73), the various capacities of men are united in Christ as they do his work, informed by his spirit, which is their bond of unity. According to Colet's metaphysics, perfection is to be found in oneness and simplicity, imperfection in multiplicity. This Platonic theme is fundamental in all Colet's writings on Scripture. It underlies his concept of the Church: "in toto non plures, sed ex pluribus partibus unum quiddam totum confectum extet" ("not a plurality of parts, but a united whole composed of the several parts"—*Romans* XII. 84; 71); of the operations of God's grace (see pp. 71–75, 179, 199,

et passim); of growth in the spiritual life (see Chap. VII below and *Romans* VII–X). In Chap. XIII, p. 259, he combines this concept with the Pauline doctrine of charity to show how the Christian can share in the activity of Christ.

4. This key phrase has several closely related meanings. The basic one is that of "form" in scholastic philosophy: the organizing principle of a thing, that which gives meaning and purpose to matter. Hence when Colet speaks of "form" in the spiritual life, he means that spiritual principle which gives meaning and purpose to human existence. This is the power of grace and the force of example offered to us by Christ: "ut per eius vivendi formam, tamquam per hostiam, in celum ingrediamus" ("through his form of living, as though by means of a sacrificial victim, we might enter into heaven" — VII, p. 169). In the deepest sense, then, the "form of living" is the way to salvation (cf. Intro., pp. 41–45). But Colet also uses "form" in relation to the two powers of a man's soul, his intellect and will (see n. 23 below). In relation to the intellect, he calls the formative principle wisdom and pictures it as light; when speaking of the will, he calls it love and warmth. So in Chap. XIII, he discusses charity as "spiritalis hominis forma intrinseca . . . et essentialis" ("the intrinsic and essential form of the spiritual man" — p. 259). The same idea operates throughout his commentary on Romans. When he speaks of "reformation" he is thinking of form as an organizing principle. To be "reformed" means to be acted upon by grace and to respond to its power to reorganize the intellect and will, just as matter is organized by its formal principle. "Quod quamdiu tenet, quasi nova tum forma effigiatus ad imaginem Dei expressius, non tam homo quam Deus videtur esse." ("So long as he retains this enlightenment, man, as though now fashioned in a new form more distinctly after the image of God, appears to be not so much man as God." *Romans* XII. 176; 59.) Obviously the transference of the metaphysical concept from the philosophical to the religious level depends more on analogy than on accuracy of terminology in the scholastic sense.

5. Colet's definitions of this important term occur in a variety of contexts throughout his works, each of which throws light upon the other. *Iusticia* (often translated "righteousness" by Lupton; "justice" is preferred here) basically means a right relation with God which fallen man, inspired by grace, can achieve through faith, hope, and love. It is a process initiated by God to which man responds. Colet's definition in *De Sac.* emphasizes faith and love: "Justicia autem est fides Deo per Christum, et caritas Dei et proximi" ("For justice is faith in God through Christ, and love of God and neighbor" — p. 79). Hope and its role in the process of justification are stressed in *Corinthians* VII, p. 156 and in Colet's letter to the Abbot of Winchcombe: "Credens et confidens deo justus est. Confidens creaturis quibusquunque impius et iniustus est. Unde justicia deo confidentia est." ("Believing and trusting in God is just. Trusting in creatures, of any kind whatsoever, is impious and unjust. Hence justice is trust in God." MS Gg. iv. 26, 62v.) But the two treatises on Romans, as might be expected, develop the concept more fully. *Edmund's Romans* stresses faith and God's initiative rather than man's merits: "Justificati gratis per graciam ipsius, sola misericordia et bonitate Dei; facti justi ex peccatoribus, non mentis et viribus nostris, nec conanime nostro, sed sola potentia et benignitate Dei, gratis, per revelationem quae est in Christo Jesu." ("Being justified freely by his grace, by the sole mercy and goodness of God: being made righteous instead of sinners, not by any merits or strength or endeavour of our own, but by the sole power and loving-kindness of God; freely, through the redemption that is in Christ Jesus." III. 239; 105.)

Faith in the whole redemptive message of Christ is essential, transcending all external practices: "Verum in hoc loco animadvertendum est, Paulum non significare gentes, ullumve gencium sine lege recte vixisse, quum ejus est proculdubio sentencia neminem nisi ex fide Christi recte vivere, et justum esse posse. Sed ut infringat illam vanam spem, quam Judei in mosaica lege habuerunt . . . asserit eciam gentes quae sine lege data fuerint, si modo recte vixissent, tam Deo gratas et acceptas fuisse quam Judeos; quibus fuit data lex ut ad virtutem praeparentur, circumcisionemque animi et mentis purificacionem prae se ferrent; in qua sola consistit hominis justificatio." ("But in this place it must be remarked, that St. Paul means not that the Gentiles, or any Gentile man, had lived rightly without the Law; since beyond doubt his opinion is that no one lives rightly or can be righteous, save by faith in Christ. But, that he may break down that vain hope which the Jews had in the Law of Moses . . . he asserts that even the Gentiles, who were without law given to them, if only they had lived rightly, were as well-pleasing and acceptable to God as were the Jews. For these had the Law given them that they might be prepared for virtue, and might exhibit a circumcision of the heart and purification of the mind; in which alone man's justification consists." *Romans* II. 138; 4–5.) Throughout both treatises Colet emphasizes the fact that justification means a real change in the sinner, an enlightenment of his mind and a strengthening of his will. In *Romans* v he amplifies this idea by stressing man's active response to God's love, which motivates him in the first place. The change that justification effects in the sinner enables him to respond. A reciprocal exchange of love takes place, so that justification is seen as a dynamic event rather than a static condition imposed from above: "Haec in Deo graciosa dileccio et caritas erga homines ipsa vocacio et justificacio et magnificacio est; nec quicquid aliud tot verbis dicimus, quam unum quiddam; scilicet amorem Dei erga homines eos quos vult amare. Item cum homines gracia attractos, vocatos, justificatos, et magnificatos dicimus, nichil significamus aliud quam homines amantem Deum redamare. In quo amore et redamore consistit hominis justificacio" (p. 143). ("This gracious love in God, and charity towards men, is itself their calling and justification and glorifying; nor do we mean anything else by so many terms than one thing, namely, God's love towards those whom it is his will to love. In like manner, when we say that by *grace* men are drawn, are called, are justified, are glorified; we signify nothing else than that men return the love of a loving God. In this love and return of love consists the justification of man" pp. 11–12). Although the observance of law (even the Mosaic law) and the performance of good works cannot of themselves suffice for justification, it follows that the works of Christian love must proceed from a man who is truly justified, if he is to be saved: "Observatio legis est ex vivificante quadam racione, et ea quae justos homines facit. Quia non sumus justi ex observata lege, sed quia sumus justi, ideo bonam legem observamus. Justi autem sumus justificati gratia, facti justi per Deum, ut juste vivamus; ut justificatio nostra precedat justam actionem, quae legis observatio est; nec prius agamus juste quam simus ipsi justi." ("Observance of the law comes by means of a life-giving principle; and it is by this that men are justified. We are not righteous through observance of the law, but we observe the good law because we are righteous. Now we are thus righteous when justified by grace; being made righteous by God, to the end that we should live righteously." *De Cor.* p. 186; p. 32.) In *Corinthians* VII, in connection with a long section on the economy of salvation and the role of faith, Colet points out that faith is "not by itself enough for righteousness, which stands above faith in love continually doing good acts" (cf. n. 16 to Chap. VII below). The need for works as

well as faith is also brought out in *Romans* XII. Throughout this work Colet stresses the fact that justification is a free gift, initiated by God; man cannot merit it; but cf. his position on *sola fide*, n. 17 to chap. vii below. It is clear from this brief discussion that isolated statements cannot give a complete picture of Colet's view of justification. One cannot conclude, for example, that he stresses one theological virtue at the expense of the other two, for in the process of justification, there is a vital interplay among all three. To get a comprehensive view of what Colet means by justice, all such statements need to be understood in conjunction with each other.

Erasmus expresses some similar views in much the same way—e.g., not as a systematic theologian using technical terminology, but as a humanistic scholar interested in promulgating Scripture as the still-living, life-giving Word of God. (See Prefatory Dedication to Leo X, NT, LB VI, *2r.) He too believes that faith is also an intellectual assent to revealed truth. He too stresses the reciprocal quality of God's love for man and man's love for God. Although, strictly speaking, we cannot merit the grace of justification in the first place, our free and active cooperation with the grace that has been given us is required for salvation. It is in this sense that "works" are essential. In a long note on I Cor. XIII, Erasmus turns his attention to the proponents of *sola fide* in order to refute them (LB VI, 723–25). Of course, Erasmus wrote much more on justification than Colet did, but his basic position can be gleaned from careful reading of the *Paraphrases* and annotations to the NT. (See the comprehensive study of this matter by John Payne, *Erasmus: His Theology of the Sacraments*, chap. v. Payne's useful notes reveal the widespread nature of Erasmus' remarks on this subject.) Erasmus was also more concerned than Colet over the issue of grace vs. free will that developed later into the controversy with Luther.

6. In his references to predestination, Colet tries to stress the salvific will of God without destroying man's freedom. Anyone is free to reject the grace that God offers to him— but the offering of grace in the first place depends entirely on God's will. This topic is treated more fully in *Romans* IX–X.

7. This refers to the whole Church united in harmony and inspired by one Spirit. Because of the primacy of Christ as source and goal, Colet often uses such expressions to mean the Mystical Body functioning in conjunction with its head. Cf. Intro., pp. 46f; VII, p. 199; XII, p. 237; n. 3 above; and *De Cor.* p. 45: ". . . the Spirit extends itself in vital tension throughout the whole Christ." In *Cel. Hier.* XVI. 37 he cites Rom. XI:36 to make this point.

8. Not one of the seven sacraments, but the whole Christian message of salvation. Colet also uses this expression to refer to it in *Romans* IV. 4 and *De Sac.*, p. 33.

9. The phrase *totam Christi rationem* is not to be understood as "system" in the modern sense of a fully worked out philosophical explanation, but rather in the scholastic sense of "form" which gives meaning, organization, and purpose to matter. Cf. n. 4 above.

10. Colet envisions a hierarchy of the participation in grace, with the Apostles at the top and the lesser members of the Church performing their various functions in appropriate gradations. Cf. *Romans* XII. 79–80, *Ecc. Hier.* I and v. But this does not mean unfair inequality, for in the lower ranks there are compensations (XII, p. 253).

11. Anointing was the sign of man's consecration to God, as in the sacraments of confirmation and holy orders. The man taken up into God's service shares in his life by the inspiration of grace. Paul has addressed his letter to the "saints"—i.e., the baptized ones, the sharers in grace, at Corinth. For an example of an Old Testament use

of the idea of anointing and the inspiration that comes with it, see Isaiah VI: 1–8. Cf. n. 2 to Chap. XVI below.

12. Cf. n. 3 above.

13. Lat. *apprehensi a Deo*; this expresses God's initiative in the operation of grace, a point which Colet continually stresses.

14. The interconnection of these attributes of the state of grace is further developed in VII, pp. 149, 161.

15. Here Colet's metaphysics and theology come together, as the principle of Christian unity is identified with the Holy Spirit giving and sustaining life in his Church. Cf. *De Cor.* where this creative and unifying power is described more specifically: "Hoc divinum vinculum ecclesiae in Christo Jesu vel spiritus ipse est Dei in Christo, vel ejus virtus conglutinans . . ." ("This divine bond of the Church in Christ Jesus, is either the very Spirit of God in Christ, or its cementing power . . ." —p. 190; p. 39). See also *Cel. Hier.* III. 15.

16. The "deification" of man is central in Colet's theology and spiritual doctrine. But it is a concept which must be made precise in order to avoid misunderstandings that could lead to pantheistic heresy or pietistic sentimentality. Colet's bare statement here needs to be amplified by what he says elsewhere. In chap. XII of *Cel. Hier.* he considers more carefully in what sense men can be called gods. The expression is of course a metaphor, and its foundation is Scriptural (Ps. LXXXII: 6; John X: 34): "Quinimmo etiam Dii idem in sacris literis nominantur ex mutacione et relacione quoad possunt deitatis." ("Nay, more, they are even called gods in Holy Scripture, by a metaphor, and by their resembling the Deity as far as possible." P. 186; p. 34.) But how does this resemblance come about? Colet's answer, expressed in a variety of ways, presents the very heart of his spirituality. *Cel. Hier.* iii offers a succinct explanation: "Totus conatus omnium spirituum est referre Deum. Deus imprimis potenter assimilat quae vicina sunt ei; assimulata deinceps assimulant. Ita pergit derivatio deitatis ab ordine in ordinem, et ab hierarchia in hierarchiam, et a melioribus creaturis in deteriores, pro capacitate cujusque, in deificationem omnium . . ." ("The whole endeavor of all spiritual beings is to represent God. God first by his power makes like himself those beings who are near him; then they make others like in turn. Thus there proceeds a diffusion of the Deity from order to order, from hierarchy to hierarchy, and from better creatures to worse, according to each one's capacity, for the rendering godlike of all . . ." —pp. 173–74; p. 15). This chapter concludes with a summary: "Deus assimulat nos ei. Impartit ut impartiamur. In impartione accepti maxime Deo assimulamur. Divinissima virtus est misericors liberalitas. Benefaciendo aliis maxime Deo assimulamur." ("God makes us like himself. He bestows that we may bestow. In communicating what we have received, we become most like God. The divinest of virtues is a tender-hearted liberality. In benefiting others we become most like God." P. 174; p. 16.) He goes on in *Ecc. Hier.* to emphasize love as the source of this power, whether in God or man. We become like God if we love him: "Amor enim principium gignendi est; et sanctus amor sanctitatis, et Dei amor deitatis." ("For love is the source of begetting; holy love, of begetting holiness; and the love of God, of godliness." II. 2.206; 62.) Cf. *Romans* VIII, where Colet explains, with the help of Ficino, how our minds are expanded by love and raised up toward God, instead of reducing him to the narrow limits of our knowledge. This likeness to God is not just a spiritual refinement; it is essential for salvation: "Voluit enim bonus Deus salvetur homo; quod quidem esse non potest certe nisi homines dei-

ficentur, reformenturque in divinum statum, diique fiant assimilati Deo, ut Deum referant." ("For it was the will of the good God that man should be saved; and that cannot be unless men be made godlike and refashioned to a divine condition, and become gods by being made like unto God, that they may represent God." *Ecc. Hier.* I. 201; 54.) The Incarnation makes this possible: "Deus homo factus medium erat quo homines dii fierent; cujus deitate deificantur omnes." ("God, made man, was the means whereby men were to be made gods. By His Godhead all are made godlike." *De Cor.* p. 190; p. 40.) Cf. *Romans* XII. 63. Hence it follows that "omnis descensio deitatis est ad ascensionem humanitatis" ("every descent of the divinity is for the ascent of humanity" *Ecc. Hier.* IV. 231; 100). No wonder the pseudo-Dionysius' explanations of these descents and ascents, even spun out so fantastically across the angelic choirs, appealed to Colet's imagination and spiritual fervor.

17. See, for example, Jer. VII: 4; Ezek. XLIII: 12; Amos VII: 13; Hab. II: 20.

18. Colet's attribution to Paul of prudence and carefulness in his dealings with the Corinthians and his adverting to the cultural attitudes of the Greeks may both be taken as instances of his humanistic approach to the Pauline texts. But he was familiar with Patristic as well as humanist precedents for rhetorical analysis and the use of non-scriptural historical sources. Cf. Chrysostom on I Cor. IV: 6 and 9, where Paul's prudence and sensitivity to the assumptions of his readers are similarly praised (*Hom.* XII, PG 61, 95–108). See also *Edmund's Romans*, p. 252, where Colet refers to Paul as "divinus orator" who uses "art" marvelously (O'Kelly). In *Romans* too he pauses to comment upon Paul's careful consideration of his hearers' probable reactions (XII, 55; XIII, 96). P. Duhamel points out ("The Oxford Lectures of John Colet," *Journal of the History of Ideas*, 14 [1953], 493–510) that Colet's attention to the historical context of the epistles was a significant departure from the usual biblical exegesis of his day.

19. Colet is probably referring here to the leaders of the factions mentioned below. Apollos was a Jew from Alexandria, although his name was Greek, and a famous rhetorician; Chloe was probably a Christian whose servants told Paul about the disorders in Corinth (I Cor. I: 11). Crispus and Gaius, whom Paul said he baptized (I: 14), are also mentioned in Acts XVIII: 8 and Rom. XVI: 23. Stephanus (I: 16) was one of the Corinthian messengers to Paul. Cephas (I: 12) is of course Peter (NCC 869i).

20. These do not seem to have been heretical or schismatic sects in the modern sense, but rather conflicting groups who each claimed the leader or teacher they preferred, as the Greeks attached themselves to a favorite philosopher or school. Apollos, for instance, had an elegant manner of speaking which some might have preferred to Paul's simpler way. The followers of Peter probably did not put Paul on the same level as the Twelve. Those who were "of Christ" might have been those who abstained from any partisanship (NCC 867j,k,l).

21. The Corinthian church was founded by Paul during his second missionary journey, between A.D. 50–52. See Acts XVIII: 1–8.

22. Colet's view of man's abilities unaided by grace is a somber one. See, for example, his denigration of man's natural powers in *Romans* XII. 83. On the other hand, these comments must not be taken out of perspective; see n. 32 below.

23. This paragraph contains an admirably concise summary of Colet's philosophy of man. These two powers enable man to operate in both the speculative and practical order (Intro., pp. 41–42; 51–52), and to respond in two important ways to God's action upon him. The theological virtue of faith enlightens his intellect, while charity moves

his will. In Chap. VIII of his lectures on *Romans*, Colet tries to relate these traditional categories to the somewhat different terminology of Ficino in his *Theologia Platonica*. In fact, Colet paraphrases a section of this work (Bk. xiv, chap. 10) in which Ficino is at pains to show that love is superior to knowledge. It is the function of the intellect to analyze, to separate something into parts in order to understand how it works. But it is the function of love to unite, to bring together what has been separated. Hence the power of love to unite man to God is greater than the power of the intellect. See P. O. Kristeller, *The Philosophy of Marsilio Ficino*, pp. 270–75, for an explanation of how the *Theologia Platonica* differs from Ficino's earlier statements on this question of primacy. Intellect and will seem to be considered ultimately as parallel means to reach God— wings, Ficino calls them, after an image in Plato: "Concludamus animam nostram per intellectum et voluntatem tanquam geminas illas platonicas alas idcirco volare ad Deum, quoniam per eas volat ad omnia." ("Let us conclude then that our mind flies to God by means of the intellect and the will, just like those twin platonic wings, so to speak, because through them it [the mind] flies toward all things." *Theologia Platonica*, Bk. xiv, chap. 3, p. 259. I am indebted to Mrs. Mary Joan Masello, a graduate student in the classics department at Loyola University, for assistance in translations from Ficino). Jayne has published some of Ficino's letters to Colet dealing with this interrelationship (Letter D, p. 82) and he devotes a chapter to the "intellect-will problem" in his introduction to Colet's marginalia on the correspondence of Ficino (pp. 56–76). Cf. *Ecc. Hier.*, where Colet is talking about the devotion of communicants who might not fully understand the sacrament they are receiving: "Ignorans amor plus potest mille modis quam frigida sapiencia." ("Ignorant love has a thousand times more power than cold wisdom." iii.2.219; 83.)

24. Origen in his *Com. on Romans* (PG XIV, Bk. vii, sec. 619), considers the question of how Christ could be called a stumbling block. First he defines the term (lapis offensionis) as a barrier impeding one's ways. Christ was such a barrier for the Scribes and Pharisees, an impediment to the broad way of perdition toward which they were heading. He was also a barrier for Paul on the road to Damascus, stopping him when he would have gone on to persecute Christians. Colet also follows this rather unusual meaning in *Romans*: ". . . quos significat crassitate mentis et ignorancia oblatam veritatem repudiasse, et recalcitrantes ad lapidem offensionis lesisse se, non sinentes ut Christus, petra scandali, id est, petra objecta labentibus in profundum, viciis eorum obstaret . . ." ("For he implies that, in their grossness and ignorance of mind, they had rejected the offered truth, and in kicking against the *stone of stumbling* had hurt themselves; not suffering Christ, the *rock of offence* (that is, the rock that was a bar to them when sliding into the abyss) to be an obstacle to their sins . . ." —ix–x. 172; 53). The rest of this paragraph in *Corinthians* continues the image of a barrier, as Christ is compared to a rock withstanding the breakers. But see p. 83, where "stumblingblock" is taken in its more usual sense. In either case, it constitutes an obstacles for the Jews.

25. The translator refers the reader to the Latin text for the force of the antithesis in this section between *actio, impatientia*, and *agere*, on the one hand, and *pati, passio*, and *patientia* on the other, finding it impossible to convey the sustained antithesis adequately in English.

26. The translator points out that the Latin has a further pun here, opposing *constantia* to *motus*.

27. Colet uses an image here which the translation cannot reproduce satisfactorily

in English: "tamen frigens odium in eis nihil potuit admittere et in bonum partem co-quere." ("Because of the chill within them, they could admit nothing—not even the numberless and altogether convincing proofs of Christ's power and divinity—into their minds and warm it so that it could be digested and turned to good service." O'Kelly.) Cf. *Romans* XII: "Ab unitate enim solliditas et potencia; a luce veritas et rectitudo; a calore bonitas et proba actio." ("For from unity comes compactness and power; from light, truth and uprightness; from heat, goodness and honest action." XII. 178; 62.) When he describes, further on in this same chapter, how the Apostles shared the light and heat that was given to them, a similar but even more vivid image occurs: "Sermo ille illorum apostolorum fuit evangelium; sermo et oratio lucida et calida ab igneis hominibus profecta, quae discussit ignoranciae tenebras, et peccatorum ac impietatis frigus superavit, fecitque quos apprehendit sapientia et amore Dei perlucere." ("The speech of those Apostles was the Gospel; a speech and language full of light and heat, as pro-ceeding from men themselves on fire; and it dispelled the shades of ignorance, and mastered the chillness of sins and wickedness, and caused those on whom it seized to be all aglow with wisdom and the love of God." *Romans* XII. 187; 75.) In *Romans* viii the action of the Spirit is described specifically as a heating action: "Eos quidem, id est, eorum summas mentes suaviter et dulciter agitat spiritus, ac mirifice quasi calefaciendo inspiran-doque primum aliquantulum amoris emollit et extenuat, et, si sic liceat loqui in talibus rebus incorporeis, quodammodo rarefacit, ut intus et intime luceant valde et concaleant." ("Upon them, indeed (that is, upon the surface of their minds) the Spirit works pleasantly and sweetly; and by heating, as it were, and breathing upon them in a way past our understanding, first thaws and liquefies some little extent of love, and (if we may use such a term in immaterial things like these) in a measure rarefies it, to the end that they may have full light and heat in their very inmost depths." Pp. 154; 27.)

28. This proverbial analogy is a favorite with Colet. In *Romans* he expresses the same thought but with the sense of taste rather than sight: " . . . ad eundem ferme modum quo egrotis salubria insalubria, et febricitantibus suavia amara . . ." (" . . . much in the same way as to sick people wholesome things become unwholesome, and to the feverish sweets appear bitter . . ." IX–X. 164; 42). He finds the source of this image in Isaiah v: 20.

29. It is "doubtful" in the sense that the reference may be taken two ways, as Colet indicates; but either way, the paradox is plain enough: to the wisdom of this world (i.e., the Greeks) it was a foolish act, a weak act, to use a crucified man for the ac-complishment of God's will; yet God did just that, thereby accomplishing what was impossible to human wisdom and might. God's revelation, thought to be foolish and weak, is therefore stronger than man's strongest work. Cf. F. W. Grosheide, *Commen-tary on the First Epistle to the Corinthians*, NIC, p. 50; NCC, 869q.

30. The allusion is to God's creative act, the only act by which something is made *ex nihilo* (O'Kelly). But of course in this context Colet is speaking of man's spiritual development, not the metaphysical structures of the universe. To express it this way, however, underlines Colet's constant stress on man's inability to do anything by his own powers.

31. This rhetorical figure of *commutatio* (Lat. "potens sapientia et sapiens potentia") seems to have been a favorite with Colet. Cf. its frequent use in *Romans*: "misericordi justicia et justa misericordia" ("merciful justice and just mercy," VII. 151; 23); "benigna Dei justicia et justa benignitate" ("merciful justice and just mercy of God," IX–X. 159; 35); "una et pulchra bonitas, et bona ac pulchra unitas, et una ac bona pulchritudo"

("one and beautiful goodness, and good and beautiful oneness, and one and good beautifulness," XII. 183; 69). But this manner of expression is for Colet more than a play on words. He wants to show the close association of the properties of things—as for example in *Cel. Hier.* when he is describing the attributes of the angels: Seraphic Spirits are "wise loves," Cherubic Spirits are "loving wisdoms," etc. (VII. 20).

32. This is one of the passages which have made some readers challenge Colet's right to be called a Christian humanist. But when he speaks of man in this way, he is not describing the human condition as one may consider it when abstracting conceptually from the existence of God and the nature of man's relationship to God. The Godless condition he describes is, as it were, a state of existence in which men are positively deprived of the necessary help of God in everything they initiate. Since God is the source of all good, there can be no good from any other source, but only the absence of good, i.e., evil, in a sense. Conversely, whenever and wherever there is true good in men's acts, this must be ascribed to the goodness of God. Colet's language deserves close attention, too. Here the antithesis is clear. In comparison with the being of God, man's being is nothingness; in comparison with God's wisdom, man's wisdom is unwisdom, and so on. From a man who believed in an infinite God, such statements are not, after all, so startling, provided one bear in mind the norm by which human being and activity are measured. There is no implicit contradiction here of the central affirmation that God created man in His own image and likeness, or that human existence and activity are of such great value to God that the Incarnation is a historical fact. All of Colet's writings bear continual and emphatic testimony to the literally immense importance of human existence and actions, an importance to be gauged by the fact of God's having chosen to become a man for the sake of all men (O'Kelly). See Intro., p. 55. Man's nothingness is here deliberately contrasted to God's perfections. By making this contrast Colet emphasizes the need for a mediator. The fact that this mediator became incarnate not only dignifies human nature, but makes possible the opening of that nature to a higher kind of life: "utque Deo assimilati, dii evadamus" ("that we . . . being made like God, may become gods"—*Corinthians*, I. p. 87). Such passages provide the perspective in which Colet's insistence on man's "nothingness" must be understood.

Chapter II

1. It is important always to note the context in which Colet speaks of the "world." Here the context embraces both the spatial and the temporal conceptualizations adverted to by Paul as antithetical to the non-spatial, non-temporal God, as in I: 27 (*mundus*: κόσμος) and II: 6 (*saeculum*: αἰῶν). Cf. VII, p. 163, and Colet's reference to I John II: 16; also Intro., pp. 31–33, 42 for the contrast between human and divine wisdom as Colet sees it; also *Romans* IX–X, and Lefèvre on I Cor. I: 13–14 (*Epistole divi Pauli apostoli cum commentariis*, Paris, 1517). But in another sense, also founded on scriptural (and liturgical) passages, the world (*mundus, rerum universitas*) is for Colet God's creation rather than an antithesis to God, and consequently entirely good, although sometimes he speaks of it as good only in its original state and to the extent that Christ is restoring and will restore it to its original state (see *De Sac.*, p. 62). Colet refers without qualification to the world as God's Temple several times in this work: pp. 39–41, 43f., 46f. There is perhaps an attempt to bridge the two views in *Edmund's Romans*: "Voco hominem

hujus mundi eum qui natus est in hunc mundum ad mortem, non renatus gracia et bap-
tismo ad immortalitatem in Christo Iesu. Qui vero regenitus est Deo ex aqua et spiritu
sancto, is homo alterius mundi est, illius celestis et superni." ("By the man of this world
I mean the one who is born into this world unto death, not born again by grace and
baptism unto immortality in Christ Jesus. But the one who is born again to God, of
water and the Holy Ghost, is a man of another world, even the heavenly and supernal."
P. 235; p. 98.)

2. Like most of his contemporaries Colet accepted the medieval tradition ascribing
four Greek treatises on Neoplatonic theology to a certain Dionysius supposedly converted by Paul's preaching on the Areopagus in Athens; hence he is called the Areopagite.
To Colet, Dionysius was therefore an important link between Paul and later Christianity, one who could help us understand Paul better. For Colet's intellectual debt to
Dionysius, see Intro., pp. 18, 40.

3. Colet does not mean by these apparently extreme statements to disparage unduly
man's God-given human nature but rather to emphasize the difference between what
is divine and what is human. Since the difference is in kind, not merely in degree, only
grace from God can bridge this gap. To "leave off being a man" means that human
powers are simply inadequate to reach God by themselves. Cf. Romans ix–x.

4. Without a spiritual re-formation, man cannot grasp the things of God. Cf. Intro.,
pp. 41–46.

5. "Θεάνθρωπος" is Origen's word, coined by him to express the very close union
of the two natures in Christ. In Letters to Radulphus IV, 182, Colet refers to the Contra
Celsum, one of the works in which Origen uses the word, but Colet may have met
it first in derivative works, although I know of no evidence for Jayne's assumption (pp.
32f) that Colet adopted the word directly from Ficino. A Latin equivalent, Deus homo
or Deushomo, is used by Colet in Edmund's Romans (p. 272) and elsewhere. See Berthold
Altaner, Patrology p. 232, on Origen's use of the word (O'Kelly).

6. Cf. Ecc. Hier. p. 226, where in an analogous account of Christ's victory Colet uses
very similar wording: "sine querela diaboli justa" ("without giving any just cause of
complaint to the devil" – p. 92). Cf. Anselm's concern in Cur Deus Homo, c. viii (PL
158) to demonstrate that Satan had no just claim to mankind.

7. Cf. n. 6 above.

8. Colet's language here recalls Rev. xii: 3–8, describing the battle between the powers
of light and darkness at the end of the world. The primeval strife between good and
evil, familiar in many cosmological myths of the Near East, was transformed even in
the OT into eschatological doctrine (cf. Isa. xi: 6–8; lxv: 25). Cf. ICC Rev., 1:318.
Here Colet gives a moral interpretation of the ancient symbolism, identifying the evil
principles with injustice and ignorance. Cf. also Cel. Hier. xvi. 43–47.

9. Lat. "predestinatum ante secula in gloria nostra." The NEB translation makes the
meaning clearer: "I speak God's hidden wisdom, his secret purpose framed from the
very beginning to bring us to our full glory" (I Cor. ii: 7).

10. Unity is a requirement for perfection; see Intro. pp. 46–48.

11. On the equation of hope with oneness or fixed being, see pp. 147–51 and n. 25
to Chap. VII below; De Sac., pp. 79–83; Ecc. Hier., p. 240; Romans xii. 182. In the
Epistles, the most clear identification of hope with stability is probably Heb. vi: 18f.,
a passage which fits admirably the context Colet establishes here and in the following

paragraph of a restless, fishlike wandering in a dark, ceaselessly moving world of water. The language is characteristically obscure, but the Vulgate text might be translated (very literally): "So that through two immovable things [God's word and His oath] by which it is impossible for God to lie, we have a most strong consolation, we who fly for refuge to the hope set before us for us to hold; this hope we have as a safe and sure anchor of the soul. . . ." For the further relation of hope with the purgative way, faith with the illuminative way, and charity with the unitive way, see *De Sac.*, p. 77 (O'Kelly).

12. Lat. *stabiliter sit* in contrast to the fragmented, distracted condition of the sinner; cf. Intro. p. 46, and Colet's deprecation of this "fluctuating world, with divided souls and scattered thoughts," below.

13. One must recall here the hierarchy of the four elements. To be moved from water to air is to have one's metaphysical state transformed for the better. What lives by nature in the air is superior to what lives in water. The further down a creature is in the water, the worse off it is, because the further removed from the air and the light. There is an interesting passage by Clement of Alexandria (*Stromata*, PG 8, 1005) on the sorry condition of the fish deepest in the water. See also the Migne editor's note 69 *ad loc.* for a passage in the letter of Barnabas: " . . . Those little fishes, alone accursed, roll themselves about in the depth, and do not swim like the rest, but dwell on the earth which is at the bottom of the sea." Cf. p. 95, where Colet, resuming his metaphor, speaks of the worst of mankind, the lowest dregs, dwelling on the bottom, far from the light (O'Kelly).

14. Lat. "O misera hominum et perdita condicio," a favorite expression of Colet's; see e.g., p. 122. It is not, of course, original with him. Among dozens of authors in whose works Colet could have seen such expressions, Ficino uses closely analogous turns of phrase in several letters marked by Colet, and in others not marked (*Epistolae*, pp. 668, 779, 815).

Here Colet's wording and thought are closer to those of Jerome: "O miserabilis humana conditio, et sine Christo vanum omne quod vivimus!" ("O how miserable is our human condition, and in vain everything that we experience without Christ!" Ep. LX, *Ad Heliodorum*, PL 22, 598). Colet may be thinking of Rom. vii: 24 (O'Kelly).

15. Colet continues to see Paul in the historical context of his preaching to the Corinthians. The city was notorious for its moral corruption, largely because of the sacred prostitution connected with the temple of Aphrodite on the Acropolis. Many Greek and Oriental cults flourished there (NCE v. 4, 325).

16. This is the reason behind the commonplace that the weak and powerless in this world are those most pleasing to God. In keeping with Colet's doctrine of form is his insistence that dispositions contrary to God prevent the re-formation of the soul by grace, which is the foundation of its spiritual growth; cf. *Romans* ix–x.

17. The implication here that without exception if a man is not acted on by God's power he is acted on by the Devil's Colet makes explicit in *Ecc. Hier.*: "Qui non est agitatus a Spiritu Dei, ut filius Dei sit, is necessario a diaboli spiritu agitatur ut filius diaboli sit." ("He that is not moved by the Spirit of God, to be a child of God, is necessarily moved by the spirit of the devil, to be a child of the devil." Pp. 218; 80.) Colet's ultimate authority for this absolutist dichotomy might well be the words of Christ to Paul as reported by Paul to Agrippa in Acts xxvi: 18: "To open the eyes [of the Gentiles] that they may be turned from the darkness to the light and from the power of Satan to

God . . ." (O'Kelly). Cf. Rom. xiv: 23; also Intro., pp. 48–50 for the relation between this absolutist dichotomy and the principles of Colet's Christian morality.

18. The link between Colet's Platonism and his spiritual doctrine is very apparent here. To be enlightened means to receive and reflect the divine. It is grace with its form-ative power that makes man capable of becoming such a reflector—and even more a participator of the divine life. Cf. Intro., pp. 42–47. Erasmus expresses a similar view in his *Enchiridion*: "Spiritum vero qua Divinae naturae similitudinem exprimimus, in qua conditor optimus, de suae mentis archetypo, aeternam illam honesti legem insculpsit digito, hoc est, Spiritu suo. Hac Deo conglutinamur, unamque cum eo reddimur." (". . . the spirit by which we truly express the likeness of the divine nature in which the supreme Builder, from the archetype of his mind, inscribed that eternal law of righteousness with his finger, that is, with his spirit. By this we are joined firmly with God and made one with him." LB V, 19B.) Payne demonstrates the Platonic basis of Erasmus' view of man, and credits Colet with having "passed on to Erasmus the revived Platonism of the Florentine Academy" (*op. cit.*, p. 36).

19. Colet's brief exposition here of the "rationes et dispositiones" contrary to those of God depends largely on the light-darkness imagery, as in Eph. vi: 18–13, for exam-ple, or Victorinus: "Hoc est enim, et lucem esse, et filium lucis esse, bonitate praestare, praestare justitia, praestare etiam veritate. Haec tria ipsa sunt lux: nam contra sunt tenebrae malitia, injustitia, falsitas: quae omnia diabolo conveniunt: at vero haec lucis sunt, quia lux est Christus." ("For this is what it means to be light and to be a son of the light: to excel in goodness, to excel in justice, to excel in truth. These three things are themselves the light, for contrary to them are the malice, injustice, and falsehood of darkness, and all of these belong to the Devil. But those others belong to the light, because the light is Christ." PL 8, 1285). Cf. Intro., pp. 45f.

20. A common metaphor for Christ which Colet uses frequently; cf. especially *Cel. Hier.* ii. 7–8, where Christ is the "Sun of the Church," the "Sun of Righteousness."

21. On the calling of the Apostles and their spiritual superiority, see also *Romans* xii, 76.

22. For an analogous development, see Ficino, *Liber de sole*, ix: "Denique sicut nihil alienus est a luce divina, quam materia prorsus informis, ita nihil a luce Solis diversius est, quam terra. Ideo corpora in quibus terrea conditio praevalet, tanquam ineptissima luci, lumen nullum intus accipiunt. Non quia sit impotens lumen ad penetrandum. . . . Ita divinum lumen etiam in tenebris animae lucet, sed tenebrae non comprehendunt, non & hoc habet simile Deo?" ("Finally, just as nothing is more alien to the divine light than utterly formless matter, so there is nothing more unlike the light of the sun than the earth. For that reason, a condition prevails in which earthly bodies, as if most unsuited for the light, receive no light from within, but not because the light is powerless to penetrate. . . . So divine light shines even in the darkness of the mind, but the darkness does not comprehend it . . ." *Opera*, I, 971). Colet, like Ficino, seems here concerned to stress the fact that where grace does not penetrate efficaciously, the explanation lies in the ineptitude of the recipient, not in any limitation of Divine power or the Divine benevolence toward men (O'Kelly).

23. Cf. *Romans* xii. 82–85, and *Cel. Hier.* v, where Colet describes this same kind of diffusion by degrees through men who are God's instruments.

24. Lat. "si fieri posit," amended by Meghen to "possit." Lupton, while keeping the reading of Gg. iv. 26, translates "if it were possible . . ." (p. 23). Apart from gram-matical inaccuracy, this translation implies that Colet believed it impossible for some

men to be saved, and this is to attribute to him an opinion which he elsewhere de-
nounces with the utmost vigor, the belief that an infinitely good God should give
any man a command which that man cannot obey (see p. 163). The contingency expressed here must, then, have regard to the extreme obduracy with which some men
deliberately oppose the truth. Perhaps the best equivalent of "si fieri posit" would be
"if they could." The next sentence makes altogether clear Colet's belief that salvific
grace is extended to all men, though not all men cooperate with it (O'Kelly). Cf.
Romans IX–X.

25. This is not just a moralistic comment, but a corollary of Colet's metaphysical
principle that stability is good and fluctuation is not (see n. 12 above).

26. See Ficino's commentary on Paul, *Ascensus ad tertium caelum, ad Paulum intelligendum* (*Opera*, I [1576]). Lupton suggests that Colet might have heard some of Ficino's
lectures on Paul in Florence, but Jayne assumes that he did not visit Ficino's Academy
(*op. cit.*, p. 18).

27. Cf. n. 24 to Chap. I above.

28. This is a common scholastic axiom which Colet has used before (p. 157). Cf.
St. Thomas Aquinas, ST I–I, Q. 75, a. 5, *et passim*.

29. Lat. "vel eligitur vel reprobatur"; but to translate the phrase "elect or reprobate,"
as Lupton does (p. 28), seems unavoidably to involve what Colet says with connotations and overtones these words acquired only after his death. Clearly Colet here is putting the question of "predestination" beyond the range of human discussion or inquiry,
while affirming the central fact of God's justice and mercy. Elsewhere he makes amply
clear his conviction that no one is damned except through his own fault, that God wills
every man to be saved, and that Christ died for all men. On the other hand, he makes
equally clear his conviction that no one can lay the least claim to responsibility for his
own salvation, since only by God's freely given grace can any man be saved. To use
Colet's terminology, then, a man's state of "reprobation" is his willing and deliberate
acceptance of "principles at enmity with God," and his failure to cooperate with God's
graces, which he does not deserve, but which are freely offered to him (O'Kelly). Cf.
Romans: "Quod si curiosius vestiget curnam salvantur alii, alii vero condempnabuntur,
nullam aliam reperiet causam, nisi salutis esse graciam, damnationis vero esse hominis
improbitatem; indignissimosque salute divina benignitate et gracia esse salvos, dignissimos
morte juste et peccati jure esse damnatos." ("And if any one were to search never so
carefully, why some are saved, and others will be condemned; he would find no other
reason than this, namely, that grace is the cause of salvation, man's guilt the cause of
condemnation." IX–X. 168; 48.)

30. Yet Colet does investigate the problem of predestination in more detail: e.g., *Romans*
IX–X with reference to the story of Esau and Jacob, *Cel. Hier.* IX. 29, etc. Erasmus comments on disputes regarding predestination in his *Annotationes* on Rom. VIII and XI: 2.
He too concentrates on God's ultimate will for the salvation of all mankind in his discussion
of the word *praescivit* (Gr. προέγνω). The prefix προ "referri potest ad aeternam illam
praedestinationem, quae fuit antequam Iudaeorum populus nasceretur, aut ad gentes
posterius vocatas ad evangelii gratiam . . ." ("can be referred to that eternal predestination, which was before the people of the Jews were born, or to the descendants later
called to the grace of the gospel . . ." LB VI, 621). God's foreknowledge of man's good
works is logically prior to his election of the saved. In this respect Payne finds that Erasmus'
position is similar to that of Occam (*op. cit.*, p. 81).

Chapter III

1. Colet begins this chapter with a diagram followed by some descriptive definitions. Other diagrams occur throughout the work. They are a reminder that we are not sure of the exact circumstances of the composition of this commentary; some of it may have been intended as lecture notes, which he later expanded. See Intro., p. 19.

2. In this metaphor of building and testing by fire, Colet somewhat amplifies Paul's text (3:15). Fire is the customary biblical figure of speech describing the power of God's judgment, and in this context it could suggest a kind of purgatory (JBC II, p. 259). But Erasmus' note on this passage (*Annotationes*, LB VI, 671) cites a number of authorities against this interpretation, and refers to Ambrose's suggestion that the testing by fire is the searching out and confutation of wrong doctrine. The work that shall be burned is false and deceptive teaching that is not in accord with Christ's revelation. Colet's condemnation in this paragraph of those who rely on themselves rather than God, seeking to add something of their own to the building of the Church, seems more in accord with this interpretation than with an idea of purgatory, although a personal, moral purgation with the Holy Spirit as agent is suggested on p. 105. Erasmus adds the quaint observation that "fire" might refer to the shame a man feels when he discovers that he has been defending what is wrong. Erasmus too refers to Isaiah, but chooses a different verse (I: 31): "And the strong shall become tow, and his work a spark, and both of them shall burn together, with none to quench them." Cf. Lupton's note, pp. 30–31. In his *Paraphrases*, Erasmus goes one step further and brings the two interpretations together by making moral strength in this life (rather than purgatorical cleansing hereafter) the object of the "searching fire," which thereby exposes false doctrine and vindicates the true in a pragmatic way: "Sed uniuscujusque opus, cum propius admotum fuerit ad lucem veritatis, & regulam Evangelicam, palam arguetur quale sit. Si doctrina, quae accessit, reddat vos invictos ad omnes humanos affectus, palam est efficacem esse: si reddit imbecilles ad ferenda incommoda, si irritabiles, si morosos, si contentiosos, si obtrectatores, si fucatos, hinc satis liquet adulterinam fuisse doctrinam." ("But anyone's work, when it has been fittingly applied to the light of truth, and the Evangelical rule, will be shown for what it really is. If the teaching which accompanies it should make you incorruptible in the face of all human passions, it is clear that it is efficacious. But if it makes [you] indisposed to bear misfortunes, or irritable, or sour, disparaging, hypocritical, false, this clearly shows it to be a false doctrine." LB VII, 868.) Lefèvre's comment on this passage also refers to the sifting of doctrine. True doctrine is gold, precious stones, and silver, which will not burn. False and pernicious doctrine is wood, stubble, etc. But the "searching" is postponed until the Day of Judgment, which will reveal those who have taught truly, and their people who have been well taught: ". . . in eodem igne iusti nichil patientur: sed salvabuntur quasi per ignem quasi indicio ignis et igne ultionis eosdem iustos demonstrante." (". . . in the same fire none of the just will suffer: but they will be saved as if through fire, as by a sign of fire, and by an avenging fire, showing them to be just." *Epistole divi Pauli apostoli cum commentariis . . .* [1517] fol. lxxxvii-r.)

3. As Lupton points out (p. 30, n.) this speculation rests on a faulty copy of I Cor. to which Colet referred. For *sic* in the phrase *ipse autem salvus erit, sic tamen quasi per ignem* (3: 15), Colet's copy must have had *si.* (Lefèvre and Erasmus read *sic*). Oddly, Lupton complicates the matter by misquoting the verse itself, leaving out the word *tamen*

in his note. The last part of the sentence, *vel significat corruptos purgatos fore, corruptores damnatos*, is written in the right margin, and beside it is the uneven line which seems always to indicate in MS Gg. iv. 26 that the words so marked are to be taken as part of the text. Neither Meghen nor Lupton reproduced this afterthought (O'Kelly). Modern translations clarify the meaning of the biblical phrase: NEB: "yet he will escape with his life, as one might from a fire;" RSV: "but only as through fire."

4. Lat. "in intelligibilibus." Erasmus draws the distinction between the intelligible world and the world of sense in his *Enchiridion*: "Duos igitur quosdam mundos imagine-mur, alterum intelligibilem tantum, alterum visibilem. Intelligibilem, quem & Angeli-cum licebit appellare, in quo Deus cum beatis mentibus: Visibilem, coelestes sphaeras, & quod in his includitur . . . Quod sol hic in mundo visibili, id divina mens in mundo intelligibile, et in ei cognata tui parte, puta, spiritu. Quod illic luna, hoc in illo coetus Angelorum, et animarum piarum, quam vocant Ecclesiam triumphantem, hoc et in te spiritus." ("Let us picture to ourselves, then, two kinds of worlds: one accessible only to the understanding, the other to the sight. The intelligible world, which we may call the angelic, is the one in which God dwells with the most blessed minds. The visi-ble is made up of the heavenly spheres and whatever is included in them . . . What this visible sun is to the visible world, the celestial Mind is to the intelligible world and to that part of you which corresponds to it, namely, the spirit. What the moon there is to the one world, the society of angels and blessed souls which we call the Church Triumphant is to the other, and this the spirit is in you." Canon V, LB V 27 E–F; trans. Raymond Himelick, *The Enchiridion of Erasmus* [Bloomington, Ind.: In-diana Univ. Press, 1963], pp. 101–102.) Pico draws a three-fold distinction in his *Hep-taplus*: "Tres mundos figurat antiquitas. Supremum omnium ultra mundanum, quem theologi angelicum, philosophi autem intellectualem vocant, quem a nemine satis pro dignitate decantatum Plato inquit in *Phaedro*. Proximum huic caelestem; postremum om-nium sublunarem hunc, quem nos incolimus." ("Antiquity imagined three worlds. Highest of all is that ultra-mundane one which theologians call the angelic and philosophers the intelligible, and of which, Plato says in the *Phaedrus* [247c] no one has worthily sung. Next to this comes the celestial world, and last of all, this sublunary one which we inhabit." Second Proem; *Heptaplus*, ed. Eugenio Garin [Firenze: Vallecchi Editore, 1942], p. 184; trans. Douglas Carmichael [New York: Bobbs-Merrill Co., 1965], p. 75.) Dionysius explains how man, through the unification of his intellectual powers, may perceive intuitively as the angels do, and thereby gain an insight into the Divine Wisdom. (*Divine Names*, VII, p. 65) See Intro., p. 40.

5. Freedom in the sense of being able to perform to the height of one's powers, and to respond fully to God's gift of grace, is one of the most positive aspects of Colet's spiritual doctrine. See *Romans* VIII where he speaks of those chosen ones who are called "ad id libertatis in hoc mundo, ut possint amare Deum, et ei confidere, ac illius liberalitatem expectare" ("to such liberty in this world as to be able to love God, and trust in him, and wait for his bounty"—p. 154; 27). See also n. 64 to Chap. VII below.

6. See *De Sac.* VIII. 79 for Colet's description of the integration of the truly spiritual man. The phrase, "loftiest part of their minds," mentioned immediately below, probab-ly refers to the intellect, which Ficino calls the "highest part of the soul" in the passage from his *Platonic Theology* (Bk. XIV) quoted by Colet in *Romans* VIII. 155.

7. The decrease of excellence as a thing moves from unity to multiplicity is a central theme in Colet's metaphysical and spiritual doctrine; cf. Intro. p. 46; VII, pp. 147,

179; XII, p. 239; *Romans* XII. 60, 65, 69–88; *Ecc. Hier.* II. 72. Ficino sees the soul as the principle that unites the diverse elements of the body (*Theologia Platonica* I. 245). In *De Cor.* Colet applies this principle to the Holy Spirit's power to unite the Church, without which it would disperse into fragments (p. 36).

Chapter IV

1. The "minister" (RSV, NEB, "steward") is charged with the administration of goods or property which belong to his master, not to himself; hence it is an appropriate designation for those charged with preaching Christ's doctrine, not their own. This emphasis on stewardship rather than power is a common theme among Church reformers of all ages; see Colet's application of it to the ecclesiastical power structure of his time in his *Convocation Sermon*: "And fyrste for to speake of pride of lyfe: howe moche gredynes and appetite of honour and dignitie is nowe a dayes in men of the churche? . . . that they seme nat to be put in the humble bysshoprike of Christe, but rather in the high lordship and power of the worlde, nat knowing nor advertisinge what Christe the mayster of all mekenes sayd unto his disciples, whom he called to be bysshoppes and prestes: The princis of people (sayth he) haue lordshyp of them, and those that be in auctorite haue power; but do ye nat so: but he that is greatter amonge you, let him be minister; he that is highest in dignitie, be he the seruant of all men. 'The sonne of man came nat to be minystred unto but to ministre.' (Matt. xx: 28). By whiche wordes our Sauiour doth playnly teache that the maistry in the churche is none other thynge than a ministration, and the hygh dignitie in a man of the churche to be none other thing than a meke seruice" (In Lupton, *Life of Dean Colet*, App. C, p. 295). Lefèvre changes "ministros" of the Vulgate into "famulos" but keeps "dispensatores." He too emphasizes the idea of stewardship. The "servus Christi" is the "organum distributionis gratiarum eius" (*op. cit.*, [1517] fol. lxxxvii–v).

2. Lefèvre's comment on 4:16 emphasizes, perhaps more than Colet does, the active element in this imitation: "Et qui vult bonus esse imitator: nunquam in exemplo quiescere debet sed in exemplo ipsam semper attendere veritatem ipsumque obiectum. Et ad hoc ipsum ut digne imitarentur Christum secundum vias Pauli: misit eis Timotheum . . ." ("And he who wishes to be a good imitator ought never to rest in an example, but in the example he ought to apply his mind to the truth itself and to the object. This was the reason why Paul sent Timothy to [the people], so that they might imitate his ways, according to Christ" *op. cit.* [1517] fol. lxxxvii–v).

Chapter V

1. Colet clarifies the sense in which Paul is using "leaven" here, to mean that which causes something to spoil, a corrupting evil influence. Behind the metaphor is the Jewish custom of destroying all leaven in preparation for the paschal feast. This usage is contrary to the Gospel sense of "leaven" as a symbol of the inner dynamism of the Kingdom of God.

2. Colet uses "form" again in the scholastic sense of that which makes a thing to be what it is. By taking on the form of Christ, the Christian's whole life is reorganized

and redirected, becoming an entirely new entity. See Intro., pp. 44f; *Romans* VI. 14; XII. 190: "In quo est valde animadvertendum quidem Deum tale, et ex talibus ex quibus ille vult hominibus, corpus ecclesiamque sibi construere, quos ipse non solum inspiravit reformavitque in parte suo corpori digna, sed preterea effecit ut ad reformacionem apti essent, et divinae formae vitaeque capaces." ("Wherein it must be heedfully noted, that God fashions for himself a body, namely the Church, such, and of such men, as he wills; men whom he has not only inspired and reformed in a measure befitting his body, but has also rendered fit for reformation, and capable of receiving the divine form and life." P. 80.) See also *Ecc. Hier.* I. 54–55.

3. In this sentence Colet deftly combines Paul's metaphor of the leaven that corrupts with his own Platonic principle of simplicity, oneness, and purity as essential to perfection, and admixture as signifying imperfection; see n. 7 to Chap. III above.

4. An example of the use of Scripture in an anagogical sense; cf. Colet's remarks on the traditional "four senses" of Scriptural interpretation in *Ecc. Hier.* V. 105–107. Lefèvre also adds a very similar anagogical interpretation to I Cor. v: 6–8: "Si enim filii Israel in figura in immolatione paschatis sui exierunt Aegyptum: tanto magis nos verum pacha [*sic*] habentes debemus exisse hunc mundum & sequi agnum nostrum immaculatum in montibus aeternitatis. . . ." ("For if the sons of Israel figuratively went forth from Egypt in the immolation of the paschal victim itself, so much more ought we, having this paschal victim, to have gone forth from this world and to follow our immaculate lamb into the mountains of eternity. . . ." *Op. cit.* [1517] fol. lxxxix-r.)

5. Lat. "si aliquid sit fermentatius," "if there be anything too far leavened" (O'Kelly). Lupton translates, "Anything less unleavened" (p. 37). Colet continues the metaphor of leaven as a corrupting influence.

6. The uncompromising attitude that Colet expresses here is reflected in other places where he talks about the malice of sin. In *Romans* VI he refers to I Cor.v: 5 as a partial answer to the question of whether a man can be saved if he relapses into sin after having once been redeemed. In spite of Paul's severity, Colet draws a positive conclusion: "Nunquam enim censuisset revocandum ad ecclesiam fornicatorem illum, quem tradidit Sathanae in prima epistola ad Corinthios, si peccatoribus post baptismum nullum penitendi locum reliquisset." ("For he would never have decided that the fornicator, whom in his first Epistle to the Corinthians he delivered up to Satan, should be recalled to the Church, had he left no room for repentance to them that sin after baptism." P. 145; 14.) Excommunication does not mean damnation; it is a drastic remedy for the protection of the community and the eventual healing of the hardened sinner.

Chapter VI

1. On the unity of the Church, which for Colet is essential to its perfection, see *Romans* XII. 71, 75; *De Cor.*, pp. 35–37; *Ecc. Hier.* II. 72.

2. Colet applies this criticism of the Corinthian church to the church of his own day, which was certainly concerned with "worldly things," property rights, etc. Cf. *Convocation Sermon, op. cit.*, p. 296. The digression in the following paragraphs is more than a conventional diatribe against the Church's well-known materialism. Colet's main point is that a temporal concern for property rights, and the legal wrangling that goes with it, lessen the Church's credibility as witness to the Gospel. Then when the Church uses

force to maintain its supposed institutional prerogatives, instead of inspiring love, it becomes unworthy of its founder and its mission. Since it was this kind of shortsightedness, as well as specific abuses, that helped to bring on the Reformation, Seebohm (Chaps. IV and VII) hails Colet's criticisms in this vein as steps toward a new Protestantism. See Intro., p. 13.

3. In this context the phrase suggests not only the whole economy of salvation, but also the Christian perspective which considers the things of this world—i.e., legal justice in human terms—*sub specie aeternitatis.*

4. Cf. p. 93 and n. 13 to Chap. II below for Colet's previous use of a similar comparison. He might also have in mind, as Lupton points out, (p. 39), Aristotle's observation (*De part. Anima* II. 14) that since fish have no eyelids, they see through a tough outer membrane.

5. Like his predecessors in the struggle against ecclesiastical corruption, Colet here recalls the Church to its only true source of power and authority. Love is its foundation and the best motivation by which its wealth is gathered. Colet goes on to show how the self-serving greed now threatening the Church ultimately defeats its own purposes too. Cf. J. L. McKenzie, *Authority in the Church*, p. 150.

6. Colet's uses of *capitium*, the opening in an ecclesiastical vestment through which the head passes, is probably intended as a synecdoche here. Lupton changes Colet's word to *caputium* (p. 187), and translates it "hoods" (p. 41) (O'Kelly).

7. In *Romans* XIV Colet repeats some of the same warnings against property that he mentions here, "Quia non est ecclesia decimae et oblaciones," (p. 218), and he quotes the same phrase from the Psalms (p. 117).

8. In *Romans* XIII, when Paul is advising the Christians in Rome how to live in the midst of a pagan society, Colet emphasizes how he urges them to return good for evil instead of insisting on their rights (pp. 92–95). See Lupton's note on *Corinthians*, VI. 43.

9. The use of *malum* here for something that falls short of the best (*ab optimo*) may seem rather severe; it almost suggests that marriage and payment for services rendered are wrong. Unrealistic as this may sound, it fits in with Colet's Platonic ideas of perfection, according to which any admixture, any diversity, detracts from the pure simplicity that perfect goodness must have. See Intro., p. 48. This idea is combined with love as the "altogether unfailing standard by which all things are to be directed" (see below). The two concepts are beautifully combined in *De Sac.*: "Hic in Deo vera bonitas est, et bona veritas; in hominis anima idem radius est fidelis amor Deo et amans fides. Sed ut nihil possit lucere et calere nisi prius sit—est autem quodque simplicitate et veritate, nam divisio et multiplicitas mors est—ut aliquid ergo illuminetur fide, et concaleat amore Dei et proximi, oportet illud recreetur prius, quasi ex nihilo, et a multiplicitate pulvereque ad simplicitatem, a divisione morteque ad veritatem et vitam contrahatur . . ." ("Here in God is true goodness, and good truth; likewise, in the soul of man this ray [of God] is faithful love and loving faith in God. But just as nothing can illuminate and warm [anything] unless it is prior [to it]—so is it in simplicity and truth, for division and multiplicity are death—if someone is therefore illuminated by faith, and warms with love of God and neighbor, it follows that he be first re-created, as if from nothing, and be drawn away from multiplicity and fragmentation toward simplicity, from division and death toward truth and life . . ."—VIII. 79). Elsewhere he explicitly views moral conduct in absolute terms; any course of action short of the best is sinful unless a man cannot possibly help it. "In not effecting what is best, there is room for indulgence;

but, beyond that, not to wish for what is best, or to refuse it when offered to us, is unpardonable" (*Edmund's Romans*, p. 110).

10. "Unjust" in the sense of pagans who have not been "justified" according to the Christian meaning of redemption—not necessarily unjust in matters of law.

11. The Book of Enoch speaks of a judgment pronounced by the Son of Man on angels and men. Associated with him, the elect will also participate in his judgment. Cf. Dan. VII: 17–18 (JBC II, 261).

12. Beginning with this text, there is a marked difference in the handwriting. It is much looser, much less disciplined. The change might indicate an interval in the composition, perhaps a long one. The reader will notice that while Colet takes up again Paul's instructions about lawsuits, he bases his comments on a different principle, although this may represent nothing other than an effort to establish the unity of Paul's chapter by making the rather abrupt VI: 12 apply retroactively to 1–8 (while anticipating its recurrence in X: 18–33) (O'Kelly).

13. In *Romans* XII Colet shows how Paul similarly exhorts the Romans to divest themselves of self and submit to the "divine reformation" (p. 58). It is in this context that the warning given below, not to attempt anything of and for oneself, needs to be read. The Romans are told that "ut non deinceps nunc propriam, sed divinam in se voluntatem habere ostendant, Deumque in ipsis regnare, quae ipsa est bonitas ipsa et perfectio . . ." ("that they should henceforth show that they have now not their own will, but the will of God in them, and that God reigns in them, who is goodness and perfectness itself . . ." XII. 176; 59).

14. A fuller explanation of this process is given in *Romans*: "Nam quo fertur una hominis pars, vel corpus vel anima, illuc statim totus homo trahitur; sic ut totus aut sursum aut deorsum tendat necesse est. Illuc si sursum tendat humilis et confidens Deo, apprehensus a spiritu trahetur altius, et supra se quadam in divina condicione sustinebitur, anima divino spiritu, corpore animae jugiter serviente . . . Nam corpore reformato anima, factoque (ut ita dicam) *animali*, id est, quatenus ejus crassitas patitur, simili naturae animae, statim ipsa deinde anima, si confidat Deo, Deumque amet, divina gracia et spiritu reformatur, fitque spiritualis et naturae Dei similis, totusque homo pulchre redigitur sursum in statum divinum, quum anima in Deum, corpus in animam incumbat, extatque in terris plane quidam Deus, quandoquidem 'qui adheret Domino,' ut est in Epistola ad Colocenses, 'unus est spiritus'." ("For in what direction one part of man is borne, whether body or soul, thither is the whole man instantly drawn; so that he must needs tend wholly either upwards or downwards. If he tend in that upward direction, humbly and with trust in God, he will be laid hold of by the Spirit and drawn still higher, and his soul will be sustained by the Divine Spirit in a divine state beyond itself; his body being the constant servant of the soul. . . . For when the body is transformed by the soul, and made, so to speak, *soul-like* (that is, so far as its grossness allows, like to the nature of the soul), then at once the soul itself, if it trust in God, and love God, is transformed by the divine grace and Spirit, and becomes spiritual and like to the nature of God; and the whole man is again brought upwards, in fair guise, to a divine state; the soul leaning towards God, the body towards the soul; and there exists upon earth a being that is plainly a god; since 'he that is joined unto the Lord,' as it is in the Epistle to the Colossians, 'is one spirit'." XII. 176–77; 60.) Lupton points out that the reference should be to I Cor. VI: 17, not Colossians (p. 60). Colet summarizes these same ideas in Paul's exhortation to the Corinthians in the paragraph that follows below. Erasmus

similarly sees a series of such transformations, by which the downward pull of the body can be overcome: "Quemadmodum enim divinus Spiritus, nostrum inhabitans spiritum, in eum redundat, et ut est potentior, eum in sese veluti transformat: ita noster spiritus immutatus redundat in corpus, domicilium utique suum; idque quoad licet in sese transformat." ("For just as the divine Spirit, dwelling in our spirit, overflows into it, and as it is more powerful, transforms it into itself: in the same way our spirit, unchanged, overflows into the body, which is, of course, its own dwelling, and in so far as it is able, it [spirit] transforms it [body] into itself." *Enarratio Ps. Beatus Vir*, LB V 192A.) See also Payne, p. 39.

15. It is so because it hinders and obscures man's rationality, as Colet explains below. Cf. St. Thomas, ST II–I, Q. 153, and St. Basil, *Liber de virginitate* (PG 30, col. 678). Augustine warns lest concupiscence negate the only good reason for marriage, the *bonum prolis* (though he does acknowledge several others; see n. 64 to Chap. VII below). After citing the case of Onan, he says, "Propagatio itaque filiorum, ipsa est prima et naturalis et legitima causa nuptiarum: ac per hoc qui propter incontinentiam conjugantur, non sic debent temperare malum suum, ut bonum exterminent nuptiarum, id est, propaginem filiorum." ("The procreation of children is in itself the primary, natural, and legitimate reason for marriage; and for this reason, those who are married on account of incontinence ought not, as things stand, abstain from the evil itself, so that the good of the marriage, that is, the propagation of children, is destroyed." *De Conjugiis Adulterinis*, PL 40, c. xii. 479.) Cf. Intro., pp. 48f.

16. The idea that left to itself the body would slip into sin is a consequence of Colet's metaphysical principles as well as of his theology. The body's downward course has been described above (n. 14). Since the body is a corruptible compound, its parts must be held together by a higher principle. Cf. n. 6 to Chap. III above. Added to the body's natural tendency to dissolution is original sin, with its destructive darkening of the mind and weakening of the will. Colet devotes almost the whole of Chap. VI of *Romans* to a description of the consequences of original sin, man's inability to cure himself, and the incapacity of the Mosaic law to help him. But this dismal picture is continually offset by the power of God's grace, which for Colet is stronger than man's sin at its very worst: "Quapropter credendum est longe plus posse in mundo graciam reconciliantem Deo, quam peccatum a Deo alienans. Quo fit ut multo plus possit justicia et obediencia Christi ad revocandos homines, qui revocandi sunt, Deo, quam peccatum et inobediencia Adae ad eosdem a Deo avocandos. Nam proculdubio vivificacior est virtus multo quam peccatum est mortificans, et auctor virtutis longe potencior est quam peccati causa." ("Wherefore we must believe that grace, which reconciles to God, has far more power in the world than sin, which estranges from God. And hence, that the righteousness and obedience of Christ has far more power to recall to God men who are to be recalled, than the sin and disobedience of Adam had to call them away from God. For without doubt virtue is a much more life-giving thing than sin is deadening, and the Author of virtue far more powerful than the cause of sin." Pp. 142; 10.)

17. Here the Platonic disparagement of corruptible and sinful flesh is lost in the Christian promise of physical resurrection. The split between soul and body is here overcome in an immortal unity. No matter how much he condemns the body and its lusts, the fact of its ultimate resurrection helps to keep Colet from falling too far into an unrealistic dualism.

Chapter VII

1. The chapter heading is missing in the MS. Colet begins instead with the first three words of I Cor. VII. The handwriting degenerates remarkably in this section; perhaps it was written in haste (O'Kelly).

2. Colet no doubt has in mind other passages where Paul alludes to the "diversity of persons" and speaks of the attitudes which the new believers should adopt toward that variety and of the manner in which each is to reconcile pre-Christian status with the new faith. Cf. Col. III: 5 to IV: 6; Gal. III: 25–29; Eph. VI: 1–9. Colet's acknowledgement that diversity has "almost always existed in the human race" is perhaps not so much an indication of historical sophistication as an echo of his belief that diversity, like private property, is a consequence of the "corrupt law of nature," a result of original sin. See *Romans*, pp. 218 ff.; *Edmund's Romans*, pp. 259 f. (O'Kelly).

3. Colet uses this phrase here to indicate their Christian membership. Paul is speaking of married couples in Corinth of whom both or only one might be Christian (vv. 12–17).

4. Lat. "plurimum et diu dubitatum." Colet seems to infer that the uncertainties in the early church over retaining former status and condition were great and long-lasting, from the tentativeness of Paul's treatment of the matter here and in similar passages, e.g. Acts XV: 1–29 (O'Kelly).

5. Colet grounds his long commentary on chap. vii in the context of the Corinthians' situation as a small group of believers living in the midst of a pagan and licentious society. Although he goes on to present the core of his soteriology in this chapter, his starting point is the practical questions to which Paul addresses himself in his letter.

6. Cf. the discussion of this question with its symbolic ramifications in *Romans*, chap. IV and *Edmund's Romans*, Chap. IV.

7. Colet's admiration for Paul was not just intellectual; Jayne conjectures that "he seems to have committed himself to a career of teaching and preaching Paul" (*op. cit.*, p. 39).

8. Cf. the metaphysical basis of Colet's discussion of Christ as exemplar, XIII, p. 261 below, and nn. 11 and 13 to Chap. XIII below.

9. Colet uses I Cor. VII: 6 as the occasion for making distinctions here that are really not part of Paul's argument. But he prefaces what he has to say on this point by a long discussion of his soteriology and Christology; he does not actually get down to the definition of these terms until p. 169.

10. It is curious that Colet, the good friend of such humanists as Erasmus and Thomas More, makes no reference to Plato's Socratic dialogues, in which the "features and countenance of the good" are directly discussed. As we have pointed out, there is some doubt about his own knowledge of Greek (cf. Intro., pp. 26f); but he certainly knew the Platonism of Ficino, who was at pains throughout his *Theologia Platonica* to show how the ancients too discussed the good and reached conclusions about it that a Christian could accept (Bk. XIV. 10). On the other hand, Colet may be using "good" here in the particular sense of salvific good, as the following sentences suggest. See also Chap. XII, pp. 249–51.

11. For a development of the metaphysical sense in which these terms are to be understood, see pp. 249–51.

12. Cf. Intro., pp. 41f. and n. 4 to Chap. I below.

13. For a discussion of this aspect of Colet's moral teaching, see Intro., pp. 48,

51–52. Colet seems not to have adverted to the scholastic distinction between the kinds of will. An act of volition directed toward an ultimate end which is desired for itself, not as a means to something else, is called *simplex voluntas*, or *voluntas ut natura*, to distinguish it from the willing of a means to a further end (*voluntas ut ratio*). (S. T. III, q. 18, a. 3) A man makes a fundamental choice of the highest good which guides his life and influences all his lesser decisions, but he need not consciously will this last end all the time. The conscious and shifting choices made on the level of means (*voluntas ut ratio*) may vary greatly, may be unpleasant, and perhaps misguided. Aquinas even shows how one can will two things at the same time (S.T. I–I, q. 12, a. 3). This distinction allows for more flexibility than Colet seems willing to admit. His view seems to be based instead on his strict interpretation of I Cor. xii: 7: "To each is given the manifestation of the Spirit for the common good." Therefore he concludes that each is obliged to do the best he can; if he doesn't, he misuses the grace that is given to him. "Oblitterat enim imaginem nepharie, qui non repraesentat id quatenus percutitur" ("For he wickedly effaces the image, who does not reproduce it as far as he is stamped with it" *Ecc. Hier.* I. 200; 53).

14. See Colet's own definition of this word below, p. 169 and and n. 54 to Chap. VII below.

15. Cf. *Romans* ix–x, 170–71. The context of the quotation from Deuteronomy is similar; Colet wants to show that there is no excuse for not following the law when God has made it evident, as he did for the Hebrews.

16. Lat. "non tamen ipsam fidem per se ad iusticiam satis esse, que consistit supra fidem, ex amore in continua actione bonorum." The syntactical relationships are important here, and translations vary. Lupton's version implies a hierarchy with love at the top: "not that faith of itself is sufficient for righteousness, since that consists of something above faith, even of love, in a continual doing good" (p. 56). Lupton's note on this passage refers to the primacy of love in Ficino's *Theologia Platonica* and Dionysius. Since, as we have seen, the relationship between intellect and love in the former is not clear-cut, Ficino's commentary on Paul is perhaps more to the point here. In speaking of gifts of the Spirit, he says that love is more effective than knowledge, and invokes Plato as well as Paul: "Quapropter in symposio Plato noster inquit, mentem nostram denique per amorem cum divina mente coniunctam ipsas rerum ideas virtutesque non modo spectare, sed in seipsa iam generare." ("For this reason our Plato says in the *Symposium* that our mind united with the divine mind through love does not only contemplate the ideas and perfections of things but even generates them within itself." *In Epistolas D. Pauli, Opera*, I, c. iv, p. 433.) He asserts that man is justified without the works of the law, but that good works must follow justification in order for a man to achieve salvation (*Ibid.*, xxii, 461). Faith and hope are inextricably bound up with love, a love which has its origin in God's love for us: "Quod si charitas in Deum nostra ab ipsa Dei erga nos charitate principium habet, merito & quae charitati necessaria sunt, fides scilicet atque spes, ab eadem divinitate procedunt." ("If our love for God has its beginning in the love of God for us, then the things which are necessary for that love, and [our] merit — namely, faith and hope — proceed from that same divinity." *Ibid.*, xxvi, 469.) Colet's own emphasis is on interaction rather than hierarchy at this point. *Justicia* stands above faith in the sense that it is more inclusive, and what it includes is the love that generates good works (*ex amore* in the sense of "issuing from"). All of this is necessary

for salvation. That Colet believed works were necessary is evident from the rest of this paragraph, in which he paraphrases James II: 14–26.

Lefèvre emphasizes the dynamic nature of this interaction between faith and love by suggesting (in his note on Rom. x: 8–10, "The word is near you, on your lips and in your heart,") that the phrase *in ore* means speaking or listening to that which concerns the salvation of ourselves and others; *in corde* refers to our own active cooperation with God. He goes further to imply that justification, once accomplished, opens the way for this cooperation, which must be a continuing and active response: "Ergo nunquam à corde & ore recedere debet: à corde quidem, ut semper iustificemur: ab ore vero, ut alios tanquam dei ministri & cooperatores salvemus, iustitiam dei in nobis adaugentes: adaugemus enim, non quod aliter, fortius, aut intensius influat deus, sed quatenus bona agentes reddimur gratiae dei & infusionis iustitiae eius capaciores." ("Therefore, it ought never to withdraw from the heart and the lips: from the heart, so that we may always be justified; from the lips, so that like ministers of God and cooperators [with Him] we might save others, increasing God's justice in ourselves — not that God's grace flows into us more strongly or more intensely, but to the extent that, doing good, we give thanks to God and become more fit for His infusion of justice." *Op. cit.*, [1531] Fvii-v.)

17. Colet's stand on the necessity for works as well as faith is made clear in *Edmund's Romans*, Chap. II. For him, justification must lead to moral and spiritual activity, namely the imitation of Christ. This does not mean, however, that works are required for justification in the first place, only that a living faith expresses itself in good works. Cf. the following note on Gal. v: 6.

18. Vulg.: "fides quae per caritatem *operatur*" (Gr. ἐνεργουμένη). This is a key passage that was soon to becom crucial in controversies over faith vs. works. The exact relation between faith and works in this context is expressed through the predicate of the phrase describing faith. Even down to our own time, translations vary: RSV: "faith working through love"; NEB: "faith active in love." Colet returns to the problem in XIII, pp. 263–65. Erasmus also cites Gal. v: 6 as an indication of the practical indivisibility of faith and love: " . . . ad Galatas describit fidem quae per charitatem operatur: opera charitatis, fidei tribuenda sunt. Qui convenit ergo charitatem à fide separare, hoc est, radicem à ramis." ("to the Galatians [Paul] describes the faith which works through love: the works of love are to be attributed to faith. Therefore whoever asserts that love is separate from faith is dividing the root from the branches." *Annot.*, NT [1535], p. 500.) Lefèvre makes a slight change in his translation: "sed fides quae per *dilectionem* operatur." His discussion goes on to stress the idea of this love as a relation of sonship between God and the believer: "Quomodo enim fides, quae filios facit & deum patrem, non operaretur per dilectionem? Operatur certe & erga deum, ut nos diligat tanquam filios, & ut per dilectionem omnia circa nos agat. Et erga nos, ut nos deum diligamus tanquam patrem, quo modo & propter Christum in cuius filatione inserimur, vult à nobis diligi, & omnia per dilectionem nos agere vult. . . ." ("For how should faith, which makes us sons and God our Father, not work through love? Certainly it operates with respect to God, that He might love us as sons, and through love He accomplishes everything concerning us; and in respect to ourselves, that we might love God as Father, as Christ did, and on His account, in whose sonship we are included. He wishes to be loved by us, and He wants us to do everything through love." *Op. cit.*, [1531] xvi-v, xvii-r.) Luther's first comment on this passage (*Lectures on Galatians*, 1519) picks up

Erasmus' idea: "That is, as Erasmus shows from the Greek, a faith which is powerfully active, not one that snores once it has been 'acquired' or one that is strong through miracles but one that is powerfully active through love" (*Luther's Works*, ed. and trans. Jaroslav Pelikan, v. 27, p. 336). In 1535 the same metaphor was still on his mind, as he paraphrased Paul with greater precision: "It is true that faith alone justifies, without works; but I am speaking about genuine faith, which, after it has justified, will not go to sleep but is active through love" (*Ibid.*, p. 30).

19. Cf. n. 2 to Chap. I above; *Cel. Hier.* VII. 21. Behind this phrase, which is not just a casual metaphor, is a whole framework of important fifteenth-century philosophical and mystical thought patterns. Ficino demonstrates its epistemological significance at some length in Bk. XII of his *Theologia Platonica*. He develops Plato's analogy in Bk. VI of the *Republic*. Just as the light of the sun enables the eyes to see objects and colors, so God enables the mind to understand and perceive the truth. He provides the epistemological link between perceiver and that which is perceived: "Itaque mentis actum Deus cum intelligibilium actu coniungit, sicut solis lumen oculi actum cum actu colorum. Et sicut in videndo triplex est actus, motus scilicet coloris, aspectus oculi, fulgor luminis connectens actus reliquos invicem, sic in intelligendo, ubi actus intelligibilium veritas a Platone vocatur, actus mentis scientia, actus utrorumque nodus apud Platonem est Deus, qui efficit ut et mens scienter intelligat et res vere intelligantur, immo facit ut ipse intelligatur." ("Accordingly, God joins the act of the intelligence with the act of the intelligibles just as the light of the sun [joins] the act of the eyes with the act of colors. Just as in seeing, the act is threefold—movement of color, glance of the eye, and brightness of light connecting the other acts reciprocally—likewise also in understanding, the act of the intelligibles is called 'truth' by Plato, and the act of the intelligence, 'knowledge,' and the act which unites them both is, according to Plato, God, who brings it about that the intelligence knowingly understands, and things are truly understood; and He even makes it so that He Himself is understood." *Opera Omnia*, I, 267–68; ed. Marcel, pp. 155–56.) Further, just as the eye perceives colors and figures, by means of the light which the sun reflects, not directly, so the mind, illuminated by the divine ray, understands the reasons of things, and ultimately God himself, by means of His reflected light: " . . . ita mens nostra, Dei radio illustrata, in eo ipso intelligit rerum omnium rationes, quarum fons est Deus, et quae Deus ipsae sunt; ideo et per Dei lumen intelligit et ipsum divinum dumtaxat lumen cognoscit." ("so our mind, illuminated by the ray of God, understands in itself the reasons of all things, the source of which is God, and which are themselves God; therefore it understands through the light of God, and to this extent it perceives the divine light itself." *Ibid.*) As the soul gradually becomes more and more purified, it can perceive God more and more clearly: "Quamvis autem per Dei lumen quotidie omnia cognoscamus et ipsum quoque lumen sub tali aut tali rerum figura refulgens gradatim percipiamus, puram tamen Dei lumen ab ideis omnibus absolutam et in suo fonte penitus infinitam, non prius videbimus, quam eum mentis purissimae statum adipiscamur, in quo lumen ipsum unico intuitu cunctarum simul idearum splendore refulgens contueamur." ("However, although we understand everything daily by the light of God, and we also perceive little by little the splendor of this light under this or that image of things, yet we do not see the pure light of God, independent of all Ideas, absolute and infinite, in its source, before we have attained the condition of a most pure understanding, in which we will be able to compass in a single insight the very light itself shining with the simultaneous brilliance of all

the Ideas at once.") Finally, as John says in his Gospel, we can see Him as He is. Ficino then adds the logical but quaintly impractical corollary that theologians then ought to be more truly "sons of God" than other people are, being in daily contact with this light: "Quamvis et in hac vita secundum Ioannem theologi filii Dei sint, quia per divinas ideas quotidie reformantur, quarum idearum series ab eo vocatur ratio Dei, vita rerum omnium, lumen mentium, non angelicarum modo, sed etiam humanarum. . . ." ("Even in this life, according to John, theologians may be sons of God, because they are daily re-formed by the divine Ideas. The series of these Ideas is called by him the reasoning or reflection of God, the way of all things, the light of the intelligences, not just angelic ones, but human as well." *Ibid.*, p. 157.) A familiar contemporary literary expression of these Platonic aspirations is the conclusion of Bembo's discourse on love in Castiglione's *Book of the Courtier*: "let us climb up the stairs which at the lowermost step have the shadow of sensual beauty, to the high mansion place where the heavenly, amiable, and right beauty dwelleth, which lieth hid in the innermost secrets of God, lest unhallowed eyes should come to the sight of it; and there shall we find a most happy end for our desires . . ." (Bk. IV; trans. Hoby; in *Major Elizabethan Poetry and Prose*, ed. Ruoff, p. 90).

20. Cf. Intro., pp. 46f; n. 3 to Chap. I above.

21. Behind this characteristic sequence is the Socratic notion that if one really sees what is true, he must will to follow it, and thereby become good. See Intro., pp. 43f.

22. The technical term *suppositum* from the philosophy of the Schools was traditionally defined as *distinctum subsistens in aliqua natura*, i.e., an individual being or substance complete and autonomous in itself, and essentially incommunicable to another. Hence Colet is here emphasizing the miraculous nature both of the Incarnation and of the Mystical Body of Christ (O'Kelly).

23. Cf. n. 2 to Chap. I above and *Ecc. Hier.* v. 105, 108.

24. In *Romans* VIII, 154–55, Colet indicates more precisely how this comes about. Only those who have been predestined receive the necessary enlightenment, which proceeds first from faith. Love then expands the soul and disposes it to receive the divine formation, to become another Christ, "to be conformed to the image of his Son, in order that he might be the first-born among many brethren" (Rom. VIII: 29).

25. In *Romans* Colet explains how the virtue of hope gathers one's forces together, and is therefore a life-giving source of unity, counteracting tendencies to dispersal and fragmentation—and therefore, in Colet's metaphysics, toward non-being: "Quae spes inicium est humanae profectionis in Deum, quae est collectio animae et counitio ac contractio in Deum ut illuminetur et incendatur. Nam divisa et dispersa per corpus, nec lumen tenere nec calorem servare potest. Primum ergo est ut a multiplici diffidentia cogatur in unam spem, ut unita illuminetur, illuminata ardeat; cogatur quidem in unum, contractu spiritus sancti, ut uni Deo speret, ut sperans credat, ut credens diligat, ut amor ex fide et ex spe fides possit proficisci." ("This hope is the beginning of man's journey towards God, a collecting of the soul, and a uniting and drawing of it to God, that it may be illumined and inflamed. For if it be divided and scattered through the body, it can neither retain light nor preserve heat. And so the first requisite is, that the soul be brought together from distrust, which is manifold, to hope, which is one; that being made one it may be illumined, and being illumined may glow with heat:—be brought together, I say, to one, by the drawing of the Holy Spirit, that it may hope in one God, and in hope believe, and believing, love; that so love may spring from faith, as faith from hope." XII. 182; 68.) Cf. also n. 11 to Chap. II above.

26. Cf. the relation between *gnosis* and *praxis*, Intro., pp. 41–43; and Colet's insistence on this point in *Edmund's Romans*, Chap. II.

27. Cf. *Romans* VIII. 153. It is apparent that for Colet, Christ as the Word is the source of our knowledge about God's will for us, rather than any private mystical experience.

28. Lupton points out (p. 63) that Colet's phrase "exacta atque expressa imago" is an effort to express the Greek *character* (from *charassein*, "to mark, engrave, or stamp" — G. Buchanan, AB, v. 36, p. 6). The Vulgate version has only *figura*: "locutus est nobis in Filio . . . qui cum sit splendor gloriae, et figura substantiae eius . . ." Erasmus' translation tries to capture the Greek meaning: "expressa imago substantiae illius" (LB VI, 984). In his annotation he explains that *figura* is an inadequate translation of Greek χαρακτήρ, which means "formam expressam ex alio." The idea of an archetype is expressed by the image of an impression made with a seal: "Nihil autem propius exprimit archetypum quam imago impressa sigillo." ("Nothing more accurately expresses an archetype than an image impressed by a seal.") For support he refers to Augustine's version, "figuram expressam" (*De Incarn. Verbi*, c. XII). Since the choice of words must convey essential truth about the nature of the Incarnation and the Son's precise relationship to the Father, these variants are not just linguistic quibbles. As Erasmus points out, "Ex hoc verba nata est magna digladatio" ("These words have given rise to great contention"), including the Arian controversy (983D). Lefèvre also turns to the Greek and uses the concept of a seal or image of the Father: "Et quid est character hypostaseos eius, nisi signaculum, & imago subsistentiae paternae, id est, personae patris. Et id, verum & consubstantialem designat ipsum esse dei filium, est enim omnis verus cuiusquam filius, character & consubstantialis imago, immo consubstantialis paternae personae. . . ." ("What is this hypostatic character but the sign and image of the paternal subsistence, that is, of the person of the Father? And so He ordained that the Son of God should be His true and consubstantial Self; for He is His Son, wholly and truly, His character and consubstantial image, indeed consubstantial with the Father's person." *Op. cit.*, OOiiij–v.) This revelation of the Father through his image in the Son has the great advantage of unity and simplicity, in contrast to the multiplicity of ways God revealed himself in the Old Testament, through visions of various prophets, etc.: "In fine autem non in multiplicitate, non per visiones, sed in unitate, & per seme ipsum in filio, qui CHRISTUS dominus est, locutus est mundo, implens suum quod in Isaia scriptum est, oraculum." ("Finally, not in multiplicity, nor through visions, but in unity, and through Himself in the Son, who is CHRIST the Lord, He has spoken in the world, fulfilling His own prophecy that was written in Isaiah." *Ibid.*, OOiij–v.) The phrase "splendor gloriae" in this context leads Lefèvre to draw a comparison which was a favorite with Colet, namely between Christ and the sun. In him the true light is revealed to men, not borrowed or reflected through the prophets. Augustine's discussion of this passage in *De Incarn. Verbi*, c. XII, to which Erasmus turns his attention, combines both images: "splendor est gloriae Dei, et figura expressa substantiae ejus (Heb. I: 3): quid de hoc sentiendum sit, videamus, Deus lux est, secundum Joannem (I Joan. I: 5). Splendor ergo lucis est unigenitus Filius, ex ipso inseparabiliter, velut splendor ex luce procedens, et illuminans universam creaturam." ("He is the splendor of God's glory and the exact representation of His substance (Heb. I: 3). Let us see what can be discerned about this. God is light, according to John (I John I: 5). The brilliance of light, therefore, is the only-begotten Son, proceeding from Him inseparably, just as brightness proceeds from light, illumi-

nating every creature." PL 42, col. 1180.) Like Colet he goes on to show how the fact that Christ is the Word of the Father in this manner makes it possible for man, his rational creature, to attain some knowledge of those divine mysteries which would otherwise be forever beyond his ken. In this intellectual sense, Christ is the way to the Father: " . . . quomodo via sit et ducat ad Patrem: et quomodo Verbum sit, arcana sapientiae et scientiae mysteria interpretans, ac proferens rationabili creaturae: quomodo etiam veritas, vel vita est, vel resurrectio est." ("even as He is the way and leads to the Father, and even as He is the Word, interpreting the arcane mysteries of wisdom and knowledge, and holding them forth to the rational creature, just so is He also truth, and life, and resurrection." *Ibid.*) It is interesting to compare modern English attempts to translate this passage. The AV of 1611 chooses "the very image of his substance" but includes a variant in a footnote, "the impress of his substance." The 1889 revision tries "the express image of his person," which the RSV then paraphrases as "He reflects the glory of God and bears the very stamp of his nature." The AB follows this, "a reflection of the glory and stamp of his nature," but the NEB tries to improve upon it: "the effulgence of God's splendor and the stamp of God's very being." The sequence of "substance," "nature," and "being" in these versions suggests some interesting philosophical implications.

29. By putting "vital spirit" (*spiritus vitalis*) in apposition with "soul" (*anima*) Colet shows that he has in mind the medieval concept of the soul as the vital, sensitive, or rational principle which sustains the life of the body.

30. This word *eternus* is apparently used inadvertently. There is no evidence that Colet believed the human soul to be eternal, unless the word is made to mean the same thing as immortal (O'Kelly).

31. Lupton's note, p. 63, points out the similarity of this argument for immortality to that of Lactantius, though it is really very much like Ficino's in *Theologia Platonica*, VI, c. 8.

32. In his commentary on Plato's *Timaeus*, Ficino discusses at some length the soul's descent into the body. In his marginalia on Ficino's *Epistolae*, Colet takes this Platonic dualism far enough to include the idea of the soul's pre-existence: "⟨Ani⟩mus primum apud deum expletus et exultans, appetitu amoreque corporis decidit in corpus, coitque cum corpore unde quasi ⟨obr⟩uto alicui aquis turbulentis nata est anime oblivio, ignaratia [*sic*] unde omnia mala nascuntur." ("The soul is at first in the presence of God, where it is satisifed and happy. Then, because of its desire for and love of the body, it falls into the body and is united with it. There, like a person drowning in a stormy sea, the soul is overcome by oblivion, the lack of knowledge [of heaven], whence all evils spring." Jayne, p. 89.)

33. By the use of this phrase Colet implies something more than a moral and spiritual mediation. Like Ficino, he seems to see Christ incarnate as a mediator between the Creator and creation as a whole. In Ficino's metaphysics, man, because of his rational soul, is the "middle species of the world" (v. *De Religione Christiana*, in *Op. om.*, p. 20); therefore Christ's taking on a human nature is "to become a middle ground" or link between the higher and lower realms, the created and the creating, or, as Ficino puts it, eternity and time. (Cf. Kristeller, *op. cit.*, Chap. VII and App. I). By seeing the Incarnation in this light of Plotinian-Dionysian metaphysics, Colet stresses Christ as Mediator more than Christ as Redeemer. There is a fine passage in his *Romans* which describes the Incarnation as the means whereby man can bridge the gap between the human and the

divine: "Hic filius Dei et hominis, Deus et homo, qui grece *theonthropon* dicitur, Jesus est Christus, mediator Dei et hominum, in se ipso utrumque extremum mire copulans; ut hoc ineffabili medio commode et gratiose extrema inter se illa copularentur. Verbum caro factum est, et Deus filius hominis, ut caro ad verbum habeat accessum, et homo filius Dei fieret. Deus induit humanitatem, ut homo divinitatem indueret. Deus se humiliavit, ut homo exaltaretur. In Christo humanitatis et divinitatis unitio, ut homines cum Deo co-unirentur." ("This Son of God and man, himself God and man (which in Greek is called *Theanthropos*) is Jesus Christ, the mediator between God and man, uniting in himself each extreme in a wonderful manner, so as for those extremes to be fitly and graciously connected together by this unutterable mean. The Word was made flesh, and God was made the Son of man, that flesh might have access to the Word, and man become the son of God. God put on our human nature, that man might put on the divine. God humbled himself that man might be exalted. In Christ there was a uniting of humanity and divinity, that men might be united with God." XII. 179; 63–64.) Cf. Colet's use of *theanthropos* in Chap. II, and n. 5 to Chap. II above; also his comment on p. 165 below that Christ "descended only to ascend." Consequently I can scarcely agree with Lupton's observation that "the Dionysian system hardly admits of the Scriptural doctrine of man's Redemption" (Intro. to *Two Treatises on the Hierarchies of Dionysius*, p. xlvi). In Colet's whole soteriology, forgiveness of sin is but the beginning of redemption; the redemptive process finds its fulfillment, and its justification, in the union with God which the Dionysian system explained for him.

34. Vulgate: "Oculi mei deficiunt desiderio auxilii tui" (Ps. cxviii/cxix: 123).

35. Lupton fails to include this sentence, although it is marked in the margin for inclusion. In a footnote (p. 64) he mentions it as a "marginal note," and remarks on the grouping of these three passages as "a passing illustration (if any were needed) of Colet's readiness in Scripture" (O'Kelly).

36. The third word in this marginal heading is entirely indecipherable to me, and has been to everyone to whom I have shown it (O'Kelly).

37. From the Vulgate, "expectatio gentium." Cf. RSV: "The scepter shall not depart from Judah, nor the ruler's staff from between his feet, until he comes to whom it belongs; and to him shall be the obedience of the peoples"; and AV: "unto him shall the gathering of the people be."

38. Cf. Colet's further explanation of the order of priority of these three theological virtues, and the nature of their interaction, in Chap. XIII, pp. 261–63, 267–69. Erasmus also deals with this relationship in his *Paraphrases*: "Fides, qua procul cernimus immortalitatem futuram: spes, qua confidimus nos illius fore participes: caritas, qua Deum sic de nobis meritum redamamus, & hujus gratia proximum. Haec tria caeteras dotes omnes antecellunt, sed tamen in his ipsis primas tenet caritas, cui fidem etiam & spem debemus, aut certe sine qua nec illae sunt ad salutem efficaces." ("Faith, by which we perceive future immortality from afar: hope, by which we trust confidently that we will be sharers of that [immortality]: love, by which we return love for love to God, who deserves [it] from us, and to our neighbor, by the grace of this [love]. These three surpass all other gifts, but yet even among these love holds first place, to which we owe faith and also hope, for certainly without love they are not efficacious for salvation." LB VII, 901.)

39. Erasmus' alteration of the Vulg. here supports the idea that Colet has been expressing, in Dionysian terms, of how man is transformed into the image of God by

becoming a progressively purer reflection of the "divine ray" (see n. 3 to Chap. I above).

Erasmus' interpretation hinges on the word κατοπτριζόμενοι, translated as *speculantes* in the Vulg.: "Nos vero omnes, revelata facie gloriam Domini speculantes, in eandem imaginem transformamur a claritate in claritatem, tanquam a Domini Spiritu." ("We all, with unveiled face beholding the glory of the Lord, are changed into His likeness from brightness into brightness, as by the Spirit of the Lord.") His revision gives the image of the purified soul reflecting God as in a mirror, not merely beholding him through it: "Nos autem omnes retecta facie gloriam Domini in speculo repraesentantes, ad eamdem imaginem transformamur a gloria in gloriam, tanquam a Domini Spiritu." ("For we all, with unveiled face reflecting [as] in a mirror the glory of the Lord are turned into that image, from glory to glory, as by the Spirit of the Lord.") He explains, "Hoc loco a speculo ductum est, non a specula: ut intelligas Dei gloriam a purgatis animis ceu speculo excipi ac reddi." ("In this passage [the word] comes from *speculo* [mirror], not *specula* [place from which to look], so that we understand that the glory of God is received and reproduced by purified minds, as in a mirror." LB VI, 761.) A comparison with the passage from Augustine to which his note refers shows an interesting correspondence, although Augustine develops the idea more fully. Since this whole concept is so important in the thought of Dionysius, Ficino, and Colet, Augustine's treatment of it here is worth quoting at length. He starts from I Cor. XIII: 12 and then asks, "Quale sit et quod sit hoc speculum si quaeramus, profecto illud occurrit, quod in speculo nisi imago non cernitur. Hoc ergo facere conati sumus, ut per imaginem hanc quod nos sumus, videremus utcumque a quo facti sumus, tanquam per speculum. Hoc significat etiam illud quod ait idem apostolus [quotes Vulg. II Cor. III: 18 as above]. *Speculantes* dixit, per speculum videntes, non de specula prospicientes. Quod in graeca lingua non est ambiguum, unde in latinam translatae sunt apostolicae Litterae. Ibi quippe speculum ubi apparent imagines rerum, a specula de cujus altitudine longius aliquid intuemur, etiam sono verbi distat omnino; satisque apparet Apostolum a speculo, non a specula dixisse, *gloriam Domini speculantes.* Quod vero ait, *In eamdem imaginem transformamur*: utique imaginem Dei vult intelligi, eamdem dicens, istam ipsam scilicet, id est, quam speculamur; quia eadem imago est et gloria Dei, sicut alibi dicit, *Vir quidem non debet velare caput suum, cum sit imago et gloria Dei* (I Cor. XI. 7). . . . Transformamur ergo dicit, de forma in formam mutamur, atque transimus de forma obscura in formam lucidam; quia et ipsa obscura, imago Dei est; et si imago, profecto etiam gloria, in qua homines creati sumus, praestantes caeteris animalibus . . . Et propter hoc addidit, *de gloria in gloriam*: de gloria creationis in gloriam justificationis . . . Quod vero adjunxit, tanquam a Domini Spiritu; ostendit gratia Dei nobis conferri tam optabilis transformationis bonum." ("If we inquire what this mirror is, and of what sort it is, the first thing that naturally comes to mind is that nothing else is seen in a mirror except an image. We have, therefore, tried to do this in order that through this image which we are, we might see Him by whom we have been made in some manner or other, as through a mirror. Such is also the meaning of the words spoken by the same Apostle: 'But we, with face unveiled, beholding the glory of God, are transformed into the same image, from glory to glory, as through the Spirit of the Lord.' He uses the word *speculantes*, that is, beholding through a mirror [speculum], not looking out from a watch-tower [specula]. There is no ambiguity here in the Greek language, from which the Epistles of the Apostle were translated into Latin. For there the word for mirror, in which the images of things appear, and the word for watch-tower, from the height of which we see something at a greater

distance, are entirely different even in sound; and it is quite clear that the Apostle was referring to a mirror and not to a watch-tower when he said 'beholding the glory of the Lord'; but when he says: 'we are transformed into the same image,' he undoubtedly means the image of God, since he calls it the 'same image,' that is, the very one which we are beholding; for the same image is also the glory of God, as he says elsewhere: 'A man ought not to cover his head, because he is the image and glory of God.' . . . Therefore, he says 'we are transformed,' that is, changed from one form into another, and we pass from an obscure form to a bright form, for though obscure, yet it is the image of God; and if the image, then certainly also the glory in which we were created as men, surpassing the other animals . . . And, therefore, he added these words 'from glory to glory,' namely, from the glory of creation to the glory of justification . . . But where he added 'as through the Spirit of the Lord,' he shows that the good of so desirable a transformation is conferred upon us by the grace of God." *De Trinitate*, Bk. xv, c. 8; PL 42, col. 1067–68; trans. Stephen McKenna, *The Fathers of the Church*, v. 45 [Washington D. C.: Catholic University Press, 1963].) The same idea can be found even more explicitly in Chrysostom, although Erasmus does not cite him here: "Nam simul atque baptizamur, supra solem anima exsplendescit, a Spiritu perpurgata: ac non modo gloriam Dei prospicimus, sed illinc quoque splendorem aliquem haurimus. Sicut enim purum argentum, ad solis radios situm, ipsum quoque radios emittit, non ob suam dumtaxat naturam, sed etiam ob solarem fulgorem: eodem modo anima defaecata, atquᵉ argento splendidior effecta, a Spiritus gloria radium suscipit, ac vicissim remittit." ("For as soon as we are baptized, the soul beameth even more than the sun, being cleansed by the Spirit; and not only do we behold the glory of God, but from it also receive a sort of splendor. Just as if pure silver be turned towards the sun's rays, it will itself also shoot forth rays, not from its own natural property merely but also from the solar lustre; so also doth the soul being cleansed and made brighter than silver, receive a ray from the glory of the Spirit, and send it back." PG 61, col. 448; *Hom. VII on II Cor. 3:18*, trans. T. W. Chambers, in *Nicene and Post-Nicene Fathers*, v. xii, p. 314.) Both Lefèvre and Valla note and comment briefly upon the difference in Greek, but their remarks might be confusing at first because they use the plural form for mirror, *specula*: "Qui autem in Christum fide illuminante respiciunt; develata facie atque retecta ut specula gloriam illam lucem illam spiritumque illum pure hauriunt efficiunturque Christi formes . . ." ("Moreover, they reflect back upon Christ with illuminating faith; with countenance uncovered and unveiled, like mirrors they drink up completely that glory, that light and that spirit, and images of Christ are thus produced." Lefèvre, *op. cit.*, [1512], p. 138v).

Valla's explanation is more specific: "Nusquam reperi speculari a speculum, ut hic est, sed a specula: quanquam graece magis est significatio passiva κατοπτριζόμενοι, hoc est, illuminati gloria Domini, tanquam specula quae lumen accipiunt: sic enim Graeci intelligunt." ("Nowhere have I found that *speculari* is from *speculum*, as this is, but from *specula*, although in Greek the passive meaning is rather κατοπτριζόμενοι, that is, illuminated by the glory of the Lord, like mirrors which receive the light; for this is how the Greeks understand it." *Op. cit.*, p. 172v.) Cf. *Cel. Hier.*, ii, 11–12.

40. The reader will catch again the antithesis here between *actio* and *patientia*. I am forcing the English word "patience," but scarely more than Colet forces its Latin forebear (O'Kelly).

41. Lat. *hac quadrata forma*. I have borrowed Lupton's ingenious translation of *quadrata* by "four-square." Probably it comes very close to Colet's intention. The connotations,

however, are perhaps misleading to some extent, since "four-square" does not carry the derived meanings of *quadratus*, "suitable, fitting, right" (O'Kelly).

42. Cf. Colet's discussion of the reciprocity of divine love in *Romans*, v: "quia amamur, Deum redamamus per spiritum sanctum, qui datus est nobis; id est, per amorem acceptum, qui impertitur nobis ex divino amore, hoc amore accepto amamus Deum, Deo confidimus, Deum speramus" ("because we are beloved, we love God again, through the Holy Spirit which is given us; or, in other words, through the love received, which is bestowed upon us from the divine love, we love God, trust in God, hope for God" — 143; 12).

43. Lat. *ita ut etiam Petrus* . . . The idea is that the disciples were so lacking in the warmth of supernatural charity that even Peter, the first and highest among them, turned instead to a physical, natural fire (O'Kelly).

44. Lat. "in cathedra pestilentiae." See Intro., p. 23 for Colet's use of the Vulgate and Lupton's version (O'Kelly).

45. Colet often expresses the traditional idea of man's place in the hierarchy of created things, which receives its dynamism from above. Cf. his marginalia on Ficino's *Epistolae*: "Nostra gloria omnis in solo illo rege glorie est, ad quem nemo ascendit sed rapitur. Gravitas terrene nature non patitur ut ascendatur [*sic*]; pati potest ut trahatur. Ut enim gravia non petunt alta nisi ab altis trahantur, ita quoque homines terrene huius orbis terrarum incole in celum gradus non ascendunt quidem, nisi eos celestis potestas attraxerit. Est res tota in tractu dei non in conatu nostro. Trahit autem ille et rapit quos amat ardentius." ("Our glory rests entirely with that one King of Glory, to whom no one ascends, but is raised. The heaviness of earthly nature does not permit [the soul] to rise of its own accord; it is capable only of allowing itself to be raised. As heavy things do not seek the heights unless they are drawn up by things above them, so also men, the earthly inhabitants of this earth, do not climb the steps to heaven unless some heavenly power draws them up. It is entirely a matter of God's raising us, not of our own effort. God lifts up and takes to heaven those whom He most loves." (Jayne, p. 107.) In *Cel. Hier.*, Colet is more explicit about the ascending scale: ". . . ut inter sensibilia et intelligibilia collocatus homo medius, per corpora ad spiritum, per sensa ad intellectum, per umbram ad lucem, per imaginem ad veritatem adduci possit; ut eam aliquando nactus, contempta tum omnino carne, et contensus in spiritum, in spiritali sola veritate conquiescat" (". . . man, placed midway between the material and the immaterial, may be led by the body to the spirit, by the senses to the understanding, by the shadow to the light, by the image to the truth; that finding truth at length, he may then wholly despise the flesh, and striving after the spirit may rest in spiritual truth alone" — I. 4). Cf. n. 68 below.

46. Colet's many references to the "freedom of the sons of God" (cf. *Romans* VIII) should not be forgotten in his assessment of man's potential, although at times this aspect of his thought is overshadowed by his constant emphasis on earthbound flesh and slavery to sin. Cf. n. 61 below.

47. This stress on the imitation of Christ was one of the hallmarks of the *Devotio Moderna* in Holland, as well as of the *philosophia Christi* advocated by Erasmus in *Paraclesis*, *Enchiridion*, and many other works, especially the *Paraphrases*. Erasmus had once been a pupil of the Brethren of Common Life at Deventer, and from them he was early imbued with an interest in practical Christianity. But it should be noted that Colet's concept of "following Christ" was often mystical — that is, Christ as the way to union with

God, as well as Christ the moral exemplar. Hence in the following paragraphs Christ appears as the heavenly guide of those who want to depart from the earth as soon as possible.

48. Colet's marginal drawing of a target with four arrows of varying lengths approaching it from different directions illustrates the text at this point. Colet appears to have adapted quite naturally to a distinctly English context Paul's later metaphor of the runners in the stadium, except that Paul's metaphor appears to permit only one winner out of several, while Colet's adaptation to archery clearly permits relative degrees of effort and achievement (O'Kelly).

49. It will be observed that the absolute moral standard which Colet advocated (cf. pp. 143–45) is here modified to the extent that some gradation of reward is allowed, provided, of course, man's will is unswervingly directed toward good.

50. Lat. "Ab omnibus sensuum delenimentis." Lupton reproduces Colet's spelling, "delinimentis," which Meghen had changed to (or mistranscribed) "delimentis." Possibly Colet intended "deliramentis," but this seems unlikely. "Delenimenta" here might be related to the "crassimus sensus," touch (see pp. 133 f. above), but not specifically to venereal pleasures, alluded to in the phrase following, "a venere castus" (O'Kelly).

51. Here Colet connects his moral standard with his metaphysics (see Intro., p. 49; VI, pp. 133–35 and n. 9 to Chap. VI above). In a hierarchical universe where good and evil are connected with upward and downward, it becomes difficult to make room morally for all the ambiguities of the human condition.

52. A good succinct statement of this aspect of Colet's Platonism; cf. n. 32 above. But there is an interesting reversal at the end of this paragraph, where Colet's thinking is obviously modified by the doctrine of the resurrection of the body.

53. Colet wrote "hostiam," which Meghen and Lupton silently changed to "hostium." Perhaps this emendation is correct; there is no way of knowing whether Colet approved Meghen's change, although in other places Meghen's readings are distinctly wrongheaded. There is a possibility that Colet wrote "hostiam" inadvertently, but I think it likelier that Colet is drawing attention to the oddly relevant pun emphasized in the fifth stanza of Aquinas' hymn, "Verbum supernum": "O salutaris hostia/Quae coeli pandis ostium . . ." (O'Kelly).

54. Colet returns here to the distinctions which he had started to make on p. 139. In the discussion which follows, he seems at the outset to be using "counsel" and "precept" synonymously; but it soon becomes clear that "counsel" is a more general term, and "precept" means a counsel which must be followed if one is to be saved. But then he rather curiously makes "precept" depend on one's ability, so that whatever a man finds he *can* do toward salvation, he then *must* do. Exactly what this is depends on the individual's own particular powers. See definitions, p. 173. "Indulgence" permits him to stop at the limit of his powers, even if he has not attained the best. Aquinas makes different distinctions: "The difference between a counsel and a commandment is that a commandment implies obligation, whereas a counsel is left to the option of the one to whom it is given. Consequently in the New Law, which is the law of liberty, counsels are added to the commandments, and not in the Old Law, which is the law of bondage. We must therefore understand the commandments of the New Law to have been given about matters that are necessary to gain the end of eternal bliss, to which end the New Law brings us forthwith: but that the counsels are about matters that render the gaining of this end more assured and expeditious" (ST I, q. 108, a. 4). Aquinas reserves

the word "indulgence" for its specialized theological meaning (ST III, q. 25). Dispensations may be allowed by proper authority when a precept of the law is applied to an individual case (ST I–II, q. 97, a. 4). It is significant that Colet places the burden of decision on the individual involved, since he knows his own capacities better than anyone else; but Aquinas states specifically that it would be "dangerous" to leave the question of dispensation from a precept up to the individual, "except perhaps by reason of an evident and sudden emergency." In spite of his many references to the darkness of man's intellect, etc., Colet reserves a healthy respect for individual judgment.

55. Cf. n. 9 to Chap. I; also Lupton's note, p. 79.

56. To call "indulgence" as he defines it above a "concession of evil" reveals Colet's Platonist tendency to see the good as an absolute, so that anything that is less good becomes, *ipso facto*, evil, to that extent. Colet's metaphysics seems to be leading him into unusual moral rigor at this point. Cf. Erasmus' annotation on I Cor. VII: 1, "It is well for a man not to touch a woman." First he cites Jerome, who is arguing against those who prefer marriage: "Si bonum est non tangere uxorem, malum igitur est tangere: quum bono, malum sit contrarium." ("If it is good not to touch one's wife, then touching is evil, since evil is opposite to good.") But then he points out that Augustine in *In epistolis adversus Hieronymum de medio inter bonum et malum*, cites Aristotle's categories to the effect that there can be an intermediate level, neither good nor bad: ". . . quaedam esse indifferentia, quae nec bona sint nec mala . . ." ("some things are indifferent, which are neither good nor evil"), but the examples given refer to acts that have no moral implications (LB VI. 685E).

57. The similarity of this sentence to a crucial passage in More's *Utopia* is interesting. More writes, "If you cannot pluck up wrongheaded opinions by the root, if you cannot cure according to your heart's desire vices of long standing, yet you must not on that account desert the commonwealth. . . . On the contrary, by the indirect approach you must seek and strive to the best of your power to handle matters tactfully. What you cannot turn to good you must make as little bad as you can. For it is impossible that all should be well unless all men were good, a situation which I do not expect for a great many years to come!" (Book I, p. 50; ed. Edward Surtz, S.J.). Of course the context is very different, for More is using this principle as an argument for realistic flexibility in the affairs of state. Still it should be remembered that Colet was More's confessor.

58. *Romans* VI develops this metaphor more fully. See Lupton's note, p. 18, on the frequency of Colet's illustrations from the art of medicine.

59. Colet was fond of using oxymoron to express the paradoxes of the Christian life. Here he adapts a scriptural image (passing through the eye of a needle) to his metaphysical concept of unity and simplicity, which has been so prominent in this chapter.

60. Cf. Homer, *Odyssey*, XII. Although probably neither Colet nor his audience had read Homer in the original, the story was obviously familiar. But his use of it as a metaphor of the Christian pressing on toward salvation may be one of the earliest instances of a Renaissance humanist's literary adaptation of the classics to sacred ends, a tendency which was to culminate in Erasmus' famous plea, "Sancte Socrates, ora pro nobis."

61. In several of his works, Colet explores the connections between grace and freedom. Although he does not present any systematic analysis of the perennial problem of predestination, he tries to maintain both God's initiative and man's free choice. (Cf. *Romans* IX–X, in which he uses Paul's reference to Jacob and Esau as a springboard for

a discussion of this point.) Colet was more concerned with man's slavery to sin and the power of grace to set him free (*Romans* VIII, pp. 153–54). When he speaks here of "a freedom by nature tending to the good," he is, of course, making use of the familiar scholastic principle that all things desire the good. Aquinas attributes this to Dionysius and explains that the will as a rational appetite desires what is suitable and good for it; hence every inclination is to something good. This "good" may be real, or only apparent, but it is always apprehended as good in some way (ST I–II, q. 8, a. 1). By freeing man from his dependence on the satisfaction of his fleshly appetites (in the broadest sense: i.e., life lived κατὰ σάρκα), grace enables him to see and choose real goods, not specious ones, and gives him the strength of will to follow his enlightened choice. Paul's classic comment on this point is, of course, Rom. VII: 18, which Colet discusses below, and which inspired Luther's famous "simul justus et peccator." Starting with the principle enunciated below, "the natural inclination of my mind is to freedom for good" (p. 189), Colet sees grace as a power allowing this freedom to operate in fallen man. Like Erasmus (see his note on Luke II: 14, LB VI, 232), Colet views the joyous announcement of the angels at the birth of Christ in this context, heralding man's new chance for freedom from his former slavery to sin: "Nato etiam Iesu, denunciaverunt angeli pacem in terra hominibus bonae voluntatis. Sed haec cogita adjumentum Dei cum vi voluntatis concurrere, in graciaque homines libere posse, ut ex utrisque simul nascatur libertas ad bonum; ut, nisi velit homo, non admittat lucem; et, nisi illuminetur, non velit admittere. Est voluntas in causa cur animus admittit; et est lux simul in causa cur animus velit. Anima calens gracia suapte libertate elegit bonum, quod eadem libertate potest recusare. Sine gracia vero nulla libertas, et in gracia quidem nihil nisi libertas." ("At the birth of Jesus also, angels announced 'on earth peace, good will toward men.' But consider thus, that God's assistance concurs with the force of our own will; and that in grace men have free power; so as for our freedom towards good to spring from both together; so that, unless a man will, he receives not the light, and, unless he be enlightened, he wills not to receive it. Man's will is the cause why his soul receives it; and at the same time the light is the cause why his soul wills. The spirit, when warmed by grace, in its own freedom chooses the good, which in that same freedom it can refuse. Without grace indeed, there is no liberty; and yet in grace there is nothing but liberty." *Cel. Hier.* IX. 183; 29.)

62. Vulg. *gratia Dei.* RSV: "Thanks be to God." Lefèvre prefers "Gratias ago Deo," because Paul uses the verb εὐχαριστῶ which means to give thanks (*Op. cit.* [1512] fol. 86r). Valla agrees: "Non est Dei, sed Deo, hoc est, gratia sit Deo . . . . Credo sic exponendum, Gratia Deo, qui ipse liberabit nos per Iesum Christum." "It is not 'of God' but 'to God,' that is, 'thanks be to God . . . . I think it should be expressed thus: 'Thanks to God, who will set us free through Jesus Christ.' " *Op. cit.*, p. 137v.) Erasmus points out that "gratias ago Deo" is also more in harmony with the context; Paul is thanking God for his liberation from the conflicts of life lived κατὰ σάρκα. This is a freedom that only the Christian message can bring: "Atqui si legisset gratia dei, non congruebat haec particula in Paulum, qui non liberandus erat, sed liberatus: . . . Igitur aut Gratia deo, legendum, aut Gratias ago, quibus verbis iam liberatus gratias agit deo, per cuius gratiam assequutus sit, quod nec naturae, nec Mosis lex, nec conscientia, nec opera praestare poterant." ("And yet if it had read 'grace of God,' this particle would not have been suitable for Paul, who was not about to be freed, but already freed. . . . Therefore one should read either 'thanks to God' or 'I give thanks.' With these words

one who is already freed gives thanks to God, through whose grace he obtained [his freedom], because neither the law of nature, nor the law of Moses, nor conscience, nor works could avail him." LB VI, 599.) A good discussion of Rom. VII: 14ff. for the non-specialist can be found in W. G. Kümmel, *Man in the New Testament* (London, 1963), pp. 49–71.

63. It should be noted that Paul himself does not draw this conclusion (VII: 3–5). As the marginal note in the MS indicates, Colet may be thinking here of Jerome's *Adversus Jovinianum*, in which he quotes Xystus (or Sextus) in this context: "Adulter est, inquit, in suam uxorem amator ardentior. In aliena quippe uxore omnis amor turpis est, in sua nimius. Sapiens vir judicio debet amare conjugem, non affectu." ("Hence Xystus in his *Sentences* tells us that 'he who ardently loves his own wife is an adulterer.' It is disgraceful to love another man's wife at all, or one's own too much. A wise man ought to love his wife with judgment, not with passion." Bk. I, 49, no. 319; PL 23. Trans. W. H. Freemantle in *St. Jerome: Letters and Selected Works* [*A Select Library of Nicene and Post-nicene Fathers of the Christian Church*, 2nd Series, vol. VI (New York: Parker & Co., 1893), p. 386].)

64. See Intro., pp. 48–50 for a discussion of this extreme position. Colet here departs from the tradition of the Church Fathers, best summarized by Augustine, who asserted a three-fold good of marriage in his treatise *De Bono Coniugali*: 1) offspring, 2) fidelity, 3) sacrament. The procreation of children was considered to be the primary good of marriage; in fact, Augustine explicitly says that the marital act performed with this intention is good and lawful, but it becomes sinful if this intention is absent. Fidelity means the right of the partners over each other's bodies, which Paul stresses in this chapter. Faithfulness to a contract is of course a general good; its opposite in this case is the evil of adultery. For the "people of God," Augustine adds a third good, which he calls the "sanctity of the sacrament." There is some dispute about the exact meaning of this term (see the intro. to the translation of *De Bono Coniugali* by Charles Wilcox in the Fathers of the Church series, no. 15). Since Augustine cites it as the reason why a divorced person should not re-marry so long as his spouse is living, it refers to the indissolubility of the marriage bond and the symbolism of this sacrament as representing the union of Christ and his Church (PL 40; Ch. 24). In this context Augustine addresses himself to the question which Colet raises on p. 189 above: if it were possible, would it not be better for everyone to refrain from marriage, thereby filling the City of God at once and hastening the end of time? (chap. 10). Like Colet, he interprets v. 7 and vv. 29–34 in this way. The answer he gives is Paul's answer: those who do not restrain themselves ought to be married. But he does not treat the permission to marry as an "indulgence" in the sense of pardon, as Colet seems to do. Since Augustine has shown that marriage is not a sin, he quite logically adds that it cannot be granted as a pardon; pardon is needed only for marital intercourse which does not have offspring as its aim. Augustine's views formed the basis of the traditional interpretation of this subject.

St. Thomas Aquinas maintains that the marriage act is not only not a sin, but meritorious for those in a state of grace (ST Suppl. q. 41, a. 3 and 4). His argument is primarily from nature: corporeal nature is good, having been created by a good God; hence we cannot hold that those things which pertain to the preservation of that nature, and to which nature inclines, are evil. To do so would be to say that corruptible things were created by an evil God. In asserting that the marital act is meritorious, Aquinas

cites I Cor. VII: 3 and calls it an act of justice. It might also be called an act of religion, if the couple are deliberately begetting children for the worship of God. These motives are virtuous and hence the marital act can be meritorious.

Erasmus is, of course, in disagreement with Colet on the interpretation of this part of Corinthians: "Eximia quaedam res est perpetua castitas, ob Christi negotium suscepta. Sed honesta res est & legitimum connubium, cujus auctor & consecrator est ipse Deus. . . . Proinde neque damnet quisquam alienum statum, neque sui poeniteat quenquam, sed quisque pro sua virili, dono, quod accepit à Deo, respondeat. Est castum conjugium, est impura virginitas." ("Perpetual chastity is a somewhat exceptional state, undertaken on account of the work of Christ. But a lawful marriage, whose author and consecrator is God Himself, is also a respectable condition. Consequently no one may condemn another's state, nor punish anyone for it, but each must be responsible for his own manhood, a gift which he receives from God. There is chaste marriage and there is impure virginity." *Paraphrases*, LB VII, 879D.)

65. Cf. *De Sac.*, pp. 73–78.

66. Cf. Rom. XII: 1–2 and Colet's comment upon it. For him, this means a complete regeneration of sinful man, a real interior renewal: "Quod quamdiu tenet, quasi nova tum forma effigiatus ad imaginem Dei expressius, non tam homo quam Deus videtur esse." ("So long as he retains this enlightenment, man, as though now fashioned in a new form more distinctly after the image of God, appears to be not so much man as God." *Romans* XII. 176; 59.)

67. Lat. "corpore in obsequelam anime intime contracto." Cf. *Romans* XII: "Nam quo fertur una hominis pars, vel corpus vel anima, illuc statim totus homo trahitur; sic ut totus aut sursum aut deorsum tendat necesse est. Illuc si sursum tendat humilis et confidens Deo, apprehensus a spiritu trahetur altius, et supra se quadam in divina condicione sustinebitur, anima divino spiritu, corpore animae jugiter serviente." ("For in what direction one part of man is borne, whether body or soul, thither is the whole man instantly drawn; so that he must needs tend wholly either upwards or downwards. If he tend in that upward direction, humbly and with trust in God, he will be laid hold of by the Spirit and drawn still higher, and his soul will be sustained by the Divine Spirit in a divine state beyond itself; his body being the constant servant of the soul." 176–77; 60.) According to Ficino, the body is, by its very nature, scattered, dispersed, subject to change, heat, cold, passions, corruption of all kinds. But contrary to its own nature, it can be held together in an effective unity by a higher principle: the soul. "Unde fit ut contra naturam corporis sit coire in unum, manere simile, et sibiipsi constare. Extensio namque ipsa quantitatis partes corporis disjunctas manere compellit. Motus perennis cogit mutari naturam, neque sua simul habere, sed aliud amittere, quaerere aliud. . . ." ("As a result, it is contrary to its nature for the body to be joined into a single unit, to remain alike and constant within itself. In fact, the very extension of quantity compels the parts of the body to be disjoined. Continual movement requires its nature to be changed, not to possess its qualities all at the same time, but to lose one and then acquire another." *Theol. Plat.*, VI, viii, 245.) This is one of Ficino's arguments for the soul's immortality: "Igitur anima neque est corpus, sed copula corporis intima, vel substantia copulatrix. Neque forma divisa per corpus. . . ." ("Therefore the soul is not the body, but its intimate link, or substance which unites it, rather than a form dispersed throughout the body." Ibid., 246.)

68. This ranking of spiritual over physical fecundity follows from the hierarchy of

beings described above. Created midway between beasts and angels, and possessing to some extent the attributes of both, man's challenge is to rise toward the angelic level, not to drop to the animal level. This is a common theme in the literature of the period, as well as in theological treatises.

Chapter VIII

1. The contrast between knowledge and love, and the relative importance of each in the spiritual life, is a dominant theme in Colet's writings. In Chap. VIII of *Romans*, for example, he draws heavily on Ficino to show how love and knowledge are both means by which man rises toward God. (See above, Chap. I, n. 23.) Paraphrasing Ficino, he emphasizes the idea that by love our minds are expanded and raised up toward God, but by knowledge we reduce him to the narrow limits of our own comprehension: "Preterea est homini magis honorificum, et divinae majestati eciam sane magis congruum, ut statim ametur pocius ab homunculis, quam aliquatenus exquisicius cognoscatur; quod contendentes ut cognoscamus Deum, conamur eum ad nostrae mentis humilitatem et angustiam contrahere quodammodo, et quasi devertere; at vero amantes, ad Deum ipsum nos attollimus, et ad immensam illius bonitatem nos ipsi amplificamus, ut magni et excelsi eam capiamus quoad possumus; nos illi non illam nobis accommodantes." ("Moreover it is more honourable to man, and also, it must be allowed, more befitting the majesty divine, that God should be loved at once by feeble men, than that he should be known in some degree more minutely; seeing that, in striving to know God, we are endeavouring in a measure to narrow, and, as it were, distort him, to the meanness and straitness of our own intellect; but in loving him, we are raising ourselves to God, and enlarging ourselves to his unbounded goodness, so as now, great and lofty, to receive it according to our measure; adapting ourselves to it, not it to ourselves." *Romans* VIII. 156–57; 31.) Cf. Ficino, *Theol. Plat.*, ed. Marcel, Bk. XIV, c. x., p. 292. In *Corinthians* XIII, pp. 257 f. he develops the idea of charity as the perfection of the spiritual man (cf. n. 6 below). Lefèvre suggests a change in the translation of I Cor. VIII: 1. Where the Vulg. has "Scientia inflat, caritas vero aedificat," he puts "cognitio inflat: dilectio autem aedificat," but does not offer an explanation for the change. In contrasting worldly wisdom to that which is a gift of the Spirit, he continually points out the limitations of human knowledge; cf. his comments on I Cor. I: 18 and III: 18.

Erasmus adds the idea that love teaches us how to use knowledge: "At caritas ubique prodesse studet, laedit neminem. Quanquam magna scientiae pars abesse videtur iis, qui nesciunt quatenus sit utendum scientia. Id praescribit caritas, è proximi commodo metiens omnia. Hanc igitur in consilium advocet oportet, qui vere scientia praeditus videri velit. At qui caritatis expers, inani scientiae persuasione tumet, tantum abest à scientia, ut nec illud etiam sit assecutus, ut sciat quatenus oporteat uti scientiae." ("Love is eager to be useful anywhere; it hurts no one. Yet a great deal of knowledge seems to be lacking in those who do not know how knowledge ought to be used. Love prescribes this, measuring everything from the benefit of the neighbor. Therefore he who wishes to seem truly endowed with knowledge ought to take this into account. Without charity, he is puffed up with an inane pretext of knowledge; he is so far from it that he would not attain it even if he were to learn how he ought to use it." *Paraphrases*, LB VII, 885C.) On the other hand, he warns against those who would twist this scriptural verse

to mean that Paul considers knowledge dangerous and is here forbidding us to follow it: "Proinde non vetat Paulus, ne non amplectemur scientiam, sed ne desit scientiae charitas, alioque nihil aeque inflat atque inscita." ("Accordingly, Paul does not forbid us to embrace knowledge, but love should not be absent from it, for nothing else puffs one up so much, and [makes him seem] foolish." *Annot.*, LB VI, 703E.) In support of his view he refers to Augustine's *Contra Faustum* on this same verse: "Utquid ergo habebat ipse quo inflaretur, nisi quia cum charitate non solum non inflat scientia, sed etiam firmat?" ("Did not he [the Apostle] have [knowledge] by which he might have been puffed up, if it were not for the fact that knowledge joined with love not only does not puff up, but strengthens?" PL 42, Bk. xv, c. viii.)

2. Cf. Ficino: "Ob id enim citius propinquiusque firmius amor, quam cognitio mentem cum divinitate coniungit, quia vis cognitionis in discretione consistit magis, amoris autem magis in unione." ("For this reason, love unites the mind with divinity more quickly, more intimately, and more firmly than knowledge does, because the essence of knowledge lies in making distinctions, but the essence of love lies rather in effecting union." *Theol. Plat.*, ed. Marcel, Bk. xiv, p. 291.)

Chapter IX

1. Lat. *simpliciter*. The other term of the scholastic distinction is *relative*. The opposite of *absolute* is *secundum quid* (O'Kelly).

2. Cf. St. Thomas, ST I–II, q. 1, a. 8; q. 2, a. 7; q. 3, a. 1; also Aristotle, *Physics*, II. 9; *Nich. Ethics*, III. vii. 6: "And every activity aims at the end that corresponds to the disposition of which it is the manifestation. So it is therefore with the activity of the courageous man: his courage is noble; therefore its end is nobility, for a thing is defined by its end." Trans. H. Rackham, Loeb ed., (London, 1934), p. 159.

3. In his assertion of these rather formidable principles, Colet departs from Paul's text. They serve to introduce the list of statements with which he concludes this short chapter (the 6th and 7th on p. 209 below). This stress on the building up of the Church could easily be misunderstood, as though Colet were making it into an absolute, in a sense quite inappropriate for an institution which has its human as well as divine element. Colet gives no indication at this point of being aware of this danger; but in his Convocation Sermon, preached at St. Paul's in 1511, he comes to grips with the serious imperfections of the contemporary church (*op. cit.* pp. 293–304). He warns the bishops of their responsibilities and exhorts them to live up to their own laws.

4. The word ἐξουσίαν, ix: 4 and 5, translated in the Vulg. as *potestatem* and in AV as "power" can be misleading here, according to IB (v. 10, p. 99). The word "right" is used instead in RSV and NEB. Erasmus finds no problem with *potestatem*, nor does Valla. In a similar context, II Cor. xiii: 10, *potestate* is translated (NEB) as "authority."

5. Lat. *feminas ministras*. Vulg., *sororem mulierem*, Gr. ἀδελφὴν γυναῖκα "a sister as wife," (IB, v. 10, p. 99). Both AV and RSV say "wife"; NEB, "Christian wife"; JB, "Christian woman." Erasmus explains that "sister" means she was a Christian. He cites Eusebius' quotation of Clement to the effect that Paul was married. Clement uses this passage (I Cor. ix: 5) as his evidence for this view. Eusebius reports as follows: "And Paul does not hesitate, in one of his epistles, to greet his wife, whom he did not take about with him, that he might not be inconvenienced in his ministry." (*Church History*,

Bk. III, c. xxx; trans. A. McGiffert, *Nicene and Post-Nicene Fathers*, 2nd series, I, p. 162.) Erasmus also cites Valla with approval, who takes a similar view, but assumes that some of the Apostles' wives remained companions in their ministry: "Quid opus est addere Mulierem, cum dictum sit Sororem? quare puto transferendum fuisse Vxorem, cum praesertim dicatur numero singulari, γυναῖκα. Ex quo datur intelligi, fuisse Apostolos suas uxores comitatas, quas ideo appellat sorores, quod tanquam non uxores iam erant." ("Why is it necessary to add 'Woman,' since it said 'Sister'? The reason is, I suppose, that it ought to have been translated 'Wife,' especially since [the word] is given in the singular number, γυναῖκα. We can infer from this that the Apostles took their wives along as companions, but called them sisters, since they were no longer [treated as] wives." *Op. cit.*, pp. 157r–v.) Lefèvre translates *sororem uxorem* and assumes that Paul was married, but separated: "Ignatius Petro & Paulo coaetaneus: Paulum habuisse uxorem testatur & fidelem quidem & ideo sororem. Sed ob evangelium Christi in opus evangelii separatam reliquit." ("Ignatius, a contemporary of Peter and Paul, attests that Paul had a wife, a faithful one indeed, and for this reason [she is called] sister. But for the sake of Christ's gospel and his labors in its behalf, he left her behind." *Op. cit.*, [1512] p. 119v.) The final version of Erasmus' annotation adds his explicit conclusion: "quam tamen non circumduxerit, consulens Evangelicae libertati, quam Petrus & Philippus circumducerent suas." ("yet he, concerned with Evangelical freedom, did not take her around [with him], although Peter and Philip used to take their wives [with them]." LB VI, 706.)

6. In *Romans* xv, Colet tempers the severity of his moral exhortations by advising the compassion that Paul suggests: "Habenda ergo est benigna racio infirmorum, et cavendum ne eis aliquod onus imponamus. Sed potius compatiamur cum ipsis, imitati Christum, qui nobiscum compati voluit, ut nos victores passionum faceret." ("We must therefore take a kindly account of the weak, and beware of laying any burden upon them. But rather let us have compassion on them; following the example of Christ, whose will it was to have compassion on us, that he might make us victors over our passions." 221; 123.)

7. Lat. *ut comprehendas*. In this and in the subsequent sentences where I have used the verb "to attain," it is entirely possible that Colet intended the double meaning of *comprehendere*: to lay hold of, and to comprehend intellectually. This is all the more likely, I think, since the entire chapter is concerned with the nature of true wisdom and true knowledge (O'Kelly).

Chapter X

1. Lat. *impietatem*—i.e., a lack of due respect toward those to whom one owes it; here, toward the "weaker brethren" who took scandal from this conduct (O'Kelly).

2. Lat. *Christi communionem*; Gr. κοινωνία; cf. Vulg., "communicatio sanguinis . . . participatio corporis." Lefèvre uses *communio* in both phrases, as does the AV: "The cup of blessing which we bless, is it not the communion of the blood of Christ? The bread which we break, is it not the communion of the body of Christ?" (The RSV changes "communion" to "participation" in both instances). Erasmus finds no difference in these words as used here, and is puzzled about the duplication (LB VI, 711). Colet takes it for granted that Paul is talking about the Eucharist here. Erasmus thinks likewise in his early annotation of 1516, but in his final version, he allows for the possibility

of looser interpretations, in accordance with the custom of early Christians to have a commemorative meal which was not always a sacrament. At any rate, it is clear that Colet is not here concerned with debates over the sacrament of the Eucharist which were to become so important shortly after his death. (Cf. Intro., pp. 9f, 40f). Erasmus' comments on this passage in the *Paraphrases* stress the idea of fellowship among believers, rather than doctrinal disputes.

3. Cf. Chap. VIII, n. 1 above on the relation between knowledge and love.

4. Lat. *fratres dominici*. Throughout this entire passage the play on *demonicus* and *dominicus* is recurrent. Although it cannot be reproduced in English, the reader should try to keep the antithesis in mind (O'Kelly).

5. Colet's use of typological allegory at this point scarcely goes beyond that of Paul himself in vv. 1–11, nor is it developed any further by Erasmus. But Lefèvre, in the 1531 edition of his commentary, uses this passage as a springboard from which to launch a whole series of allegorical correspondences, in which the Rock is Christ transfixed upon the Cross, the wilderness is this world, the Promised Land is the heavenly kingdom, and various forms of punishments are conceived for the idolators of v. 14. Lefèvre wants to indicate how the typology of the OT shows us the way to the NT: ". . . omnem enim Paulus typum in propriam aptat revocatque veritatem, & in veritate videt typum & in typo veritatem" ("Paul accommodates and refers every type back to its proper truth; in the truth, he sees the type, and in the type, the truth" fol. xcv-v). This passage is a good illustration of Lefèvre's contention that fundamentally the spiritual and the literal sense are one; cf. Obermann's discussion of this point in *Forerunners of the Reformation*, p. 291; also Lefèvre's introduction to his *Commentary on the Psalms*, in which he shows how the literal and spiritual senses "coincide," making one true sense, that intended by the Holy Spirit (reprinted and trans. in Obermann, *op. cit.*, pp. 297–301).

6. The meaning ought to be "Or are we going to provoke the Lord to anger?" (O'Kelly). As Lupton points out (p. 106n.), Colet misinterprets *aemulari* in v. 22 of the Vulgate. The Greek word παραζηλοῦμεν is translated as "provoke to jealousy" in the principal English versions from Tyndale to the AV, except for Reims, which has "emulate." Valla points out that this word has two senses, depending on whether it is used with the accusative or dative case, and he rejects the Vulg. reading: "Quidem hoc exponunt, quòd invidemus Domino, quae sententia longè abest à vero . . ." ("Some interpret this to mean that we envy the Lord, which meaning is far from the truth . . ." p. 159v). Erasmus corrects the Vulg. *aemulari* to *provocamus*, citing the scholion of Theophylactus as his precedent. Colet's further effort to explicate this passage (see pp. 215, 217, and n. 9 below) might indicate his uneasiness with the reading of the Vulg. Lefèvre translates "An ad zelum provocamus dominum?" ("But do we provoke the Lord to anger?") and calls his version "intelligibilior interpretatio" ("a more intelligible interpretation"—p. 122r [1512]).

7. This identification of charity with wisdom is made more clear in Chap. XIII; see n. 6. Cf. *Romans*, VIII: "Non est enim amor scienciae finibus contentus, sed pro sua excellenti vi longius progreditur, et lacius vagatur, nec ei satisfactum est, donec est nactus primum illud immensum et infinitum bonum in quo solo conquiescat." ("For love is not confined within the limits of knowledge, but advances farther, in keeping with its transcendent power, and takes a wider sweep, not satisfied till it has attained that first boundless and infinite good, wherein alone it can repose." 157; 31–32.)

8. Colet is still making use of the scholastic doctrine of form, but here he relates

it to the Mystical Body of Christ (cf. n. 3 to Chap. I above). It is the Eucharist which provides the new formative principle enabling the Christian to be "of the same form" as Christ—a true spiritual transformation, not just a pious wish. This passage is a good example of the way in which Colet combines scholastic doctrines with the data of faith and revelation. In the following paragraph the "oneness" so highly favored by the neo-platonists becomes elevated into the unity of the Mystical Body in communion with its Head, with the Eucharist as the principle of unity.

9. Lat. "id dictum a Paulo non minus obscure quam breviter." Lupton misread *obscure* as *obstare* (p. 237), and while he presents an ingenious translation for the phrase so read (p. 108), he overlooks Colet's uneasiness over his reading of v. 22 (O'Kelly). See n. 6 above.

10. Colet departs at this point from the literal meaning of the text to a related allegorical interpretation, which he (or someone) tried to illustrate by a drawing in the margin of MS Gg. iv. 26 (here reproduced). See Lupton's note, p. 109.

11. Lupton, "President of the banquet," p. 109; Lat. *magister convivii*, which Colet also describes as *architriclinus* a few lines below.

12. See Lupton, p. 109, n. 3 for other uses of this figure.

13. In his zeal for absolute purity and "simplicity," Colet here sets up a dichotomy between Christian and pagan which is, in a sense, contrary to his own practice. The statutes of St. Paul's School, which he founded, prescribe pagan as well as Christian authors for the curriculum; in fact, St. Paul's served as a model for the classical curricula that were soon to become such a prominent feature of Renaissance schools. Lily wrote his famous Latin grammar for the children of St. Paul's. Pagan authors were widely read and quoted by the Italian humanists whom Colet admired. Ficino, for example, devotes his *Platonic Theology* to a harmonizing of Christian and pagan religious themes. Pico set out to combine the best of ancient philosophy with Christianity in *De Ente et Uno*; and of course Erasmus did not hesitate to "spoil the Egyptians" or to ask for the prayers of Socrates. Colet's own use of Platonic and neo-Platonist themes has been frequently observed in these notes. But I doubt if he was even aware of these inconsistencies in the absolute exclusion that he advocates here. Rather, he seems to take for granted that the structure of reality in which the Christian dispensation takes place is that which the ancients also described for us, in their limited way. For him, the neo-Platonic doctrines of unity, simplicity, etc. simply describe the way things are; they are not merely pagan beliefs, any more than the scholastic doctrine of form and matter would be, for Colet, merely a scholastic belief. Hence he can use these concepts—especially as drawn from the pages of the pseudo-Dionysius—without feeling that he is borrowing specifically pagan notions. An important phrase in the following paragraphs is "beyond the truth." For Colet, truth was what counted; pagans might have had glimmerings of it, but it was to be found in its fullness in Holy Scripture. If all this seems contradictory, we must remember that Colet was not, after all, a systematic or profound philosopher; he was a teacher and a preacher.

Chapter XI

1. Colet's emphasis on unquestioning obedience in this chapter is a logical consequence of his stress on hierarchy and the subjection of the lower to the higher. It is basic to

his cosmology and metaphysics (see Intro. pp. 52–57). Institutional and social hierarchies are thus seen as reflections, in the microcosm of the human context, of the universal order. See *Cel. Hier.*, c. XVI.

2. The following summary of female subjection is entirely in accord with the traditional interpretation of male and female roles in the history of the Church. Colet finds no reason to feel uneasy with Paul's strictures on women here; however, he does throw the emphasis on "propriety and fittingness" within the Corinthian context. Then he goes on (as Paul does not, at this point) to assert the basis for a kind of "equality" of the sexes before God.

3. Colet's extension of the veil symbol to a metaphor of the appropriate Christian stance before God in a sense elevates the feminine role. Obedience and subjection are required of men as well as women in their most important relation, that is, to Christ and God.

4. Colet supplies another definition a few lines farther down (p. 225), which is substantially the same except that it seems to put more stress on the direct inspiration of the Holy Spirit. The fact that he troubles to define it twice suggests that this more scriptural meaning was perhaps a secondary one for Colet's audience. But it was not new; its use in this sense in English goes back as far as Wyclif's Bible (1382) and is frequently to be found among the Puritans of the sixteenth and seventeenth centuries (OED).

5. Lat. *viragines*. This is another instance of Colet's feeling for words and the relationships between them. Lupton found a difficulty with the sentence (p. 114 and n.), but I do not think the problem he describes is really there (O'Kelly).

6. Lat. *heresis*, as in Vulg.; RSV, "factions," not generally interpreted as "heresy" in the modern sense (JBC II. 51:70). But Colet seems to understand it as heresy, even calling it "deadly" (*mortiferum*). For a similar statement of the idea of testing through false doctrine, see I Cor. III: 13 and Erasmus' note (c. III, n. 2). In his note on this passage (I Cor. XI: 19), Erasmus, following Chrysostom, says that the Greek conjunction ἵνα does not signify cause, but event (LB VI 715)—so he changes the Vulg. *ut qui probati sunt* to *quo qui probati sunt*. Colet, however, paraphrases and extends the idea in the rest of his paragraph.

7. Lat. *facibus*. Meghen changed the word to *faucibus*, and Lupton followed him, recording in a footnote (p. 115) that "in the original [MS] it looks more like *in facibus*," and suggesting "amid the broken lights." The word *fax* means not only a torch, a firebrand, but carries very apposite connotations in some of its derived meanings. Apart from the fact that it is normally a short-lived sort of flame (classically, it is often used for a meteor or shooting star), it is employed metaphorically of people who inflame and incite others, and who are a cause of ruin (O'Kelly).

8. Lat. *consecratum est*. This is Meghen's reading also; but if it were not for the context, one would almost certainly take this word for *conservatum* in the MS, and this is what Lupton reproduces, translating "has been preserved" (O'Kelly).

9. Colet states the substance of this covenant as he sees it very simply and straightforwardly here—not in the terms of a confessional creed, but as the motivating principle behind his soteriology. The emphasis is upon the general activity of a Christ-like life, rather than upon specific precepts, and the fulfillment of the covenant is nothing short of an actual participation in the glory of God. (Note his "examination of conscience," p. 229). This helps to explain why hope plays such an important part in Colet's discussion of these matters; see, for example, the weight he gives to it in chap. VII.

10. Lat. *Christus moriens in ipsos*, which looks like a nominative absolute. Perhaps the explanation is simply that Colet began with a construction in which "Christus" was to be the subject, and then changed his mind (O'Kelly).

11. Cf. n. 3 to Chap. I above on Colet's concept of the Mystical Body. The paradox with which he begins the next paragraph depends, of course, on this symbolism.

12. Lat. *ipsi Dei immolati in ara crucis*. I have translated this phrase on the assumption that *Dei* is the genitive singular; if *ipsi* is not a slip for *ipsius* (and I think it almost certainly is), it must be a nominative plural intensifying and in apposition with *omnes*. It is possible, however, that *Dei* in the phrase is a nominative plural, and then the phrase would mean that we are ourselves offered upon the altar of the Cross as gods (O'Kelly).

Chapter XII

1. Lat. *novum esse*. This is another of many instances in which Colet stresses the newness, the complete regeneration, of the redeemed life. Cf. his comments on Rom. vi: 5–8 in *Romans*, vi. 144–45.

2. Gr. κατὰ σάρκα. In his understanding of this important Pauline term, Colet departs for the moment from the Platonic dualism that has been dominating his thought: "By 'the flesh' Paul almost always means man in his entirety: man, whose knowledge is death, whose wisdom is at war with God" (p. 231). Colet's choice of quotations from Rom. and I and II Cor. in this section shows his grasp of the Hebraic idea that σάρξ means man in his weakness and mortality, his distance from God. To live according to *sarx* is also sinful, "not because the flesh is evil or impure, but because such an attitude is a denial of the human situation over against God . . . a distortion of the fundamental relationship of the creature to God. . . . As such it is the final denial of the human situation, and must be utterly shattered." (John A. T. Robinson, *The Body: A Study in Pauline Theology*, pp. 24–26.) It is significant that at this point Colet does not describe the "new creature" (καινὴ κτίσις) of II Cor. v: 17 in the usual scholastic terminology of form and matter (see nn. 4 to Chap. I, 2 to Chap. V, 14 to Chap. VI) but in the biblical sense of one who has undergone μετάνοια. Man becomes this new creation, he explains, "by the whole man being turned to the Spirit" (p. 233).

3. Colet here superimposes his own hierarchical vision of the world upon Paul's words. Paul is at pains to point out that the relative value of the gifts he enumerates here is to be estimated by their usefulness to the Church, but Colet's diagram of ascending and descending orders is straight out of Dionysius. Compare his diagram of p. 235 below with that in *Cel. Hier.* xvi. 42; also his elaboration of it in *Ecc. Hier.* vi. 128–30 and *passim*. Of course, he thought that Dionysius, presumed to have been a disciple of Paul's, was expounding Paul's views. Still it seems rather paradoxical that immediately after having presented this elaborate and detailed schema, Colet admits, in effect, that the "Spirit of God" is not bound by any of this but "breathes where he wishes, and as much as he wishes, and as long as he wishes" (p. 233). The diagram itself is not easy to reproduce exactly. (See comments on the text, Intro., pp. 19–21.) O'Kelly explains, "The schemata which follow . . . I have reproduced as closely as possible from the MS (fol. 133r). The spacing does not correspond exactly, but I have made it closer to Colet's than Meghen did. I cannot conjecture with any degree of certainty what differences in relationship

Colet intended to indicate by his use of solid lines in some instances and broken lines in others."

4. This is but another instance of Colet's deprecation of man when he is seen in relation to the divine; see also n. 32 to Chap. I above. It is important not to lift such passages out of context, for by themselves they could give a distorted view of Colet's thought. For an example of such distortion, see Eugene Rice, op. cit.

5. This remark is another evidence of the highly relative way in which Colet intends this paragraph to be interpreted. The "man" in question here is man as *sarx* (see n. 2 above), man without God in the world, subject to all the distresses outlined by Paul in Rom. I: 18–32; the "old" man who must be put to death in order to live anew in the spirit. (Cf. Robinson, op. cit., chaps. 1 and 2.)

6. Lat. *sanctitum*. Colet clearly intends this word as a past participle of *sancio*. Lupton writes *sancitum*, for which there is some classical authority. Meghen writes *sanxitum*. One can see why Colet did not want to use the established form, *sanctum* (O'Kelly).

7. Colet's Platonism is evident here in a Christian context. For Plato, spiritual reality was the only reality. In spite of his firm belief in the Incarnation, Colet comes close here, as elsewhere, to a denial of the flesh on metaphysical as well as moralistic grounds. Cf. also his comment on II Cor. III: 18 in *Cel. Hier.*: ". . . in quaque erunt tandem in ipsa veritate, quam nunc quam melius possunt, imaginario ordine et actionibus, referunt spiritu; credentes Christo, et expectantes avide ipsam cum angelis plenam et perfectam veritatem." ("And in this image they will at length be in the reality itself; which now, as best they can, they spiritually represent in a figurative order and acts, believing in Christ, and eagerly looking for the full and perfect reality they will have with the angels." Chap. II., p. 170; 8–9.)

8. Lat. *et est quisque . . . est*. Colet has a comma after *quisque*, and I have translated the clause on the assumption that he had a reason for putting it there. It is possible, however, that the rendering ought to be: "And each man is himself to the extent that he is in them" (O'Kelly).

9. Colet's stringent moral precepts (see n. 13 to Chap. VII above) should be viewed in light of such paragraphs as this, which provide the philosophical background for them. If one really believes that the only reality is spiritual, then the disparagement of the flesh, the rejection of earth-bound attractions, etc. follow logically.

10. See Lupton's note, p. 122. Democritus, called the "Aristotle" of the 5th c. B.C., upheld an ideal of cheerfulness or serenity of soul, as the ultimate moral good; Heraclitus of Ephesus emphasized continual change, or metaphysical strife in the constant interaction of opposites; he also denied immortality.

11. Gr. ἐντελέχεια. See Lupton's note, p. 123, for the difficulties of translating this word into English. "Actuality" is often found in standard modern versions of the *De Anima*; see, for example, the Loeb Classical Lib. edition, trans. W. S. Hett, p. 67. Lefèvre presents the same idea of the unity of the Mystical Body endowed with diverse gifts under the image of a circle: "Christus & spiritus sanctus sunt ut circuli centrum / fideles ut innumerae a centro exeuntes lineae et ex circumferentia in centrum refluentes. Virtus autem Christi et spiritus eius: ut circumferentia omnia continens conservans atque fovens. Et ut in lineis quaedam sunt summae quaedam mediae quaedam imae et una non est alia / sed in uno tamen unitae unum continent circulum: sic in corpore Christi quaedam membra sunt summa quaedam media & quaedam ima et unum non est aliud / unita tamen omnia corpori Christi unum corpus sunt / quod omnes cum Christo sive (ut

sic dixerim) concentrati Christo fideles constituunt." ("Christ and the Holy Spirit are like the center of a circle, the faithful like the countless lines going forth and flowing back from the circumference into the center. The power of Christ and his Spirit enables the whole circumference to be sustaining, preserving, and fostering. It also ensures that among the lines [going to and fro], some are higher, some are in the middle, and some are lower. None is separated from any other, but joined into one unit, they form a single circle. So in the body of Christ, some members are higher, some in the middle, and some are lower; and yet none is separate from another, but all together they form one body in the body of Christ, composed of all the faithful with Christ, or (just as I have said), joined together in Christ." Op. cit., [1531] fol. xcviii-v.)

12. The connection between the hierarchical structure of Colet's universe and his view of morality becomes clear in comments such as this. Anger, cupidity, etc. are wrong because they upset the proper order of things. Here, however, it is not the traditional order of passions properly subservient to reason, but the more sweeping subordination of all "human principles," as he calls them, to divine purposes. He goes on to lament the disorder, in this sense, of the Church of his own day. This subject formed the basis of one of his most famous sermons, preached at St. Paul's to a convocation of bishops and clerics in 1511 (see n. 1 to Chap. IV, n. 2 to Chap VI). In it he castigates them for putting their own principles—i.e., worldly desires and greed—ahead of God's purposes in the Church. It was one of the few works of his translated into English during his lifetime.

13. See *De Corp.*, p. 190; also Lupton's note, p. 124, in which he cites Porphyry's theory about the operation of the magnet.

14. See vii, n. 39 above. The ultimate goal envisioned by Colet is not a vague blessedness, but a more specific state in which man loses all his earthbound attributes, which are fundamentally "unreal" anyway; as pure spirit he then takes on the divine life to the extent of his capacity.

15. Lat. *in subsidium angelorum*. At this point Colet departs from Paul on an excursion into the Dionysian hierarchy of which he was so fond. That Christ came into the world to aid the angels makes sense, as a purpose of the Incarnation, only in this Dionysian context. The process of enlightenment proceeds from the top downward; hence, angels must be purified and perfected before men, and then they in their turn must work to purify the next order below them, namely mankind. Among men, the highest (Apostles) are purified and enlightened first, so that, having become spiritual, they may work with spirits (angels) for the betterment of all the orders of creation. "In angelorum ordine quod prostremo exprimitur Deitatis, agunt ipsi sedulo ut id idem inferant in homines, hominesque in imitacionem sui et Dei traducant; ut sub ipsis quoque extet triplex quaedam hierarchia; hominum scilicet in terris; alludens ad id quod est in angelis. Hoc moliti sunt diu angeli frustra, hominis ineptia repugnante, donec in subsidium venerit magnus ille et (ut vocat Isaias) magni consilii angelus, Iesus Christus; de cujus nativitate exultantes cecinere angeli Gloria in excelsis Deo et in terra pax hominibus." ("Such attributes of the Deity . . . as are expressed in the order of Angels, it is their constant business to introduce among men, and to bring men also to an imitation of them and of God; that beneath themselves there may exist a threefold hierarchy, to wit, of men on earth, answering to that which there is among the angels. This was long assayed in vain by the angels; the unfitness of mankind being an obstacle, till there came to their aid the mighty Angel, the 'messenger of the great counsel,' as Isaiah calls him,

Jesus Christ; of whose nativity the angels sang in gladness, 'Glory to God in the highest, and on earth peace toward men.' " (*Cel. Hier.* IX, p. 182; 28.)

16. This analogy between the Apostles and the heavenly spheres—it is, of course, something more than an analogy—leads into Colet's exposition of the Human Hierarchy, established by Christ to put an end to the disorder and chaos which existed among men, alone of all the beings in the universe (O'Kelly). Cf. *Cel. Hier.*: "Hic virginis filius hierarchiam ad angelorum formam, ad suae veritatis exemplar instituit, et ex quibus voluit vivis lapidibus edificavit, quos non solum digessit in ordine, sed etiam vivificavit in se, ut vivi in ipso ordine digerantur." ("He, the Virgin's Son, established a hierarchy after the model of the angels, according to the pattern of his own truth, and built it up of those whom he would, as living stones; whom he not only arranged in order, but also quickened in himself, that as lively members they might be arranged in him who is Order itself." Ibid.)

17. The Ptolemaic astronomical system, not yet seriously challenged in Colet's day, underlies and sustains the imagery in this section. On the order and movement of the spheres, see Lupton's lengthy notes, pp. 126–30; also *Cel. Hier.*, XVI, p. 41.

18. The saving principle here, which gives necessary value to even the lowest beings in the hierarchy, is their function in the building up of the Church, as Paul himself makes clear in this chapter.

19. The human hierarchy is a microcosm of the heavenly one, which in turn is paralleled by the spheres of the Ptolemaic system. Cf. *Ecc. Hier., passim*. For a full discussion of Colet's view on this, see Intro., pp. 52–57.

20. Lat. *religiosus*. Saturn came to be associated, in astrological systems, with the brain, which was generally recognized in Colet's time as the center of the soul's activities. We still have, in the word "Saturday," evidence of the early association between the Jewish Sabbath and Saturn's Day (O'Kelly).

21. It would have been more logical, perhaps, for Colet to have listed these characteristic qualities within each triad in reverse order. Love belongs to the highest and best rank in each system, wisdom to the next highest, and so on, with disintegration marking the lowest and last (O'Kelly).

22. Cf. Dante's use of number nine as a symbol, *La Vita Nuova*, XXIX.

23. The idea here is that the perfect thing from each class of things should be offered to God. Colet's remark below, that "Moses and the theologian-prophets betokened it all by allegory," indicates that he was probably thinking of the custom of tithing: "And Abraham gave him a tenth of everything" (Gen. XIV: 20). Allegorically, Mosaic tithes were a type of Christ offered to the Father, as he explains on p. 249. See Pico, *Heptaplus*, I, vii.

Chapter XIII

1. Lat. *preclaris*. I am not at all sure of this ill-written word in the MS, but this is what both Meghen and Lupton read (or conjecture), and I cannot think of anything else it is likely to be (O'Kelly).

2. For Colet's knowledge of Greek, see Intro., pp. 26f. One of the four forms given here, χαριτόω, is written in Latin characters, *charistoo*. The others are written without accents. Peter Meghen left blanks for all four (O'Kelly). Lefèvre defines the word in

Latin: ". . . charitas quae dilectio dicitur et dei dilectio. . ." (*Op. cit.*, [1531] fol. xcix-v).

3. Lat. *Amor est hec charitas.* Colet also uses these words interchangeably in *Romans*; see especially the conclusion of Chap. VIII. Valla discusses variant forms for the word "love" in Greek and Latin in his note on John XXI: 15: "Varietas haec verborum diligo et amo, non ab interprete est, sed e Graeco: nam diligo redditur illi, ἀγαπῶ, amo illi φιλῶ, quae verba nunc & fere semper ab Ecclesiasticis indifferenter accipiuntur tam Latine quam Graece, ut ex ipsa loci huius inspectione datur intelligi. Itidem dilectio & charitas, quarum altera verbo φιλῶ, altera verbo ἀγαπῶ, ab interprete redditur, etsi nonnunquam idem utatur Amor, veteres tamen aliter distinxerunt, & amo & diligo, & item amorem & charitatem . . . qui ait inter dilectionem & charitatem hoc differentiae esse, quod dilectio Latinum nomen est, charitas graecum: cum charitas nusquam apud Graecos reperiatur, nec aliter a charus fiat, quam a clarus claritas, a sanus sanitas, a bonus bonitas." ("This variation of the words 'diligo' [to love in the sense of preferring, hence to esteem highly] and 'amo' [to love passionately or fondly] is not made by the translator, but is found in the Greek: ἀγαπῶ is translated 'diligo' and φιλῶ is translated 'amo.' These words are now almost always used indiscriminately by the Ecclesiastics both in Latin and in Greek, as shown by our inspection of this passage. Also 'dilectio' [love in the sense of preference, esteem] and 'caritas' [love in the sense of something being highly prized] are used to translate ἀγαπῶ and φιλῶ; if 'Amor' is sometimes used likewise, yet the ancients distinguished between 'amo' and 'diligo,' and also between 'amor' and 'caritas'. . . . [According to Remigius], the difference between 'dilectio' and 'charitas' is that 'dilectio' is a Latin noun, and 'charitas' a Greek one; since 'charitas' is found nowhere among the Greeks, it may be formed from 'charus,' [dear, expensive, prized], just like 'claritas' [clarity] from 'clarus' [clear], 'sanitas' [soundness, health] from 'sanus' [sound, healthy], 'bonitas' [goodness] from 'bonus' [good]." *Op. cit.*, pp. 108v–109r.)

4. The initiative is always with God; man's love for God follows from God's prior love for him. In *Romans*, Colet uses *amor* and *ama-* plus the prefix *red-* to indicate this reciprocity: "Item cum homines gracia attractos, vocatos, justificatos, et magnificatos dicimus, nichil significamus aliud quam homines amantem Deum redamare. In quo amore et redamore consistit hominis justificacio." ("In like manner, when we say that by *grace* men are drawn, are called, are justified, are glorified; we signify nothing else than that men return the love of a loving God. In this love and return of love consists the justification of man." v. 143;12.)

5. Lat. *cognitus . . . approbatus.* Cf. I Cor. VIII: 3. Lefèvre translates: "At si quis deum diligit: is ab eo cognitus est."

6. Colet no doubt has in mind here the root meaning of the word as well as its more modern connotations. *Per + facio* means to finish, bring to completion; hence it applies here, because charity is the virtue which completes, and in fact validates, all the others. He uses the word directly in its root sense a few lines below: "perfectus et forma consummatus," i.e., "finished in form."

7. Again Colet is using the scholastic doctrine of form, an understanding of which is essential to the grasp of his meaning here. (See nn. 4 to Chap. I, 2 to Chap. V, 14 to Chap. VI, 2 to Chap. XII). Colet's treatment of the relationship of the Holy Spirit as informing agent and *causa principalis* to man as *materia informata* (with regard to spiritual operations) is a fine instance of his use of traditional Aristotelian Scholastic terminology in combination with more directly Platonist concepts (O'Kelly). Lupton quotes exten-

sively from Pico's *Heptaplus* in his note on this passage (pp. 138–39) to show how closely Colet parallels Pico here, but there is a slight error in his reference. The passage is
to be found in Bk. I, Chap. I, p. 1r (*Opera*, 1557).

8. Lat. *decoctionis flos.* A term from alchemy, which has an odd ring in this context
(O'Kelly). Lupton translates this as "quintessence." He points out the popularity of
alchemy at the time Colet was writing (n., p. 139).

9. In *Theol. Plat.*, Bk. II, Ficino explains this neo-Platonic concept of substantial causality: "Omnis causa per aliquam agit formam et agit effectum ipsius in forma quodammodo similem, ideoque oportet effectus formam a causa comprehendi. Cum vero Deus
sit omnium causa, necessarium est in eo omnium formas esse. Est ergo Deus essentia
omniformis." ("Every cause acts through some form and produces in the form an effect
similar to it in some sense. That is why it is necessary that the form of the effect be
comprehended by the cause. Since God is the cause of all things, the forms of all things
must be in Him. Therefore God is in essence omniform." Marcel, I, p. 105; *Opera*,
I, p. 105.)

Combining Plato's "Idea" with Aristotle's doctrine of immanent form, Ficino asserts
that the form within things is derived from the form above things. By communicating
itself to individual things, the Idea is the cause of the intrinsic form. Ultimately this
participation goes back to one primary cause, as Ficino tries to show through movement: "Oportet tamen ad aliquam essentiam pervenire quae sit et fons et receptaculum
motionis et vitae, quemadmodum ad aliquam pervenitur quae lucis et ad aliquam quae
caloris radix est simul et fundamentum." ("It is necessary, however, to reach a kind
of essence which is both the source and the receiver of motion and of life, just as one
comes to an essence which is both the source and foundation of light, and another which
is the source and foundation of warmth." Bk. VI, x. xii; Marcel, I, p. 254; *Opera* I,
p. 169.) Soul, sun, and fire are all active causes of movement, light, and warmth, but
of course they are not absolute in themselves, as God is. (Cf. Kristeller, *op. cit.*, Chap.
VIII, and Lupton's note, p. 140.) Colet easily bypasses the more complex steps in an
explanation of causality that a philosopher would have to go through and rises immediately
to the divine causality. But some understanding of a position like this of Ficino's is
necessary if a reader is to grasp, in the rest of this paragraph, how a man can "act by
his own form" and yet still be "a living and perfect instrument" of another, i.e., God.
This gets at the heart of the paradox of Christian freedom (Augustine's "Love God,
and do what you will," or the complete obedience of Mary's free response, "Be it done
unto me according to Thy word.") It also helps us to understand, on a practical level,
why it is that love is primary, and how this free response of love can be, at the same
time, the "fulfilling of the law" (Rom. XIII: 10).

10. Lat. *vel ipsa inflata*—i.e., "puffed up." Although God may use them to bring about
the building of His Church, they themselves are not "built," for without charity they
remain dead instruments.

11. The addition of "exemplar cause" to the Aristotelian scheme of four causes comes
from the neo-platonic attempt to include the Idea in this scheme. But Ficino defines
God as efficient cause, end, and exemplar of the world; causality is an aspect of the divine
essence. (Cf. Kristeller, *op. cit.*, pp. 122–23.) To show how efficient, final, and exemplar
cause can be one, Ficino first proves that the efficient cause must come from outside
the thing caused; then he goes on, "Neque afferat quispiam solam habere finalem causam.
Habet enim eam, cum ad bonum tamquam ad finem recte feratur. Cum vero ad id frustra

non moveatur, aliquid certe boni ab illo consequitur. Accipit autem secundum essentiam, quandoquidem secundum essentiam appetit atque movetur. Igitur ab eodem accipit esse, a quo essentialem accipit bonitatem. Itaque causa illa tam efficiens est quam finis. Est et exemplar. Si enim mundus certa ratione fertur ad bonum, certe Deus illum certa ratione tamquam exemplari ad bonum illud continue dirigit." ("We are not saying that [a thing] has a final cause only. Certainly it has one when it is brought directly toward the good as toward its end; but in fact, since it is not moved [toward its end] in vain, it certainly acquires some good from that. Now it receives [this good] according to its essence, since it is according to its essence that it desires [the good] and is moved [toward it]. Therefore it receives existence from that same [principle] from which it receives essential goodness. Therefore that cause is both efficient and final cause. It is also an exemplary cause. For if the world is brought toward the good by a definite plan or idea, then certainly God directs it continually toward the good according to that idea as its exemplar." *Theol. Plat.* Bk. xviii, c. 1; Marcel, III, pp. 176–77; *Op. om.* I, p. 397.) Ficino approaches the argument from a somewhat different angle in his unfinished commentary on Paul's Epistles. Commenting on Rom. i: 20, Ficino asks what is meant by "invisibilia Dei" and responds with the concept of exemplary cause: "Praeterea invisibilia Dei dicuntur exemplaria rerum omnium in ipso Deo, quae & sensum, & imaginationem prorsus exuperant. . . . Intelligimus aptata esse secula verbo Dei, ut ex invisibilibus visibilia fierent. Nempe in ipso intelligentiae divinae conceptu ideales omnium eorum rationes extendunt, fecit enim coelos in intellectu. Ex his ideis, velut exemplaribus visibilia omnia sunt effecta, ut ipsae meritò philosophicae tanquam per imagines cognoscantur. Duo quidem secula sunt aeternitas atque tempus. Verbum igitur, id est divina ratio, rerum artifex, ita haec secula coaptavit, ut ab aeternis temporalia dependerent, item ut imagines idearum in aeternitate micantium in temporali seculo refulgerent. . . ." ("Moreover, the 'invisible things of God' are said to be the exemplars of all things within God himself, which utterly surpass both sense and imagination. . . . We understand that the world is harmonized by the word of God as visible things are made from the invisible. Indeed, in the very conception of the divine intelligence, the Ideas include the grounds and reasons of all things, for He fashioned the heavens in His mind. From these Ideas, as from models, all visible things are brought into being, just as philosophical [truths] are recognized through images. Indeed, there are two worlds: eternity and time. The Word, therefore, that is, the divine reason, the creator of things, so arranged these worlds that the temporal depends on the eternal, as the images of ideas sparkling in eternity reflect upon the temporal world." *In Epistolas D. Pauli, Op. om.* I, p. 436.) See Chap. XIII, n. 13 below for more on God as exemplary cause.

12. Cf. Chap. IV, n. 1 above.

13. According to Ficino, "whatever good or vital act is transferred from the cause to the effect is first developed within the cause" (Kristeller, p. 138). Following this principle, he assumes that God develops within Himself the model world of Ideas before producing the world of real things: "Decet etiam sicut res omnes duos habent actus, internum scilicet atque externum, et ille est vita aequalis agenti, hic vero posterior, ita ipsum quoque rerum opificem foetum vita aequalem intra se continere, partum vero extra se posteriorem producere, ut non minus aeternitas quam perfectiones aliae deficiat in effectu." ("It is fitting that just as all things have two acts, internal and external, and the former is equal in life to the agent, whereas the latter is inferior; so also the Creator bears within himself a fruit equal to him in life, but produces outside of himself

an inferior progeny, so that eternity, no less than other perfections, is lacking in the effect produced." *Theol. Plat.* Bk. XVIII, c. 1; *Op. om.*, I, p. 399.)

14. Although Colet's reference is to I Cor. IV in the margin, he is doubtless thinking of the context of the verse he has just quoted from I Cor. III, which is preceded by the comment on testing with fire: ". . . the fire will test what sort of work each one has done. If the work which any man has built on the foundation survives, he will receive a reward. If any man's work is burned up, he will suffer loss, though he himself will be saved, but only as through fire" (vv. 13b–15; see also Chap. III, n. 2 above).

15. This is the idea, also developed by Ficino, that causality is an essential and inseparable aspect of the doctrine of hierarchy. The lower grades are passive in relation to the higher, receiving what they have from above and passing the effects of their own force and substance to the grades below them. Hence "anterior" becomes almost equivalent to "superior," and "posterior" to "inferior" (Cf. Kristeller, p. 139). In the present context, man's charity is posterior and obviously inferior to God's, from whence it comes. By the same principle of operation, that which is prior/superior can exist in its inferior, even if it is not further communicated, since it must include, at least virtually, all the attributes of the inferior orders. This explains the apparent paradox that the charity of God can exist in man without the charity of man.

16. There is no indication here that Colet was aware of the bitter conflict that was to develop later on the question of faith vs. works. The "man so loved" actually has charity in himself by his participation in God's love; it now belongs to him, and so do the works that are its fruits; hence to Colet it follows logically that these works should be meritorious for him. In the following paragraphs he makes this point even more forcefully, going so far as to claim that the spiritual man, together with God, is "the parent of good works, which are now assigned not to the Spirit only, but in the Spirit to the man also, who is loved and makes the return of love . . ." (Lat. *qui amatus, redamans*).

17. Jerome indicates the variant reading and points out that there is a difference of only one letter between the Greek word translated as *ardeam*, καυθήσωμαι, and *glorier*, καυχήσωμαι. He assumes that there has been an error because of this similarity (PL 26, col. 425). Erasmus acknowledges Jerome's note but prefers the first reading, though he changes *ardeam* to *comburar* in his own translation (LB VI, 725–26). It is interesting that Colet, with his presumably scanty and tardy knowledge of Greek (see Intro., pp. 26–27), should have made this observation on the text, many years before either Erasmus' pioneer edition of the NT or his edition of Jerome appeared.

18. Lat. *ego interea expers fructus*. Unless one imagine and supply a form of *esse* here, this phrase can be only a nominative absolute (O'Kelly).

19. Lat. "nisi vivificata et inter se et cum Christo uniatur charitate." Lupton changes the verb to *vivificatur*. One might supply *sit*, but it is hardly necessary; the subject, of course, is *ecclesia* (O'Kelly).

20. Lat. "Erant quidam Rome qui ex contentione Christum annunciarunt, non sincere, existimantes se pressuram sustinere Paulo." See Lupton's note, p. 144, on Colet's deviation from the Vulg. here.

21. Lat. *in angustiis perdite*. Cf. Lupton's translation: "If you are no more than a receiver, you are lost in your own cold exclusiveness" (p. 145).

22. Lupton: "indulgently worded" (p. 146). He refers to Lefèvre's interpretation of Eph. IV: 26 quoted above: "let not the sun go down" means "let not clouds of passion

darken your mind," because "Ratio, oculus est; veritas, sol et lumen ejus" (*op. cit.*, [1512] p. 168v). Cf. also Ficino's development of the imagery of the sun as the light of truth, Chap. VII, n. 19 above. This is one of the places in Lefèvre's commentary where he allows an allegorical interpretation to be spun out at some length: Christ is the day, the devil and his works are the night, etc.

23. In Colet's scheme there is no possiblity of a real conflict between charity and justice, because all of these attributes must be perfectly united. In God they are one; hence in us they will be also, to the extent that we become like God—which is, of course, the point of Colet's whole treatise.

24. Lat. *titubent*. The word in the MS looks more like *tutubent* than anything else. Meghen reads *intubent*, while Lupton has the form that I have given here (O'Kelly).

25. Faith will eventually give way to open vision; hope will be swallowed up in realization; but love remains unchanged in its nature even when it attains perfection. (See F. F. Bruce, NCB *Comentary*, n. 37, p. 129). Since it is a participation in the nature of God himself, it belongs to the realm of the eternal, not just the temporal, and therefore it is the "greatest." See below, "charity . . . will then be the same," p. 269, and Erasmus' comment on this passage in the *Paraphrases*, n. 38 to Chap. VII above.

26. Colet presumably means here to be recognized and accepted by God, in the sense that we achieve our fulfillment as persons through charity, by becoming what God intended we should be. He "recognizes" us then when we have achieved this full identity. See below, "when we are men," p. 269.

27. Cf. Ficino: "Plato Plotinusque res veras esse duntaxat ideas existimant, formas autem naturales rerum verarum, id est, idearum imagines esse, ex influxibus invisibilium idearum in ipsa mundi materia, quasi speculo resultantes ad sensum. Quarum aspectu vides homines ita falli, ut res veras existiment, perinde ac si infantes imagines apparentes in speculo pro rebus omnino veris accipiat . . . Philosophi vero, praesertim Platonici, formas in materia mundi considerantes, agnoscunt eas esse similitudines idearum. . . . Ad quas quidem ideas in alia vita convertentes vultum, perspicaciter, ut inquit Paulus, facie ad faciem contemplantur, ita ferme cum Propheta clamantes, Domine Deus virtutum converte nos. Illumina vultum tuum super nos, & salvi erimus." ("Plato and Plotinus think that real things are actually Ideas, that is, that the natural forms of things are images of the Ideas, coming from the influx of the invisible Ideas into the very matter of this world, rebounding upon the senses as if from a mirror. You see that men are so deceived by these appearances that they consider them to be real things, just as children take images appearing in a mirror for real things. . . . But the Philosophers, especially the Platonists, observing forms within the matter of the world, realize that they are the likenesses of Ideas. . . . Turning our faces toward these Ideas in the next life, we see them plainly, face to face, as Paul says, and so almost shout with the Prophet, 'Lord God of Hosts, convert us. Let your face shine upon us and we shall be saved.' " *In Epistolas D. Pauli*, c. VII; *Op. om.*, pp. 437–38.)

Chapter XIV

1. Lat. *facultate linguarum*. Colet seems to have been unfamiliar with the phenomenon of glossolalia, which Paul is referring to in this chapter. It was not a skill, but an emotional response to religious stimulation, a kind of ecstasy. Paul clearly differentiates it here from intellectual gifts.

2. Another instance of Colet's practical emphasis on deeds as well as words; cf. Chap. VII above, p. 145; *Edmund's Romans*, Chap. II, pp. 215–19.

3. Lat. "et sumis testimonium tuum per os meum." Vulg. "Peccatori autem dixit Deus: Quare tu enarris iustitias meas? Et assumis testamentum meum per os tuum?" Both Meghen and Lupton reverse the pronouns, restoring the text to the form in which it is to be found in the Vulg. (O'Kelly). The NEB has a good rendering of this verse: "God's word to the wicked man is this: what right have you to recite my laws and make so free with the words of my covenant?"

4. Lat. "Nolite pueri effici sensibus, sed perfecti." In addition to the more obvious meanings here, Colet no doubt fully intended the sense "full-grown," in antithesis to "children" (O'Kelly).

5. Beneath this line in the text of Gg. iv. 26 is to be found "Finis xiiii," and immediately beneath this, "In Capud xiiii." The "xiiii" has been crossed out, probably by another hand, since the ink is of a different sort, and "xv" has been written in, the formation of the characters as well as the ink indicating another hand at work. Certainly what follows belongs to Chapter XIV, and both Meghen and Lupton take no note of the break. It perhaps indicates a lapse of time in composition (O'Kelly). As far as the content of this passage is concerned, Colet naturally does not disagree with Paul. Neither does Lefèvre, but he adds, "Ad turbam infidelem aut non satis in fide instructam: quid prohibebat si a spiritu sancto monebantur publicum habere sermonem? Id enim divinae non obviat ordinationi, Sed eam quam ponit circa praesentem materiam a deo esse ordinationem. . . ." ("Before a crowd of unbelievers, or those insufficiently instructed in the faith, what is to prevent them, if they are prompted by the Holy Spirit, to have public preaching? For this is not opposed to the divine ordination, but that which he [Paul] asserts concerning this present matter is ordained by God. . . ." *Op. cit.*, [1512], p. 128v.)

6. Lupton adds an interesting note here (p. 150) regarding the impact of Colet's own preaching on the common people who came to St. Paul's to hear him.

7. Lat. *particulatim*. (This presumably paraphrases the Vulg. "secundum duos, aut ut multum tres, et per partes" (v. 27). Erasmus changes this to "fiat per binos, aut ad summum ternos, idque vicissim" ("let it be done by twos, or at the most threes, and in turn"). He explains that Paul was objecting to the confusion that occurred when everyone was talking at once (LB VI, 733–34). From what Paul says about the frequency of glossolalia, perhaps this was the usual condition of the Corinthian church (JCB II. 79). As for *per partes*, Erasmus merely asks, "Quid autem est per partes?" ("But what is 'by parts'?") and points out that Ambrose read this as *particulatim*. Cf. Lefèvre's version: "Sive quispiam lingua loquitur: ad duos aut summum tres & separatus loquatur: & unus interpretetur" ("If any man speak in an unknown tongue, let it be by two, or at the most three, and that by course; and let one interpret" AV).

Chapter XV

1. For Colet's concept of causality, see pp. 259–61 above and nn. 9, 11, 13, and 15 to Chap. XIII.

2. The fallen angels were not led astray by weakness and ignorance, but by their own choice, in which they rejected God and His grace, as Colet explains below (O'Kelly).

3. Colet does not mean that there are some sins so bad that they cannot be forgiven. He refers rather to a freely-chosen state of mind and will of a sinner who deliberately rejects every grace.

4. Cf. n. 2 to Chap. I.

5. Colet here applies his doctrine of form (cf. n. 4 to Chap. I, n. 2 to Chap. V) to the change from physical to spiritual that Paul describes in connection with the resurrection. See below his reference to Phil. III: 21, "who will change our lowly body to be like his glorious body" (Erasmus: "ut conforme reddat corpori suo glorioso" — LB VI, 876).

6. After this sentence in Gg. iv. 26 is written the word, "Finis," and the next folio (151) is headed "Capud xvi." At the end of 151v, however, are to be found the words "finis xv," and 152r is headed "In capud xvj & Ultimum." The uncorrected mistake may indicate, I think, that Colet was copying this part, at least, from a previous draft (O'Kelly).

7. Vulg. "omnes quidem resurgemus, sed non omnes immutabimur." Colet seems unaware of the various readings of this passage, which Erasmus details at length in his annotation (LB VI, 740–43), drawing largely from Jerome's "Epistola CXIX Ad Minervium et Alexandrum" (PL 22, 966–75). Although Erasmus prefers the reading (which has since been adopted by modern scholars) "non omnes quidem dormiemus, omnes tamen immutabimur," he is at pains to point out that neither reading leads to heresy and that both readings have support among the Fathers. Erasmus takes the verse in its total context, assuming that "we shall all be changed" refers to the just, who are to be glorified; "we shall not all sleep" refers to those who will be still alive at the time of Christ's second coming. Colet does not seem to notice the implicit contradiction of the Vulg. reading with v. 52 and the rest of Paul's context. Erasmus defends his interpretation at length in his *Apologia* on this reading, LB IX, 433–42. Lefèvre, also basing his revision on the Greek, makes the following change: "non omnes quidem dormiemus: omnes autem immutabimur in indivisibili," explaining that all who die must rise incorruptible, since our faith maintains the resurrection of the body (*op. cit.*, [1512] pp. 132v–33r). Valla asserts that in v. 51, what the Latin affirms is negated by the Greek, and conversely, what the Latin denies, the Greek affirms. He too relies on Jerome's interpretation and the whole context, especially v. 52. Paul is considering what will happen to those who are still alive when Christ comes again (*op. cit.*, p. 167v). See also Lupton's note, p. 153.

8. Lat. "Qui erit tunc ut sine fine non sit infeliciter in se ipso." Cf. Lupton's version: "For his existence, then, will be an endless non-existence of unhappiness in himself" (p. 153).

Chapter XVI

1. He was a prophet who came down from Jerusalem to Antioch and predicted a famine during the reign of Claudius (A.D. 41–54). He also foretold the imprisonment of Paul (Acts XXI: 10).

2. Lat. *sanctos*, Gr. ἁγίους. This is the Pauline term for the members of the early Christian community. Paul adapts the OT expression, miqrā' qodes, or "holy gathering," which designated the Israelites as a people set apart and dedicated to Yahweh (JBC

II. 53:16). The Christians too are set apart by their holy calling. Cf. n. 11 to Chap. I above.

3. Colet writes this word with Latin characters as *Elogia* (O'Kelly). His use of this term here is not entirely accurate. The word referred to in II Cor. VIII: 6 is χάριν (Vulg. *gratiam*). RSV translates it as "gracious work." Lupton traces the history and meaning of *eulogia* in Colet's context here, pp. 154–55, nn. 1 and 2. The *charis* in the early church was the opportunity of contributing to the collection for the Jerusalem community; it is a "grace" because it is an opporunity for doing good, a participation in the ministry of service to those in need (JBC II. 52:27).

4. This Aramaic word was probably a primitive liturgical formula. Spelled Maran atha, as above, it meant "Our Lord has come" and was probably a credal declaration; spelled *marana tha*, it meant "Our Lord, come," and would signify an eschatological prayer (JBC II. 79:61). Colet's use of *venisse* indicates that he read it in the first sense. Erasmus points out, however, that the eschatological sense was preferred by Jerome, Ambrose, and others (LB VI, 747–48). Lefèvre also reads it in this way, and cites Jerome (*op. cit.*, [1512] 135r).

Note on the Translations

Whenever possible, standard translations have been used, as indicated above. In making the others, I acknowledge the assistance of Mrs. Mary Joan Masello, a graduate student in classics at Loyola University, Chicago.

General Index

Scriptural Index

General Index

Scriptural Index

John Colet's commentary on Paul's First Epistle to the Corinthians is here presented in a new translation with fully annotated text and an interpretive introduction. Of major importance as a Renaissance humanist, teacher and preacher, he was a close friend of Erasmus and the confessor of Thomas More. His work was inspired by the Platonism of Marsilio Ficino and Pico della Mirandola and the cosmology of Dionysius the Areopagite. Colet's explications of the epistles are distinctive because he understands Paul's text as a scholar of the Renaissance who is still untouched by the theological conflicts soon to follow; thus he tries to present Paul in the context of apostolic times, treating the letters as historical compositions rather than as sourcebooks for disputation.

Recent scholarship on the theology of Erasmus and other Renaissance humanists has aroused new interest in John Colet, who was well known for his educational work (he was Dean of St. Paul's and founder of St. Paul's school) and for the intellectual inspiration he provided to other, more famous people.

Bernard O'Kelly is Dean of the College of Arts and Sciences and Professor of English at the University of North Dakota, and has edited *The Renaissance Image of Man and the World* (Ohio State University Press, 1966). He is past president of the Council of Arts & Sciences and of the Federation of Public Programs in the Humanities. **Catherine A. L. Jarrott** is the author of articles on Erasmus and Colet, and is Professor of English at Loyola University, Chicago.

mRts

medieval & Renaissance texts & studies
is the publishing program of the
Center for Medieval & Early Renaissance Studies
at the University Center at Binghamton.

mRts emphasizes books that are needed —
texts, translations, and major research tools.

mRts aims to publish the highest quality scholarship
in attractive and durable format at modest cost.